THE CORN LAWS

THE CORN LAWS

The Formation of Popular Economics in Britain

Edited by
ALON KADISH

VOLUME III

FREE TRADE AND IRISH NATIONALISM II

JAMES WILSON AND *THE ECONOMIST*

Routledge
Taylor & Francis Group
LONDON AND NEW YORK

First published 1996 by Pickering & Chatto (Publishers) Limited

Published 2016 by Routledge
2 Park Square, Milton Park, Abingdon, Oxon OX14 4RN
605 Third Avenue, New York, NY 10017

Routledge is an imprint of the Taylor & Francis Group, an informa business

BRITISH LIBRARY CATALOGUING IN PUBLICATION DATA
Corn Laws: Formation of Popular Economics
in Britain
I. Kadish, Alon
941.081

Set ISBN 1 85196 410 X

ISBN 13: 978-1-13875-888-9 (hbk) (Vol-3)

LIBRARY OF CONGRESS CATALOGING-IN-PUBLICATION DATA
Kadish, Alon, 1950–
The corn laws : the formation of popular economics in Britain / Alon Kadish.
p. cm.
Includes bibliographical references and index.
ISBN 1–85196–410–X (set)
1. Corn laws (Great Britain) 2. Free trade––Great Britain. 3. Anti-Corn-Law League. I. Title.
HF2044.K33 1996
v. 1. Whig free trade I –– v. 2. Whig free trade II : Free trade and Irish nationalism I –– v. 3. Free trade and Irish nationalism I : James Wilson and the economist –– v. 4. Free trade and religion –– v. 5. Provincial free trade I –– v. 6. Provincial free trade II : Free trade farmers.
382.7'3'0942––dc20 98–1232
CIP

CONTENTS

THE

"COMMERCIAL INJUSTICES."

EXTRACT FROM APPENDIX OF

A REPORT TO THE REPEAL ASSOCIATION,

ON THE GENERAL CASE OF IRELAND FOR A

REPEAL OF THE LEGISLATIVE UNION.

Appendix References in the following pages will be explained to the reader by the above.

The Report itself, with its various Appendices, is nearly ready for publication.

JOHN O'CONNELL.

DUBLIN:
PRINTED BY J. BROWNE, 36, NASSAU-STREET.
1843.

John O'Connell (1810–58)[1]

John O'Connell was the third son of Daniel O'Connell, the 'Liberator', and Mary. He was called to the Irish bar at the King's Inns, Dublin, and was elected to Parliament for Youghal by 22 votes to 5. His return was unsuccessfully petitioned and he sat for the constituency until 1837 when he was returned unopposed for Athlone. In 1841 he succeeded Joseph Hume as representative for the borough of Kilkenny, and in 1847, having been elected for both Kilkenny and for Limerick, he chose to represent the latter.

John O'Connell acted as his father's lieutenant in the repeal agitation, and prepared a number of reports for the Repeal Association including on "*Commercial Injustices*". In 1844 he stood trial with his father, and shared his imprisonment in Richmond. John O'Connell became the practical head of the Repeal Association in Ireland in which he was opposed by the "Young Ireland" party to whom he objected as irreligious and lawless.

Following Daniel O'Connell's final departure from Ireland the Association, under John O'Connell's leadership, rapidly declined for want of funds, and in June 1848 it was dissolved. At the time of the 1848 rebellion John O'Connell retired to France, and on his return took the Whig side in politics, becoming a Captain of militia. He voted against Lord Russell's ministry in February 1851 and was censured by the corporation of Limerick. O'Connell accepted the Chiltern Hundreds, thereby creating a vacancy for the Earl of Arundel, and was elected in 1853 for Clonmel. But his position in the House of Commons was by then insignificant and in 1857 he retired from politics by accepting a position of Clerk to the Crown.

[1] Based on John Andrew Hamilton, Lord Summer of Ibstone, in *D.N.B.* vol. 14, pp. 834–5.

THE

"COMMERCIAL INJUSTICES."

English testimony as to English commercial jealousy of Ireland.

The following recorded evidences of the ungenerous spirit in which England has acted towards Ireland in points affecting her commercial and manufacturing prosperity, are taken from English sources.

The first is from Anderson's History of Commerce. It shows that the more favourable conduct of England in the points alluded to, previous to the 17th century, was subsequently a subject of regret. Anderson has not noted the reason of that early favour. It was simply because the commerce and trifling manufactures of Ireland were in towns that were mere English fortresses along the Irish coast. But when the Irish began to have a share, she commenced her oppressions, and gave free vent to her ungenerous and cruel jealousy of Irish prosperity.

"In those early days commerce was not so perfectly understood as to be made subservient to the political interests of princes and states. Of this we have an instance under the year 1289, being the 17th of King Edward I., when an act passed relating to Ireland, the 4th section whereof gives 'leave for all kinds of merchandize to be exported from Ireland except to the King's enemies.' Certainly, then as well as now, there were some Irish commodities that interfered with those of the same kind in England, and particularly wool and leather. Even much later than this time, we find another law to the like effect in the 34th year of King Edward III., being the year of our Lord 1360, cap. 17, 'giving leave for all kinds of merchandize to be exported from and into Ireland, as well by aliens as denizens; and also cap. 18 of the same year enacts, that all persons who, have lands and possessions in Ireland might freely import thither, and also export from that kingdom their own commodities,' *which liberty, in our days, would be deemed unsafe and dangerous.*—1763, p. 321, vol. 1, *Anderson's Commerce.*"

This was written in 1763, but there are earlier proofs of the evil disposition of England. Sir William Temple, writing in 1673, thus advised the then Lord Lieutenant of Ireland:—

"Regard must be had to those points wherein the trade of Ireland comes to interfere with that of England, in which case the Irish trade ought to be declined, so as to give way to the trade of England."

This policy was very effectively followed up. Indeed ten years before Sir William Temple wrote, Irish commerce got a cruel blow from the Navigation Acts of Charles II. She was cut off from all direct trade with the colonies, just as she was beginning to find it most profitable.

For details we refer the reader to a subsequent part of this article, as well as for the details of the ruin of our woollen manufactures, by the compliance of William III. with the grossly and tyrannously unjust demand to that effect, made upon him by the British Parliament. We proceed with our authorities. The cruel effect of the act of William III. was well described by the historian, Barlow:—

"From the establishment of the act of settlement and explanation, Ireland had rapidly increased in wealth and improvement, to the admiration and envy of her neighbours, till it was again laid waste by the revolutionary wars under William III., and even from this calamity it was recovering with such quickness, that in 1698 the balance of trade in its favour amounted to between *four and five hundred thousand pounds.*

"But the effects were permanent of restricting laws, insurmountable by the fertility of the soil, the ingenuity of the inhabitants, navigable rivers, and a multitude of harbours."—(vol. 1, p. 290.)

The 17th century having thus closed, we give, from a pamphlet published in London in 1727, an evidence of the continuance, in the 18th century, of the same arrogant and insolently selfish spirit, with which our interests were treated.

"*Seasonable Remarks on Trade, with some Reflections on the Advantages that might accrue to Great Britain by a proper Regulation of the Trade of Ireland, wrote in London*, 1727.

"P. 36.—The situation of Ireland for an extended trade is more advantageous than that of any other nation in Europe. Its harbours are many and commodious, its inhabitants numerous and hardy, inured to want and labour, and able upon poor fare to run through a great deal of work.

"Their near situation renders intercourse between us very easy, and enables us to protect their trade, and to take such care of our interest there as would be almost impossible, had they been more remote. The politeness, the gaiety, the power of our court, allure all those who are studious either of improvement, of pleasure, or of preferment. This drains from them the penny-rents of most of the great estates of that kingdom, and every increase of their wealth will (by enlarging the rent-rolls of those already settled here, and by enabling others to taste the delights of a court, who by the narrowness of their present fortunes are confined at home) greatly enlarge this inlet of their money, and *increase our* drafts upon them, which together with the restrictions on the exportation of their wool, and the other advantages which we already have of them in trade, will cause to centre in England all, or the most part of, their acquisitions on the general balance.

"I am sensible that the proposition which I here advance is a very bold one; as it is so opposite to the universally received opinion, that it were better for England if Ireland were no more. But, if we consider (apart from prejudice and particular interests) how greatly we are already gainers by the trade and industry of that country, poor as it is, we shall perhaps give into a notion so greatly exploded, and begin to think that the wealth and prosperity of Ireland is not only compatible with that of England, but highly conducing also to its riches, grandeur, and power."

The writer of the pamphlet had actually to apologise for thinking that Ireland ought to exist at all, and this although he only contemplated her existence as a means of giving England more plunder!

Referring for all details to the citation that follows, of acts of the English parliament, marking the subsistence of their spirit of injustice, we crowd together our remaining English authorities.

"British legislation, on all occasions, controlled Irish commerce with a very high hand—universally on the principle of monopoly; as if the poverty of Ireland were her wealth."—*Tour of Arthur Young*, 1776-7.

"From the Revolution till within these few years, the system had been that of debarring Ireland from the use of her own resources, and making her subservient to the interests and opulence of the English people."—*Pitt*, 1785.

Mr. Dempster (on the same occasion), in the English parliament, said, that "England had always been miserably jealous of Ireland."

On another occasion, Mr. Grenville (afterwards Lord Grenville) said, "If England were heavily taxed, she had now, and had had for a whole century past, the benefits of a widely-extended trade, *from which she had excluded Ireland*—and the latter had already given to England all that she could have made, if by a barbarous and equally absurd policy she had not been debarred from those advantages that God and nature had given her."

"Ireland had long felt the narrow policy of Great Britain, who, influenced by views of trade and commercial advantage, and stained and perverted with selfish motives, had treated her with partiality and neglect, and never looked on her prosperity as that of the empire at large."—*Pitt*, 1799.

Similar testimony after the Union.

Such being some of the principal testimony, up to the Union, as to English jealousy of Ireland's prosperity, there need but two extracts more to show that it has not been denied since.

"Is it not well known that, till 1780, the agriculture, internal industry, manufactures, commerce, and navigation of Ireland, were all held in the most rigid subserviency to the supposed interests of Great Britain? In 1778 there was a proposal to allow her to import sugar direct, and to export every thing but woollens to pay for it; and this proposal was almost made a question of allegiance by the great towns of Great Britain, and so it was lost! In 1779 a more limited concession to her was also lost! *But towards the close of that year the disasters in North America, and the state of things in Ireland, produced a different feeling in the British parliament—state necessities, acting under a sense of political danger, yielded without grace, that which good sense and good feeling had before recommended in vain; and in* 1782, *under the like pressure, those concessions were rendered irrevocable."—Mr. Huskisson, March* 21, 1825.

Ireland was under our old colonial system—prohibited from any direct trade with British colonies. This system was maintained with all its vigour till 1780, when, after the close of the American war, it became imperatively necessary to look to the rising spirit of discontent in Ireland, much fomented by the illiberal and unjust policy of this country (England) in respect to commerce. Every liberal relaxation encountered violent opposition by strong petitions from Manchester, Glasgow, and Liverpool; the merchants of the latter place said that if Ireland were placed on the same footing with England, the port and town of Liverpool would fall back to its former state."—*March* 12, 1841—*Labouchere, President of the Board of Trade.*

Leaving these general testimonies as to England's jealousy of our commercial progress, we come to details. By the infamous Lord Strafford, her active hostility in this respect seems to have been evoked. In Wallace's Essay on the Trade and Manufactures of Ireland (Dublin, 1798), an extract is given from a letter of his, dated July 25, 1636, on the subject of the report he had made to the King and Council respecting the manufacturing prospects of Ireland. The extract is as follows:— First conception of the project of crushing Irish manufactures.

"That there was little or no manufacture among them (*scil.* the Irish), but some beginnings towards a clothing trade which I had, and so should still discourage all I could, unless otherwise directed by his Majesty and their Lordships, in regard it would trench not only on the clothings of England, being our staple commodity, so as if they should manufacture their own wool, which grew to very great quantities, we (*scil.* the English) should not only lose the profit we made now by in-draping their wools, but his Majesty lose extremely by his customs. And in conclusion, it might be feared they might beat us out of the trade itself, by underselling us, which they were able to do."

He added, that he had endeavoured to turn the attention of the Irish to the manufacture of linen. His interference was utterly unjustifiable. Ireland, like every other nation, had a right to follow whatever manufactures she best liked, or found most convenient. Wool was her natural staple, the material being in excellence and abundance at home.

If she afterwards took of her own accord to the more exotic article of linen, there was no reason why she should be confined to that alone. But such was the design, and although Strafford failed, and that the internal dissensions and disorders which prevailed in England for nearly a quarter of a century after, prevented his suggestions being immediately acted upon by England, they were carefully kept in mind, till a favourable concurrence of circumstances in the very last years of the century gave her the long desired opportunity of carrying them into effect.

1660. First legislative attack on our manufactures. Woollen goods forbidden to be exported to England. Attack followed up; colonial market shut.

In the reign of Charles II. begun the direct legislative interference with the commercial prospects of Ireland, which is alluded to in the quotations we have given from English writers and speakers. By the 12 Chas. II. chap. 4, duties equal to a prohibition were laid in England on the import of Irish woollen goods. This was little noticed at the time, our manufacture, in that respect, not being just then very extensive. But it was the beginning of a cruel system rigorously carried out and persevered in for nearly 120 years, and which speedily and severely forced itself on the notice of the Irish. The act we have mentioned was speedily followed up by the 15 Chas. II. chap. 7, (1663,) prohibiting the import of Irish cattle into England, and *all export* of value from Ireland to the colonies. Then came the 22 & 23 Chas. II. chap. 26, (1770,) forbidding import into Ireland of sugar, tobacco, cotton, indigo, steel, or Jamaica wood, fustic, and some other articles from the colonies, unless *first unloaded in an English port*. This act contains an intimation that its prohibitions had been *intended* in the act of 1663, but not sufficiently expressed in the clause of the latter act, which forbade import of colonial articles from an English port into Ireland, unless the ship had first unloaded in that port.

Aggression by way of prevention of our prosperity.

So active was the miserable jealousy that dictated these and other aggressions upon our commercial liberty, that they were, for the greater part, made more to guard against an *anticipated*, rather than against any immediately existing, success of Irish enterprize. This was particularly the case with the two first of the acts we have mentioned. Our wool manufacture, although certainly making advances, was very far from being in such a flourishing condition in 1660, as to justify the jealous fears of competition with England, that prompted the 12 Chas. II. chap. 4. Nor was the English dread of decrease in the value of land, from extensive import of Irish cattle, better founded, when in 1663 that article of import was forbidden upon such a pretence.

At the same time there is no doubt that Ireland was progressing. We have already quoted the testimony of the historian Barlow, to that effect. In 1692, Lord Deputy Sydney, in his speech from the throne to the Irish Parliament bore similar testimony, from his own knowledge.* Much of this increased prosperity has been attributed, and with justice, to James, first Duke of Ormonde. In an excellent publication (the authorship of which is in some doubt), entitled "The Commercial Restraints of Ireland considered," printed in Dublin, in 1779, this nobleman and his efforts are thus spoken of:—

Improvement of Ireland up to 1688.

"To heal the wound that this country (Ireland) had received by the prohibition of the export of her cattle to England, Lord Ormonde obtained from Charles II. a letter dated 23rd March, 1667, by which he directed all restraints on export of Irish goods to *foreign*† parts, to be taken off......and the import from Scotland of linen, woollen, and other commodities to be stopped, as drawing large sums out of Ireland. His Grace successfully executed his schemes of national improvement, having by his own constant attention, the exertion of his extensive influence, and the most princely munificence, greatly advanced the woollen, and revived the linen manufactures."

Efforts of the Duke of Ormonde to promote this improvement.

This result was also in some degree, accelerated by one of those very instances of *anticipatory obstruction*, on the part of Great Britain, which we have noticed a couple of paragraphs ago. The particular instance in question was, that in which, by one part of the act of 1663, Irish cattle were prohibited from being sent into England. The Irish, having the English market thus closed for their cattle, turned their attention to increasing and improving their breed of sheep, for the sake of the wool, which they began to manufacture very largely; and although here again met by the cruel operation of the other part of the same unjust law, which shut their woollen manufactures from the colonies, yet foreign exports very considerably increased.

Accidental impulse to it from England herself

The framers and followers out of the cruel policy we

* Other evidence can be abundantly had—as that of Archbishop King in his State of the Protestants of Ireland; Lord Chief Justice Keating's Address to James II. and his Letters to Sir John Temple, &c.

† The *English* possessions abroad remaining shut against our commodities.

are exposing, did not expect this result; and seeing it, only became the more determined to crush the manufacture in question. This, as we have before noted and shall presently shew more in detail, they succeeded in doing before the end of the century.

England's care of her own interest.

By the Act 1 William and Mary, chap. 32, while the prohibition was continued against woollen goods from Ireland, the import of the raw material from that country into England, which had never been interrupted, was limited to certain ports therein named. This limitation was by no means with a view to prevent or check the Irish raw wool from coming; for England was very glad to take it to work up herself; but would appear to have been designed in order to ensure the more easy detection of the manufactured article, should an attempt be made to smuggle it, under cover of the free import of the raw material.

Aggressions resumed.

Colonies totally shut.

Our woollen manufactures crushed.

In the reign of William the aggressions upon us recommenced by the 7 and 8 Will. III. chap. 22; which extended the prohibition of *direct* import of certain colonial articles into Ireland, enacted in Charles II.'s reign, to *all* colonial articles whatsoever. In the succeeding year, 1697, a bill was openly brought in, in the English parliament, to forbid all export from Ireland of her woollen manufactures. It passed the Commons; but although favourably received in the Lords and much debated there, it did not pass the Upper House before the dissolution of the parliament, which occurred in the July of that year. There was very little reclamation against this conduct from the Irish parliament; partly because the attention of the latter was a good deal diverted and distracted, by the passing of an English act in the previous session, which admitted Irish linens, hemp, and flax into England. But one other cause prevailed. The Irish Catholics (by the infamous breach of the treaty of Limerick after their gallant army on the faith of that treaty had expatriated itself, and so rendered safe the violation of the treaty) were laid prostrate, but were still formidable. The dominant party knew that their only hope of securing and permanently establishing their ascendancy was, by ensuring the constant aid of England; and to propitiate her, they had to countenance her aggressions upon the commercial interests of their country. We will do them the charity to say, that they did so with reluctance, but they did so most certainly. In 1698-9 they not only allowed the long meditated and final blow to de-

Details of this iniquitous proceeding.

scend upon our woollen manufactures; but at the imperious demand of England, actually gave it strength, and certainty themselves; by anticipating the English legislature, and enacting (by the 10 Will. III. chap. 3,) their own disgrace and the commercial ruin of their country!

Addresses of the English Houses of Parliament to William III. in 1698, to this effect.

The English parliament *began* the matter, but as we have said, the so-called Irish parliament anticipated them in its completion. In England it commenced in June, 1698. On the 9th of that month, the House of Lords addressed King William, stating (*English Lord's Journals* 1698, pp. 314-315.):—

"That the growing manufactures of cloth in Ireland, both by the cheapness of all sorts of necessaries of life, and goodness of materials for making all manner of cloths, doth invite your subjects of England with their families and servants to settle there, to the increase of the woollen manufactures in Ireland, which makes your loyal subjects in England very apprehensive, that the further growth of it may greatly prejudice the said manufacture here, by which the trade of this nation, and the value of lands will greatly decrease, and the number of your people be much lessened here.

"Wherefore we humbly beseech your most sacred majesty, that your majesty would be pleased, in the most public and effectual way that may be, to declare to all your subjects of Ireland, that the *growth and increase of the woollen manufacture there hath long been, and will be ever looked upon with great jealousy*, by all your subjects of this kingdom, and if not timely remedied, may occasion *very strict laws totally to prohibit and suppress the same.* And, on the other hand, if they turn their industry and skill to the settling and improving the linen manufacture, for which, generally, the lands are very proper, they shall receive all the countenance, favour, and protection from your royal influence for the encouragement and promotion of the linen manufacture, to all the advantage and profit they can be capable of."

The address of the Commons was in the following terms:—

"Your Majesty's most dutiful and loyal subjects, the Commons in Parliament assembled, being very sensible that the wealth and power of this kingdom do in a great measure depend on the preservation of the woollen manufacture, as much as possible entire to this realm, think *it becomes us*, like our ancestors, *to be jealous of the increase and establishment of it elsewhere, and to use our utmost endeavours to prevent it;* and therefore we cannot without trouble observe that Ireland, which is dependent on, and protected by England in the enjoyment of all they have, (and which is so proper for the linen manufacture, the establishment and growth of which there, would be so enriching to themselves, and so profitable to England,) should of late apply itself to the woollen manufacture, to the great prejudice of the trade of this kingdom, and so unwillingly promote the linen trade, which would benefit both themselves and us; the consequence whereof will necessitate your Parliament of England to interpose to prevent the mischief that threatens us, unless your Majesty, by your authority and great wisdom, shall find means to secure the trade of England, by making your subjects of Ireland to pursue the joint interests of both kingdoms. And we do most humbly implore your Majesty's protection and favour in this matter, that you will make it your royal care, and enjoin all those you employ in Ireland, to make it their care, and use their utmost diligence, to hinder the exportation of wool from Ireland, except to be imported hither, and *to discourage the woollen manufacture*, and encourage the linen manufactures of Ireland, *to which we shall always be ready to give our utmost assistance.*"

King William gave the following reply to the House of Commons:—

His answer.

"*I shall do all that in me lies to discourage the woollen manufacture in Ireland*, and to encourage the linen manufacture there, and to promote the trade of England."

False statements of these addresses.

In these addresses there were three false averments; first, that Ireland was more fitted for linen than for woollen manufacture; second, that the latter was recently set up; and third, that its establishment in Ireland was of great prejudice to English interests.

As to the first—which is rather suggested than distinctly stated—its inconsistency with truth cannot for a moment be doubted, when we recollect that Ireland had the raw material for woollen manufacture in abundance and excellence at home. Not so in the case of linen. Flax-seed, the foundation of the material, was to be imported; its culture here was always precarious, owing to the humidity of the climate. And again, wool employed more hands, and yielded a greater profit to the public and to the manufacturer—considerations, of course, of great importance in any country, but particularly so in one so unfortunately circumstanced as Ireland. Anderson, in his History of Commerce, vol. iii. p. 194, remarks as follows on this point:—

"It requires about 20 acres of land to breed wool for setting on work the same number of hands which one acre of flax would employ; and yet in the end, the woollen manufacturer will be found to employ by far the greater number of hands, and yield the most profit."

The second averment, to the effect that the Irish had only recently taken up this manufacture, can be quickly disposed of. A glance at the Report of the commissioners of enquiry into the condition of the hand-loom weavers, printed in 1840, by order of the House of Commons, will give, on parliamentary authority, the fact of Irish woollen goods being in demand and high repute in foreign countries, so early as 1357. Anderson's History of Commerce records several successive notices of this manufacture in acts of parliament, or otherwise, during the succeeding three centuries. In 1655, it was mentioned along with the wool manufacture of England herself, in one of the articles of a treaty then negociating between Cromwell and the ministers of Louis XIV. And wherever mentioned, whether in the many acts of parliament of both countries relative to the subject, or in treaties, or by individual writers, it is spoken of as a manufacture of good foreign demand, and giving abundant employment at home.

The third averment, viz.—that of injury to British interests, had no foundation in the existing state of matters. Adam Smith in his "Memoirs of Wool," (vol. 2, p. 244,) states, "that though the amount was increasing, yet, that the Irish in 1698 had not recovered one-third of the woollen trade which they had before the war." No market could be shewn from which Ireland had excluded England as to woollens, or where she was even a notable competitor. No proof was attempted of the allegation in any one way. The English commissioners of trade did, indeed (in 1698) report that the difference between wool and labour in the two countries respectively, amounted to an advantage for Ireland of one-third; and that to reduce Irish woollens to an equality with British, so high as 44 *per cent.* might be laid on the former above what was on the latter in export duties. But in the proof of this they utterly failed, notwithstanding which failure, such was the remorseless and reckless selfishness of the English parliament, and the interested obsequiousness of what was called the Irish parliament, that crushing duties were laid on all Irish woollens, (except friezes before taken off the loom,) and on all materials, and everything used in working up the material, even to the working utensils!

King William's letter to the Irish government on the subject.

In pursuance of his reply, King William wrote immediately after (on the 16th July, 1698,) to one of the Lords Justices of Ireland, Lord Galway, as follows:—"The chief thing that must be prevented is, that the Irish Parliament take no notice of this here, and that you make effectual laws for the linen manufacture, *and discourage as far as possible the woollen. It never was of such importance to have a good session of parliament.*" (*Rapin, vol.* 17, *p.* 417.)

How the matter was pushed in Ireland.

The work we have before noticed, viz. "The Commercial Restraints of Ireland Considered," so well describes the manner in which the affair was pushed in the Irish Parliament, that we shall here insert its description at length. (pp. 99 to 105.)

"The Houses of Parliament in England originally intended, that the business should be done in the Parliament of Ireland, by the exertion of that great and just influence which King William had acquired in that kingdom. On the first day of the following Session,* the Lords Justices in their speech, mention a bill transmitted for the encouragement of the linen and hempen manufactures, which they recommend in the following words: 'The settlement of this manufacture will contribute much to people the country, and will be found *much more advantageous to this kingdom* than the woollen manufacture, which being the settled staple trade of England, *from whence all foreign markets* are supplied, can never be encouraged *here* for that purpose; whereas the linen and hempen manufactures will not only be encouraged, as consistent with the trade of England, but will render the trade of this kingdom both useful and necessary to England.'

"The Commons in their address,† promise their hearty endeavours to establish a linen and hempen manufacture in Ireland, and say that they hoped to find such a temperament in respect to the woollen trade here, that the same may not be injurious to England. They referred the con-

* 27th September, 1698. vol. ii. p. 994. † Com. Jour. vol. ii. p. 997.

sideration of that subject to the committee of supply, who resolved that an additional duty be laid on old and new drapery of the manufacture of this kingdom* that shall be exported, friezes excepted, to which the House agreed.† But there were petitions presented against this duty, and relative to the quantity of it, and the committee appointed to consider of this duty were not, it seems, so expeditious in their proceedings, as the impatience of the times required.‡

"On the second of October, the Lords Justices made a quickening speech to both Houses, taking notice, that the progress which they expected, was not made in the business of the session, and use those remarkable words: 'The matters we recommended to you are so necessary, that the prosperity of this kingdom depends so much on the good success of this session, that since we know his Majesty's affairs cannot permit your sitting very long, we thought the greatest mark we could give of our kindness and concern for you, was to come hither, and lesire you to hasten the dispatch of the matters under your consideration; in which we are the more earnest, because we must be sensible, that if the present opportunity his Majesty's affection to you hath put into your hands be lost, it seems hardly to be recovered.'§

"On the second of January, 1699, O. S., the House resolved, that the report from the committee of the whole House, appointed to consider of a duty to be laid on the woollen manufactures of this kingdom, should be made on the next day, nothing to intervene. But on that day a message was delivered from the Lords Justices in the following words: 'We have received his Majesty's commands‖ to send unto you a bill, entitled, an Act for laying an additional duty upon woollen manufactures exported out of this kingdom; the passing of which in this Session his Majesty recommends to you, as what may be of great advantage for the preservation of the trade of this kingdom.'

"The bill which accompanied this message was presented, and a question for receiving it was carried in the affirmative by 74 against 34. This bill must have been transmitted from the Council of Ireland. Whilst the Commons were proceeding with the utmost temper and moderation, were

* Ib. vol. ii. p. 1022.

† October 24, 1698.

‡ Com. Jour. vol ii. p. 1007, 1035.

§ Com. Jour. p. 1032.

‖ Com. Jour. vol. ii. p. 1082.

exerting great firmness in restraining all attempts to enflame the minds of the people,* and were deliberating on the most important subject that could arise, it was taken out of their hands; and the bill passed, though not without opposition,† and received the royal assent on the 29th day of January, 1698.

"By this act an additional duty was imposed, of 4*s*. for every 20*s*. in value of broad-cloth exported out of Ireland, and 2*s*. on every 20*s*. in value of new drapery, friezes only excepted, from the 25th of March, 1699, to the 25th of March, 1702;‡ the only woollen manufacture excepted, was one of which Ireland had been in possession before the reign of Edward III., and in which she had always been distinguished.§ This law has every appearance of having been framed on the part of administration.‖

"*But it did not satisfy the English parliament, where a perpetual law was made, prohibiting from the 20th of June*, 1699,¶ *the exportation from Ireland of all goods made or mixed with wool, except to England and Wales, and with the licence of the commissioners of the revenue; duties*** *had been before laid on the importation into England equal to a prohibition, therefore this act has operated as a total prohibition of the exportation.*

"Before these laws, the Irish were under great disadvantages in the woollen trade, by not being allowed to export their woollen manufactures to the English colonies,†† or to import dye-stuffs directly from thence; and the English in this respect, and in having those exclusive markets, possessed considerable advantages."

The accounts given by Lord Oriel in his "Paper on the Linen Trade," and by other authorities, of the leading facts connected with this fatal measure to Ireland, thoroughly correspond with what we have given.

* Com. Jour. vol. ii. p. 1007. † Com. Jour. 1104, by 105 against 41.

‡ 10 Will. III. chap. 5. § And. on Com. vol. i. p. 204.

‖ The Commissioners of Trade in England, by their representation of the 11th October, 1698, say, (Eng. Com. Jour. xii. vol. 437,) "they conceive it not necessary to make any alteration whatsoever in this act," but take notice that the duties on broad cloth, of which very little is made in Ireland, is 20 per cent; but the duty on new drapery, of which much is made, is but 10 per cent.

¶ Eng. Stat. 10 and 11 Will. III. chap. 10, passed in 1699.

** 12 Charles II. chap. 4, Eng. and afterwards continued by 11 Geo. I. chap. 7, Brit.

†† By an Eng. act, made in 1663, the same which laid the first restraint on the exportation of cattle.

Injustice ever comes back ultimately upon its authors; and accordingly England herself suffered from the ungenerous and cruel destruction of our woollen manufactures. We here again quote the work from which the preceding extract is taken.

"Mr. Dobbs, who wrote in 1729,* affirms that by this law of 1699, our woollen manufactures were forced away into France, Germany, and Spain; that they had in many branches so much improved the woollen manufacture of France, as not only to supply themselves, but to vie with the English in foreign markets, and that by their correspondence, they had laid the foundation of the running of wool thither, both from England and Ireland. He says, that those nations were then so improved, as in a great measure to supply themselves with many sorts they formerly had from England, and since that time, have deprived Britain of millions instead of thousands that Ireland might have made.

"It is now acknowledged that the French undersell the English, and as far as they are supplied with Irish wool, the loss to the British empire is double what it would be if the Irish exported their goods manufactured. This is mentioned by Sir Mathew Decker,† as the cause of the decline of the English, and the increase of the French woollen manufactures; and he asserts that the Irish can recover that trade out of their hands. England, since the passing of this law, has got much less of our wool than before.‡ In 1698 the export of our wool to England, amounted to 377,520¾ stone; at a medium of eight years, to Lady-day, 1728, it was only 227,049 stone, which is 148,000 less than in 1698, and was a loss of more than half a million yearly to England.. In the last ten years, the quantity exported has been so greatly reduced, that in one of these years§ it amounted only to 1,007 stone, 11lb., and in the last year did not exceed 1665 stone, 12lb.‖ The price of wool under an absolute prohibition is £50 or £60 per cent. under the market price of Europe, which will always defeat the prohibition.¶

* Essay on the Trade of Ireland, p. 6, 7.

† Decline of Foreign Trade, p. 55, 56, 155. ‡ Dobbs, p. 76. § In 1774.

‖ Nor was this deficiency made up by the exportation of yarn. The quantities of these several articles exported from 1764 to 1778, are mentioned in the Appendix, No.

¶ Smith's Memoirs of Wool, vol. ii. p. 554. The only way to prevent it, is to enable us to work it up at home. ib. 293.

"The impracticability of preventing the pernicious practice of running wool is now well understood. Of the thirty-two counties in Ireland, nineteen are maritime, and the rest are washed by a number of fine rivers that empty themselves into the sea. Can such an extent of ocean, such a range of coasts, such a multitude of harbours, bays, and creeks, be effectually guarded?

"The prohibition of the export of live cattle forced the Irish into the re-establishment of their woollen manufacture; and the restraint of the woollen manufacture was a strong temptation to the running of wool. The severest penalties were enacted, the British legislature, the government, and House of Commons of Ireland, exerted all possible efforts to remove this growing evil, but in vain, until the law was made in Great Britain* in 1739, to take off the duties from woollen or bay yarn exported from Ireland, excepting worsted yarn of two or more threads, which has certainly given a considerable check to the running of wool, and has shewn that the policy of opening is far more efficacious than that of restraining. The world is become a great commercial society—exclude trade from one channel, and it seldom fails to find another."

To these sensible remarks, we add those of Anderson, as little a friend to Irish commercial interests as any of his countrymen.

"Concerning these laws, (viz. the restrictions on Irish cattle and Irish woollens,) many think them hurtful; and that it would be wiser to suffer the Irish to be employed in breeding and fattening their black cattle for us, than to turn their lands into sheep-walks, as at present; in consequence of which, in spite of all our laws, they supply foreign nations with their wool." *(Anderson, vol. 2, p. 645.)*

The linen manufacture no equivalent for the loss of the woollen.

The Irish part of the arrangement of 1688–9 being carried out by those who were acting as representatives of Ireland, it is to be seen how the English did their part. And first it is to be here remarked, that nothing can be more unfounded than a notion very prevalent with English writers, and adopted by some Irish, to the effect, that the linen manufacture was left us *as an equivalent* for the taking away of that of woollens. In the first place, why should a country be restricted from any manufacture, in

* This was done for the benefit of the woollen manufacture in England. *Eng. Com. Jour.* vol. xxii. p. 442.

which its inhabitants might consider they could profitably embark? In the next place a manufacture that co-existed with another, can scarcely be considered a proper and real equivalent for the destruction of that other. If a robber deprive his victim of a portion of the contents of his purse, and leave him the remainder, that remainder would not be considered by the victim, or by any body else, as an equivalent for what was taken away. It is true, the linen manufacture had not gone so far as the woollen, but that very circumstance ought to have been an additional reason not to confine Ireland to it alone.

Desirous, when practicable, to quote from documents of the present day, particularly from such as have received the parliamentary stamp of acceptance, we insert the following, taken indifferently from the reports of Messrs. Otway and Muggeridge, assistant commissioners. Co-existence of both.

"In a curious little poem written in the reign of Henry VI., about the year 1430, by Haklayt, in the enumeration of the commodities of every country, he mentions the *linen-cloth* of Ireland. Report of R. M. Muggeridge, Esq.

"In 1533, the act 24 Henry VIII. chap. 4, required 'every person occupying 60 acres of tilled land to sow a quarter of an acre yearly in flax or hemp, for the purpose of protecting and encouraging the linen manufacture by an adequate supply of the raw material.'" Hand loom enquiry.

"The linen-trade was enumerated as one of the principal branches of Irish manufacture, in the thirty-third of Henry VIII. 1542. . . . . . . In an act of the thirteenth year of Elizabeth's reign, it was recited, that Irishmen had been exporters of linen for more than 100 years. . . . . . Lord Strafford adopted extensive measures to encourage the linen manufacture. He sent to Holland for flax-seed, and to the Netherlands for competent workmen. To animate others, he embarked in the business £30,000 of his private fortune. (N. B. This "*private fortune*" mainly consisted of his lion's share of the plunder of Ireland.) But the troubles that then broke out, put a stop to the enterprize. The Duke of Ormond, Charles the Second's lieutenant, sought to revive it, and procured several acts for its encouragement and for inviting Protestant strangers to settle in the kingdom. He sent Irishmen to be instructed in the details of the linen manufacture in Flanders, and brought over 500 Brabant families, expert in the business, and also operatives from Rochelle, the Isle of Report of C. G. Otway, Esq.

Rhé, Jersey, &c., &c. . . . . . His example was followed by many others, and Lord Dungannon, in Ulster, gave encouragement with great success to the Scotch settlers. . . . . Laurence, in his work, entitled 'the Interest of Ireland,' published in 1682, says, 'My opinion is, that there is not a greater quantity of linen produced in the like circuit in Europe,'" &c. &c.

The linen manufacture, then, having co-existed with the woollen, could not properly be an equivalent for the latter, and above all, when, as we have before remarked, it was a more difficult, costly, and uncertain manufacture; and also one yielding much less employment.

Did England keep her promise to favour our linen trade?

But such as it was, did England do her part towards the so-called international agreement of 1688–9? She was to encourage our linens, and the declaration of her Houses of Parliament to that effect in 1698, were taken as decisive assurances of her determination to follow out the policy indicated in an act of 1696, the 7 & 8 Will. III. chap. 39, which recited "that great sums of money were yearly exported out of England for the purchasing of hemp, flax, and linen, and the productions thereof," which might be prevented by being supplied from Ireland; and therefore natives of England and Ireland were to be allowed to "import into England, free of all duties, hemp, flax, linen, and all the productions thereof."

No steps taken for years.

No further encouragement, however, was given in this respect until the year 1705, when the act 3 & 4 Anne, chap. 8, passed, allowing us to export our white and brown linens to the colonies—a thing which, before the 15 Chas. II. chap. 7, we could do with *all* our commodities, and which proved nugatory as to benefit now, inasmuch as the restraint on our imports from those colonies prevented interchange, and thereby most seriously crippled the trade that otherwise might have taken place.

This restraint on our imports from the colonies had, as we have seen, originated in 1670, by the 22 & 23 Chas. II. chap. 26, and applied to a number of valuable commodities. But its scope was enlarged, and made to include *all* commodities by an act in 1696, the 7 & 8 Will. III. chap. 22. It is true these acts allowed us to get colonial commodities still, but not unless first unloaded and then taken on board again in an English port, and carried in an English vessel.

And then only

Any encouragement really given by England to our

linen manufacture, was directly with a view to her own benefit—of ours she was little regardful. A duty was indeed placed upon foreign linen, but it was allowed to be drawn back again on exportation from England, and the drawback was found in practice to operate as a *premium* upon German and Russian linens. The bounties given later on the export of Irish linens from England, were confined to those of 1*s*. 3*d*. per yard, and *if stamped*, they forfeited the bounty, although allowed to German stamped linens. * The retailing and stamping of our linens in England gave great employment there; and the bounty on Irish export to England was in fact an advantage to the British merchant, as he got into his own hands the business of the re-exportation to foreign countries, to which Ireland ceased to export direct.

with a view to her own interest.

So little was England really disposed to keep her promise, that our linens painted, striped, chequered, printed, stained, or dyed, were practically excluded by her so early as 1711, by the act 10 Anne, chap. 19, which was directed against all such linens made in *foreign* parts, and was, by a strained construction, made to apply to Ireland.

Some valuable kinds of our linens shut out from England,

The striped, chequered, &c. linens of the latter country were thus shut out (we have used the word "*practically*" in the preceding paragraph, as the import duties of 30 per cent. imposed by the tenth of Anne, and confirmed by the 11 & 12 Anne, chap. 9, amounted, in practice and effect, to an exclusion) from England; and, by the Navigation Act 15 Car. II. chap. 7, had before been excluded from America and the British West Indies, into which latter they were not admitted until 1777–8, when the British act 18 Geo. III. chap. 55, passed, allowing them to go there, but without the advantage of the bounty on export, given to similar goods from England to all parts of the world, by an act dated eight years earlier. The admission then allowed was of little practical value, as the restrictions on direct import from the colonies still existed as to many important articles, and of course rendered the colonists very indifferent as to commerce with us.

as before from colonies and plantations.

We got indeed, *nominally*, equal bounties on export to foreign countries of our white and brown linens, by the 15 Geo. II. chap. 29, but the benefit was infinitely less to us than to England, as we could only get that bounty by exporting from an *English* port, and the expense of freight, insurance, commission, &c., in this first transit of our

Advantage to the white and brown linens of England over ours.

linens was computed to deduct 4, and sometimes even 5 or 6 per cent. from the 12 per cent. amount of the premium, whereas the English manufacturer, having comparatively no preliminary charges, was not subject to deductions.

Our market at her command for every species of linen she chose to manufacture.

We are by no means done with the exposure of the delusion respecting English encouragement of our linen-trade. While England took away her own market, and that of every part of the globe in which she held power, from our chequered, &c., linens, she endeavoured to deprive them even of our own home market. This she in a great degree accomplished, owing to the inefficiency of the duty on her chequered, striped, &c., linens coming into Ireland. It was no more than 10 per cent. *ad valorem, and the linen not valued.* The power which she had until 1782, of controlling our legislation, by the necessity we were under of submitting all projects of law for the approval of the *English* privy-council, before discussion in the Irish parliament, of course enabled her to prevent all attempts at even making the existing duty effectual.

But England had the benefit of *a bounty* in addition, and its effects were not only to increase the advantage of English linens of the above kind over those of Ireland, but by raising the price of yarn, to inflict a heavy discouragement on *all* species of Irish linens. A committee of the Irish Commons reported in 1771, "on the linen manufactures of Ireland, and her title to encouragement thereof," and we take the following from one of the papers laid before them by the Trustees of the Linen Manufacture:—

"Cheques and striped linens, such as are exported, are generally made of yarn, about 10*d.* or 11*d.* value in the pound, great part of which is imported into Britain from Ireland; and as 1lb. of yarn will, on a medium, make upwards of three yards of those cheques or striped goods, a bounty of ½*d.* per yard is a premium of upwards of 1½*d.* on the pound of yarn, in favour of the manufacturer in Britain over the manufacturer in Ireland, from which bounty the Irish cheques striped, or printed linens, &c., are totally excluded, their importation into Britain being prohibited."

Meantime England had before secured our market for her other linens. This was done by the 3 Geo. I. chap. 21, passed in 1716, whereby the act of the 3 & 4 Anne, allowing export of our linens to the colonies, was enacted to be continued "*so long as the merchants* and others *of Great Britain shall be permitted to import into Ireland, free of all duties, white and brown linen-cloth*".*

Breach of her promises.

Thus, so far as we have gone, we have seen that England not only deprived us of the manufacture most suited to us, viz., the woollen, and made us confine ourselves to the more expensive and precarious manufacture of linen, but she virtually broke her promise of peculiar encouragement to that, by not passing one law in its favour that she did not give the benefit of, in more ample measure, to herself, and by keeping the Irish market open for her own linens, while she crippled and restricted the entry of those of Ireland into her market.

Our sail-cloth manufacture destroyed.

She did yet more than this to benefit her own interest in this branch, at the expense of Ireland. By an act of the year 1750, the 23rd Geo. II. chap. 32, she heavily taxed the import of sail-cloth made of *Irish* hemp. The consequence to us was this; that whereas in 1750 we exported more sail-cloth than we imported, matters so changed, that in 1784 we were exporting none, and imported 180,000 yards. And for several years after, England herself reaped no benefit from this wanton injury to us, as the trade thus lost to the Irish, fell into the hands of the Russians, Germans, and Dutch,† notwithstanding three or four acts encouraging the manufacture in England and Scotland.

Further restriction on our linen trade.

Again, lest by any possibility Ireland should reap much benefit from the act of 1742, (delusive as it was to a great extent,) which gave bounties on the export of Irish, as well as English linens, exported from England, an act of the year 1756, the 29 *Geo. II. chap.* 15, provided, that no Irish linen so exported should be entitled to the bounty, if it were the property of a resident in Ireland!

Encouragement of Scotch linens.

But it was not alone her own linen trade which England encouraged, and gave advantages to, beyond what she did to redeem her engagement of fostering that of Ireland. The Scotch were also brought into the field, to compete with the Irish in that trade. This was immediately a necessity of the times after the union with Scotland, when it was important to do all that could be done, to calm down

* Clause 4 of this act transferred to the Crown, that portion of the penalties in former acts, on export of Irish wool, which had previously been applied "to the encouragement of the linen manufacture of Ireland!"
† See Journals, H. Com. Ireland, years 1774—1784.

the irritation in that country, produced by the carrying of that measure.

Accordingly a portion of the sum given to Scotland, under the terms of the Act of Union, as an "equivalent" for her assuming joint fiscal responsibility with England, was specially allocated for the encouragement of her manufactures, including her linen.*

Special legislation for the same purpose followed, particularly by the Act 13, Geo. I. chap. 26; and from thenceforward every advantage which England gave her own linen and hempen manufactures, she gave equally to those of Scotland; and therefore of course placed those of the latter, in the same position of advantage as her own, over the similar manufactures of Ireland. Nay, in 1753, she gave the Scotch an advantage to some degree over herself, by the act 26 Geo. II. chap. 20, which withdrew the export bounty on English and Irish coarse linens, and enacted that £3000 a year for nine years, should be given as bounty upon that export from Scotland.

Our complaint not against favor to Scotland, but against oppression of us.

Our complaint is not against the abstract fact of Scotland's being brought into the field as a competitor with us. No such false view of political economy, or social justice, is taken in Ireland, as that either of the other portions of the empire should be, or should have been, debarred from seeking their national prosperity, by all the means placed at their disposal by the bounteous providence of heaven. Our proper and real ground of complaint is, that we should have been deprived of one manufacture, while

* This grant, given under the act of Scotch Union, and confirmed and explained by the 13 *Geo I.* chap. 30, was of the amount of £2000—a very large sum at that time to so exceedingly poor a country as Scotland. It was to be an annuity redeemable at any time by the English parliament, *on payment of* £40,000. What occurred? The "Board of Commissioners for encouragement of Scottish Manufactures," which was created for the management of this fund, "did not begin operations till 1727; by which time (i. e. 20 years from the Union) £40,000 had accumulated, on which, after termination of the series of years, Government have, EVER SINCE, paid £2000 *a year as interest.*" The words in inverted commas are from a letter written in February, 1841, by Sir Thomas Dick Lauder, "Secretary to the Royal Board of Manufactures, Edinburgh," addressed to "J. R. Mallet, Esq. Capel-street, Dublin," and published, it is to be supposed with the consent of both gentlemen, in the Dublin papers of the above month. One thing seems to be omitted in Sir T. Lauder's statement, viz.—that the "series of years" which he speaks of, was only determinable on the payment of £40,000. Now as he states that this series *did* terminate, it follows, that not only have the Scotch manufacturers had the benefit of the annual £2000 for 116 years; but that while yet in their infancy, they got in a lump sum, £40,000. (See section 14 of the Act 13 Geo. I. chap. 30.)

the other portions of the empire were left at liberty to pursue it, as well as all other branches of industry.

Circumstances that facilitated the depression of our manufacturing industry.

Mr. Assistant Commissioner Otway, in his report to the hand-loom weavers' commission, (part iii. February, 1840,) has ascribed to its true cause, the rapidity with which, before the mere breath of the legislature, Irish manufactures, though long established, and apparently vigorous in growth, declined and disappeared. His remarks on this subject well merit perusal, and therefore we insert them at length, although that length is considerable for our limits, and that we do not altogether concur in one or two of the positions laid down by him:—

"One great and fatal error in the system of colonization to which I have adverted was, that it became a fixed principle of policy to exclude the native Irish from the benefits of all the improved arts introduced by the new settlers. It had been found, that the Anglo-Norman Lords who had obtained estates from the Plantagenets, became, in the course of time, alienated from English allegiance and usages; to use the phrase of the day, they were "*Hibernis ipsis Hiberniores.*" To prevent such a result from the new settlement was perversely regarded as an object of greater importance than the settlement itself; it was said to be essentially necessary "to preserve and maintain an English interest in Ireland." But for the unhappy difference of religion between the settlers and the natives, this exclusive system would not have been long maintained; the Irish and the English would gradually have amalgamated, like the Normans and the Saxons; but the distinction of religion gave strength and permanence to the distinction of race, and rendered the line of demarcation scarcely less broad than if it had been perpetuated by difference of colour and physical organization.

"The hand-loom weavers, the wool-combers, the clothiers, the dyers, the white-smiths, and even the mariners, in the South of Ireland, were so extensively Protestant, that they would not allow a Roman Catholic apprentice to be received in any of their trades. The only branch of manufactures permitted to "the mere Irish" was that of brogues or common shoes; and even this trade was not permitted to be carried on within the precincts of walled towns. Hence, these manufactures were, and continued to be, exotics; they struck no root in the soil.

"The early settlers were long a flourishing and numerous

body. In 1689 William and Mary were proclaimed in several small towns in Munster; and the Protestant artizans raised a respectable army to resist James. At an earlier period the desertion of the royal cause by the Munster Protestants, under Lord Broghill and Inchiquin, was the principal cause of the easy conquest by Cromwell. It may be added, that James II., in his letters, ascribes his failures in Ireland to the fact that the Protestants alone understood the art of making and mending gun-locks, and that in consequence he never was able to keep his partisans supplied with serviceable arms.

"During the reigns of William and Anne this exclusion of the Irish from all manufactures was rigorously continued; but to compensate for this, great encouragement was given to the immigration of foreign Protestants, esperially the Huguenots, who had fled from France on the revocation of the edict of Nantes. The bigotry of Louis the XIV. upset the magnificent schemes of his minister, Colbert, by the expulsion of his Huguenot subjects; and numbers of these men brought their arts, their industry, their capital, and their faith into Ireland—they established several branches of trade in various parts of the country—the woollen manufacture in the south—linens and cambrics in the Counties of Down and Armagh, and the silk manufacture in Dublin. In support of these refugees, and the arts they carried with them, the Irish landed proprietors were very active—a subscription was raised, as appears from Primate Boulter's letters, for establishing the cambric manufacture in the town of Dundalk, amounting to £30,000., and a Monsieur De Joncourt was appointed to collect French operatives, and conduct the establishment. But the Huguenots adopted the baneful system of exclusion, and exerted themselves to prevent the Irish from learning their arts or profiting by their industry. The Duke of Ormond, following the example of the Earl of Cork, also prohibited the instruction of Roman Catholic apprentices, as did the principal landholders, who encouraged foreigners to settle on their estates.

"Now this exclusive system at once destroyed the basis of all manufacturing property—the home market. The fabrics introduced by the English and French settlers were of a superior quality, for which the native Irish could only gradually acquire a want, as they were raised in the scale of civilization. But instead of thus raising them, the foreign manufacturers, aided by the legislature, employed every possible means to depress them, and thus blindly drove from their market a whole nation of customers, and confined them to the use of the rude and cheap fabrics which were woven amongst themselves. The manufacturers were thus forced to rely on their foreign trade; but here they came into competition with the English merchants, and aroused the spirit of commercial jealousy.

"The act of William, prohibiting the export of Irish wool and woollens, destroyed the Irish woollen manufactures, simply because they depended almost solely on foreign sale for their support. There was no independent peasantry, or respectable wealthy and middle class, for them to supply.

"The Irish legislature saw this decline of manufactures, but could not discover a remedy; it attempted to supply the want of a home market by bounties, duties, and premiums. These, of course, aggravated the evil. The manufacturers looked to the premiums and the parliament, instead of their own industry and the market, and expected that customers could be created by a statute. The manufactures in most places sunk by the sure process of gradual decay. Even where they maintained a lingering existence, the fabrics they produced became greatly deteriorated in quality.

"It may be asked why the manufactures of the North did not share the same fate of those of the South; but the question is easily solved by a glance at the state of the population in the province of Ulster. The settlement in Ulster was more complete and extensive than that in any other part of Ireland. The natives had been either wholly exterminated or driven into mountainous and remote districts. The landlords and tenants in the manufacturing districts of the North thus belonging to one class, they did not regard each other as hereditary enemies; there was no legacy of oppression on one side, and revenge on the other. The Ulster tenant felt (and feels) he had a property in his farm—something on the earth he could call his own; and the fruits of his industry would be allowed to accumulate into a small capital, and in point of fact, such an accumulation did take place; for the greater part of the capital in the linen manufacture of Ulster, was derived from the savings of agricultural industry, and hence arose the numerous class who were each at the same time a farmer, a weaver, and a linen-dealer (jobber). In the south of Ireland the title to property was unsettled; for more than a century confiscation and re-confiscation followed each other, until the Acts of Settlement and Explanation secured the followers of Cromwell in their estates; there was no community of feeling or interest between the proprietor and the occupants brought about by these acts. The great object was to establish an English interest in Ireland; and to accomplish this hereditary policy, the two last Stuarts, while they patronized Roman Catholics in their own courts, rigorously maintained the new Protestant proprietary in the South of Ireland. It was not until James the 2nd was driven from England, that he would allow even of an enquiry into the Act of Settlement, and it is doubtful whether he would have consented, even in Dublin, to its repeal, if a large portion of the re-confiscations had not reverted to the crown. The repeal of the Irish Act of Settlement, by the parliament of James the 2nd, gave the Protestant proprietors a fright from which they have not perfectly recovered even to this day; since that time they have been persuaded that every change of policy, or isolated disturbance, threatens their titles; they deem that they only garrison their estates, and therefore they look upon the native occupants (I cannot call them tenants) as persons ready to eject them upon a favorable opportunity. Hence, the Munster landlord was afraid to give the persons who occupied his ground a permanent hold upon the land, or a beneficial interest in its occupancy.

"The old struggle of title, in natural course, produced the new contest of tenure; and Captain Rock and Lady Clare were as legitimately descended from the Catholic Lords of the Pale, as Jack Straw and Wat Tyler were from the Saxon Thanes, who fought at Hastings. *There is, and, until the relations between landlord and occupant are altered, there can be no accumulation of savings in the South of Ireland from agricultural industry*—and hence there was not and can be no spontaneous growth of manufactures from small capitals.

"Another reason for the greater prosperity of the linen manufacture in the North of Ireland is, that in Ulster a moderate modus was established for the tithe of the flax; but all efforts to have the same modus extended to the rest of Ireland were defeated by the pertinacious opposition of the ecclesiastical authorities. Without at all entering on the general question of tithe, or the policy of taxing the raw materials of industry, it is enough to state that the import on flax proved to be so heavy, that the farmers found it to be an unprofitable crop, and it was never cultivated, except in very small patches, in the South of Ireland.

"In the present day the principal impediments to the growth of manufacturing industry arise from the want of a comfortable middle class, and the condition of the agricultural population."

Inquiry to the cause of truth from the one-sided reports to the Imperial Parliament.

In all this mass of rational remark, and clear-headed tracing out of cause and effect, it is singular that there should be only one sentence given to those active efforts of English commercial jealousy, the facile and successful operation of which he so well attributes in the main, to the narrow basis to which sectarian bigotry restricted our manufactures. The reason of his avoidance of this topic, must simply have been, because his report was to be presented to an English parliament. Ever since the Union, this circumstance has exercised an influence most injurious to the interests of Ireland, and of truth and justice, over the reports of committees and commissioners of enquiry, into matters affecting the international relations between the two countries. Mr. Otway's report is one of the very few honorable exceptions, in which that influence has not been allowed to extend as far as the *suggestio falsi*, however partly chargeable with the *omissio veri*.

The unavoidable length to which we have already gone necessitates as brief a handling as possible, of the remainder of our subject.

England's jealousy consistent.

The commercial jealousy of England was consistent throughout. We have seen that our woollen goods were practically excluded from her ports, while she had the command of ours. Nay she had been able to obtain from the Irish parliament in 1662, before the first fervour of its interested loyalty after the restoration of Charles II. had subsided, the prohibition by the Irish Act 14 and 15 Chas. II. chap. 8, of foreign woollen goods in Irish ports; a concession in her favour that her conduct two years before, in shutting her ports to our woollens, very little deserved. But the same miserable spirit actuated that parliament, as prevailed in that of King William—namely, that of making any sacrifice of national interests to obtain security for their own particular interests; so many of its members being persons who had acquired their properties

Exercised against our woollens.

by rapine and murder in the time of Cromwell's blood-stained rule over Ireland.

Against our linens.

We have also seen how scarcely even colourable the promise to encourage our linen manufacture was proved to be. The historian Barlow well denominates it as "*moonshine*," and says that "England departed from the letter and the spirit of that compact."—(vol. i. chap. 10.)

Cottons.

By the Acts 15 Chas. II. chap. 5—3 and 4 Anne, chap. 4—4 and 5 William and Mary, chap 5, Irish cotton manufactures were subjected to 25 per cent. on import into England; and lest this enormous charge should not be enough to exclude them, the Act 7 Geo. I. chap. 7, enacted penalties on the *wearing* of any such manufactures in Great Britain, unless there made. On the other hand British cottons went into Ireland in immense quantities at only 10 per cent.

Beer and malt.

Irish beer and malt were excluded from England, and her beer and malt sent into Ireland at almost a nominal duty. The 9th Anne, chap. 12, prohibited us from importing hops from any other place but Great Britain, styling such importation "a public and common nuisance." So determined were the English parliament that we should not otherwise be supplied in this particular, that when the prohibition of direct importation from the colonies and plantations of colonial goods was first relaxed, (which it was by the 4th Geo. II. chap. 16, passed in 1835, and declared to be so passed, not on account of the hardship of the previous restrictions to us, but of "*great prejudice to the trade and navigation of Great Britain and the said colonies*," a statute was specially passed the year afterwards, (viz. the 5th Geo. II. chap. 2,) declaring that the trifling relaxation enacted by the before-mentioned act should not be construed to allow hops into Ireland from those quarters, and four years afterwards the 7th Geo. II. chap. 19, further enforced and strengthened the restrictions.

Import of hops.

This injustice will appear gross, and yet it is not all stated. Not only were we prevented supplying ourselves with hops elsewhere than from England, but the duty on their export from thence was not allowed to be drawn back in favour of the Irish consumer, and the money thus most unfairly wrung from him, was appropriated to the payment of an English debt !

The exclusion of our cattle, by the act of 1663, has been mentioned before. It had not, indeed, excluded them in words, but the high duties then enacted, operated as a prohibition, and, with the additional precaution that marked the carrying out of all these injustices, another act was passed shortly after, (the 18th Chas. II. chap. 2,) specially, and in terms, prohibiting our cattle, and declaring that their import into England was "a public and common nuisance!"

Export of cattle.

We have before given an extract from Anderson, vol. xi. p. 1645, describing these laws as unwise, and now quote him again.

"Ireland is really a mine of treasure to Great Britain, and is so perhaps in a much greater degree than our American plantations; since so much of what is gained in Ireland, centres at length in Britain. Every severe step taken by us with regard to Ireland, has been advantageous to our foreign rivals. It is now clearly seen that the prohibition of live cattle from Ireland, in order to raise the price of our lands, was not well-judged. Even the restrictive laws on the woollen manufactures of Ireland forced the Irish workmen to settle in France; and thereby laid the foundation for the great woollen manufactures of that kingdom."

It is instructive to observe, in these and other extracts we have given, the quiet way in which every thing is argued for, and on account of, English interests; those of Ireland being totally left out of the question. This of course is natural; but is also very significant.

The English parliament excluded our cattle, but it was the wish of the English people to have them; and accordingly "they set about defeating the intentions of the legislature." This is proved by the confessions in the angry preambles of successive acts passed to enforce those of 1663 and 1666. At length the legislature had to give way under this pressure; and Irish cattle, and the provisions, &c. manufactured from them, (which also had been excluded by an act of 1680,) were, in the reign of George the 2nd, admitted again into England; at first temporarily, but the acts opening the ports to them were continually and easily renewed.

Hats, glass, gunpowder, coals, bar-iron, iron-ware, and several other matters, some of which Ireland had not to export, and others of which she had very little, were at

Other miscellaneous articles.

different times the objects of English restrictions; whensoever it was fancied that English interests were at all threatened by them. One of the most important of these articles, was that of glass; which, by an act of the 19th year of George the 2nd., Ireland was prohibited from importing from any country but Great Britain, and could not export the article at all.

Also silk.

In addition to the discouragements affecting our silk manufacture, in common with our other manufactures, it had the further discouragement that coming to us as the raw material did, through England, the sum of three-pence in the pound was retained there, of the original import duty in that country; and the price thereby so much enhanced to us—in addition to the benefit at our expense, to the English revenue.

The results affected not only Ireland, but the British colonial, &c. possessions.

It was impossible for a country thus hampered and restricted, not only in every point where competition with her jealous and powerful neighbour was at all likely, but in many where the apprehension of it was utterly without foundation, to make any real advances towards commercial prosperity. From the British possessions in both hemispheres, she was shut out, (from the East Indies by a clause in the 7th George I., chap. 21, but practically before,) as although she still could import their commodities through England, the trade was unable to bear the delays and expense of the double journey. These restraints were ultimately injurious to the British possessions; as Ireland, unable to supply herself from them, had to get from foreign countries the materials for ship-building, some of those articles used in perfecting her staple manufacture, and other valuable imports. But of course the weight of the injury was upon Ireland, and to it was owing her poverty and embarrasments of the greater part of the eighteenth century.

Reference to testimonies, as to the injury to Ireland.

We have quoted at an early period of this article, authorities as to the prosperity of Ireland previous to the destruction of her natural staple, the woollen manufacture. After that the story was different. In the session of 1703, the Irish Commons laid before Queen Anne a true state of the deplorable condition of the country. They complained of vast decay and loss of its trade—its being almost exhausted of coin—of the poor having become very numerous—of the foreign trade and its returns being under such restrictions and discouragements as to be then become impracticable; *although the kingdom of Ireland had by its blood and treasure contributed to secure the plantation trade to the people of England.*

At the end of the session, Mr. Speaker Brodrick, (afterwards Lord Chancellor) declared in his speech to the Lord Lieutenant, that the representations made by the Commons were their unanimous voice; and that they hoped they might be allowed such a proportion of trade, that they may recover from the great poverty they now lie under. (*Irish Com. Jour.* 3 *vol. pp.* 149—208.)

In the journals of the Irish Commons, from thenceforward till within the last 20 years of the eighteenth century, will be found declaration after declaration, admission after admission, complaint after complaint, of the poverty and wretchedness of Ireland—the want of employment among her people—the wretched condition of her trade—the consequent inability of the country to support her public burthens, and the cruelty of the restrictions that fettered and crippled her industry. Scarcely two years elapsed during the interval we have mentioned, without some of these disheartening records. The Irish parliament was impotent to redress the evils, whose existence they thus recorded, not only as contained in resolutions and remonstrances of their own, but as admitted and acknowledged in speeches to them from the vice-throne. They were then under the fetters of Poyning's law, and the acts confirming it; and no bill for effectual relief of these distresses, by opening up the restricted and impeded sources of industry, would get the sanction of the English Privy Council, to which the laws in question compelled every legislative project to be submitted for approval, ere it could be introduced into the Irish parliament. This was the state of things until 1780—2.

But we need not delay upon this part of our subject, when we have the strong English testimony bearing upon it, with which this article commences.

Forcing of the linen manufacture.

Meantime the linen manufacture undoubtedly increased; but there was little of natural vigour and stability about it. What progress it did make was mainly owing to the unremitting care and attention of the Irish parliament, so far as lay in their power; and to the impulse it received by the large immigration of foreign Protestants, versed in the manufacture, who were driven from France by the execrable revocation of the edict of Nantes. In the hand-loom weavers' report it is stated, that the Irish parliament from 1700 up to

1777, expended in the encouragement of the linen trade, the sum of £1,295,560.

In the speeches from the vice-throne to the Irish parliament throughout the century, exhortations to the encouragement of that trade, coupled, as it invariably was, with that of the Protestant Charter Schools—the phrase being "those sources of honest industry and pure religion," are to be found as regularly recurring as the "phrases banales" of royal speeches in our own days respecting the "assurances from foreign powers," and the "economy with which the "estimates are framed."

The decisive proof, were, such wanted, that the linen trade was not a healthy natural effort of the industry of the country, and exercising a genial influence on the national prosperity, is given by the very fact of its having required this constant encouragement and attention.

Additional injustice of England.

To the enumeration in detail of English injuries to our trade, we have unfortunately to add one striking instance, general in its effect. From 1740 to 1759 there were no less than 24 embargoes in Ireland! One of these lasted three years, viz.: from 1776 to 1779, when Irish provisions were restrained from being sent any where, but into England—nor was this altogether relaxed even in the latter year, as they were still restrained from being sent to America, the West Indies, or indeed any place out of Europe.

Thus, by all possible means—namely, by direct and actively oppressive legislation—by false interpretation and forced construction of laws supposed to have no such object—by real breach under a seeming observance of international engagements—and even by an unconstitutional exercise of the prerogative, Irish industry and enterprize were cruelly restrained and repressed to the verge of ruin.

Remarks. 1st, Our religious discord enabled her to tyrannize.

We now approach the time when England had to retrace her steps. Ere, however, leaving the first branch of our subject, we would make two short remarks. The first is, that the wretched history we have been detailing, ought to make an impression upon every honest Irishman, and warn him from that execrable religious discord which so divided the nation against itself, as to render it incapable of resisting these monstrous outrages.

2nd, She allowed us to follow the linen trade only

Secondly, it is to be remarked generally on the conduct of England towards the only manufacture she allowed us any freedom in following, viz. the linen, that what freedom she gave, it was little other than that which the cat gives the mouse; whom she releases for an instant, certain of being able to put her paw on it, when she pleases. England was not inclined towards the linen manufacture herself, at the close of the 17th century, and to remove a rival in the woollen, had no objection to allow Ireland to follow the former; reserving to herself, as we have seen, advantages over the Irish linens, (not only by restrictions and cramping regulations of our export, and greater bounties and facilities in that respect for herself, but also by the complete command of our ports,) so as that whenever her own manufacturers should please to turn their attention to linen, they would have little need to dread Irish competition. In either country the woollen manufacture was the natural staple. In either it was the most profitable. The similarity of climate rendered flax-seed an equally precarious crop in both countries—and in both it was of course a crop equally exhausting to the soil. Was it not cruel that the poorer country, Ireland, should be forced to confine herself to the more difficult and costly branch of manufacture; *and yet have no security even in the pursuit of that?* during her pleasure.

The inevitable necessity of things, and not the considerations of justice and humanity, compelled England to retrace many of her steps in her course of commercial, as she did subsequently with regard to political oppression. She began to find out that she had been hurting herself in her over-eagerness to dominate over Ireland. We have before mentioned the first indications of this discovery, when, so early as 1739 (by the act 3rd Geo. II. chap. 3) she had so far to relax her restrictions on our products, as to allow import of Irish woollen or bay yarn, as her own manufacturers were beginning to feel grievously the impetus given to the French woollen-trade by the immense smuggled export of Irish wool to that country.* It had Relaxation in her injustices owing to necessity, not benevolence.

* Mr. Ray, (Secretary to the Repeal Association,) in a brief but most excellent Report drawn up by him in 1840, on the Trade and Manufactures of Ireland, treats of the occurrence of 1739 as follows:—

"In 1739 it was found that Irish woollens were making their way to foreign ports, notwithstanding the stringency of the prohibitory laws. Permission was therefore given to export woollen and bay yarns to England, 'as it may be a means,' says the act, (12 Geo. II. chap. 11.) 'to prevent export of wool and woollen manufactures from Ireland to foreign parts, and may also be of use to the manufactures of Great Britain.' And more strict provisions against export of Irish woollen goods to foreign parts were embodied in this statute."

After this the reader can judge for himself of the degree of "*benevolence*" that suggested this first relaxation.

then been ascertained, that (to use the expression of the writers of that day) "one pack of Irish wool became two or three on the continent," as it enabled the foreigner, by admixture, to work up his own wool. Sir Mathew Decker, in his "Decline of Foreign Trade," and Dr. Smith, in his "Memoirs of Wool," both show how England suffered in this respect, and record, that though Irish wool sold at about 50 per cent. advance on the price in England, yet that labour in foreign countries was so much cheaper, and the advantages derivable by foreigners from mixing the Irish wool with their own, that they were enabled to undersell England in foreign markets.

The authorities we have mentioned (and various other writers) equally reprobated, and for similar reasons, the acts restricting import of Irish cattle and provisions into England, as we have earlier stated; it was in the same reign (viz., Geo. II.) in which Great Britain found it better for her interest to admit them, to exclude Irish wool and yarn, that she made the same discovery as to the articles of cattle and provisions.

English testimony to this effect.

These relaxations were prompted, as we have said, by a better understanding of her own interests, and were far more benefical to the latter than to Ireland. Of the same description were those which succeeded them in 1778 and 1779, the one admitting Irish manufactured cotton yarn, and the other admitting Irish hemp.* The *manufactures* of Ireland *from* the woollen and cotton yarn, and from the hemp, were still rigorously excluded. At length came the time that no words of ours can so well describe, as it is described in the extract we have given at the commencement of this article, from the speech of the celebrated Mr. Huskisson in 1825—the time when "state-necessities, acting under a sense of political danger, yielded without grace that which good sense and good feeling had before recommended in vain!"

The following is a summary of the events of this time :

The "necessity" pressing on her in 1779.

On the failure of the attempt in 1779, (mentioned by Mr. Huskisson,) to effect a real, though partial, opening of the colonial trade to Ireland, the citizens of Dublin, the

* We purposely omit here the 18 Geo. III. chap. 55, allowing *some* direct export from Ireland to the British colonial possessions—first, because of its insultingly limited extent, and second, because it was futile in practice, owing to the restrictions on *our direct import in return*. We also omit two acts of Geo. II. which mocked us by *nibbling* at those restrictions, &c.

grand juries in many parts of Ireland, and the people throughout the country, met and passed strong resolutions in their different assemblies, condemnatory of the "avarice and ingratitude" of Great Britain—her "illiberal and contracted policy," &c., &c., and pledging themselves to Irish manufacture. The author of "Collectanea Politica," (in the first volume of which, pages 161–2, will be found some of these resolutions,) after remarking, that in consequence of this resolve, Irish manufactures began to revive, and the demand for British goods greatly decreased," dryly observes that "*this circumstance tended to produce a disposition in Great Britain, to attend to the complaints of this country, different indeed from that which Ireland had hitherto experienced.*"

External circumstances hastily ripened this disposition; France had joined her arms with those of struggling America, and the scale was turning against British interests in the new hemisphere. The combined fleets of France and Spain "rode triumphant in the channel." "The affrighted maritime towns made application to the Government for protection; part of the established forces of the nation having been called away to support the war in America, the Chief Governor was obliged to confess himself unable to afford assistance. . . . . The people of Ireland therefore resolved to defend themselves,—volunteer corps were formed in every part of the kingdom; their force and respectability saved the country from ruin. The fleets of the enemy, alarmed at our military preparations, beheld the banners of defiance, and fled with precipitation from our coasts. Parliament bore testimony to the services and loyalty of these patriotic guardians of Ireland, in votes of thanks to the several volunteer corps, for their spirited exertions, at this time so necessary in defence of this country."—(*Collectanea Politica, or, The Political Transactions of Ireland*, from 1760 to 1800, vol. i. p. 166.)

The Irish Parliament meeting on the 12th of October, 1779, the Lord Lieutenant, the Earl of Buckinghamshire, in his speech from the throne, drew attention to "the extraordinary decline of the revenues, notwithstanding the very liberal supplies of the last session," and called upon the country for new efforts. The commons, however, after a warm and interesting debate, replied by an address to the King, as follows:—

Address of the Irish Commons.

"We beg leave humbly to represent to your Majesty, that it is *not by temporary expedients*, but by *a free trade alone*, that this nation is now to be saved from impending ruin. And from your Majesty's gracious declaration—imprinted in our hearts in characters of indelible gratitude, that '*anxious for the happiness of all your people, you will most cheerfully co-operate with your parliaments in such measures as may promote the common interests of all your subjects*,' we draw the happiest presages in favour of a measure *essential* to the *existence* of this kingdom, and which appears to us conducive to the interests of Great Britain.

"Permit us to assure your Majesty, that we have every disposition to go as far as the national abilities will, in making a provision for the honourable support of your Majesty's government, but with hearts glowing with the warmest wishes for the prosperity and glory of the British empire, and full of zeal against the common enemy, we have the mortification to find, that the limited state of our trade and commerce must, by narrowing our resources, set bounds to our liberality, very far short of our earnest inclinations."—(*Irish Commons' Journal*, vol. xix.)

They were fully born out by facts in the matters they thus advanced. Irish debt had enormously increased in consequence of the falling of the revenue, and so also had her drains. The profits of Ireland on *all* the trade that she had, were not estimated higher than £600,000 a year, while her remittances to England were computed at more than double that amount. But it is unnecessary to go into proofs of the distress of Ireland, when we have the admissions in the English parliament, not only on the occasions and by the persons which are mentioned in our first pages, but *general* admissions in 1778–9, as will be seen by reference to the debates in the English parliament during those years. In the latter year the ministry of the day, in defending themselves against the charge of having occasioned the grievances of Ireland, declared "*that her grievances originated many years before, in the general system of trade laws—that the restrictions then laid on arose from a narrow, short-sighted policy, which, though conceived in prejudice, and founded on ignorance, was yet so strengthened by time, and confirmed by the habits of a century, that it seemed at length wrought into, and became even a part of the consitution*"—(*Coll. Pol.* p. 173.)

Notwithstanding these things, nothing was done in the way of relief at that moment. Immediately after, however, the Irish parliament took the strong measure of limiting the supplies to six months; and this was effective where argument failed, and accordingly the British minister at length proceeded to give relief. The various propositions for the purpose, from the first starting of the matter in 1778, were as follows: England coerced into relaxation.

In 1778, Lord Newhaven moved, in the English parliament, that Ireland should be allowed freedom of export, except of her woollen manufactures; and should have liberty of trading to and from America, the West Indies, and the Coast of Africa.

From this position he was gradually beaten down; until in March 1779, he had to reduce his motion to one for a repeal, in so far as related to the article of sugar, of that part of the Navigation Act of 1663, which compelled sugar intended for Ireland, to be first landed in England. This he at first carried by a majority of 47 to 42—but being afterwards deserted by the minister on account of the violent outcry of English and Scotch great towns, the motion was finally lost on a division of 62 to 58. Details.

In November of that year, the Irish parliament resolved unanimously—

"That the export from this kingdom of its woollen and other manufactures to all foreign places, would materially relieve its distresses, increase its wealth, promote its prosperity, and thereby advance the welfare of Great Britain, and the common strength, wealth, and commerce of the British Empire.

"That a liberty for this kingdom to trade with the British Colonies in America and the West Indies, and the British Settlements on the Coast of Africa, in like manner as trade is carried on between Great Britain and the said colonies and settlements, would be productive of very great commercial benefits—would be a most affectionate mark of the regard and attention of Great Britain to our distresses —and would give new vigour to the zeal of His Majesty's brave and loyal people of Ireland, to stand forward in support of His Majesty's person and government, and the interest, the honor, and the dignity of the British empire."—*Commons Journal, Vol.* 19.

The British minister, coerced by the gathered force of public opinion, and the powerful additional stimulant of the short money-bill from Ireland, accordingly moved on the 13th December, 1779, three propositions—first, for the repeal of those laws which prohibited export of Irish woollen goods and wool flocks, to any part of Europe; second, that so much of the Act 19, Geo. 2, as forbade import of glass into Ireland, save of British manufacture, and also forbade export of glass from Ireland, should be repealed; and third, that Ireland should have freedom of trade to all the British Colonial Settlements, subject to such limitations and regulations as the parliament of Ireland should impose.

The "Free Trade" of 1779-80.

The two first were quickly passed into law—the third was delayed till the next session, on the plea of some inquiry being necessary into its probable effect in Ireland. In the latter country the partial concessions were received in so good a spirit, that the supplies were immediately granted for a year and a half more.

Fresh invasions of Irish rights.

But this satisfaction was by no means unalloyed or lasting. England, unwisely for her own views of policy, had provoked the question of her right to control the legislature of Ireland—a question which had always been present to the Irish mind; and towards the discussion of which that mind had been of late strongly tending, with the determined purpose of asserting independence of legislation. The Privy Council in England altered a mutiny bill, (by making it perpetual,) sent over as usual for their approbation, from Ireland. This was altogether an unconstitutional proceeding, and woke up at once the smouldering flame. In this article we have to deal only with commercial matters, so do not go into the details of the constitutional agitation and demand, which then arose, further than in so far as commerce was concerned. The alteration in the mutiny-bill was accompanied by a nearly equally exasperating alteration in a bill respecting the import of sugars. The business of sugar-refining had recently taken great head in Ireland, and the parliament here sought to defend it against the English monopoly by an import duty on refined sugar; while they sought to give it a fair stimulus by admitting raw sugar at a low rate. This the Privy Council reversed, reducing the duty on refined sugar 20 per cent under the drawback allowed in England to the English refiner on export, and thereby giving the latter a virtual *premium* to that amount—and also increasing the duty on the raw sugar.

The time was ill-chosen for further invasions on Irish rights. Irritation had long been rankling in Ireland at the restrictions on her commerce; and it had indeed already broken out into an overt act. One of the Dublin Corporation, Alderman Horan, resolved to test the question, whether the Irish woollen trade could be *legally* bound by the *English* act of William's reign, restricting it from foreign export. The act passed by the obsequious Irish parliament of that time, for the same purpose, had long before 1771 become extinct. Accordingly he tendered for entry *outwards*, at the Custom-house, Irish woollen goods. He was dissuaded from pressing the point at the moment: but the affair made great sensation—and (as we see from official documents copied in the laborious and most interesting memoir of his father's life, from the pen of Henry Grattan, the excellent member for Meath,) drew the serious and alarmed attention of the government. Their consequences.

These points of alterations in the mutiny bill and the sugar bill, were not considered in the Irish parliament till August 1780; and the delay by no means tended to calm the existing irritation—but grievously to impair the feelings of satisfaction and gratitude, which the Irish people had been disposed to demonstrate, after the commercial relaxations we have mentioned, as enacted in the English parliament in the month of February. Several minor circumstances concurred to exasperate them still further, and to render irrevocable, and soon after irresistible, their determination to have a free parliament, without which they saw they never could obtain the full extension of their trade, amongst other benefits sought, nor even be sure of preserving what had been conceded to them.

The Irish parliament disgraced itself at this juncture, by sanctioning the alterations in question. Their conduct in this respect excited great indignation against themselves, and the Merchants' Corps of Volunteers, the Independent Dublin and Liberty Corps, and several other corps, and the general body of the citizens of Dublin, passed strong resolutions in their several meetings, condemnatory of the conduct of their legislature—which, in its turn, passed a vote of censure on these proceedings, and addressed the Viceroy to prosecute their authors.

In the short session of the year 1781 the chief matters of debate were the obstructions given to our woollens and printed linens in the ports of Portugal, and the disastrous Irish interests neglected and sacrificed.

effects to our sugar-refineries of the measure of the preceding year. On this point several members of the mercantile body were examined at the bar of the commons, and their evidence of the mischief done was strongly supported and urged by Grattan, Flood, and other patriots, but without any good result. The other matter, the dispute with Portugal, had its origin in a measure of the preceding session, which raised the duties on port wine; at the same time, however, that the previous advantage which that wine had possessed over those of France was proportionately preserved, by an equal increase upon the previously higher duties on the latter. In the two months of the session of 1782, the attention of the government was several times called to the dispute, but without success. Early in the ensuing session, however, viz., on the 6th of February, 1782, the House unanimously adopted an address to the Throne, calling the royal attention to the conduct of Portugal, and soliciting his Majesty's interference to procure an abatement of the grievance complained of. The royal answer received, March 5th, promised compliance with the request, but further than the giving of this promise nothing was done.

In another article of this Appendix we treat of the glorious achievement in 1782, of legislative independence; at present it is not properly within our scope to speak of it, as we are dealing with the *commercial* relations of the countries alone.

Really limited nature of the "FREE TRADE" of 1782.

We have now seen the full extent of the relaxations obtained by Ireland up to 1782, in the rigid exclusion-code which England had enacted against our manufactures. Ireland by them obtained liberty of trade with foreign countries and the dependencies of Great Britain, (excepting the *East Indies*), but trade with Britain herself remained in nearly as unequal and unjust a condition as ever; she took from us little else but our inferior linens and our linen yarn, which we could have worked up more profitably at home; and the whole sum she spent upon our products was estimated not to exceed half-a-million at the utmost. On the other hand, we took largely of her manufactures, and paid her about two millions of money for them. Some idea of the discrepancy of the customs rates between the two countries may be formed from the fact, that English cloths were charged only with 6*d*. per yard on entering Ireland, whereas Irish were shut out of British ports by the enormous charge of £2 0s. 6d. per yard. In fact the "Free Trade" obtained in 1782, although an immense improvement on the previously existing state of things, was a most maimed and halting measure, and almost altogether justified the assurances that the British minister, Lord North, found himself compelled to give, in circular letters, to the manufacturing towns of England, to the effect that "*nothing effectual had been granted to Ireland!*"

Proof of deceits of the English ministers.

Yet, neither these assurances, nor the facts that to a considerable extent bore them out, were successful in satisfying the griping spirit of the English manufacturers and traders. The concessions, "ineffectual" as they were thus represented to be, and limited most unfairly, as they undoubtedly were, yet looked too large in the eyes of selfish monopoly; and in three years from their date, Mr. Pitt, who had in 1782 declared them to be nothing more than what Ireland had the merest and purest right to demand, had to conciliate public opinion in England, by stigmatizing them as "ignorant and unsystematic," and such as required limitation.

Examinations of the propositions of 1785.

The occasion on which he did so, was in 1785, when bringing forward the celebrated "commercial propositions" of that year. Whether those propositions had any better foundations in "British generosity" than any of the preceding changes proposed, or effected, in the commercial relations of the two countries, will be seen on perusing the account we now proceed to give of them.

The "commercial" propositions as originally proposed.

In Ireland they were, and have been up to the present day, usually styled, "Orde's propositions," from their having been first brought forward by Mr. Orde, Secretary for Ireland. On the 17th of February, 1785, he introduced them to the Irish House of Commons, in the following shape:—

I.—Resolved—"That it is the opinion of this committee, (committee of the *whole House*,) that it is highly important to the general interest of the British Empire, that the trade between Great Britain and Ireland be encouraged and extended as much as possible, and, for that purpose, that the intercourse and commerce be finally settled, and regulated on permanent and equitable principles, for the mutual benefit of both countries.

II.—"That towards carrying into full effect so desirable a settlement, it is fit and proper that all articles not the growth or manufacture of Great Britain or Ireland, should be imported into each kingdom from the other reciprocally, under the same regulations, and at the same duties, if subject to duties, to which they are liable when imported directly from the place of their growth, product or manufacture; and that all duties originally paid on the import into either country respectively, shall be fully drawn back on export to the other.

III.—"That for the same purpose, it is proper that no prohibition should exist in either country, against the importation, use, or sale of any article, the growth, produce, or manufacture of the other; and that the duty on import of every such article, if subject to duty in either country, should be precisely the same in the one as in the other, except where an addition may be necessary in either country, in consequence of an internal duty on any such article of its own consumption.

IV.—"That in all cases where the duties on articles of the growth, product, or manufacture of either country are different on the importation into the other, it would be expedient that they should be reduced in the kingdom where they are highest, to the amount payable in the other; and that all such articles should be exportable from the kingdom into which they shall be imported, as free from such duty as the similar commmodities, or home manufacture of the same kingdom.

V.—"That for the same purpose,. it is also proper, that in all cases where either kingdoms shall charge articles of its own consumption with an internal duty on the manufacture, or a duty on the material, the same manufacture when imported from the other, may be charged with a further import-duty to the same amount, as the internal duty on the manufacture, or to an amount adequate to countervail the duty on the material; and shall be entitled to such drawbacks, or bounties upon export, as may leave the same subject to no heavier burthens than the home-made manufacture; such further duty to continue so long as the internal consumption shall be charged with the duty or duties, to balance which it shall be imposed, or until the manufacture coming from the other kingdom, shall be subjected there to an equal burthen, not drawn back, or compensated on exportation.

VI.—"That in order to give permanency to the settlement now intended to be established, it is necessary that no prohibition, or new additional duties should be hereafter imposed in either kingdom, on import of any article of the growth, product, or manufacture of the other, save such additional duties as may be requisite to balance duties on internal consumption, pursuant to the foregoing resolution.

VII.—"That for the same purpose, it is further necessary that no prohibitions, or new and additional duties, should be hereafter imposed in either kingdom, on export of any article of native growth, product, or manufacture, to the other; except such as either kingdom may deem expedient, from time to time, upon corn, meal, malt, flour, and biscuit; and also except where there now exists any prohibition which is not reciprocal, or any duty not equal in both. In every such case the prohibition may be reciprocal, or the duties raised, so as to make them equal.

VIII.—"That for the same purpose, it is necessary, that no bounties whatever be paid in either kingdom, on export of any article to the other, except such as relate to corn, meal malt, flour, and biscuit; and such as are in the nature of drawbacks, or compensation for duties paid; and that no bounty be granted in this kingdom on export of any article imported from the British plantations, or any manufacture made of such article, unless in cases where a similar bounty is payable in Britain on export from thence; or where such bounty is merely in the nature of a drawback, or compensation for duties paid, over and above any duties paid thereon in Britain.

IX.—"That it is expedient for the general benefit of the British empire, that the import of articles from foreign states should be regulated from time to time, in each kingdom, on such terms as may afford an effectual preference to the import of similar articles of the growth, product, or manufacture of the other.

X. "That it is the opinion of this committee, that for the protection of trade, whatever sum the gross hereditary revenue of this kingdom (after deducting drawbacks, repayments, and bounties in the nature of drawbacks) shall produce annually, over and above the sum of £——— should be appropriated towards the naval force of the empire, in such manner as the parliament of this kingdom shall direct."

Mr. Secretary Orde introduced these propositions with many praises of the liberality of England. "The moment," said he, (page 119 of the 4th vol. Irish Parliamentary

Secretary Orde's Speech introducing

his propositions, 7th Feb. 1785. Register,) "is, I trust, come, when she will make her victory over herself complete—when the reservation even of a just preference will be given up, and thereby every obstacle removed to the interchange of the commodities of the world.........The same principle which induces Great Britain to sacrifice a partial interest to the great object, a generous reciprocity, will influence your estimation and acknowledgement of her unequivocal liberality, &c., &c."

Attempts at delusion. He praised the second resolution, as enabling Ireland to "supply the British market, on the same terms as the British merchants could." Of the third, he said—"that it secured the English market for Irish goods, linens, tabbinets, poplins, &c." And he added, "at this day how large a portion of what Britain takes from Ireland is Irish produce! and how small a portion of what Ireland takes from Britain is produced there!" But the part of his speech most to be noticed, was that concerning the tenth resolution, viz.—"Great Britain will thus generously sacrifice her monopolies; she gives up the hope of being the emporium of trade, at a time when her burdens press upon her; and she groans under the weight of a debt incurred by the general defence of the empire. I hope we will meet her with a like liberality of spirit. If in consequence of this adjustment a great increase of revenue arise to Ireland, it will not be thought unreasonable to appropriate a part to the protection of the trade from which it arises; and by our contributing to the support of the naval force of the empire, Britain will still be enabled to afford protection."

Manner in which the plan was received. The Right Hon. William Brownlow, M. P. for Armagh County, rose next, and denounced the tenth proposition, as tending to make Ireland a tributary nation. The whole plan was however received with something like favor by the House. The Right Hon. Luke Gardiner, (afterwards Lord Mountjoy,) one who at that time held a prominent position in the patriotic ranks, went so far as to express some gratitude for the "*liberal principles*" that the English ministry seemed disposed to act upon. He made however a general objection, that these resolutions would go to prevent protecting duties, which he considered necessary to the manufactures of Ireland, to balance England's advantages of "long-established trade, large capitals, and extensive credit." And he concluded by calling attention to the failure of reciprocity as regarded mutual interchange

Objections noted.

of the raw material of each other's staple, viz.—linen yarn for Ireland, and wool for England; the latter being strictly guarded against export from England, while Irish linen yarn was to go free into that country.

Mr. Foster, Chancellor of the Exchequer, (afterwards, and until the Union, speaker of the Irish House of Commons—and subsequently an official in the united parliament, until raised to the peerage by the title of Lord Oriel,) gave no answer to these objections, than that our linen manufacture was of the greatest importance to us; and would now be secure of the English market. *and evaded.*

The matter was then adjourned to Friday, the 11th of February, on which day— *Adjournment to 11th Feb.*

Petitions were presented against the propositions—one from the Dublin Chamber of Commerce, to much the same effect as Mr. Gardiner's objections—and a similar one from the woollen, silk, cotton, and mixed goods manufacturers of Dublin. *Petitions against.*

Mr. Flood and others complained of being hurried into consideration of the matter.

He complained that the people of Ireland had asked for protection; and the answer was, the 4th proposition, which was to do away with all protection—and insisted on the necessity of preserving our home-market. *Flood begins his opposition.*

With much debate but no division, the propositions were passed, until the 7th, when Mr. Gardiner moved that neither country should prohibit export of the raw material of its staple. He said "Irish woollen yarn was best for the *weft*—and English for the *warp*. Now the English get our yarn, of which they make their weft—but send none of theirs to us to make our warp—which surely was no reciprocity." *Grattan's attempt to secure real reciprocity.*

The Committee divided— *Failure.*

For the amendment, ... 33
For the original resolution, 178

It was then proposed that the following should be the 10th resolution:—

"That it is essential to the commercial interest of this country to prevent, as much as possible, an accumulation of national debt; and that therefore it is highly expedient that the annual revenues of this kingdom should be made equal to its annual expences." *Change at the end of the resolutions, made with the concurrence of Grattan, who de-*

And that the 11th should be,—"That for the better protection of trade, whatever sum the gross hereditary refends them. venue of this kingdom, (after deducting all drawbacks, repayments, or bounties in the nature of drawbacks), shall produce over and above the sum of £656,000 in each year in peace, wherein the annual revenue shall equal the annual expense; and in each year of war, without regard to such equality; should be appropriated towards the support of the naval force of the empire, in such manner as the parliament of this kingdom shall direct."

The Chancellor of the Exchequer stated that in these he had the advice and assistance of Mr. Grattan.

It was objected, that the first of these made no provision for *reduction of expenditure*—but for increased taxation. And that the second was, in fact, a subsidy to England.

Allusion to the "Surplus" question of 1753.

Mr. Grattan defended them on the grounds that "by making the surplus not applicable to the general expenditure till all expenses were paid, both British and Irish ministers would be interested in Irish economy, and the Irish parliament would have the control." This latter provision decided, he said, "the great question of 1753," (which was a controversy as to whether the Irish parliament had, or had not, the power of disposing of surplus revenue, after clearing off the debt—an occurrence that took place in that year.)

Resolutions passed at an advanced hour in the morning, in Mr. Flood's absence.

The "propositions," or resolutions were then passed.

On Monday, February 14, Mr. Flood re-opened the subject, commencing by stating he had been obliged by illness to leave the House, at a comparatively early period of the previous discussion, and had gone with the impression that the promise of Mr. Foster to "ameliorate" the concluding resolution would have been otherwise carried out than it was.

He complains thereof March 14, and accuses the Government of fraud.

Ireland ought to have a navy of her own.

He accused Foster of seeking unfairly to create the "*casus*" of the 11th resolution, by not including in the deductions excepted in it, the corn-bounty, and the charges of management of the revenue. He contended that Ireland ought not thus to give away her money for ever to the navy of the empire, but, if need were, to create and support a navy of her own; and showed what a bad precedent she had, in the provision she had been called upon, since 1769, to make for the army of the empire, which had caused her debt ever since to accumulate. He said that a part of the hereditary revenue was already appropriated to a sea-guard—that a time when England herself was in every way retrenching, was no time for us, instead of reducing our heavy military establishment, to add to our expenses by this naval contribution, and to her debt also as she could not borrow all she would want at home, but should do so in England, and so create *absentee debt*, the interest being, of course, paid and spent out of the country. He concluded by moving, "That an immediate and effectual retrenchment is necessary." An amendment to defer (and thereby, of course, defeat) his motion was then moved by Mr. Mason, (M.P. for the borough of St. Canice, or Irishtown, county Kilkenny.)

Ought not to be made to incur more debt, and an *absentee-debt*; also moves amendment.

Division for the amendment, ... 131
For Mr. Flood's motion, ... 43

Defeated.

No sufficient answer appears to have been given—nor, indeed, could be given, to Mr. Flood's eloquent and most cogent arguments. The arrangement then, as proposed in February, 1785, stands charged with the following injustices towards Ireland:—

General remarks on the whole scheme.

First, That by resolution 4 (and others), she was to deprive herself at once, and for ever, of all protection against the tremendous rivalry of the long-established manufactures of England, supported as they were by an immensely superior capital, and of course a system of long credits. And the concluding provision of this resolution opened the way for England to seize on the export trade of Ireland.

Its binding Ireland against any protection to her manufactures.

Second, That by resolution 6, England was to be enabled to supply herself at her own terms with our linen-yarn, that is, the material of our staple manufacture,—while resolution 7, allowed the continuance of *her* prohibition of export to us of *her wool*, the material of *her* staple manufacture, *and an article which we much desired to have.*

Also perfect reciprocity, not established, England being favoured as to her wool.

Third, That we should (by resolution 9) pledge ourselves to give English goods a preference over foreign, no matter how much more advantageous to us to deal with the foreigner; England, to be sure, was to be similarly bound; but our staple manufacture, that of linen, had a powerful rival in the Scotch linen in her market, and we had nothing else of consequence which she would take.

Against profitable treaty with foreigners.

Fourth, That the resolution No. 10, (as last proposed and carried,) went to sanction the scarcely concealed purpose of the minister to increase our burthens, without any reference to the propriety of reducing our expenses.

To heavy increase of taxation and to a tribute.

Fifth, That the final resolution, No. 11, violated all constitutional precedent, by pledging the country, without limitation of time, to pay a certain fixed amount of money to England, upon the occurrence of a contingency, the great likelihood of which was enhanced by the fraudulent working of the clause providing for it.

The proviso giving the Irish parliament control over the details of the disposition of the grant was a mockery, when they were to preclude themselves from meddling with its general application.

But these injustices did not appear to the parliament of England to be sufficient.

English parliament however not satisfied even with these grievances to Ireland.

Pitt contradicting Orde.

Mr. Pitt, in submitting the resolutions to the British parliament for their adoption, (which he did on the 22nd February, 1785,) found it necessary to endeavour to remove from the minds of his hearers the impression which his deputy in Ireland (Mr. Orde) had laboured to make upon the Irish parliament; viz., that the contemplated arrangement was a pure benefit to Ireland, out of the liberality of England.

In the first place he sought to have it considered that Ireland had required this arrangement. "What has been done" (said he, alluding to the concessions of 1780–2) "was still viewed by the Irish people as insufficient, and clamours were excited, and suggestions published in Dublin and elsewhere, of putting duties on English produce and manufactures, under the name of protecting duties."

The real design of the scheme coming out through the clumsiness of the device.

This last branch of the sentence discloses at once and thoroughly the *real* reason why the proposed arrangement was brought forward by the British ministry. They could not show one petition to prove that Ireland wished for it. In fact and truth the secret of the matter was, the desire to prevent the Irish from giving their own manufactures some protection against the crushing rivalry of England.

Compelled by the somewhat indiscreet anxiety of the representatives of the manufacturing interests of England, to speak plainer than exactly consisted with the language of Mr. Orde in Ireland, he asked—"What was likely to be the extent of this boon to Ireland? was it likely she would become the mart of the empire? He could not believe it ever would be the case. . . . . . It was not probable that Ireland ever could furnish England with colonial produce in any great degree. . . . . . As to the equalization of the duties on mutual intercourse, a country like Ireland, not capable of supplying herself, never could meet us in our markets. . . . . . With the disadvantage of being loaded with heavy taxes at home, still our manufactures had always been able to triumph over the Irish in their own markets, paying the low duties there on import, and also the charges. . . . . . Would Ireland's cheap labour enable her to undersell us? Manufacturers thought otherwise; there were great obstacles to the planting of any manufacture. It would require time for arts and capital, which could not increase without the demand; and in an established manufacture improvement was so rapid as to bid defiance to rivalship. In some of our manufactures too, there were natural and insurmountable obstacles to their competition. In the *woollens*, for instance, *by confining the raw material to this country*, the manufacture was confined also."

Mr. Fox made the following significant remarks on this occasion: "It had struck him as a singular instance of ingenuity, that in opening the outlines of the plan, the Right Honourable gentleman (Mr. Pitt) had done away with a good deal of what had been said upon the subject in another speech, to another assembly. Indeed his (Mr. Pitt's) speech had been little else than an answer to that of Mr. Secretary Orde, in the Irish House of Commons. . . . . . It was curious to observe how differently the minister in Ireland, and the minister in England had recommended the same propositions to two different Parliaments. In Ireland they had been stated as highly advantageous to that country—putting it on the footing of Great Britain, and rendering it an emporium of trade, and the source and supply of the British markets. In England and in that House they were told that the propositions were such as this country (England) might gladly accede to. Why? 'because it gives Ireland nothing but what it had before—because Ireland cannot rival you— because Ireland is poor and feeble; and because Ireland must remain so, if not for ever, at least for a considerable length of time.'" Fox's eloquent denunciation of the pretences put forward.

It was agreed upon that time should be given for the presentation of petitions respecting these resolutions, hearing of counsel at the Bar of the House on the subject, &c. &c.; in consequence of this, it was not till Thursday, 7th May, 1785, that the propositions were debated, with a view to definitive adoption. Time for petitions, &c. allowed. The propositions brought on again in the English parliament 7th May, 1785.

In moving them, Mr. Pitt took occasion to state as follows, the then position of Ireland:—

"Ireland could, at this moment, trade with unlimited freedom to every foreign state in Europe, supply them with her own produce and manufacture, and carry home Pitt exposes the then condition of Ireland.

She had free foreign trade and colonial trade, and could carry colonial goods *direct* to Great Britain.

theirs in return. She was also at liberty to supply the British colonies in the West Indies, and, by a direct trade homeward, furnish herself with the West-India goods. But this was not all, she could also, at this moment supply the British market by a direct trade to Britain, with the produce of the British Islands. Relative to West-India commodities, the only question now was, that the Irish should be permitted to bring into England, circuitously through Ireland, those goods which they were at present at full liberty to import into this country direct from the West Indies."

The opposition to this was from the West India planters, who feared that foreign sugars would be imported under cover of it.

Her exclusion from the East Indies.

Proposed *boon* in this respect.

Mr. Pitt said that Ireland "had no better right to complain of exclusion from the East India trade, than any one of our own outports. He would, however, allow her this, that 'the East India Company should be empowered to take in such part of their outward bound cargo *as they might find convenient*, in the ports of Ireland, and also to import directly from the East Indies into Ireland, whatever they might think proper.'"

He condemned the petitions against his plan, saying, that "the greater part of them had been drawn up without due attention to the subject. . . . . . They seemed (the petitioners) not to know that the liberties and privileges to Ireland, of which they complained, and her rivalry in foreign markets, subsisted by the laws already in existence."

Pitt further shows how Ireland could not rival England.

He then went on to combat the doctrine "that Ireland, from the cheapness of labour, must necessarily undersell the English manufacturer. . . . . It did not depend on that sort of work which was required for the most rough and rude occupations of agriculture, whether a nation was to flourish in manufacture or not. . . . . . The fears of the manufacturers were extremely far-fetched and ill-founded. . . . . . They had declared themselves to be afraid that the Irish should be able to draw over all their workmen, all their trade and capital, and undersell them in their own markets by, at least, 13 per cent. Now, he desired the committee to attend to that single subject. The Irish cotton trade was to enter England by this plan, at £10½ per cent. duty, and yet it was said they were to undersell the English cotton manufacturer by 13 per cent.!

States the then Irish duty on cotton import from

Besides this, England had hitherto imported into Ireland at a duty of £10½ per cent. These three sums together would make £34 per cent.; therefore if these petitions deserved credit, they had, at that disadvantage, engrossed almost exclusively the Irish market, in which their dealings had increased and flourished to an extent hardly to be equalled by any other branch of trade known, a thing perfectly beyond the reach of belief. . . . . . In another branch there was the same exaggerated representation by Mr. Wedgewood, the earthenware manufacturer, who had given a very copious testimony at the bar, in the most collected and deliberate manner, and yet the House could learn nothing from him than his having wished to engross every market to which he had ever thought of sending his wares; and, by the by, he did not know well how to send them to Ireland for fear of damage by breakage and other losses. At all risks of credibility and consistency, he sought to find nothing in these propositions but ruin to his manufacture."

England, 10½ per cent., notwithstanding which the Englishman beat the Irish cotton manufacturer.

Ridicules the jealousy and fears of the British manufacturers,

After ridiculing the idea of comparing a poor with a rich country, and showing that notwithstanding the great advantages predicted to Scotland from her union with England, *the latter had been "more benefitted by it,"* and that the result of that union *"had been such as not to make England averse to a repetition of the experiment;"* he proceeded to open "that part of the plan which was entirely and exclusively favourable to this country (England), and which was to be the gratuity given by Ireland for whatever benefit she was to derive, and the compensation to England for whatever advantage she might give up. . . . . . This compensation was the surplus of the Irish hereditary revenue, over and above £654,000 for her own uses. This would bear an exact proportion to the benefit she was to reap from the new arrangements; her hereditary revenue was by customs on almost every thing imported, by excise on the most general articles of consumption, and by a house-tax, levied on the number of hearths in each. . . . . . . The committee would see, therefore, that this revenue would increase necessarily as soon as the new arrangement had effect, and in exact proportion to that effect, every article of which it was composed being so closely connected with commerce, wealth, and population. It was his idea that the supply should be taken in provisions and stores."

especially as Ireland was a poor country. Confesses that the union with Scotland benefitted the latter less than England, *who, therefore, would "not be averse to repeat the experiment,"* (viz., *with Ireland.*) The "Tribute" said by him to be a fair purchase by Ireland of a benefit.

He concluded with submitting an "amended" and extended list of "propositions," increasing the number greatly,

Increase of the number of the

propositions and their stringency.

Fox asks the justification of so great a change, if the first plan were all it had been pretended.

And shews his own jealousy of Ireland.

and materially altering and adding to the substance. Mr. Fox, speaking to the question a little later, remarked severely upon the high-handed manner in which the first list had been sought to be pressed upon the House, and praised for their perfection; whereas now, the minister had been forced practically to admit their great faultiness—that by them, as they first stood, England would have lost the monopoly of the East India trade, hazarded the revenue arising from spirituous liquors—no distinction having been made between native and foreign spirits—nor any protection provided against the latter. That they would have sacrificed the navigation laws, and thereby given up "the great source of commercial opulence, the prime origin of our maritime strength," in trust to Ireland, leaving English interests totally dependent on her policy and her bounty. That a door would be opened to most extensive smuggling—no bonds, cockets, &c. &c., being required. And that Ireland having the power of giving bounties, or allowing drawbacks on goods exported to the colonies, might beat England in the colonial market, while she could also injure the colonies, by letting in foreign colonial goods cheap.

Inadvertent confession of hardship to Ireland.

He continued thus: "I need not state to the committee a fact so universally known, as that the *produce of our colonies is dearer than that of the foreign islands.* Nevertheless, we have given them the home-market, on account of the natural interest we have in them, and we must continue to do so. But Ireland has no such obligation; *on the contrary, her interest would as forcibly lead her to the foreign colonies.*"

He supports the new propositions because of their stringency.

Aware of this fact with regard to Ireland, and in order to prevent her from thus consulting her own interest, Mr. Fox supported the new form of the "propositions."

Mr. Pitt succeeded in carrying his resolutions, and sending them to the Lords. After some amendments there, and subsequent amendments, unnecessary to be detailed, in tne Commons on return, both houses finally agreed to, and passed them in the following shape:—

The propositions as they finally passed in England.

I.—"That it is highly important to the interests of both countries, that the commerce between Great Britain and Ireland should be finally regulated on permanent and equitable principles, for the mutual benefit of both countries.

II.—"That a full participation of commercial advantages should be permanently secured to Ireland, whenever a provision equally permanent and secure, shall be made by the parliament of that kingdom, towards defraying, in proportion to its growing prosperity, the necessary expenses in time of peace, of protecting the trade and general interests of the empire.

III.—"That towards carrying into full effect so desirable a settlement, it is fit and proper that all articles, not the growth or manufacture of Great Britain or Ireland, except those of the growth, produce, or manufacture of any of the countries beyond the Cape of Good Hope to the Streights of Magellan, should be imported into each kingdom from the other reciprocally, under the same regulations, and at the same duties (if subject to duties) to which they would be liable, when imported directly from the country or place from whence the same may have been imported into Great Britain or Ireland respectively, as the case may be; and that all duties originally paid on importation into either country respectively, except on arrack and foreign brandy, and on rum, and all sorts of strong waters not imported from the British colonies in the West Indies, shall be fully drawn back on exportation to the other. But, nevertheless, that the duties shall continue to be protected and guarded, as at present, by withholding the drawback, until a certificate from the proper officers of the revenue, in the kingdom to which the export may be made, shall be returned and compared with the entry outwards.

IV.—"That it is highly important to the general interests of the British empire, that the laws for regulating trade and navigation, should be the same in Great Britain and Ireland; and therefore, that it is essential towards carrying into effect the present settlement, that all laws which have been made, or shall be made, in Great Britain, for securing exclusive privileges to the ships and mariners of Great Britain, Ireland, and the British colonies and plantations, and for regulating and restraining the trade of the British colonies and plantations; such laws imposing the same restraints, and conferring the same benefits on the subjects of both kingdoms); should be in force in Ireland, by laws to be passed by the parliament of that kingdom, for the same time, and in the same manner, as in Great Britain.

V.—"That it is further essential to this settlement, that all goods and commodities of the growth, produce, or manufacture of British or foreign colonies in America of the

West Indies, and the British or foreign settlements on the coast of Africa, imported into Ireland, should, on importation, be subject to the same duties and regulations, as the like goods are, or from time to time shall be subject to, upon importation into Great Britain; or if prohibited from being imported into Great Britain, shall in like manner be prohibited from being imported into Ireland.

VI.—" That in order to prevent illicit practices, injurious to the revenue and commerce of both kingdoms, it is expedient, that all goods, whether of the growth, produce, or manufacture of Great Britain or Ireland, or of any foreign country, which shall be hereafter imported into Great Britain from Ireland, or into Ireland from Great Britain, should be put, by laws to be passed in the parliament of the two kingdoms, under the same regulations with respect to bonds, cockets, and other instruments, to which the like goods are now subject in passing from one port of Great Britain to another.

VII.—" That for the like purpose it is also expedient, that when any goods, the growth, produce, or manufacture of the British West India islands, or any other of the British colonies or plantations, shall be shipped from Ireland for Great Britain, they should be accompanied with such original certificates of the revenue officers of the said colonies, as shall be required by the law, on importation into Great Britain; and that when the whole quantity, included in one certificate, shall not be shipped at any one time, the original certificate, properly endorsed as to quantity, should be sent with the first parcel; and to identify the remainder, if shipped at any future period, new certificates should be granted by the principal officers of the ports in Ireland, extracted from a register of the original document, specifying the quantities before shipped from thence, by what vessels, and to what ports.

VIII.—" That it is essential for carrying into effect the present settlement, that all goods exported from Ireland to the British colonies in the West Indies, or in America, or to the British settlements on the coast of Africa, should from time to time be made liable to such duties and drawbacks, and put under such regulations as may be necessary, in order that the same may not be exported with less incumbrance of duties or imposition than the like goods shall be burthened with when exported from Great Britain.

IX.—" That it is essential to the general commercial interests of the empire, that so long as the parliament of this kingdom shall think it advisable, that the commerce to the countries beyond the Cape of Good Hope shall be carried on solely by an exclusive company, having liberty to import into the port of London only, no goods of the growth, produce, or manufacture of any countries beyond the Cape of Good Hope should be importable into Ireland from any foreign country, or from any settlement in the East Indies belonging to any such foreign country; and that no goods of the growth, produce, or manufacture of the said countries should be allowed to be imported into Ireland but through Great Britain; and it shall be lawful to export such goods of the growth, produce, or manufacture of any of the countries beyond the Cape of Good Hope to the Streights of Magellan, from Great Britain to Ireland, with the same duties retained thereon as are now retained on their being exported to that kingdom; but that an account shall be kept of the duties retained, and the net drawback on the said goods imported to Ireland; and the amount thereof shall be remitted by the receiver-general of his Majesty's customs in Great Britain to the proper officers of the revenue in Ireland, to be placed to the account of his Majesty's revenue there, subject to the disposal of the parliament of that kingdom; and that whenever the commerce to the said countries shall cease to be carried on by an exclusive company, in the goods of the produce of countries beyond the Cape of Good Hope to the Streights of Magellan, the goods should be importable into Ireland from countries from which they may be importable into Great Britain, and no other; and that no vessel should be cleared out from Ireland, for any part of the countries from the Cape of Good Hope to the Streights of Magellan, but such as shall be freighted in Ireland by the said exclusive company, and shall have sailed from the port of London; and that the ships going from Great Britain to any of the said countries beyond the Cape of Good Hope, should not be restrained from touching at any of the ports in Ireland, and taking on board there any of the goods of the growth, produce, or manufacture of that kingdom.

X.—"That no prohibition should exist in either country, against the importation, use, or sale of any article, the growth, produce, or manufacture of the other, except such as either kingdom may judge expedient, from time to time, upon corn, meal, malt, flour, and biscuits; and except such qualified prohibitions, at present contained in any act of the British or Irish parliaments, as do not absolutely prevent the importation of goods, or manufactures, or materials of manufactures, but only regulate the weight, the size, the packages, or other particular circumstances, or prescribe the build or country, and dimensions of the ship importing the same; and also, except on arms, ammunition, gunpowder, and other utensils of war, importable only by virtue of his Majesty's licence; and that the duty on the importation of every such article (if subject to duty in either country) should be precisely the same in one country as in the other, except where an addition may be necessary in either country, in consequence of internal duty on any such article of its own consumption, or in consequence of internal bounties in the country where such article is grown, produced, or manufactured, and except such duties as either kingdom may judge expedient, from time to time, upon corn, meal, flour, malt, and biscuits.

XI.—"That in all cases where the duties on articles of the growth, produce, or manufacture of either country, are different on the importation into the other, it is expedient that they be reduced in the kingdom where they are the highest, to an amount not exceeding the amount payable in the other; so that the same shall not be less than ten and a half per cent. where any article was charged with a duty on importation into Ireland, of ten and a half per cent. or upwards previous to the 17th day of May, 1782; and that all such articles should be exportable, from the kingdom into which they shall be imported, as free from duty as the similar commodities or home manufactures of the same kingdom.

XII.—"That it is also proper, that in all cases where the articles of the consumption of either kingdom shall be charged with an internal duty on the manufacture, the said manufacture, when imported from the other, may be charged with a further duty on importation, adequate to countervail the internal duty on the manufacture, as far as relates to the duties now charged thereon; such further duty to continue so long only as the internal consumption shall be charged with the duty or duties, to balance which it shall be imposed; and that, where there is a duty on the importation of the raw material of any manufacture in one kingdom greater that the like duty on raw materials in the other, such manufacture may, on its importation into the other kingdom, be charged with such a countervailing duty, as may be sufficient to subject the same, so imported, to burdens adequate to those which the manufacture composed of the like raw material is subject to, in consequence of duties on the importation of such material in the kingdom into which such manufacture is so imported; and the said manufacture so imported, shall be entitled to such drawbacks or bounties on exportation, as may leave the same subject to no heavier burden than the home-made manufacture.

XIII.—"That in order to give permanency to the settlement now intended to be established, it is necessary that no new or additional duties should be hereafter imposed in either kingdom on the importation of any article of the growth, produce, or manufacture of the other, except such additional duties as may be requisite to balance the duties on internal consumption, pursuant to the foregoing resolution, or in consequence of bounties remaining on such articles when exported from the other kingdom.

XIV.—"That for the same purpose it is necessary further, that no prohibition, or new or additional duties, shall be hereafter imposed in either kingdom, on the exportation of any article of native growth, produce, or manufacture, from one kingdom to the other, except such as either kingdom may deem expedient from time to time, upon corn, meal, malt, flour, and biscuits.

XV.—"That for the same purpose it is necessary that no bounties whatever should be paid or payable in either kingdom, on the exportation of any article to the other, except such as relate to corn, meal, malt, flour, and biscuits. And except also the bounties at present given by Great Britain on beer and spirits distilled from corn, and such as are in the nature of drawbacks, or compensations for duties paid. And that no bounty should be payable on the exportation of any article to any British colonies or plantations, or to the British settlements on the coast of Africa, or British settlements in the East Indies, or any manufacture made of such article, unless in cases where a similar bounty is payable in Great Britain on exportation from thence, or where such bounty is merely in the nature of a drawback or compensation of or for duties paid over and above any duties paid thereon in Great Britain; and where any internal bounty shall be given in either kingdom, on any goods manufactured therein, and shall remain on such goods when exported, a countervailing duty adequate thereto may be laid upon the importation of the said goods into the other kingdom.

XVI.—"That it is expedient for the general benefit of

the British Empire, that the importation of articles from foreign countries should be regulated from time to time in each kingdom, on such terms as may effectually favor the importation of similar articles of the growth, produce, or manufacture of the other, except in the cases of materials of manufactures, which are, or hereafter may be allowed to be imported from foreign countries duty free; and that in all cases, where any articles are, or may be, subject to higher duties on importation into this kingdom, from the countries belonging to any of the States of North America, than the like goods are or may be subject to when imported as the growth, produce, or manufacture of the British colonies and plantations, or as the produce of fisheries carried on by British subjects, such articles shall be subject to the same duties on importation into Ireland, from the countries belonging to any of the States of North America, as the same are or may be subject to on importation from the said countries into this kingdom.

XVII.—" That it is expedient that measures should be be taken to prevent disputes touching the exercise of the right of the inhabitants of each kingdom to fish on the coast of any part of the British dominions.

XVIII.—" That it is expedient that such privileges of printing and vending books, as are or may be legally possessed within Great Britain, under the grant of the Crown or otherwise, and the copyrights of the authors and booksellers of Great Britain should continue to be protected in the manner they are at present by the laws of Great Britain; and that it is just that measures should be taken by the parliament of Ireland, for giving the like protection to the copyright of the authors and booksellers of that kingdom.

XIX.—" That it is expedient that regulations should be adoped with respect to patents to be hereafter granted, for the encouragement of new inventions, so that the rights, privileges, and restrictions thereon granted and contained, shall be of equal duration and force throughout Great Britain and Ireland.

XX.—" That the appropriation of whatever sum the gross hereditary revenue of the kingdom of Ireland (the due collection thereof being secured by permanent provisions) shall produce, after deducting all drawbacks, repayments, or bounties granted in the nature of drawbacks, over and above the sum of £656,000 in each year, towards the support of the naval force of the empire, to be applied in such manner as the parliament of Ireland shall direct, by an act to be passed for that purpose, will be a satisfactory provision, proportioned to the growing prosperity of that kingdom, towards defraying, in time of peace, the necessary expenses of protecting the trade and general interests of the empire."

Mr. Pitt moved an address to the Throne, relative to these resolutions.

Lord Beauchamp opposed, on the ground of the hurry and insufficiency of the plan. He denied that Ireland was impatient for it.—"It might crush the infant manufactory of Ireland in the first instance, and ultimately injure those of Great Britain. . . . . . The vindication of it, on the allegation that the Irish parliament was determined to lay on protecting duties, was not well grounded. . . . . . . In none of four instances produced was there hostility. . . . . Beer was raised because the Irish inland excise on it was raised. The duty on wire was pointed against Dutch wire, not British, and was only to last a year. . . . . . As to muslins and calicoes, there was only the application of an old law of Charles II.; and the increase of duty on sugar arose from the different principles on which the drawback of our last duty was calculated, of which the Irish parliament made the application, and fixed their port-duty accordingly. . . . . . In the case of woollens the Irish parliament had recently disclaimed the principle; and indeed the whole history of their rates is a proof that they have carried their commercial preference for Great Britain to as great a length as one country can expect from another. . . . . . No reciprocity in these arrangements. British prohibitions on wool and fuller's earth perpetuated, while Irish bay yarn, linen yarn, and raw hides secured to British market for ever. In beer and spirits bounties are reserved, to give a decided superiority against Ireland." He further observed, that the 11th and 12th propositions would also militate against her, and that the coast regulations of "bonds" and "cockets" would embarrass and tend to restrict that trade, which the Irish parliament desired to extend. That the 7th inconvenienced Ireland only, and as to the linen trade, the plan gave "no new security." "England's previous policy was founded on the wisest views of the subject for her own interest. By suffering Irish linens to come in free, she secured the best materials for her own printing trade; and by granting a bounty on their export,

Lord Beauchamp opposes the propositions.

Shews how fair the conduct of Ireland had been,

and the unfair character of these arrangements to her.

England's encouragement to Irish linen had been, in fact, a

benefit to herself. she insured to the London factors the commission and other advantages of sending them to every part of the world."

Mr. Eden states the nature of the whole plan. Mr. Eden professing to speak "as one of the agents for the British manufacturers, and for the landed interests, and stock-holders of England," thus described the general nature of the plan :—

"Great Britain was to give: First, the carriage from Ireland to this kingdom, of colonial produce, after landing in Ireland. Second, an access to the British markets. Third, a national compact not to raise the duties on Irish linens."

It must be clear to the reader, that the first of these *boons* to Ireland was a mockery. England having, of course, the power to import direct from her colonies, would not of course, prefer to pay an increased price on their commodities coming through Ireland.

As to the second *boon*, Ireland was to compensate for it, by thoroughly opening her market to England, then and for ever.

That the third was but the continuance of a matter of advantage to England herself, we have seen confessed in Lord Beauchamp's words already quoted.

So much for the "boons to Ireland." In return England, according to Mr. Eden, was to obtain :

1.—"A control and superintending power of legislation in matters of trade and commerce.

2.—"Acquiescence of Ireland in the perpetual duration of the East and West Indian monopolies.

3.—"A confirmation in British prohibitions of exports, without the power of making them reciprocal." To which, (added Mr. Eden, with astonishing *candour,*) "perhaps I ought to add, *the contribution in proportion to the increasing opulence of Ireland.*"

Fox declares its injustice to Ireland. We shall take leave of the English discussion, with the opinion of Mr. Fox, expressed in the same debate, that by this plan, "*Ireland would lose her constitution, and again become a dependent, subordinate kingdom.*"

The English Lords and Commons having agreed to the propositions in the middle of July, they were submitted to the Irish parliament in their altered shape, upon the 12th of August.

The resolutions being returned to Ire- Mr. Flood sought to anticipate them, upon the 2nd of August, by a resolution—"That we will maintain, in full and undiminished force, the legislative supremacy of "the parliament of Ireland, to legislate for Ireland in all cases —internally, commercially, and externally!"

land are vigorously opposed by Flood, Grattan, &c. &c.

Mr. Grattan and he condemned in most forcible terms the English resolutions; and said they thought no man would have ventured to think of bringing such resolutions before the Irish parliament.

Mr. Flood's motion was evaded by the minister, (Mr. Orde) on a point of form; but was again brought forward by him, in nearly the same words, on the 11th of August, to which day the house had adjourned. After some further strong condemnation of the English resolutions by him and Mr. Grattan, it was agreed that the motion should be adjourned, until Mr. Orde should have the opportunity which he contemplated having the succeeding day, of endeavouring to shew the house that he did not wish to compromise the legislative independence of Ireland.

He, accordingly, made this attempt next day; but the pretexts he put forward for the purpose were too shallow to deceive for a moment, and such as it were a waste of time to record.

Mr. Grattan eloquently and indignantly denounced the attempt; and went into details to shew the various injustices of the whole scheme.

The proofs must be so evident to the candid reader, on the face of the propositions themselves, and indeed in the remarks we have before given, of Mr. Eden, the advocate in the English parliament of the English interests, which considered themselves imperilled even by the shadow of benefit to Ireland, that it is unnecessary to go into them.

One sentence of Mr. Grattan's so well expresses the whole history of our commercial relations with Great Britain, that we quote it, although limited to space:

Grattan on the commercial relations of the three countries.

"Whence the restrictions on Irish trade and commerce? Whence the old misconstruction of the act of navigation? Whence, but from the evil of suffering one country to regulate the trade and navigation of another, and of instituting, under the idea of general protectress, a proud domination, which sacrifices the interests of the whole to the ambition of a part, and arms the little passions of the monopolist with the sovereign potency of an imperial parliament. For great nations, when cursed with unnatural sway, follow but their nature when they invade; and human wisdom has not better provided for human safety than by limiting the principles of human power."

A sentence that dropped from a supporter of Mr. Orde, Mr. Mason, M. P. for St. Canice, deserves also to be recorded, for obvious reasons:

Allusion to a Union.

"The house should recollect they were not going to form an indissoluble contract, like the treaty of union between England and Scotland; for, the moment the act of union passed, the parliament of Scotland was annihilated, or rather merged in that of Great Britain; and if the *articles of union had proved highly oppressive to the people of Scotland, they were left without resource: except what they should find in the moderation of the British parliament, (!)* or the hazards of a civil war!"

Having given these, some extracts from the admirable speech of Flood cannot be omitted.

Flood's final denunciation of the 'propositions.

"I do not wonder at all that this system should end in an open attack upon the rights of Ireland in commerce and constitution—because in its origin it appeared to me to be a covered attack on both.

"The King's speech declared that this system was only to adjust matters not before adjusted—yet the very second of the original ten propositions, in contradiction to this, went only to objects that had been before adjusted in 1780 and 1782—namely, foreign trade and British colonial trade."

"As to foreign trade, one word dispatches that, viz.—the word Independence. Independent Ireland has every right of foreign trade that Britain herself possesses. For this, therefore, she had no compact to make with Britain. This had been adjusted in 1782. British colony trade was adjusted in 1780. The British parliament then declared, that the unshaken loyalty of Ireland entitled her to participate in every advantage of British colony trade. The British act of parliament in pursuance of this resolve, authorized Ireland to trade to the British colonies with like advantages as Britain herself. In equity, and good faith, what can we have to ask that these did not give? Or can Britain, without impeaching her own candour, now say that she then withheld anything? She then boasted the liberality of that transaction. * * * * *
* * * * * * * * * *

"As to Ireland's not having paid for the transaction of 1780, I say the argument would be a sordid one, were it founded on fact—which it is not. The sentiment of the British parliament in 1780, was a wiser and more statesmanlike conception. It was, that the unshaken loyalty of Ireland entitled her to those advantages; and surely that is a price above all prices. But Ireland paid for it in two ways beside; and in each of them more than the value of the object. Firstly, she gave to the British colonies, a monopoly of her consumption in those articles in which she then obtained that free trade. Now I say universally, that any nation pays too dear for one market, when she gives up all other markets for one. And particularly, that the nation pays too dearly for the sugar market of the British colonies, who gives up all other sugar markets for the British, which is neither the best, nor the cheapest. Secondly, I add, that Ireland paid in taxes for the direct trade more than it was worth; and I prove it thus:—£10 per cent. is a good profit in general on trade, and no trade can afford to pay the whole, nor the greater part of its clear profit in tax. To apply this:—we paid for that direct trade an estimated sum of tax to the amount of above £100,000 per annum. Now this would be the whole clear profit, at £10 per cent, of £2,000,000 worth of trade. Could the whole clear profit be afforded in tax; or can the whole increase of traffic, by the direct trade, amount in any series of years to anything like the enormous sum of Two Millions? Most certainly not."

* * * * * * * * * *

* * "The boldest stroke was, in the very moment Ireland was soliciting higher duties on import, in order to give protection to her manufactures, to compel her to propose in the 4th of the original ten resolutions, that she should never have such protecting resolutions. The 4th does this by requiring that the lowest existing duties, viz. the Irish, shall, hereafter, be the port-duties for both kingdoms. Now experience proved these too low to protect Ireland, and therefore she had prayed to have them raised, but the 4th proposition made her negative her own application. Notwithstanding this, a fear began to be entertained in England, that by some possibility these low duties might suffer some Irish manufacture to escape into the British market. Therefore an expedient was adopted, at the latter end of the 3rd proposition, by which Britain should have higher protecting duties, without appearing to mean it. This was by '*countervailing duties*,' that is to say, that the port-duties, though too low for the protection of Ireland, should be equal; but that the country that had

the highest internal duties on consumption, might add to the port-duty a countervailing-duty, in proportion to its internal imposts, whereby the before equal duties would become unequal. Now we have only to ask, which of these kingdoms now has, and which of them, as richer, must always be able to have, the highest internal duties on consumption?—Undoubtedly Britain. What follows? That Ireland was made in the countervailing principle to propose, that Britain should have higher duties against Irish imports, than Ireland against British imports. Certainly the weaker country required more protection than the stronger, though she would be content with a protection equal to what Britain had long enjoyed, and by the long enjoyment of which Britain had gained such advantageous ground as Ireland could never recover, nor Britain ever lose."

Last fallacy, as to these propositions being of benefit to Ireland, upset.

The Attorney-General, Right Hon. John Scott, argued that these resolutions would confirm to Ireland the benefits she now held only at England's pleasure, under the 20th Geo. III., chap. 10, (passed in 1780, and known by the title of the Act of Free Trade.)

Mr. Ogilvie, M. P. for Bullyshannon, said that this was not correct, but had been advanced by the Attorney-General, because he knew "that the bill now introduced by the British minister, clashed with the act of 1780, and could not be passed while the latter continued in force, and that he had, of consequence, seen the necessity of representing this act as a favor granted by Great Britain, held at her discretion, and revocable at her pleasure. He (Mr. Ogilvie) positively denied that it was so revocable, for in it there was enacted 'that the importation and exportation allowed by this act, shall have continuance so long, and in such respective cases only, as the goods or any of them, &c., shall be liable by some act or acts of parliament, to be made in the kingdom of Ireland, to equal duties and drawbacks, and shall be made subject to the same securities, regulations, and restrictions, as the like goods, &c., exported from, or imported into Great Britain, from the British colonies in the West Indies, America, and Africa. Thus it was for Ireland to terminate the act, by not performing the conditions annexed to the grant of its advantages. He was ready, however, to admit with the Chancellor of the Exchequer, (Mr. Foster,) that the principle of the present bill was the same as that of the

20th Geo. III. chap. 10. But that act expressly provided against the extending of the principle to the trade enjoyed by Ireland *previously*, but only to the import and export which were given by itself. This was the Magna Charta of Irish trade, but was now to be destroyed.

* * * * * * * * * *

* * * "As to trade with foreign colonies, Ireland was not restricted by the act of 1780, but he agreed, that upon an equal and fair construction of the navigation laws, as adopted by Yelverton's act, Ireland was restrained from intercourse with foreign colonies; but then gentlemen must admit, that this construction put Ireland on an equal footing with Great Britain, and opened British ports to Irish ships, as it did Irish ports to British ships. If this was denied, the Irish nation was not restrained from trading with foreign colonies; if it were admitted, she had a right to the intercourse which was made the pretence for the present settlement, and was considered as one branch of the price that she was to receive for the numerous disadvantages she was to submit to in return."

The debate ended with a majority for the government—the numbers being—

Ayes, ...	127
Noes, ...	108
Majority for the Resolutions, ...	19

Propositions though carried, yet abandoned by government, with indecent shew of vexation and disappointment.

This majority, however, was considered too small especially taking into account the personal importance of those who composed the minority, to justify further progress with the measure, and so it was dropped; the minister making his retreat with a motion on the 15th of August, to read a first time, print, and then leave before the country, the bill founded on the resolutions thus passed.

A most animated debate occurred on that occasion; Mr. Grattan, Mr. Flood, Mr. Curran, and other bright names of Irish history, expressing eloquently their joy at the result, and their hope that this would be the last attack on the constitution of Ireland. The ministerial speakers gave way to much ill temper; and used the most unworthy language in reference to the capabilities of their country. Mr. Flood well remarked at the end of the discussion, that "he had never heard more mischievous, or more inflammatory language, nor more saucy folly." The Chancellor of the Exchequer (Foster) resented the expression, and moved that it should be taken down.

Whereupon Mr. Flood said, "Let my words be taken down. I do not retract my expression; I am ready to maintain and defend it."

And his words were *not* taken down. The government knew too well that he spoke what would be the feeling of the country, when the debate should come before them.

General remarks.

It is unnecessary to make more extended comment on the whole transaction, than to say:

1.—That we have found it confessed, that these propositions originated in the fear of Ireland protecting her manufactures, in return for the high duties on her imports in England.

2.—They went to fetter Ireland in her foreign and colonial trade; and to make England's commercial legislation virtually control us. Also, to raise our taxation, and to pledge this country irrevocably, and most unconstitutionally, to a tribute.

3.—To appease the English manufacturers, (whose jealousy was pronounced by the English minister himself, to be ignorant, unreasoning, and excessive; as well he might so designate it, when the propositions went to fetter Ireland in their favor,) the scheme was advocated in England as a gain to her, while the Irish parliament were assured that it was a gain to Ireland.

4.—Ireland was promised free access to the British market, which she would have got in name, but not in reality, as the internal taxes of England were to justify heavy "countervailing" or balancing duties on Irish goods entering her ports—while Ireland was to continue for ever her then low duties on British imports; notwithstanding, that the English manufacturer was able, after paying them, to undersell the Irishman at home.

In short, the propositions, whether in their original or final state, went to counteract the commercial freedom and legislative independence, which England had been compelled to concede to Ireland a few years before.

Their defeat was, consequently, a triumph for Ireland, but, owing to the unreformed state of her legislature, a FATAL triumph. Failing to obtain her ends by treaty, England resolved upon the Union, in order thereby to regain, and extend her old domination. Parliamentary corruption unfortunately gave her the means; and by that, and the demoniacal expedient of fomenting a rebellion to distract the country, and give excuse for military violence, she reversed our triumph only fifteen years later; and destroyed our commerce, our manufactures, our legislative independence, and our national prosperity.

Obstructions to prosperity of Ireland.

Besides the points already mentioned, in which circumstances still existed, after the arrangements of 1779–82, unfavourable to the full developement of the resources of Ireland, her advance towards prosperity was a good deal impeded by the heavy public expenses to which the profligacy of the government continually subjected her; yet she progressed with what, considering every thing, was an extraordinary rapidity, and in a manner that fully justified the expression of Lord Chancellor Clare, in 1798, when reviewing the occurrences of the previous sixteen years. "There is not," said he, "a nation on the face of the habitable globe, which has advanced in cultivation, in agriculture, in manufactures, with such rapidity, within the same period, as Ireland." The present Lord Grey recorded his opinion to the same effect, in 1799, as did also Lord Plunket and others. As we have touched upon this subject, we will add here one or two remaining testimonies to the prosperity of Ireland under her own parliament. On the 18th December, 1798, the bankers of Dublin had a meeting, in which they passed these resolutions:—"Resolved, that since the renunciation of the power of Great Britain, in 1782, to legislate for Ireland, the commerce and prosperity of this kingdom have eminently increased." "Resolved, that we attribute these blessings, under providence, to the wisdom of the Irish parliament." The Guild of Merchants resolved as follows, (on 14th January, 1799:)—"That the commerce of Ireland has increased, and her manufactures have improved, beyond example, since the independence of this kingdom was restored by the exertions of our countrymen in 1782."

Yet it made progress.

After Repeal those obstructions would not exist.

When under all the disadvantages of the remaining restrictions and inequalities in her commercial relations with England—of the profligate expenditure of a corrupt and hostile government, unchecked, because her parliament was unreformed—and of the terrible and wasting wars which marked the latter years of the period 1782—1800, Ireland still so wonderfully prospered, what may not be expected from her, when her reformed and freely-elected parliament shall be legislating for her interests with the lights and experiences of the present day, and a perfect and ever present sense of their speedy accountability to the intelligent and high-minded constituent body: when thus a potent check and control can be constitutionally had over the executive

—when English influence over our legislation shall be attainable only by evidences on her part of a real disposition to conciliate and be friends—and when disputes with foreign countries will be rendered most unlikely, first, by the pacific and *honest* policy which the people of Ireland will dictate to their representatives; and, second, by the respect which a country of such immense and developing resources, and such vast growing strength, will impress upon other nations.

Occurrences between 1785 and the Union.

The commercial events from 1785 to the Union need not delay us long. Neither the English nor the East India markets had been opened to us, by the "Free Trade" Act of 1780. The latter remained altogether shut, notwithstanding the renunciation by England of her claim to hold us bound by her laws. Mr. Corry, member for Newry, essayed to draw the attention of the Irish Commons to this in 1783–4, but the matter was evaded on the part of government by their assurances, that in the new commercial system, the plan of which was in preparation, (viz., that brought forward in the "Propositions" of 1785,) there would be found a satisfactory arrangement with regard to the India trade. The reader has seen how futile were these assurances.

Ireland seeks to get free trade to East.

Mr. Ponsonby's motions on this subject.

In 1791, and again in 1792, Mr. George Ponsonby, M.P. for the borough of Innistioge, brought the subject forward again. The arguments having been similar, a notice of them on the latter occasion will suffice. Mr. Ponsonby and his supporters considered the time to be most appropriate, inasmuch as the East India Company were about to apply for a renewal of their charter. He said that with the British possessions in the East he did not want to meddle, but that England had no right to exclude Ireland from trade with China and Japan. He estimated that Ireland paid to England for Eastern goods about half-a-million annually—an amount much swelled by the charges on re-exportation, which would of course be done away with if Ireland imported direct into her own ports. It was answered, that if we meddled with this trade, we would raise the hostility of England against us—that we would injure her without benefitting ourselves—that we had not money for the trade—that our capital was too small for the existing investments at home, and that if we could even increase it, it would be far better to employ it at home: and finally, that the system of taking those goods from

England, if a sacrifice by us, was a "tribute of affection," a mark of "gratitude and friendship," due to England from us, on account of the concessions she had made, and the advantages she gave our linens in her market!

These fallacies were ably refuted by Curran (then member for Rathcormac) and Grattan.—(*See the Irish Debates, vol.* 12, *p.p.* 110—111. Speeches of Grattan and Curran.

Mr. Curran adverted to the distinction that had been made, that this was not giving up a right, but making a voluntary concession of the exercise of that right; this, he said, "was not merely submitting to subjugation, but coming forward to demand the chain with the meanness and servility of a Capadocian. Other gentlemen had said, 'dont engage the country in a trade that has ruined all that have ever adventured in it,' as if gentlemen thought that the motion went to engage them to create commissioners to to send the bread of the country to India to be eaten. No act of parliament can prescribe the channels in which commerce shall flow—it was the object of the motion only to leave the field of commerce open to the merchant, and let him avail himself of advantages as he can. The smallness of our capital had been urged against the motion;—that objection, he said, amounted to this—'You have but little money; therefore buy at London for £200, what you can import directly into Dublin for £50.'—He desired the House to consider whether, as men of common faith and common probity, they could refuse to their fellow-subjects the exercise of this right, which all acknowledged them to possess;—for his part, he thought not; and by the determination of the House on this question, their character would stand or fall, if Ireland was not a besotted nation: on those who held out the threat of hostile retaliation, if the House should agree to this motion, he was particularly severe; he protested that his blood run cold when he conceived, even for a moment, this country in such circumstances, that she dreaded hostility from a sister kingdom for asserting and exercising what was acknowledged her undoubted right. Really, the question was not at all between Britain and Ireland; but between the people of Ireland together with the unchartered people of England, and a small number of chartered monopolists. The present he conceived to be a question of general liberty, and as a friend to the liberties of the people of England and Ireland, he should vote for it."

Mr. Grattan followed Mr. Curran, and supported the motion: he said that "the House of Commons of Ireland were not justified—had no power to reject the principle of a bill, which, like the present, was to confer a benefit to the people of Ireland—to liberate the commerce and constitution of the kingdom, which, from what had been advanced by gentlemen, appeared to hang and depend from the constitution and commerce of Britain. Parliament had, he granted, a right to modify and regulate trade, but they had none to destroy it, as they did the India commerce."

The obligation of this country to Great Britain was little; he mentioned her modification of the channel trade, and her interpretation of the navigation act, as instances of unfair conduct on the part of Britain. "As to the profits of this or any other trade, parliament had no right to take them into consideration: to leave the trade open was their duty, that of the merchant to consider of its profits. The want of capital was a frivolous objection, for if the bill passed, there would be imported capital; he knew that there was a very large foreign capital ready to be embarked to-morrow in the trade, if it were opened; and he called to the recollection of gentlemen, that the principal arguments ministers had used in favour of the propositions was, that foreign capital would be immediately imported, if these propositions passed."

Motion defeated.

Corruption had already begun to blast the once vigorous shoot of Irish parliamentary independence, and so these and other arguments were unavailing, and ministers defeated the motion on a division of 156 to 70.

Illusory modification of it prepared in 1793, by government, in order to get the Irish parliament to renew the East India Company's Charter.

Still to have asked the Irish parliament for their consent to a renewal of the India Company's Charter, would have been too gross even for the government of the day; and so, when in 1793 it was necessary to procure this renewal, a modification of the restrictions on Irish commerce to the East, was offered by Mr. Secretary Hobart, by a bill which he introduced in the month of June of that year, enacting that an Indiaman of 800 tons should be sent to Cork, or some other Irish port, annually, to take on board Irish exports to that amount for the countries beyond the Cape of Good Hope, and to do so at the reduced rate of freightage of £5 per ton.

The boon was illusory. In the first place, the Irish merchant should give previous notice of the quantity and quality of the goods he purposed to have ready for the ship; and such notice reaching the London merchants, prior to her sailing for Ireland, they had it of course in their power to forestall the Irishman in the vessels that went direct from London. In the second place, he could not get returns from the East directly back to his own ports: but should receive them through London, grievously surcharged of course, in consequence of their circuitous, slow, and (owing to the difficulties of the Channel navigation) perilous voyage.

But it was enough for the minister, and the venal herd who supported him, that there was even the appearance of a concession; and on the strength of that appearance, vague and shadowy as it was, he forced the measure upon the country, and obtained the renewal of the East India Charter.

And carried.

In the debates on the subject, the abstract right of Ireland to trade to the East, was not contested; but the old fallacy of its not being a trade likely to be of any benefit to her, was again brought forward and insisted upon. It was urged too, as before, that her consenting to abandon it would be only a proper proof of gratitude to England, not only for the concessions of 1779–80, but for an act just then passed in the British parliament, giving, as it was said, "the full construction of the navigation act" to Ireland, by allowing her to re-export to England, such goods of Asia, Africa, and America, as she did not want for her own consumption. This matter had been mooted by Mr. Grattan in 1787, but then rejected; as ministers then had not an India bill to carry.

Notices of the debates on the subject.

In fact Ireland had purchased this privilege long before; and at a price far outweighing the very limited advantages which it could give her. In 1785, she had at the beginning of the session, granted £140,000 in new taxes, on expectation of this, and other concessions, which she was to get from the settlement of the "commercial propositions" of that year. And ever since the year 1763, she had maintained 3,000 men for the defence of the West Indies; although until 1780 denied trade with them, and not being entirely freed from restriction in that respect, until the year 1793 itself. Again, she had in 1780 consented to adopt the enormous English duty on import of raw sugars, and to exclude foreign—a tremendous sacrifice for so poor a country, in regard of such an important necessary. And

Unrequited concessions of Ireland.

finally, she had at the same time, while restricted as to the *advantages*, adopted all the *penalties* of the navigation act, in particular that which restricted her from providing her trade with foreign shipping: which for a time would have been her best and most economical policy.

We have little to delay us now from the consideration of the arrangements in commercial matters at the time of the Union. Any minor regulations from 1785 to 1800, concerning them, whether adopted by England to bolster up her monopolies, or by Ireland to modify her infant manufactures, the effect of their nearly total exclusion from English ports, will be found sufficiently noted in the debates of that period. We therefore here make no further delay than to mention, that on the 20th February, 1794, Mr. Grattan made a last and unsuccessful effort to induce the parliament to demand admission for Irish manufactures into England, on terms as favourable as English commodities were allowed on entry into Ireland. He was ably supported by Mr. Duquery, colleague of Curran, in the representation of the borough of Rathcormack, who recapitulated the commercial injustices of England, and the concessions of Ireland, and alluded to some of the details of disparity of duties between the two countries—woollen cloths, or "*old drapery*," being charged with £2 0*s*. 6*d*. in English ports, and only 50*d*. per yard in Irish. Woollen stuffs, and mixed goods, or "*new drapery*," (as they were styled,) being 6*s*. per yard on import into England, and only 1*d*. here. Irish cotton goods being shut out by a duty of 30 per cent., while we took English at only 10 per cent.; and finally, all but our plain linens being charged with 65 per cent. by her, while the duty in our ports was no more than in the case of cottons.*

Grattan's last attempt to procure a fair commercial arrangement.

Mr. Grattan was obliged to content himself with the old hollow plausibilities, and indeed proved and insulting fallacies respecting English generosity, past and future, put forward by Mr. Secretary Douglas and the Chancellor of the Exchequer, and the motion was withdrawn.

Attempt baffled.

On the fatal 22nd of January, 1799, the Lord Lieutenant's speech broached the subject of the Union. On this

The "Union" broached in 1799.

* A Report of the Lords of the Committee of Council in England, in 1785, states that all woollens, stuffs made or mixed with wool, cottons of all kinds, linen printed, leather manufactures, candles, soap, and refined sugar, were prohibited in English ports; while in Irish they paid but a trifling duty. Also cheese, gold and silver twist and lace, laces, all kinds of silks, ribbons, gauzes, velvets, gloves, glass, earthenware, &c.

occasion, Mr. Geeorge Ponsonby moved an amendment to the "address in answer" to the effect that Ireland would maintain her parliament. The amendment being lost by a majority of one, (the numbers being 105 and 106,) and a division, two days afterwards, on the same subject, having also gone against the friends of Ireland, the Union measure itself was shortly after introduced by Lord Castlereagh, but that session rejected, to the great joy of the nation.—It was a short-lived joy—the recess was spent by ministers in corrupting the parliament · many were got to promise to reverse their patriotic votes of the past sessions; others to resign to make room for nominees and tools of the minister; and in consequence an anti-union amendment proposed by Sir Laurence Parsons, to the address, on the opening of the session, January 15th, 1800, was lost by a majority of 42, (in a house of 234 members,) although many of the government nominees had not taken their seats.

The commercial arrangements of the Union, as finally carried in that year, were as follows:—

"*Article* 6.—That it be the sixth article of Union, that his Majesty's subjects of Great Britain and Ireland shall, from and after the 1st day of January, 1801, be entitled to the same privileges, and be on the same footing as to encouragements and bounties on the like articles, being the growth, produce, or manufacture of either country respectively and generally, in respect of trade and navigation, in all ports and places in the united kingdom and its dependencies; and that in all treaties made by his Majesty, his heirs, and successors, with any foreign power, his Majesty's subjects of Ireland shall have the same privileges, and be on the same footing as his Majesty's subjects of Great Britain.

"That from the 1st day of January, 1801, all prohibitions and bounties on the export of articles, the growth, produce, or manufacture of either country to the other, shall cease and determine, and that the said articles shall thenceforth be exported from one country to the other without duty or bounty on such export.

"That all articles the growth, produce, or manufacture of either country, (not herein after enumerated as subject to specific duties,) shall from henceforth be imported into each country from the other free from duty, other than such countervailing duties on the several articles enumerated in the schedule to said act annexed, or such other countervailing duties as shall hereafter be imposed by the parliament of the United Kingdom, in the manner hereinafter provided; and that for the period of twenty years from the Union, the articles enumerated in another schedule thereunto annexed, shall be subject, on importation into each country from the other, to the duties specified in the said schedule; and the woollen manufactures, known by the names of old and new drapery, shall pay on importation into each country from the other, the duties now payable on importation into Ireland.

"Salt and hops, on importation into Ireland from Great Britain, shall be subject to duties not exceeding those which are now paid on importation into Ireland; and coals, on importation into Ireland from Great Britain, shall be subject to burthens not exceeding those to which they are now subject.

"That calicoes and muslins shall, on their importation into either country from the other, be subject and liable to the duties now payable on the same, on the importation thereof from Great Britain into Ireland, until the fifth day of January, 1808; and from and after the said day the said duties shall be annually reduced by equal proportions as near as may be in each year, so as that the said duties shall stand at ten *per centum* from and after the fifth day of January, 1816, until the fifth day of January, 1821; and that cotton-yarn and cotton-twist shall, on their importation into either country from the other, be subject and liable to the duties now payable upon the same on the importation thereof from Great Britain into Ireland, until the fifth day of January, 1808; and from and after the said day the said duties shall be annually reduced by equal proportions as near as may be in each year, so as that all duties shall cease on the said articles from and after the fifth day of January, 1816.

"That any articles of the growth, produce, or manufacture of either country, which are or may be subject to internal duty, or to duty on the materials of which they are composed, may be made subject, on their importation into each country respectively from the other, to such countervailing duty as shall appear to be just and reasonable in respect of such internal duty or duties on the materials, and that for the said purposes the articles specified in the said schedules shall be subject to the duties set forth therein, liable to be taken off, diminished, or increased in the manner herein specified; and that upon the export of the said articles from each country to the other respectively, a drawback shall be given equal in amount to the countervailing duty payable on such articles on the import thereof into the same country from the other; and that in like manner in future it shall be competent to the united Parliament to impose any new or additional countervailing duties, or to take off or diminish such existing countervailing duties as may appear on like principles to be just and reasonable, in respect of any future or additional internal duty, on any article of the growth, produce, or manufacture of either country, or of any new or additional duty on any materials of which such article may be composed, or of any abatement of duty on the same, and that when any such new or additional countervailing duty shall be so imposed on the import of any article into either country from the other, a drawback, equal in amount to such countervailing duty, shall be given in like manner on the export of every such article respectively, from the same country to the other.

"That all articles, the growth, produce, or manufacture of either country, when exported through the other, shall in all cases be exported subject to the same charges as if they had been exported directly from the country of which they were the growth, produce, or manufacture.

"That all duty charged on the import of foreign or colonial goods into either country, shall, on their export to the other, be either drawnback, or the amount (if any be retained) shall be placed to the credit of the country to which they shall be so exported, so long as the expenditure of the United Kingdom shall be defrayed by proportional contributions; provided always, that nothing herein shall extend to take away any duty, bounty, or prohibition, which exists with respect to corn, meal, malt, flour, or biscuit, but that all duties, bounties, or prohibitions on the said articles may be regulated, varied, or repealed from time to time, as the united parliament shall deem expedient."

The Speaker of the Irish Commons, the Right Honorable John Foster, (afterwards Lord Oriel,) was the chief among several able opponents of these regulations. In 1799 and in 1800 he made powerful speeches in opposition, and went largely into the subject of the commercial relations of the two countries, and exposed their past future inequalities and injustices towards Irish interests. His objections to the 6th Article of Union were briefly as follows: The union commercial arrangements.

Foster's denunciation of them.

That they lowered all protecting duties that were above 10 per cent. to that amount; and thus exposed the infant manufactures of Ireland (which the Irish parliament had in latter years began to protect) to the overwhelming competition of the great capital and long established skill and ability of England. That no less than seventy articles of our manufacture would thus be injured, and our cotton manufactures in particular, in which we had begun to make most promising advances, would be nearly ruined. That no preference over foreign goods in the British market was given. That the "new and excessive" duties on salt were made perpetual, those on hops and coals unalterable; that our brewery was left unprotected, &c. &c.

He added, that what little protection remained in any particular, was herein provided to cease and determine after the lapse of a specified number of years.

The commercial position of Ireland at that time.

To rightly understand the effect of these arrangements, it is necessary to review, very briefly, the leading circumstances of Ireland's commercial position.

She had, by the acts of 1779–80, obtained the freedom of foreign and colonial trade, both of export and of import.

By the act of 1793 she had obtained liberty to re-export foreign and colonial goods from her own shores to England.

She had, by an English act of the same year, got the loudly vaunted, but utterly illusory privilege of having an eight-hundred-ton East Indiaman, to make up a cargo for the East, in her ports.

But she had not free trade to the East, nor had she admission to English ports for her own goods.

This latter she had been, and was very desirous of obtaining. In the hope that England would have made the concession, the Irish parliament, for some years after 1780, refused the solicitations of their own merchants, to retaliate on her, by raising the Irish import duties. So eager were they to obtain it, that they jumped at the propositions of 1785, and, notwithstanding the violations of justice and the constitution which those propositions involved, had nearly adopted them, when Flood, aided speedily and powerfully by Grattan, woke up the public mind against them, and caused their abandonment.

She had not re-

It was not till after a fair experiment and delay that the Irish parliament, despairing of getting England to terms

by fair means, commenced retaliation. To this we have the incontestable testimony of the Commissioners of Revenue Enquiry in 1822—an authority by no means disposed to be over-favorable to Irish interests, or over-anxious for the credit of the Irish parliament. In their Fourth Report, speaking of the system of restrictions on English goods, and bounties on their own, to which that parliament had had recourse; they say,

stricted English commerce with her till driven to do so.

"Ireland was, undoubtedly, instigated to the adoption of this course by the exclusive spirit of the commercial policy of England. It will be found, that few exceptions in favor of the sister-kingdom were inserted in the list of goods absolutely prohibited to be imported into this country (*England*), in which list, all goods made of cotton-wool, every description of manufactured woollen, silk, and leather, together with cattle, sheep, malt, stuffs, and other less important articles, were at one time comprehended. In this embarrassing situation of exclusion from the markets of Great Britain, and deriving little assistance from foreign trade, Ireland had no other course to pursue for the protection of her own industry, except that of maintaining, by restrictive duties on the importation from Great Britain, the manufacturing means she possessed for the supply of her own markets."

English acknowledgment of this.

What the Irish parliament wanted was of course, not an absolute *free-trade* with England, which they knew well would cause the ruin of their struggling, though growing manufactures, but some such arrangement as the following, suggested in the year 1780, by no less an authority than the English Board of Trade itself:

"The best plan is, that the two kingdoms lay on certain moderate duties, to be imposed on the manufactures of the other; such as will secure a due preference in the home-market to like articles of its own growth and manufacture; and yet leave to the sister kingdom, advantages though not equal to its own, yet superior to those granted to any foreign country. The duties payable on British goods imported into Ireland, seem by their moderation, as well adapted to answer the purpose, as any that could be devised; but to make this system complete, there should be added proper regulations with respect to bounties in future, and with respect to the duties on raw materials imported into each kingdom.

"It is in the judgment of the committee, a great recommendation of this plan, that if it should be carried into execution, and become the system in which both countries shall be bound hereafter to conform, it will secure them in future from the unpleasant contests, to which, in pursuit of their respective interests, they may be otherwise exposed; and his Majesty, as sovereign of the two kingdoms, will be relievod from the disagreeable situation of having laws presented to him by the respective Houses of parliament, for his assent, which, though beneficial to one of his kingdoms, may, in their opinion, be highly detrimental to the interest of the other."

But it suited not the temper of the manufacturing interests in England to make any such arrangement, and their influence on the legislature prevented any step being taken on this recommendation. However, the retaliatory measures to which Ireland was at length driven, alarmed the selfishness of those interests, and compelled them to abandon the system of "leaving things as they were." The question then was, how to change them without granting too much to Ireland. It was seen that such a change could be effected only by a Union, which, while it granted in appearance the commercial advantage that Ireland required, would, as we shall immediately shew, nullify it *in effect*, by operation of the accompanying regulations. And this project of a Union had the further recommendation, that Ireland, in return for the apparent advantage alluded to, was to reduce at once to an utterly inefficient and insignificant amount, the import duties that had hitherto saved her home manufacturers, and finally to abolish those duties altogether—and furthermore was to be subjected to the ruinously exhausting drains of capital, which were easily foreseen to be the inevitable consequence of the measure in agitation.

The consequence of her doing so.

Commercial motives of England to accomplish the Union.

Its provisions nugatory as to good to Irish commerce.

The advantage to Ireland of admission for her goods into English ports, was nullified by the provision, by which "*countervailing*" duties were put on them there, to balance the heavier excise duties which such goods of English manufacture had to pay. On the other hand English goods going to Ireland, got a drawback on export from England of the heavy English excise duty they had paid, and entering Ireland, met a much lower rate of excise, and had consequently, only a very moderate "countervailing" duty put upon them nere.

The "*drains of capital*" alluded to, as occasioned by the

Its absence leaves no hope for our manufactures.

Union, have been spoken of at large, in the article on the "Taxation Injustice;" and therefore need not be dwelt upon here. They consist of the surplus revenue taken from Ireland—the payments for foreign goods received now through England, which formerly we received direct—and, above all, the millions spent out of the country by the absentee proprietors. These last had no attraction to remain in their native land, when the parliament was gone; and the consequence has been, that they have emigrated in such numbers, that whereas a million and a half was the amount of this drain in 1801, it is now generally believed to exceed four millions and a half—a sum equal to the whole revenue that Ireland is able to contribute to the state!

Irish capital drained away.

The aggregrate of annual "drain" from Ireland at the present moment, is nearly nine millions—or double her public revenue!

When money was thus constantly, and in an annually increasing amount, flowing out of Ireland, without return, during the period of years allotted by the act of Union for the gradual cessation of the remaining protecting duties, it can well be conceived that commercial enterprize, and all the operations of industry declined and grew less. In the twenty years then that elapsed ere the commercial arrangements of the Union were re-considered in 1821, the manufactures of Ireland may, at the best, be said to have dragged on a sickly and precarious existence, rather than to have maintained, much less improved, the vigour that had marked their early growth before 1800. They were no longer formidable, yet the cruel spirit of commercial monopoly was not to be satisfied so long as any vitality remained; and though the cries of the perishing artizans of Ireland did, by some strange chance, reach the ears of the English parliament in 1821, and procure some extension of the time originally marked out for the duration of the "Union Duties," as they were called, yet in the very next year a commission was appointed, as it would seem, to *find excuses* for getting rid of them, and on its report their doom was sealed, and they were got rid of with as much haste as decency at all allowed.*

* Scant as was the decency observed towards us in these respects, it was still less, or rather none at all, in others, since the Union. Notwithstanding, that in 1825, a committee (of course of the imperial parliament) had, after a patient and full enquiry, reported that "Ireland had undoubtedly strong claims for every encouragement to her linen manufacture, at least to the

If we do not altogether deny the truth of the remark in the report alluded to, to the effect that the "Union

extent of the annual grant of parliament;" (viz. £20,000, the remnant of the old promised encouragement to that manufacture.)—Notwithstanding this deliberate opinion, twice expressed in their report, the grant was reduced three years afterwards one-half, and the succeeding year withdrawn altogether!

In the same way a grant of £10,000, voted annually since the Union to the Wide-street Board, and defended by Sir Robert Peel, (when secretary for Ireland,) as no more than a fitting partial compensation to Dublin, for the evil consequences of the Union to that city, was withdrawn, a short time before the withdrawal of the linen grant, with quite as little apology or warning. And no later than last year (to pass over some other instances of particular injustice) we had one general sweeping blow made at all the charitable institutions of Dublin, that received any aid from the public purse. A commission was issued to enquire into the claims of such institutions in Dublin, to receive aid not given elsewhere. The report of the commissioners—conservative gentlemen of great respectability and most undoubtedly *no Repealers*—is an admirable rebuff to the petty prying jealousy that instigated such an enquiry. It would have been more dignified for a government to have sought information on the subject privately, ere committing itself by an overt act, betraying malice prepense; and malice too that is now defeated of its object. The following is some of the main part of the report:—

"Immediately after the Union, Dublin, it may be said, ceased to be a metropolis as regards the wealthy, while it continued a metropolis as regards the poor; and in no inconsiderable degree it has remained so since. The causes, therefore, which induced those who framed the articles of Union to introduce stipulations into that measure as regards Dublin, appears to us to be still in extensive operation. Other causes likewise (not, however, having effect on Dublin alone)—the increase of population, without a corresponding increase in wealth, the want of capital, the decay of manufactures in Ireland, operating to increase the proportion of poor—have operated likewise to increase rather than diminish the cogency of those reasons which led to the stipulations in the articles of Union.

"In evidence of this we beg leave to notice the increased accommodation which the governors at different periods, and with the sanction of government have been compelled to supply in most of these institutions, and the increased grants, notwithstanding the financial difficulties of the empire, which various governments have deemed it necessary to make for their support.

"In further evidence of this disproportionate increase of the poorer classes in Dublin, we have to observe that, notwithstanding the support thus rendered by government to certain institutions, others of a similar character, arising principally out of the exigencies of the lower classes, have been established and are supported, some by private means alone, and some partly from private means and partly from local assessment.

"We therefore submit that the necessity which was found to exist previous to and at the time of the Union for extraneous support as regards Dublin, in aid of its principal charitable institutions, (arising, in our opinion, from the disproportion between the wealthy and the poorer classes of the community,) has, as was anticipated, increased since that period, and still continues, although, we trust and believe, it may be now gradually diminishing.

"Dublin, therefore, with its population of upwards of 250,000, is, in our opinion, an exception to all other cities in the empire; and we respectfully urge, that because in London and the other large towns in Eng-

Duties" operated to "enhance the price of the most indispensable instruments of agricultural labour; and of those implements and materials in most general request by the various classes of artizans and mechanics; and at the same time, to make almost all manufactured articles from 15 to 20 per cent. dearer than in England," we are by no means to be understood as agreeing, that the measure of abolishing them was the proper remedy. We impute this injurious action of theirs, not to intrinsic evil, but to the absence of the money capital of Ireland, which, had it remained at home, would have vivified enterprize and industry, and enabled our manufacturers to take advantage of the moderate protection still left to them, to produce at as cheap a rate at least as the Englishman, the goods required.

If restored they will revive.

Since the abolition of these duties, the Englishman has had complete command of our market. The instances are many in which attempts in Ireland to restore some waning or perished manufacture, have been crushed by means of the temporary sacrifice of profit which the superior wealth of the English capitalist enabled him to make, to undersell his rash Irish competitor. The worm at the vitals of Irish enterprize, is the want of capital, and till the latter is restored, there is little hope for our manufacturers and artizans.

But to restore this capital. the Repeal of the Act of Union was and is necessary. The parliament must be at home; 1st. to give the absentees an inducement to come home; 2nd. to enable us to stop the drains of revenue, by getting rid of the unjust burthen of English debt; and 3rd. to give us the means of making our own commercial arrangements with foreign countries, whereby we can not only prevent the recurrence of such reckless injury to our commercial interests, as was involved in the recent commercial negotiations of England with France and Portugal, but we can obtain advantages, which our being bound now to the high tariffs of England, prevents us from obtaining

It will be restored by Repeal.

land, private charity may have been found amply sufficient for the support of their public charitable institutions, it by no means follows that in Dublin, where the poor are so numerous, and the rich comparatively are so few, it would be reasonable or just to expect from her citizens an extent of liberality which neither their numbers nor circumstances could fairly warrant."

This answer shamed the government out of their plan of stopping the grants, which, after all, have been found not to have amounted since 1800, to more than £120,000 in the whole!

in foreign countries; and furthermore, shall have all the duty paid by us on foreign imports credited to our own revenue, instead of, as now, going to swell the receipts of the English exchequer.

Under this altered state of circumstances we should have a sum of from eight to nine millions of money, at the very least, annually spent in the country, which is now drained out of her, and as much lost to her as if thrown into the sea!

Question as to whether duties on English goods then necessary.

Whether, after the Repeal, duties should be levied here on English imports, is a question we are not now called upon to discuss. If England readily yielded to the incontestable justice of our claim to be relieved from our present most unjust responsibility for her debt, we might, in return, show our good will, by letting in her commodities duty-free. Our taxes would become so very much lighter than hers, that our manufactures would have virtually the same advantage they now expect from import duties. But if we must continue under this unjust responsibility, nothing could be fairer than that we should seek revenue wherewith to meet it, from taxes on English goods. It may be considered as an established axiom, that import-duties,* if kept below the point at which smuggling (with all its long train of immoralities and crime) can begin, are the fairest source to which the government of a country can look for the revenues necessary to carry on the public business, and to support the public burthens.

In either of the cases mentioned, viz., of lighter taxes than in England, or of revenue duties on English manufactured goods, there would be, at this side of the water, a prospect of profitable investment opened for the surplus-capital of England. At present there is no such thing—as the Englishman who should attempt an enterprize in Ireland, has, of course, no better protection against the combinations of the monopolists than the native manufacturer. Failing thus of a field in Ireland, and that at home being even overstocked, English surplus capital has been forced to seek investments in countries in the other hemisphere, where the circumstances of natural position, or of peculiar legislation, or of both combined, ensured advantage for goods produced in the country, over imported articles.

The contemptible fallacy, that "Agitation has kept Eng-

* Such import-duties not however to be on the *materials* of manufactures.

lish capital out of Ireland," falls to the ground at once, when we consider the continued civil distractions and endless and sanguinary revolutions of the South American States, into which English capital has so largely and steadily flowed.

Summary remarks in conclusion.

Our sketch of the *many* commercial *injustices* inflicted upon this country by Great Britain, is now done. We have shown how uniformly intolerant has been the conduct of the latter. Every interest of ours checked, repressed, put in abeyance, when thought to come at all in contact with hers —delusive promises held out—lasting and reckless injury inflicted.

At the beginning of the last century her cry was, that we were not fit for the woollen manufacture; but that if we devoted ourselves to linen, we should have the highest encouragement in that branch. It has been the object of these pages to prove how she kept that promise "to the ear, but broke it to the hope," by giving greater encouragement to the Scotch linen, and to her own. The cry since the Union has been, that we ought not to think of *any* manufacture, but to devote ourselves to the supplying Great Britain with our agricultural produce. The tariff of last year proves that she does not hold herself bound to us in this particular either.

In truth, she has done what, after all, was but natural; attended to her own interests, and to her own interests alone. The misfortune to us has been, that she has had the power of controlling *our* interests. This power must be got rid of, if we would ever hope to see our country attain to that prosperity, of which Providence has so abundantly given her the means, but of which she has so long been cruelly deprived by man.

ADDENDA

TO THE

"COMMERCIAL INJUSTICES."

No. 1.

The progress of the Linen Trade of Ireland was as follows: Taking our figures, partly from M'Culloch's Commercial Dictionary, *(article "Linen,")* but mainly from the Report of the Hand-loom Weavers' Enquiry; and taking also the seven years averages stated in that Report, to be the proper measure by which to estimate such progress, we find that—

EXPORT OF IRISH LINEN.

The averages of 7 years, including and ending respectively with the years	1147	1,665,486	Increase in this period of 66 yrs. 17,890,893 yds.
	1780	19,556,379	Ditto, 2nd period, 18 yrs. 22,114,593 yards.
	1798	41,670,972	Ditto, from 1800 up to 1825, 5,917,735 yards.
	1825	47,588,707	

A very short calculation will shew, that had the linen trade progressed in the first period as it did in the second, it ought to have shewn an increase above the statement for 1714, of not less than eighty millions, instead of eighteen. And, similarly, had it progressed since the Union in the manner in which it did during the same second period stated above, it ought to have shewn an increase over that period, of not less than thirty millions, instead of being short of six millions!

But the defect since the Union, is not only on comparison with the period that Ireland had the free management of her commercial concerns, but even in comparison with the period *previous* to 1780. It will be seen that at the rate of progression in the period since the Union, nearly *eighty years* should elapse ere the linen trade could make the same advance, that under the guidance even of her fettered and restricted parliament before 1780, she had made in sixty-six years!

One of the assistant Commissioners of the Enquiry, whose report we quote, seeks to make it appear that the increase since the Union is more valuable than the mere figures would denote: his remark is:

"Ireland lost in a great measure her coarse linen trade, owing to the prohibition placed on export of yarn in 1784, which forced the English manufacturers to turn their attention to providing yarn at home; which they did so successfully as not only to be able to be independent of a supply from Ireland, but also to drive the Irish out of the market in those coarse fabrics to which their mill-spun yarn was capable of being applied. The exports of linen since 1800 were chiefly of the finer linens, and therefore indicate a greater degree of prosperity of the linen trade than would at first appear."—*Otway's Report, H. L. Enquiry, p.* 620.

The over-anxiety of Mr. Commissioner Otway to prove that the Union has done every-thing for us, has here led him into a mis-statement. If he were correct, then must the English manufacturers of 50 years ago, have been very different men from the keen, active, and enterprising class they are at this day; inasmuch as they must have taken not less than sixteen years (viz from 1784 to 1801) to provide themselves elsewhere than from Ireland, with a material so much needed as linen-yarn! But the fact is, as Mr. Otway might have seen had he consulted the debates of the Irish Parliament during that time, and the publications in Ireland having relation to commerce, that the English market became almost immediately shut to the Irish coarse linens, after the export of yarn to that market was stopped; and that consequently the export from Ireland during much the greater part of the period 1784—1801, was of the finer description.

It may be argued that the small proportion which the *post-Union* increase of linen-export bears to that between 1780 and 1798, is mainly owing to the fact that there was not room for much further improvement; the linen, like every other trade, having its limits. This however is in fact only another testimony to the beneficial influence of Irish *home* legislation, since under its short-lived auspices, the utmost limit was so nearly attained. And it remains for the advocates of the Union to shew, that had that measure never been carried, the six millions increase up to 1825 would not have occurred by the mere force of the increase of demand in England, caused by the increase of population in that country, to say nothing of the continuance of that beneficial influence which, on such good ground of indisputable figures, we ascribe to "*home-legislation*."

It is unanimously acknowledged and declared, that since 1825, when the traffic between the two countries was assimilated to a coasting trade, and consequently official records ceased to be kept, all estimates of the commercial progress of Ireland are, at best, but *good guesses*. In the truly valuable "Irish Railway Report" drawn up by the lamented Mr. Drummond, this deficiency is spoken of, and deplored. He sought to supply it by taking the exaggerated reports of individual merchants; who naturally enough wished to make their dealings appear as large as the wide range of probability at all allowed. With all his candour Mr. Drummond was not adverse to these exaggerations: it was a point with him, as with British writers in general, and persons reporting to the Imperial Parliament in particular, to make out as far as possible a "*prosperity-case*" for the Union. He therefore sets down our linen export to have been in 1835, 70 millions of yards, without however attempting to say that that was a seven-years-average. We can afford to admit, for the sake of argument, that the average *was* so high; and yet the period 1780—1798 will be found to have proportionably exceeded it. If those 18 years gave an *increase* of 22 millions of yards, the 35 years of the Railway Report ought to have given an *increase* of 43 millions. But they actually gave no higher amount than 28,600,000 yards!

No. 2.

MISCELLANEA HAVING REFERENCE TO THE COMMERCE, MANUFACTURES, INTERNAL PROSPERITY, &c. &c. OF IRELAND, BEFORE AND AFTER THE UNION.

The "Balance of Trade," or relative proportion to each other of a country's exports and imports, was a test in much vogue in the last century, when the advantages or disadvantages of external trade were to be estimated. Sounder notions of political economy have, to use an expressive French phrase, much "*discredited*" this test. The idea is exploded, that an import trade is bad for a country, merely because she pays in money for what she receives. Money has been recognized as to the full as much a "marketable commodity," as the "goods," or "produce," ordinarily so considered; and where importation has been found in any case really disadvantageous, it has been, because of some peculiarity in the *quality*, not because of the *quantity* abstractedly speaking, of the articles received. Again, a great exportation has been seen not to be, *of necessity*, a great benefit. On the contrary it has come sometimes to be considered a great evil—as in the case of export of commodities wanted by the population at home—or where a valuable return is not certain and immediate.

To come then to a proper judgment of the real commercial *status* of a country, the *nature*, as well as the quantity of her exports and imports must be enquired into; and their effects, generally, upon the condition of the inhabitants.

Our space limits us to a very brief and cursory examination of these points.

We have seen in the article to which this is appended, how wretched was the commercial condition of Ireland before 1780; and some evidences have been recorded of her extraordinary advance subsequently. The rate of Exchange was after 1780 steadily in her favor, in her dealings with England; (as recorded in the report of a committee of the Imperial Parliament in 1804, upon the currency, &c. &c. of Ireland.) The committee to which we refer, although an *English* committee of an English Parliament, did themselves confess the prosperity of Ireland after 1782. They, to be sure, ascribe that prosperity to the mere fact of the establishment of the Bank of Ireland in 1783; but this inadequate cause for so great an effect, as the "*rapid advances of trade*, manufactures, and agriculture," which they speak of, (Report, page 12,) we need not delay to discuss: being satisfied with their confession of the fact of those advances.

The excess of the exports of Ireland, over what she received in return from England, (namely as more than two to one, see Foster, debate in committee 1799,)—would of itself be enough to demonstrate the activity of her manufactures—her export of unmanufactured produce being comparatively nothing; and her home-consumption being, in a very great over-proportion, supplied by herself.

Comparisons will best shew the state of her home-consumption of those foreign articles, whose use is generally taken as the scale by which to estimate the degree of prosperity of a people. The following comparisons are not only the quantities consumed in Ireland at periods before and after the Union—but between those quantities and what were consumed in England at corresponding periods. The figures verifying them in detail will be found in the report of the committee of 1830, on the "State of the Irish Poor,"—Mr. Spring Rice, the present Lord Monteagle, chairman—(see Appendices, G. 1. and Geo. 2. p.p. 112—125, No. 667 of 1830 *Reports*.)

"Period from 1785 to the Union:—

Tea—Increase of consumption in Ireland,		84	per cent.
	In England	45	do.
From 1786 to the Union.			
Tobacco—Increase in Ireland, - -		100	do.
	In England	64	do.
From 1787 to the Union.			
Wine—Increase in Ireland, - - -		74	do.
	In England	22	do.
From 1785 to the Union.			
Sugar—Increase in Ireland, - - -		57	do.
	In England	53	do.
From 1784 to the Union.			
Coffee—Increase in Ireland, - - -		600	do.
	In England	75	do.

"Period from the Union to the year 1827:—

Tea—Increase in England,	- -	25 per cent.
Increase in Ireland,	- -	24 per cent.
Coffee—Increase in England,	- -	1,800 per cent.
Increase in Ireland,	- -	400 per cent.
Sugar—Increase in England,	- -	26 per cent.
Increase in Ireland,	- -	16 per cent.
Tobacco—Increase in England,	- -	27 per cent.
Decrease in Ireland,	- -	37 per cent.
Wine—Increase in England,	- -	24 per cent.
Decrease in Ireland,	- -	45 per cent.

As to all these items, the latest official information is of the year 1825—the records of trade between the two countries having ceased to be kept in that year; and by far the greater part of the commodities enumerated coming to us through England.

We have, in the preceding Addendum, shewn the progress of the linen trade in the period of legislative independence, as advantageously contrasted with the preceding and subsequent periods.

The defenders of the Union ordinarily lay much stress on the increased export of cattle, sheep, and provisions, since that measure. This export, however, is *from a starving people;* and being so, the argument as to its great value to Ireland is not one to waste much time in considering. A curious fact has come out with reference to this subject. A return appeared in all the Dublin papers, last November, of the number of sheep and horned cattle at the great Fair at Ballinasloe, every year from 1790 to 1842. The following extract from it, we put in the same table, with figures, from a Parliamentary Return of 1834, and the Irish Railway Report, shewing the *export* of the articles mentioned in two of the years included. We have no return of the export last year.

Years.	Sheep.	Export of Ditto.	Horned Cattle.	Export of Do.
1799	77,900	800	9,900	14,000
1835	62,400	125,000	8,500	98,000
1842	76,800		14,300	

The question naturally arises—what became of the 77,000 surplus sheep in the first year, as well as the sheep at other fairs?—*They were eaten at home.*

As to oxen, 14,000 went away in 1799, and 98,000 in 1835; yet if we test the product of all Ireland in the former year, by the most sufficient criterion of the amount at Ballinasloe fair, we shall find that Ireland had then *more for sale than in* 1835, and consumed the greater part of the surplus over her export—exporting the remainder in the more valuable form of *provisions.*

The parliamentary documents quoted before, enable us to shew what the export of provisions was in the years 1799 and 1835—

Year.	Export of Cattle.	Swine.	Beef and Pork, Barrels.
1799	14,000	4,000	278,000
1835	98,000	76,000	140,000

There has then been since the Union, a *decrease* of the *more* valuable export, (viz., provisions—valuable because of the labour employed at home in their manufacture,)—and an *increase* of the *less* valuable, viz. the live animals—less valuable to a country as an article of export, by reason of the small quantity of employment which is given in the preparing of it.

As the diminution of the number of barrels of beef and pork will not, by any means, account for the great increase of the live export—while the whole number of cattle produced in Ireland in 1835, was, at any rate, *not greater* than in 1799—it follows, that much of the excess of live-export in 1835, must have been by *deduction from the number previously consumed at home*—and therefore, that the home-consumption in the latter year, was considerably *less than in the year before the Union, notwithstanding the cent. per cent. increase of population.*

But it may be said, that the market for Irish cattle and provisions was probably "a *forced* one" before the Union. So far, however, was this from being the case, that there were actually *duties on their export;* yet so active and profitable was the home-demand, that not only was there no complaint from parties in that trade, but on being offered by Mr. Foster, when Chancellor of the Exchequer, to have the exports made free, those parties actually *declined the offer.*

The war could not be said to have forced the demand in 1789; for in the years 1787, 1788, and 1789 there was no war, and the average export of those years was 227,564 barrels—on which the amount given above for 1799, was no more than a natural and moderate increase.

Since the Union, the home-market for these commodities has become extremely limited; and what advantage was gained by the extended market in England is now passing away. The tariff-reform of last session was one severe blow to our Irish *monopoly*, as it was called, of supplying the English market in these respects. A strange *monopoly!* which amounted to no more than the privilege of sending over cattle and provisions, at of course heavy charges for freight, &c. &c. to compete in the English market with the same articles of native produce. This competition of course prevented the Irish dealer from charging his expenses in his prices, and therefore his profits were considerably reduced from what they would have been had the so-called "*monopoly*" really existed. In fact he but supplied the gap that the Englishman or Scotchman could not help leaving open. The measure of last session tends to narrow his market still more—and this year these interests have received another heavy blow by the most unexpected reduction of the government contracts, from 26,000 tierces of beef and pork last year, to no more than 1200 tierces!

Mr. Foster in 1799 said, that "Ireland exported no unmanufactured wool; *it worked up all it had*, and there was little reason to suppose the quantity would be enlarged, as the *great increase of agriculture and of the linen-manufacture*, gave a better profit in the land, than sheep afforded."

Ireland has, since the Union, ceased for several years to work up all, or a considerable portion of her own wool. She exports the greater part of it now—and exports it in a way the least profitable to her, namely, on the back of the live animal.

The following extract from a speech by a high conservative authority, was read by Mr. O'Connell, when opening the Repeal Debate in the Dublin Corporation, on the 28th of February, 1843. It bears on the general state of Irish commerce since the Union.

"I am now about to read for you an extract from a speech pronounced by the Rev. Doctor Boyton, on Saturday, the 23d of February, 1833:—

"'The exports and imports, as far as they are a test of a decay of profitable occupation—so far as the exports and imports are supplied from the parliamentary returns—exhibit extraordinary evidences of the condition of the labouring classes. The importation of flax-seed (an evidence of the extent of a most important source of employment) was—in 1790, 339,745 barrels; 1800, 327,621 barrels; 1830, 168,458 barrels. The importation of silk, raw and thrown, was—in 1790, 92,091lbs.; 1800, 79,060lbs. 1830, 3,190lbs. Of unwrought iron, in 1790, 2,971 tons; in 1800, 10,241 tons; in 1830, 871 tons. Formerly we spun all our own woollen and worsted yarn, We imported in 1790 only 2,294lbs.; in 1800, 1,880lbs; in 1826, 662,750lbs. An enormous increase, There were, I unde.stand, upwards of thirty persons engaged in the woollen trade in Dublin, who have become bankrupts since 1821. There has been, doubtless, an increase in the exports of cottons. The exports were—in 1800, 9,147 yards; 1826–7,793,873. The exports of cotton from Great Britain were—in 1829, 402,517,196 yards, value £12,516,247, which will give the value of our cotton exports at something less than a quarter of a million—poor substitute for our linens, which in the province of Ulster alone exceeded in value two millions two hundred thousand pounds.'"

Having given a *conservative* authority, we now give that of a liberal, much about the same time. It is that of Mr. Staunton. In one of those admirable articles which he has, from time to time during the last twenty years, put forward in his journal, he thus remarked on the same subject:—

"The great increase of our imports has been in articles once manufactured in Ireland, and of our exports in corn and live cattle. Of refined sugar we imported only 4,200 cwts. in 1801, but we imported 66,392 cwts. in 1825. Of hardware and cutlery we imported to the value of £144,812 in 1801, but to the value of £264,944 in 1825. In 1801, our haberdashery was of the value of £57,626 but it was £337,208, or nearly *six times the former amount*, in 1825. Our woollen increased from 2,000,000 yards to 3,380,000 yards in the interval, and our cotton from 44,000 to twelve times that amount. In the miscellaneous articles the increase was cent. per cent. All this is indicative, not so much of increased consumption, as decreased manufactures at home."

The Report of the "Commissioners of Enquiry into the collection and management of the revenue arising in Ireland, &c. &c." (1822,) cannot be read by an Irishman without feelings of melancholy. Although the Union, with all its drains from this country, had then been twenty-one years in operation, the effects of the impetus Irish enterprise had received during the eighteen years of her free parliament, had not entirely passed away; and manufactures still remained, (though in a sickly state,) several of which have since totally departed from Ireland. The cotton manufacture was yet in a state to bear competition in some points with England, upon equal terms—woollen, silk, glass, cabinet-ware—the making of carriages, of hats, &c. &c. were all active businesses, and declared capable of much immediate prosperity, in the event of the recommendations of the commissioners being carried into effect. Those recommendations went to abolish the "protecting duties" left by the Union; which was accordingly done by the British Parliament—the advantage being at any rate *certain* to England herself, as the duties in question operated against her commodities under the above heads.

The result may be taken from the Reports of the Railway and Hand-Loom Weavers' Commissions of enquiry, 1838—1840:

"The only town in Ireland in which the cotton manufacture is established to any extent, is Belfast; and it is represented as declining even there. With regard to the woollen trade a considerable diminution appears to have taken place since 1822...... Mr. W. Willans of Dublin, the most extensive woollen manufacturer in Ireland, states that then there were forty-five manufacturers in and about Dublin; and the value of the cloth annully produced by them would, at the present prices, be £200,000. The value now manufactured may be about £90,000. The manufacture has also declined in Cork, Kilkenny, Moate, Carrick-on-Suir; the value produced now in those districts being supposed not to amount to £20,000. The flannel trade of Wicklow and Wexford may now be considered as extinct...... Mr. Willans calculates that the consumption of woollens in Ireland does not exceed in annual value £1,400,000, being about 3*s*. 3*d*. per head on the population; whereas the total consumption of England cannot be less in value than from £18,000,000 to £20,000,000, which would amount to 20*s*. per head."—*Railway Report, Ireland.*

"The silk trade is now confined to one fabric—the tabinets. There can be no doubt the trade in weaving whole silk is extinct, and that the manufactures of velvets, handkerchiefs, and ribbons, are reduced to a few looms."—*Mr. Otway's Report, Hand-Loom Enquiry.*

Mr. Muggeridge (also of the hand-loom enquiry) corroborates what is given above respecting the cotton trade; and one of his principal witnesses, Mr. Moncrief of Belfast, made the significant remark, that "if all the capital *of all* the manufacturers in Belfast was combined, it would not equal that employed by one large establishment in England.

Even the linen-manufacture is not shewn to be flourishing by the Reports we have quoted; although it is well known that ingenuity was tasked to the utmost in their compilation to infer a "post-union prosperity—*post-hoc, propter hoc*—in Ireland. Mr. Commissioner Muggeridge declares his inability, "in common with all who have attempted the enquiry before him, to say whether it is flourishing or not—and he states that opinions are divided on the subject in the north itself.

The very controversy which exists as to the state of that trade is an unfavourable sign. When a branch of industry is really flourishing in any country, do we usually find, even among those at a distance from a scene of action, doubts and disputes existing on the subject? Yet they are to be found rife among *persons intimately conversant* with the linen trade in the North, as will be seen by the following extracts:—

"Mr. William Kirk, a member of the linen committee of the county Armagh, says—'I *think* the linen trade is increasing.'

"Mr. William Miller, a member of the linen committee of the county of Antrim, states—'There has been an increase in the linen trade of Ballymena within the last seven years, but nevertheless there has been, generally speaking, a decrease in the linen trade of Ireland during the same period.'

"Mr. Edward Sproule, a member of the County Tyrone Committee, states—'That the linen trade of Ulster is not so extensive as it was twenty years ago.'

"Mr. John Walker, of Magherafelt, writes—'I *am of opinion* the linen trade of Ireland is increasing in quantity, though the last two years make an exception.'

"Messrs. William Orr and Sons, linen manufacturers at Loughgall, county Armagh, writes—'We consider it decreasing in many particulars, and that the Scotch are taking a great deal of it from us.'"—*Mr. Muggeridge's Report, Handloom Weavers' Inquiry.*

The annual Report of the Directors of the Provincial Bank of Ireland, contained last year a passage to the effect that "the linen manufacture of the North could not be said to be flourishing."

A large proportion of the export at present consists of *yarn*, instead of being all of the fully manufactured article, as it ought to be, were the trade really at the high pitch of prosperity which the advocates of the Union would pretend.

The principal manufactures of Ireland being in this condition, it is unnecessary to go into details as to minor articles. The glass manufacture is notoriously perishing, if not altogether gone. The Commission of 1822, reported ten large glass-houses in activity. The 20th Report of the Commissioners of Excise Inquiry, shewed that the number had fallen to six, and since then it has been further reduced one-half. The hat manufacture, &c. &c. have similarly gone down.

The tradesmen of Dublin have, from time to time, put forward statistics of painful interest, connected with the condition of their various trades in 1800 and since. In 1834 they did so to a considerable extent, but still more fully in the last three years. A statement of theirs in the year 1841, has the following:—

WOOLLEN TRADE IN DUBLIN.

Master manufacturers in 1800, ...	91
Do. in 1840, ...	12
Number of hands employed in 1800, ...	4938
Do. in 1840, ...	682

WOOL COMBING.

Master wool combers in 1800, ...	30
Do. in 1834, ...	5
Number of hands employed in 1800, ...	230
Do. in 1834, ...	66

CARPET MANUFACTURERS IN DUBLIN.

Master manufacturers in 1800, ...	13
Do. in 1841, ...	1
Number of hands employed in 1800, ...	720
Do. in 1841, only the men employed by Mr. Sheridan.	

BLANKETS.

Blanket manufacturers in Kilkenny, in the year 1800,	56
Do. in 1822, ...	12
Operatives employed in 1800, ...	3000
Do. in 1841, ...	925

RATTEENS AND FRIEZES.

Number of persons supported by the woollen manufacture at Roscrea in the year 1800, ...	900
In the year 1841 not one comber permanently employed.	
Persons deriving employment and maintenance from the cotton manufacture at Belfast, and within ten miles round it. in the year 1800, ...	27,000
Do. in 1839, ...	12,000 to 15,000
whose wages were miserably reduced, almost to the standard of a day labourer.	
Number of calico looms at full work at Balbriggan in 1799, ...	2000
Do. in 1841, ...	226

SILK MANUFACTURE IN DUBLIN.

Number of broad looms in 1800, ...	2500
Do. in 1840, ...	250

HOSIERY.

In Dublin the number of hosiery frames was, in 1800,	329
Do. in 1840, ...	80
In Cork the number of hosiery frames was in 1800, ...	200
Do. in 1840, say	12

The hosiery trade has become almost extinct at Belfast, Lisburn, Clonmel, Limerick, Waterford, Carrick, Kilkenny, Carlow, Portarlington, Maryborough, Newry, Dundalk, Armagh, aud Drogheda.

STUFF SERGE IN DUBLIN.

Master manufacturers in 1800, ...	25
Do. in 1841, ...	1
Number of hands employed in 1800, ...	1491
Do. in 1834, ...	131

FLANNEL MANUFACTURE.

Looms at work in the county Wicklow in the year 1800,	1000
Do. in 1841, ...	01

N.B.—The county Wicklow was the principal seat of this trade.

When to all these statements, (which, if space and time permitted, we could easily increase in number, and equal in force,) we add the accumulated evidence and declarations, by individual writers and royal commissions, parliamentary committees and speakers, as to the appalling destitution of *one half* of the population of Ireland, the assertion of "*giant-stride prosperity since the Union*" becomes a cruel insult! The assertion of *any general* prosperity is scarcely better. And where any particular interest can be shewn to have thriven to any degree of importance, such a result can in no way be rightfully ascribed to the operation of the Union, until it be first shewn that the same would not have occurred, had the Irish parliament been still in existence.

JOHN O'CONNELL.

September 8, 1843.

J. BROWNE, PRINTER, NASSAU-STREET, DUBLIN.

INFLUENCES

OF

THE CORN LAWS,

AS AFFECTING

ALL CLASSES OF THE COMMUNITY,

AND PARTICULARLY

THE LANDED INTERESTS.

BY

JAMES WILSON, Esq.

THIRD EDITION.

LONDON:
PUBLISHED BY LONGMAN, ORME, BROWN, GREEN, AND
LONGMANS.

1840.

James Wilson (1805–60)[1]

James Wilson was the third of fifteen children of William Wilson (1764–1832), a successful woollen manufacturer and Elizabeth nee Richardson (d. 1815) of Hawick, Roxburghshire. James was educated at Friends' schools in Ackworth and Colne, Essex. At first he planned to become a schoolmaster, then read for the Scottish bar which, he soon discovered was contrary to the rules of the Society of Friends to which he belonged. At the age of 16 James was apprenticed to a hat manufacturer in Hawick. The business was purchased for him and his older brother William by their father, and in 1824 the two brothers moved to London setting up, again with their father's help, the firm of Wilson, Irwin, & Wilson. In 1831 the firm was dissolved and James carried on as James Wilson and Co.

In January 1832 James Wilson married Elizabeth Preston of Newcastle, thereby leaving the Society of Friends, and the young family moved to Dulwich Place. In 1836 Wilson began speculating in indigo. At first the investment paid off, but within three years Wilson lost nearly all his capital. Rather than declare bankruptcy, Wilson reached an agreement with his creditors to pay all his debts. The firm continued under another name, with Wilson remaining a partner until his retirement from business in 1884.

In 1847 Wilson was returned for the borough of Westbury, Wiltshire, by 170 votes to 149. He was reelected in 1852 by six votes, and in 1857 was returned for Devonport. He soon acquired a reputation in the House and in 1848, not long after entering Parliament was appointed joint secretary of the Board of Control. From 1853 to 1858 Wilson served as financial secretary to the Treasury while declining offers to become Vice President of the Board of Trade (1855) and chairman of the inland revenue (1856). In 1959 he accepted Palmerston's offer of the Vice Presidency of the Board of Trade and the position of Paymaster, and shortly afterwards the post of financial member of the Council of India. Wilson left England for India in October, 1859. In India he began to reform the system of public accounts before he died of dysentery on 11 August 1860.

[The bibliography of James Wilson is printed on p. 250.]

[1] Walter Bagehot, 'Memoir of the Right Honourable James Wilson (*Supplement to the Economist*, 17th November, 1860)', in Walter Bagehot, *Literary Studies (miscellaneous essays) with additions* vol. 3, London: Longmans, 1913, pp. 304–57, Emilie I. Barrington, *The Servant of All. Pages from the family, social and political life of my father James Wilson. Twenty years of mid-Victorian life*, London: Longmans, 1927, and entry by William Prideaux Courtney in *D.N.B.* vol. 21, pp. 571–3.

INTRODUCTION.

In offering the following remarks to the public, on a subject which at the present moment deservedly attracts so much attention and excites so much interest, I am fully aware of the difficulties by which it is surrounded, which have been increased in no small degree by the determined and often violent spirit in which all parties have conducted their arguments; and, in consequence of which, society may be said to be now divided into two great sections, having equally, deeply-rooted and extravagant prejudices on this important question.

Disclaiming any participation or fellowship with the popular views on either side, uninfluenced by any private or party considerations, prompted only by a desire to arrive at a just and true view of so important a question as the supply of the first necessaries of life must ever be, I have approached the subject without reference to the generally existing opinions, and carefully endeavoured to consider it simply on its own merits.

To those, therefore, who are in search of arguments for the purpose of supporting the partial views of either side, which have hitherto prevailed, I can hold out no encouragement to take the trouble of perusing the following pages: they will not there find one single word declaiming the land-owners as selfish, monopolizing law-makers, or the manufacturers as sordid, avaricious beings, grasping at the riches of the great, and treading on the rights of the poor: the subject has already been handled too much in this way.

But to those who know no distinctions in the true interests of different portions of society, who feel and believe that the whole community can only be prosperous in proportion to the prosperity of its different parts, and that all these parts can only derive their individual prosperity from the well-doing of each other; who know no principle by which the operation of a law could benefit one important portion of society, and injure the remaining; or that could injure one important portion, and benefit the remaining,—to such, if a perusal of the following pages prove of any service in reconciling the facts of this subject to these principles, then will my chief object be accomplished.

The subject being essentially an agricultural one,

I have considered it *chiefly* and *particularly* in relation to that class, and *generally* in relation to the manufacturing, mercantile, and other portions of society; and, while I have endeavoured to reconcile into one general policy the best interests of all parties, I have not done so by requiring any compromise whatever at the hands of any one: but, on the contrary, only by sustaining and increasing all our present sources of national wealth and greatness; for on such broad and enlightened principles alone can this great question ever be satisfactorily adjusted.

Dulwich Place, Surrey,
March 1, 1839.

PREFACE

TO THE

SECOND EDITION.

In presenting this edition to the public, the author has taken the opportunity of explaining, in an Appendix, two objections which have been raised to the principles and views contained in this work:—first, that the extreme low price at which Continental wheat has sometimes been sold in this market appears incompatible with the estimate given of the charges necessarily incurred in importing it; and, secondly, that, from the admitted and well-ascertained fact, that the prices of wheat have fluctuated even more in the Continental countries where there are no corn-laws, and on the Continent generally, than in England, the fluctuations here cannot be attributed to the existing corn-laws.

As the consideration of these two points adds material strength to the general views of the author on this important subject, he is glad of the opportunity afforded of showing still further the mischievous tendency of these laws. In a short time he hopes to present to the public a second series of this work, pursuing the consideration to the influences which these laws exercise over the *currency*, the commerce and manufactures, and the moral and physical condition of the country, and the general influence which they exercise over the Continent of Europe.

INFLUENCES

OF THE

CORN LAWS, &c.

NOTWITHSTANDING the immeasurable importance which must necessarily attach to every principle and circumstance which tends to regulate the production and price of the first necessary of life, it is to be feared that no subject has suffered more than that which is proposed to be embraced in the present inquiry, for want of a patient investigation of the real facts connected with it, and the application of such principles, to which a knowledge and due appreciation of such facts must necessarily have led; in place of which, certain opinions and principles have been received and adopted by all parties, and have been tacitly admitted as the foundation of all reasoning on the subject, but which, I believe, I shall be able to show, in the course of the following investigation, to have very little or no foundation in reality, and that the conclusions derived therefrom by all parties must be correspondingly incorrect.

The two great parties with opposed views respecting the laws which regulate the production and supply of corn are, 1st., the landed and agricultural interest generally, who, from the commonly admitted opinions, could not sustain the present value of their property, pay the public burthens which the wants of the country and the state entail upon them, or maintain with integrity the existing contracts among themselves in the character of leases, &c., or with others, in the character of mortgages, loans, &c., unless the law afforded them a strong protection against the competition of the foreign landed interest, by high and almost prohibitory duties on all foreign agricultural produce :—and, 2ndly, the mercantile, manufacturing, and mechanical interests generally, who, from the same admitted opinions, have been impressed with the belief that, but for this protection extended to the landed interest, the price of the first necessaries of life, which must tend considerably to regulate the value of labour, and consequently the cost of their productions, would be greatly reduced from the present rates, and which, in that case, could not fail to exert a most beneficial influence on their different pursuits.

To find two opposing parties so well agreed as to the grounds of their dispute is a very uncommon circumstance : indeed, it would be difficult to say which of the two has been most industrious in circulating and insisting on the same facts in support of their different views and claims. At every agricultural meeting the greatest influence and talent have been exerted to show that, but for this prohibitory protection, and the consequent remunerating prices, the country must soon cease to produce food sufficient for one-half of its population, the value of property would vanish like a dream, the treasury would become an empty name, and famine and bankruptcy be the lot of the nation : while, on the other hand, it has been insisted that this protection has been the chief cause of almost every difficulty that has clouded our manufacturing prosperity; that to it alone may be ascribed every effort at competition and advance in the manufacturing arts which have been made by our continental neighbours since the peace; that by a removal of this protection the value of food and the price of labour would be reduced one-half, and the demand for it doubled; and it has even been stated that a free trade in corn would produce a saving to the country, by the reduction in prices, equivalent to one-half of our entire taxation. Thus, between these two parties, and on these grounds, equally admitted by both, the question has hitherto been chiefly confined; and the only point to determine has been, whether or not it was justice or good policy to afford the protection required by the one, to the apparent injury of the other.

I have, however, long been convinced that the common opinions, thus generally received and admitted by all parties, have either no foundation at all in truth, or so little, as to exert the most insignificant influence on the subject; and that, consequently, the fears and apprehended dangers on the one hand, and the continued irritating and inflammatory discontent on the other, are equally groundless: but that, nevertheless, the interference of the legislature, with the intention of accomplishing the wishes and objects of the landed interests, has had the most baneful tendencies on all classes of the community, beginning with the wealthiest landowner, and running through every grade and profession of life, down to the meanest labourer; and that the whole are consequently deeply interested in laying aside all party feelings on this important subject, and undertaking its consideration in a spirit of fairness, having no other desire than to arrive at the truth; as I believe I may safely say, that every interest has in its turn experienced and acknowledged the baneful influence of the present state of the laws, and perhaps none with so much reason as the agricultural interest itself. To collect all the facts connected with this interesting subject, and to combine them in such a way as to show the operation and tendency of the present laws and regulations affecting the price and production of wheat, as proved by the experience of the past, is the object of the following pages.

We cannot too much lament and deprecate the spirit of violence and exaggeration with which this subject has always been approached by each party, which no doubt has been the chief cause why so little of real truth or benefit has resulted from the efforts of either: the arguments on either side have been supported by such absurd and magnified statements of the influences of these prohibitory laws on their separate interests, as only to furnish each other with a good handle to turn the whole argument into ridicule. It therefore appears to be necessary to a just settlement of this great question, that these two parties should be first reconciled to a correct view of the real influences thus exerted over their interests, and the interests of the country at large; to a conviction that the imaginary fears of change on the one hand, and the exaggerated advantages expected on the other hand, are equally without foundation; that there are in reality no differences in the solid interests of either party; and that *individuals*, *communities*, or *countries* can only be prosperous in proportion to the prosperity of the whole.

To attempt this important object I do not propose to spend much time in abstract reasoning on the subject, which has been nearly exhausted by a succession of able productions from the days of Adam Smith to the present; but I propose to proceed at once to an examination of the matter practically, as shown by the statistics and historical facts of the operation of the *Corn Laws*, chiefly confining my considerations to the period from 1815 to the present day; and I will here remark that, throughout this inquiry, I shall have recourse only to the well-authenticated government returns, when they can possibly be applied, and in other cases to the best authorities extant on the subject.

I propose to confine this inquiry chiefly to the period above-mentioned; first, because during that time the greatest effort has been made by the law to regulate and control the subject: secondly, because during that period we have had uninterrupted peace; and thirdly, because going further back would lead into many considerations which influenced the prices and production of corn, not necessarily connected with itself, such as long and protracted wars, changes in the value of money, &c., &c.

I shall now proceed by dividing the subject into the following distinct propositions: first, that the present Corn Laws, as well as those which existed from 1815 to 1828, have been productive of consequences most prejudicial to all classes of the community, but more especially so to the landed and agricultural interest generally; in the course of which I propose to show in what manner they have been injurious to each separate interest, and to the country at large.

Secondly, that the agricultural interest has derived no benefit, but great injury, from the existing laws; and that the fears and apprehensions entertained of the ruinous consequences which would result to this interest by the adoption of a free and liberal policy with respect to the trade in corn are without any foundation; that the value of this property, instead of being depreciated, on the aggregate, would be rather enhanced, and the general interests of the owners most decidely benefited thereby.

Thirdly, that, while incalculable benefit would arise to the manufacturing interest and the working population generally, in common with all classes of the community, from the adoption of such policy, nothing can be more erroneous than the belief that the price of provisions or labour would on the average be thereby cheapened but that, on the contrary, the tendency would rather be to produce, by a state of general increased prosperity, a higher average rate of each;—and,

Fourthly, a consideration of what change in the present laws would best suit the interests of all parties at this particular time; and an examination of the benefit which would be derived by the establishment of a government institution for the purpose of collecting and furnishing periodically to the agricultural interests all the statistical facts connected with their pursuits, similar to those which the Custom House documents furnish to the mercantile interests.

PROPOSITION THE FIRST.

That the present Corn Laws, as well as those which existed from 1815 to 1828, have been productive of consequences most prejudicial to all classes of the community, but more especially so to the landed and agricultural interest generally, &c. &c.

In taking a general survey of the history of wheat during the period proposed, from 1815, to this time, the most striking feature is the great inequality and fluctuation of price, the average of some years being double that of others. This feature is not, however, more striking in the great extent to which it exists than it is remarkable at first sight that it should exist at all. Although long habit and experience may have caused us to cease to feel wonder at an event so common, very little consideration will, however, suffice to show that no article of extensive consumption in this country ought to be, from the nature of its production and consumption, so free from fluctuation as wheat. Natural fluctuations in the prices of commodities of any kind can only be the result of great and frequent changes in the relation of the supply of, and demand for, the article; and this may be effected in two ways,—either by a variation in the former or the latter.

It is very plain that the consumption and consequent demand of no article can possibly be so equal as that of wheat, the chief and first necessary of life. As far as regards the whole of the upper and middle ranks of life, and even a large portion of the lowest orders, the same quantity of wheat would be consumed at all times. The great bulk of the population will eat the same quantity of bread at all times: when it is cheap other articles are cheap in proportion, they therefore eat no more; when it is dear, it is the last article the consumption of which can be abridged: a thousand articles of comparative luxury will be given up before the first great necessary. There is, no doubt, a portion of the lowest orders which can command bread when cheap, that is obliged to exist more on lower fare, such as potatoes, &c., when it is dear; but this proportion is extremely small, and smaller now than at any former period of the history of this country.

It has consequently been remarked by many observers on this subject, that, owing to this necessary equality of consumption, the *limits* between surplus and deficiency are not far apart: that surplus stock and lower prices do not, to the same extent as other articles, stimulate increased consumption, and that a deficiency, with higher prices, does not like other articles materially abridge the consumption. It is, therefore, quite plain that inequality of demand cannot be the cause of the fluctuation of price;*

* It may be said by this reasoning that the very equality of consumption is one of the causes of the extreme prices; for if, with lower prices, the consumption increased, it would tend to maintain prices, and if, with higher prices, the consumption diminished, it would tend to keep prices down. This is true; but this is first to suppose that the supply is necessarily fluctuating. It is only an aggravated effect, and not a cause of fluctuation.

for, should any difference have existed in this respect, the consumption must certainly have been largest in years of the greatest cheapness and plenty, and least during the year of the highest prices : it therefore could not be diminished demand which produced the low prices, or increased demand the high prices.

It becomes obvious, therefore, that the inequality must have arisen in the supply ; but at first sight this seems almost impossible. When we consider that a chief cause of an equal supply of any article is an equal and unvarying demand ; that for the supply of this article we are dependent, almost exclusively, on our own home production, with a climate comparatively so equal, and a soil which is not only highly cultivated, but is sufficiently varying in its character, as to be adapted to any little variation of season ; with a greater amount of skill and capital, to avert the consequences which even the slight fluctuation of seasons might produce, than is enjoyed by any other country, or the cultivation of any other article ; —when we consider such a combination of causes to produce supply equal to the demand, we cannot but feel surprised that it should prove so varying as to cause such extreme fluctuations—fluctuations much greater than have been experienced in any of the chief products of our distant colonies, notwithstanding they are subject to the influence of climates and circumstances much less certain, to hurricanes and disasters, to droughts and inundations, and to a train of vicissitudes, natural and political, wholly unknown in the production of wheat.

We are induced to dwell thus minutely on this feature of the subject of our investigation, for we believe it to be the secret source of the whole mischief of the present system. We therefore think it of the greatest importance to discover the real cause of serious facts so well established, but differing so essentially from that course which all general and admitted principles would have led us to expect. In order to show what these fluctuations really have been, and at the same time to show that they have been regulated by some general and uniform principle, we submit the following table, divided into distinct periods, of rising and falling prices :—showing, first, the quantity of home-grown wheat which has arrived at *Mark Lane,* the chief market in the kingdom ; secondly, the average prices of wheat in the whole kingdom ; thirdly, the quantity of foreign wheat entered for home consumption ; fourthly, the average prices of wheat at Dantzig ; and fifthly, the average price of *South Down wool,*—in each of the last twenty-one years :—

FIRST PERIOD.—1817 to 1822.

Increasing Supplies and falling Prices.

Years.	Qrs. of wheat, British and Irish, arrived at Mark Lane.	Average price in Great Britain.	Quarters of Foreign and Colonial wheat and flour entered for consumption in Great Britain.	Average price at Dantzig.	Average price of South Down wool.
1817	290,479	94/	1,020,949	75/8	19d.
1818	205,907	83/8	1,593,518	64/7	24
1819	257,951	72/3	122,133	43/9	24
1820	395,889	65/10	34,274	33/3	17
1821	443,803	54/5	2	31/7	14½
1822*	512,152	43/3†	.. .. ..	29/1	13

SECOND PERIOD.—1822 to 1829.

Diminishing Supplies and rising Prices.

Years.	Qrs. of wheat, British and Irish, arrived at Mark Lane.	Average price in Great Britain.	Quarters of Foreign and Colonial wheat and flour entered for consumption in Great Britain.	Average price at Dantzig.	Average price of South Down wool.
1822*	512,152	43/3†	.. .. ..	29/1	13d.
1823	393,177	51/9	12,137	26/8	14½
1824	348,007	62/	15,777	22/9	12
1825	413,171	66/6	525,231	23/3	16
1826	271,120	56/11	315,892	23/1	10
1827	241,729	56/9	572,733	22/5	9
1828	312,610	60/5	842,050	24/4	9
1829‡	188,150	66/6§	1,364,220	36/10	8

THIRD PERIOD.—1829 to 1835.

Increasing Supplies and falling Prices.

Years.	Qrs. of wheat, British and Irish, arrived at Mark Lane.	Average price in Great Britain.	Quarters of Foreign and Colonial wheat and flour entered for consumption in Great Britain.	Average price at Dantzig.	Average price of South Down wool.
1829‡	188,150	69/6§	1,364,220	36/10	8d.
1830	224,887	64/3	1,701,885	34/3	10
1831	208,329	66/	1,491,631	37/3	12
1832	300,073	58/8	325,435	37/7	18
1833	388,171	52/11	82,346	29/4	16
1834	418,431	46/2	64,653	25/5	17
1835*	468,338	39/4†	28,483	23/	18

FOURTH PERIOD.—1835 to 1839.

Diminishing Supplies and rising Prices.

Years.	Qrs. of wheat, British and Irish, arrived at Mark Lane.	Average price in Great Britain.	Quarters of Foreign and Colonial wheat and flour entered for consumption in Great Britain.	Average price at Dantzig.	Average price of South Down wool.
1835*	468,338	39/4†	28,483	23/	18d.
1836	414,145	48/6	30,554	28/7	19
1837	321,735	55/10	244,619	29/	14
1838	296,500	64/7	*1,853,018	.. ..	17½

* Maximum Supply. † Minimum Price.
‡ Minimum Supply. § Maximum Price.

* It must be borne in mind that these quantities include the *Colonial* Imports, which in many years constitute by far the greatest portion.

In framing this table we have been desirous first to ascertain the annual supply of home-grown wheat from year to year. In the absence of any knowledge on this important and vital subject, beyond vague report and conjecture, we have, after much consideration, taken the arrivals at Mark Lane, as the most accurate criterion of the progress of cultivation and supply from year to year; not that these quantities bear in themselves any fixed proportion to the whole amount produced, but that they furnish the best index of the general progress of production. Being the chief market in the kingdom, supplying not only by far the largest and the wealthiest population in its own immediate vicinity, but also being the channel through which the surplus produce of one part of the country is sent to another part in want of it, we have selected it as the most satisfactory evidence on this point. In the next place we have shown in what way the average prices for the *whole kingdom* are influenced by the supply from year to year, which, corresponding so accurately with the index of the general supply which we have selected, proves that it is not far wrong. In the third column we have examined the quantities of foreign and colonial wheat and flour cleared for consumption (in each year) in the whole kingdom, in order to show how the great apparent deficiency in some years has been supplied. In the fourth column we have furnished the average price at Dantzig, the chief continental market, in each year of the same period;—and in the sixth column we have furnished the average price of South Down wool, as a criterion of the value of British wools, generally, and which appears to bear some relation to the production of wheat.

In the first years of the period, while the price of wheat was very high, it will be observed that wool was also dear, in relation to its general average price in after years:—but it will be remembered that at that time a considerable duty was paid on the importation of foreign wool, which tended to keep prices higher here; and when that duty was repealed, and the present small duty substituted, the relative value of the article was thereby lowered. It will however be remarked as an interesting fact, that from 1822 to 1829, as the production of wheat gradually fell off and the price advanced, the production of wool appears to have increased, and the price consequently diminished: so that in 1829, when wheat had reached the highest point, wool was at the lowest point; and that, from that period forward, as wheat gradually declined in price, wool gradually advanced.—There can be no doubt that these two subjects have some relation to each other, and that the increased cultivation of wheat from 1829 forward was greatly aided by the reduction of extensive sheep-walks particularly in the southern and western counties, into wheat-fields. It is at the same time evident that the prices and consumption of wool must depend on so many other circumstances, such as the general state of trade, the amount of the supplies from other countries, &c., quite distinct from any relation that it may bear to wheat, that no great practical result can be gathered from this comparison.—It is worthy of observation that, notwithstanding the crisis of 1836-37, and notwithstanding the immensely increased supplies of foreign and colonial wool, the prices have not fallen, while wheat has been rising so rapidly;—which is a cheering evidence of the rapid increase of our consumption of wool since the former period.

With this explanation of this table we will proceed to examine how far the statistical facts which it exhibits will enable us to discover a satisfactory reason for the fluctuations which, we shall hereafter show, are so prejudicial to the interests of all.—In looking at this table, it will be seen that a regular operation of increasing supplies with falling prices, and of diminishing supplies and rising prices, have been going on during the whole four distinguished periods.

The following are the extreme points, between which however the operation is gradual and regular to a wonderful degree :—

	Supply.	*Price.*
1817 . .	290,479 . .	94*s.*
1822 . .	511,152 . .	43*s.* 3*d.*, a fall of 54 per cent.
1829 . .	188,150 . .	66*s.* 6*d.*, a rise of 53 „
1835 . .	468,338 . .	39*s.* 4*d.*, a fall of 41 „
1838 . .	296,500 . .	64*s.* 7*d.*, a rise of 64 „

We cannot view this table without at once arriving at a conviction that changes so uniform have been brought about by some cause as uniform and unerring as the effects produced, and must at once banish from our mind the commonly-received opinion that the fluctuations of prices are caused by favourable and unfavourable seasons, or any other accidental reason. To suppose this would be to believe that from 1817 to 1822 the seasons were every year rapidly and uniformly improving, and that from that year till 1829 they were as rapidly and uniformly becoming worse, and so on during the whole period. As it is therefore plain that these fluctuations of supply cannot arise from the accidental variations of the seasons (though upon some occasions the natural operation may be aggravated by this cause), it follows that they must arise from an increased or diminished cultivation, either in the extent of surface or in the amount of capital and labour employed thereon; and we believe the whole cause will be most satisfactorily explained by a consideration of the natural and imperative influence of the Corn Laws which have been in operation during this period.*

From 1810 to 1813 inclusive the average price of wheat for the four years was 106*s.*, being in 1812 as high as 122*s.* 8*d.* per quarter; in 1814 the average fell down to 72*s.* 1*d.*, and in 1815 to 63*s.* 8*d.*:—these reduced prices created so much alarm amongst the agricultural interest, that they procured a parliamentary inquiry in 1814 as a preliminary to some enactment for the purpose of reviving and protecting their sinking interests. The evidence given before this Committee of the House of Peers, by Mr. Arthur Young and several eminent agriculturists, went to show that, in order to retain the cultivation of Great Britain in the extent in which it then was, it would be necessary that the average price of wheat should be 90*s.* to 100*s.* per quarter, barley 40*s.* to 45*s.*, and oats 30*s.* to 35*s.* On this evidence the Corn Laws of 1815 were founded, which entirely prohibited the import of foreign wheat until the aggregate average of the whole country for three months had reached 80*s.* per quarter. The low prices (comparatively for that period) in 1814 and 1815 had the effect of materially discouraging production, and this cause, followed by the unparalleled bad season of 1816, produced the high price of 1817, with which we commence our periods of fluctuations. In this year the average price, for the

* See Note 1, at the end.

whole kingdom, of wheat was 94*s*. This extreme price, supported by a law which was intended and supposed would at least have the effect of preventing wheat from sinking below 80*s*. per quarter, could not fail to have an important effect in stimulating a general increased production. This was effected in all possible ways. A larger breadth of land in cultivation was diverted to wheat, new lands were called into cultivation moors and morasses were reclaimed, and capital was in every way most lavishly expended to secure the glittering advantages of such high prices. To use the expression of an eminent person of the day, the surface of the land was strewed with guineas to reap wheat. Eighty shillings per quarter was the standard of all calculations, and therefore every piece of ground which could be brought into cultivation to raise wheat at this price was submitted to the plough. At this period a similar process was going forward on the Continent, caused by the high prices which resulted from the extensive supplies to this country in 1817 and 1818.

We cannot, therefore, be surprised that each year succeeding these efforts we should find a rapid increase of supply. J. H. Von Thuenen of Tellow, an eminent Continental agriculturist, in a letter addressed to Mr. Jacob, and presented in his report to the *Board of Trade* in 1827, states, "The harvests of 1821, 1822, and 1823 were so abundant, that history scarcely accords the like for a single year, much less for a series of three years; the increased production of the soil by the *application of marl,* combined with the fertility of the seasons, yielded such rich harvests, that the cost of production was much less than in former years."

This increased production and supply could not fail to affect prices materially, and consequently we find that a gradual decline took place, until the whole average price of 1822, with a supply at Mark Lane of 512,152 quarters, was only 43*s*. 3*d*. per quarter—less than half the price in 1817, when the supply was only 290,479 quarters. It is extremely worthy of remark that this change was caused only by the competition amongst our own home-growers, as it will be seen that from 1818 forward for some years the most trivial quantity of foreign wheat was imported; and it is impossible, therefore, to say that the great depression had any connexion with foreign supplies or competition.

It is evident that the influences which induced such an extended and forced cultivation, viz., the high prices of 1817, and the prohibitory law, which had for its only object the maintenance of these high prices, were the real and only cause of the ruinous prices which ensued in 1822; and it is as evident that great loss must have been sustained by those who, in the delusive hope of reaping the advantages promised by these prohibitory laws, had been thus induced to expend so much capital and labour in the improvements which took place, and who thus found that, just when the invested capital began to show its fruitful results, the prices began proportionally to diminish, until at length they did not receive one-half of the rates which had induced them to expend so much money, notwithstanding the promise of protection which the law held out.

But no article can long remain below the cost of production: we accordingly find, immediately after this year, evidences of the contrary tendency. We see that low prices did not fail to produce the exactly opposite tendency of the high prices—a curtailment of cultivation in every way in which it had previously been extended. Many of the inferior soils, which had been dragged into cultivation, were now abandoned for this purpose; and we consequently find that the supply diminished every year, and the average price gradually improved. This process went forward until 1829, when we find that the quantity of home-grown wheat brought to Mark Lane had fallen from 512,152 quarters, in 1822, to 188,150 quarters in this year, and the price had in the same time risen from 43*s*. 3*d*. to 66*s*. 6*d*. per quarter. There can be no doubt that this change was only the natural reaction which followed the glut at the former period: such a course was quite imperative, by the fact that over-supply had pressed prices below the cost of production. The cause, therefore, which influenced the over-production must necessarily be deemed the original cause of the ensuing scarcity. We now find that we have, consequently, three years of high prices, but, unfortunately for the home-grower, he had an extremely limited quantity to sell: his *large bulk*, 512,152 quarters, was sold at the minimum price, 43*s*. 3*d*.; and now his minimum bulk, only 188,159 quarters, secures the maximum price, 66*s*. 6*d*.; and it will be seen that during these three years nearly double the quantity of foreign wheat was imported and retained for consumption of that in the whole preceding ten years: the quantities being 4,559,736 quarters in 1829, 1830, and 1831, while only 2,440,229 quarters had been thus imported in the whole preceding ten years: showing an average of

1,519,245 quarters annually in the former case, and only 244,022 quarters annually in the latter case.

The ruinous consequences of these fluctuations became at this period the subject of general remark and attention, and the government, acknowledging the failure of the law of 1815, its inadequacy to produce the intended effect, and its general baneful influence, admitted that some change was needful, chiefly for the object of producing a greater equality of prices, and preventing such ruinous fluctuations. It still, however, appears not to have been clearly understood from what cause these fluctuations had really arisen; and, therefore, on the consideration of the question, they were treated more as the result of natural accidents, to which the cultivation was necessarily liable, than really as solely the consequence of the protective enactment.

To accomplish the two-fold objects of giving protection to the landed interest and of maintaining prices more equal, two modes were proposed: one, that of a fixed duty at all times; the other, a fluctuating scale of duties, which was adopted, and has since been the law.

The latter theory was received with great favour, and much lauded as possessing the important element of steadying prices: for, as it was urged, the principle of ascending duties as the price fell, and of diminishing duties as the price rose, must have the effect of equalizing the supply, and consequently prices, by gradually excluding foreign grain, when our stocks or production were increasing, and by gradually admitting it when our stocks or production were diminishing; and thus that prices could not sink very low, or rise very high. At first sight, this enactment looked most ingeniously calculated for the intended purpose.

Provided there were in the nature of the article itself the necessary elements of fluctuation, which it has been shown do not exist, then such a regulation might possibly have been useful; but if, instead of such a tendency, it is found that, if left to itself, it has the directly contrary tendency, that of maintaining an equality of value; that this ingenious device was only an attempt to cure an evil which would not have existed but for the interference of the legislature; that this attempted cure was not only a sufficient cause for the creation of the evil, but must exercise an infallible effect in prolonging and extending it,—then much of its beauty and ingenuity, acknowledged at first sight, must vanish.

Without apparently referring to what the home competition in the production of wheat, uninfluenced as has been shown by any external competition, had produced as an average price, the government aimed at again securing to the growers prices which they could never maintain; and then it was considered, very falsely, that the continental farmer could really pay a considerable duty, even 20*s*. per quarter, and successfully compete with the home-grower; and, therefore, this scale of duties was fixed throughout at such rates as to provide for this. For example, suppose the average price to be 53*s*. per quarter: if the foreign grower could profitably send his wheat at that price, and pay, as many supposed, a duty of 20*s*., the government, as a protection to the English grower, made the duty 14*s*. 8*d*. higher, viz., 34*s*. 8*d*.; and so on. It was, therefore, quite evident that prices might be maintained at a very high average without admitting any foreign competition: for example, when the average price was 60*s*. per quarter, the du., fixed was 26*s*. 8*d*.; and when the average price rose to 66*s*. 6*d*., the highest average which it has ever reached for any one year since 1819, the duty was fixed at 20*s*. 8*d*. So great an encouragement and apparent protection to maintain the high prices of the time could not, therefore, fail to produce a repetition of what had occurred from 1817 to 1822. If it had been understood that these consequences had arisen only from the previously attempted protection of high prices, we cannot believe that these rates would ever have been fixed; but there was one other great error in the principle of this fluctuating scale of duties, which must also have rendered them of no benefit in effecting their professed object.

If such a principle were applied to regulate the supply of an article which could be produced instantly, when required, and the production of which could, without loss, be instantly abandoned, then it might have a tendency to keep a very uniform supply and price; but when it is considered that the arrangements for the production of wheat require two or three years to come into full operation, either in extending or diminishing the cultivation, it is quite clear that any influence which could be given to production by the operation of this principle would not come into effect until the whole face of affairs might be changed, and its supposed adaptation to provide against famine or extreme high prices on the one hand, or a glut on the other, would entirely fail. For example, from 1833 to 1837 the average price for any one of the three years never reached 49*s*., at which price the duty is 38*s*. 8*d*., leaving only a difference of 10*s*. 8*d*. per quarter between the duty and the whole price; and in one year, 1835, the whole average price was only 39*s*. 4*d*., at which rate the duty is higher than the whole price obtained. The influence which such a state of the market was likely to produce on those growers, on whom the law supposes we must depend in case of necessity, is obvious. All cultivation must cease beyond their own wants, and in the course of two or three years after, as soon as the arrangements came into operation, their production would only be adequate thereto; but, in that time, the average price may have risen in this country, and a foreign supply become necessary, as has really been the case in the present instance, just at the moment when our own acts had annihilated the supply: or, to take the reverse case, at the present moment, our free admission of wheat to meet the scarcity which exists has raised the price to 65*s*. per quarter in many parts of the Continent, where the usual price is about 33*s*.; but it is clear that even this high price cannot instantly call production into existence to meet the urgency of the case, though it were ten times greater than it is: still it cannot fail to stimulate every effort to increase supplies as soon as possible, not only by the encouraging prices, but, also, by the additional capital which is thus unexpectedly put into the hands of the growers for their present crops. But these efforts will not produce their full effects till perhaps the end of two or even three years, by which time the urgency of the demand has passed away, and increased cultivation at home has lowered the value and raised the duty ; but, as this impulse to production on the Continent has caused a supply far greater than is required for themselves, the markets are glutted, and prices forced far below the cost of production; and thus the operation of our own Corn Laws is the chief cause of the extreme low prices which sometimes prevail on the Continent, and serve to excite the fears and astonishment of the growers in this country; which low prices, it ought to be borne in mind, are no more remunerating to them than the prices of 1822 and 1835 were to the English grower, pressed down as they were by similar causes. It thus appears that the very nature of the production of wheat must ever have excluded any benefit which was anticipated from this apparently ingenious contrivance.

By reference to the table we find (not to our astonishment) that the same process went forward from 1829, under the influence of the new law, as had done from 1817, under the influence of the law of that day. The supplies gradually increased and prices gradually fell; until, in 1835, we find a supply at Mark Lane of 468,338 quarters, with an average price, of the whole year, of 39*s.* 4*d.* against the supply in 1829 of 188,150 quarters, and an average price for the year of 66*s.* 6*d.*

Then again, true to the principle already explained, the tide once more turns, and we find supplies each year diminishing and prices increasing, until, in 1838, the former has fallen down to 296,500 quarters, and the latter risen to 64*s.* 7*d.* It is really most curious and interesting to observe in the table with what strict uniformity and regularity these changes take place; and it is just as certain that the same uniform changes must take place for the next twenty years, should the same causes continue in existence, as if the period had passed over and the figures stood recorded on the same table extended over that time.

We will just shortly glance at one of the causes which have often been urged for the variations in the prices of grain:—viz.,

The changes in the value of money, by an extended or restricted circulating medium at different times. There can be no doubt that an extension of the currency, either paper or metallic, must at all times tend to enhance the general money value of all property, and that, on the contrary, its restriction cannot fail to reduce the money value; but apply these undoubted truths to the subject of our investigation, and let us see how far they will assist us in accounting for the strange fluctuations we have pointed out. From 1822 forward to 1824 a considerable depreciation took place in the currency by an inordinate issue of country one-pound notes, which produced the panic of 1825. Prices of wheat ought, therefore, by this law, to have risen; instead of that, they remained at the lowest rates. From 1826 forward to 1829 the currency was greatly curtailed by the withdrawal of all one-pound notes from circulation, and property of almost all kinds suffered an immense depreciation; but wheat, on the contrary, was highest throughout the very year when this depreciation may be said to have reached the climax—1829. Well, then, from 1830 to 1835 the currency again experienced a great extension by the establishment of joint stock banks, and the value of money fell in 1835 to the lowest point experienced for many years, and credit and speculation were equally rife, which led to the panic of 1836.

Property and produce generally assumed then a very high relative value, but wheat still, unlike all other articles, was at the lowest point in 1835, in the very year it ought by this rule to have been highest—the Gazette average price for six weeks having at one period in that year sunk down to 35*s*., and for the whole year to 39*s*. 4*d*. per quarter. We do not say that wheat is unlike all other articles, and not subject to these influences of the currency—we know it is; but, because it is and must be, it only affords an additional proof that the fluctuations which have really taken place were not caused by that agency, but some other principle, which proved strong enough to reverse entirely the otherwise natural effects of these influences.

We, therefore, submit that we have shown sufficient to prove that these rapid changes in price have only arisen from the necessary tendency of an attempt to foster and protect high prices by restrictive laws; and we think we have shown the principle sufficiently to prove that just in proportion to the extent of the protection which might be aimed at would be the fluctuation: for example, had the law, instead of fixing 80*s*. as the price below which wheat could not be imported, been pleased to make it 100*s*., it is quite clear that, that standard being taken instead of 80*s*. by the growers, they would have brought as much more land into cultivation, and spent as much more capital on that already in culture, as had promised remuneration at this price: this increased inducement to produce could not fail to call into existence an over-stock proportionably greater, and prices correspondingly depressed. The reaction of this greater depression must also have been in exact relation to its cause, and in the proper time have produced a still greater scarcity than did actually ensue, so as to have reached the price supposed, or perhaps higher. In like manner, had the price been fixed at 60*s*. instead of 80*s*., the inducement to over-produce being abridged, depression to the same extent could not have followed, and the reaction would have been correspondingly less; but in a relative degree they must still exist, and it would not be until the attempted protection was altogether abandoned that this necessary consequence would become extinct.

We have been thus particular in endeavouring to prove that the extraordinary fluctuations which have taken place of late years in the price of wheat, which, as we have shown, ought to be the least fluctuating of all commodities, have been, and must ever continue to be, the result of protective and prohibitory laws; because we believe that from this necessary tendency the whole of the evils of the present system have arisen.

We shall therefore now proceed to examine the consequences which these fluctuations must entail generally on the interests of the whole community; and then more particularly, first, on the agricultural, and secondly, on the mercantile interests.

Many will be apt to think that, if fluctuation is the only result, the evil of the Corn Laws must have been most extravagantly exaggerated; for they may think that the high and low years may make a fair average both to consumer and producer, and what is lost by either party at one period is made up by the reverse period. Nothing can be more fallacious, which, we think, can be easily shown by a close examination of the subject.

No principle is better understood among political economists than that an over-abundant use of capital and labour, in any one pursuit or direction, must not only be in itself a waste and loss to the community, but must also be prejudicial by withdrawing these elements of national prosperity from other objects where their application would produce a positive benefit; and that it must therefore ever be of the greatest importance to a community that its capital, skill, and industry shall be directed in a way exactly apportioned to all the wants of the public, which could not fail generally to be very nearly the case, were all production left to regulate itself by the natural effect of competition and self-interest, but which must always run a great hazard of misdirection by the interference and attempted protection of government to partial objects.

It has been shown that the influence of protective duties must always be to induce a great excess of capital and labour to be for a time employed in the cultivation of grain, and that therefore, in this respect alone, they must be injurious to a great extent.

In the first place, a great excess of production and stock is the consequence, accompanied by extreme low prices, ruinous to the growers. It never can be advantageous for the community at large that they should consume the produce of any one party below the cost of production, for a period is not very far distant when the consequences must react and infallibly produce very high prices and great scarcity; and we will show that the evils of the reaction are far greater than any advantage derived from the low prices.

We find that from 1829 till 1835 the supply at Mark Lane increased from 188,150 quarters to 468,338 quarters; and that the prices fell from 66*s*. 6*d*. per quarter to 39*s*. 4*d*. per quarter. During this period there was evidently too much capital and labour employed in the production, and a great excess of supply ensued. If, therefore, such a quantity of wheat had been produced as could not be consumed in the proper period for which it was intended, but a large portion must be kept over for the consumption of future years, it follows, as a matter of course, that the value of that surplus stock (and which would consequently fix the price of the whole by the common laws of competition), which must, therefore, be held over for the chance of future demand, must be sold as much below the cost of production (which would, in all likelihood, regulate the prices in the future) as would pay the interest of the capital invested in it, the expense of keeping it, the deterioration in quantity and quality, and a profit to the holder.

The producer, by thus submitting to a great loss, is deprived of the inducement and the means to continue the same extent of production; the supply gradually dwindles below the quantity required for consumption, and the surplus held over from former years has at length an opportunity of coming into consumption by the high prices occasioned by restricted production.

But was the loss thus occasioned to the grower a gain to any one? It seldom occurs, such is the enormous cost and waste of holding grain, that, if bought in the lowest years and sold in the highest years, much if any profit attends it.—It will therefore appear that the great losses submitted to in low years are wasted in the interest of money, the cost of keeping, turning, &c., the support of vermin, and the natural decay of time. No one therefore can fail to see how great a general loss must be thus entailed on the whole community by diminishing the aggregate amount of its capital; and when it is considered how huge is the amount implicated in this important article, the loss thus sustained must be of a fearful magnitude. But many will say it is far from being all loss:—one man receives interest for the capital, another a rent for the granary, another the wages for turning and keeping, &c.; but these being all unproductive applications alike of labour and capital, must, notwithstanding this distribution, be a total loss to the community.

By way of illustration, suppose that in a certain town a great demand had existed for habitations. Streets were erected to supply the demand, but when the demands ceased the erection of new streets was still going forward;—a builder, finding himself with an elegant range of houses without a single tenant, applies to a capitalist to purchase his property.—The capitalist has no more chance of finding immediate occupants than the builder, and he therefore says, " Yes, I will purchase your houses, but only at such a price as will remunerate me for the interest of my money, and the expenses of keeping the buildings in repair, until such a time as I can hope to obtain suitable tenants to occupy them: because I see no reason to suppose that the expense of erecting such buildings will be greater some years hence, when they may be required, than at this moment." No one can therefore suppose that this loss, which would thus fall on the builder in the first place, notwithstanding the whole of the difference between the cost and the price paid by the capitalist might ultimately be paid to the slater for repairing the roofs, to the glazier for repairing the windows, to the painter and the plasterer for their necessary assistance to keep these tenements in repair, till required for habitations, would nevertheless to the full amount be a loss to the whole community by so much abridgment of the general stock.

So it is exactly with grain or any other commodity; and the case is not altered one whit though the farmer should be the holder of the wheat, or the builder the retainer of his houses:—in the first case the rents of granaries, or his own building must still be paid, the labour of turning and keeping must still apply, time would still continue to decay, and vermin would still continue to be created and fattened by that which was destined as the best support of human life:—in the last case, the roofs would still require the slater, the windows the glazier, the whole the painter and the plasterer to preserve the buildings; and in both cases the capital would be locked up and remain dormant, which might otherwise have been usefully engaged in the reproduction of other things required by the community.

But, besides this, such extreme excess of stocks and of low prices cannot fail to produce a lavish and inconsiderate use of this great necessary of life: — waste and profusion must ever accompany such a state of things. Who has forgot the numerous inferior uses to which wheat was applied in 1835? It was employed for distilling to a great extent; and in many places to no less an extent in feeding cattle; for which purposes much inferior articles, of much less prime cost, would have been more suitable; but which had been partially pressed out of cultivation by the over-production of wheat. Barley, for example, which, by the law of cost, ought to rule about half the price of wheat, was at that period nearly the same price. Green food in Ireland was in like manner dearer in proportion than wheat even for the purposes of feeding cattle; and therefore in many places wheat was used as a substitute for these products. In like manner the range of elegant houses, with their fluted and pillared porticoes, with their marble halls, and their richly-corniced rooms, suitable only for the occupation of the rich and the great, are used as the deposits of lumber or merchandise, or cut up into small tenements for the occupation of the poor, who would be more comfortable and more at home in neat ten-pound cottages.

A great part, therefore, of the surplus is wasted and unappropriately applied; the time of reaction, of scarcity and high prices, is thereby accelerated, and then the whole community are to suffer a period of want and extreme prices.

But if such are the baneful consequences to the community at large, with what a fearful degree must they apply to the landed interests, who must not only, in common with all, share in the losses thus sustained, but who are in themselves the individual objects through whom the whole evils reach the community; and who therefore *personally* and *particularly* incur all the *losses* which the public does *generally*.

This point, being one of the most important in our investigation, deserves close attention.

We have already seen how the high prices of 1817 and 1818, of 1828 and 1829, accompanied by prohibitory enactments to secure their continuance, had the effect of increasing the production and supplies: now it is clear this increase could only have been accomplished by a greatly-increased application of labour and capital, in reducing poor lands into cultivation, and in forcing the productiveness of those already in cultivation. This was all done by the farmer, stimulated by the natural hope of securing the high prices which the legislature in effect promised should be permanent; a natural competition arose for farms, and the rents accordingly advanced;—the farmer went on year after year improving and cultivating, but he found that year after year the prices were lowering. With a view of paying his enhanced rent and his increased expenses, he pressed his production further and further, to make up in quantity what he lost in price. His efforts, however, only recoiled upon himself; his increased quantity only produced greater and greater depression, until he arrived at the points of 1822 and 1835. He now found that all along the object of his pursuit had eluded his grasp, and that to go on would only have sunk him deeper and deeper in losses; that the investment of capital,—that the extraordinary application of skill and labour, to secure what had been held out to him at the commencement of his efforts as the sure reward of his industry and enterprise,—had all ended in losses and disappointment, and, in many cases, in utter ruin and despair.

He has arrived at the period when his surplus stock presses severely on the market; he has, in fact, not only produced for the wants of the present, but has anticipated the consumption of the future: he must, therefore, as before shown, sell his commodity as much below the cost of production as will enable the buyers to hold it over till the time it is required for use, and pay all the necessary charges in so doing.

It is therefore evident that the farmer personally suffers the whole loss of capital stock which the community does generally, incurred in the interest of capital necessary to hold this surplus till it is required, of the whole expenses of granary-rent, of turning and keeping in order, of producing and fattening the vermin which swarm amongst his produce, and of whatever profit may attach to the merchant by the operation. The whole of these charges and losses are only a part of the capital and industry which the farmer had been induced to invest upon the soil. Just as the difference between the cost and the diminished price which the builder received for his range of elegant houses was to him alone a personal loss, so the diminished prices paid for wheat in years of excessive supply must alone be the personal loss of the grower; and with the producer there is this greatly aggravated fact:—he is obliged not only to accept the reduced and ruinous price for the surplus quantity which must be held over for years, but he is obliged also to accept the same low prices for the whole of his produce,—not only for that which is in excess, but also for that which is absolutely required for consumption. The natural competition which prevails among all the growers to have their produce bought and consumed must always have this natural tendency. They cannot receive one price for that which is to be kept, and a higher for that which is to be consumed the following day.

The huge loss which is thus entailed on the farmer deprives him of the means and of the inducement to go on producing at the same rate. His cultivation consequently becomes curtailed, the amount of labour and capital which he expends is greatly lessened, his lands fall into a comparative state of unproductiveness, and become applied to other purposes, requiring much less capital than that of raising wheat. This operation goes on for some time, until his production gradually sinks below the average rate of consumption; the old surplus stocks become gradually, and silently and unwittingly consumed, as the prices advance; and, before long, the diminished cultivation and exhausted stocks are brought to view by rapidly-enhancing prices and increasing scarcity, which only a short time before were little apprehended, and for which, therefore, no provision had been made. This brings the grower to the points in the table of 1828 and 1838, when the prices rose so high as to admit foreign wheat without any duty, or only a nominal one.

It is true the farmer now participates in these high prices,—but to what extent? Refer to the table, and it will be seen that in 1822 the English grower receives at Mark Lane for 512,152 quarters of wheat only 43*s*. 3*d*. per quarter; and in 1835, for 468,338 quarters, only 39*s*. 4*d*. per quarter; while in 1828 he receives 66*s*. 6*d*. per quarter for only 188,150 quarters, and in 1838 he receives 64*s*. 7*d*. for only 296,500 quarters, the difference of these being supplied by the accumulated surplus produce of the Continental grower. Thus, for example, the supplies of wheat at Mark Lane were as follows in the last three months of the following years:—

Supplied	1835.	1836.	1837.	1838.
	Quarters.	Quarters.	Quarters.	Quarters.
British	124,871	102,109	84,902	56,283
Foreign	None	16,450	24,287	94,433
Total	124,871	118,559	109,189	150,716
Average price of three months	35*s*. 6*d*.	53*s*.	51*s*. 4*d*.	70*s*. 9*d*.

It will be seen, therefore, that while the English grower, by the operation of these laws, secures to himself the supply of the whole of Great Britain when the prices are ruinously low, he compels the foreign grower to hoard up his surplus produce until a scarcity arrives; and then the English farmer, having only a very limited quantity to sell, allows the foreign grower to participate in all the advantages of the high prices. It is, therefore, so ingeniously contrived, that, when prices are high, the English grower shall be only to a very limited extent advantaged thereby, and when prices are low the whole loss and ruin shall devolve upon him.

But, not knowing or not acknowledging the secret and real cause of all his misfortunes, little dreaming that the very laws which have been enacted for his protection are the real causes of his misfortunes, we see that he again, as recklessly as ever, enters the arena of competition to produce: the high prices of two or three years furnishing him with more capital, he is again tempted to a similar operation as that which before brought him to the brink of ruin. And thus we see that, notwithstanding the effects which were produced from 1817 to 1822, the same race was as eagerly run from 1828 to 1835; and the same race is now with as great eagerness at this moment commenced, which, if things remain unaltered, will end in the same results some three or four years hence.

Notwithstanding the depression only three years ago, the competition to take farms is so great, that at this moment some land, which only a year ago was worth 25*s*. per acre, has let for 44*s*. By a careful inquiry we find that the demand throughout the country for manure of every description, to force cultivation, is so great, that the produce of the government horse-barracks is engaged for many months forward at high prices; and in some cases we have found that it has been engaged for farms at a distance of fifteen and sixteen miles from the spot; whereas, in many instances, three years ago, it was with difficulty disposed of.

This shows the expensive mode which is used to force production; but such is the natural and unavoidable results of the present system, and will continue as long as the delusive cause continues. Yet it cannot fail to produce the most painful feelings to any one taking an accurate view of the subject, to contemplate the necessary results which must attend these efforts, dictated by motives so fair and so natural, the loss of capital and labour which will be experienced, and the severe disappointments which must again for a time wither the hopes and destroy the energies of the honest and laborious cultivator of the soil.

While this train of cruel effects is experienced by the farmer, the landowner, contrary to a general opinion, does not escape a large share of the evil.

In the first place he lets his lands at comparatively high prices, and for a year or two, while the high prices continue, he may obtain them; but he soon finds a diminishing ability to pay the rents: he is obliged to make deductions from year to year, to make a merit of necessity, and accept a fourth, a third, or even a half less than contracted for: he must do this or break up and ruin his tenantry without any hope of replacing them. It must be still fresh in the recollection of every one that from 1821 to 1823, and again from 1832 to 1836, the greatest portion of the landed proprietors were obliged annually to give a reduction of twenty, thirty, or forty per cent. of the stipulated rents, or submit to ruin and lose their occupiers; and even then many estates were with the greatest difficulty tenanted in those years, and some were obliged to become the occupiers themselves of large districts. All lands that are newly let at such times are let at rates corresponding with the low prices of the day: the cultivation is only suited to these prices; their productiveness is thereby materially diminished, the intrinsic value of the property is proportionably reduced, and thus the loss which is sustained by the landowner by this reduction of rent, being sunk in a lessened productiveness, is gained by no one, but, so far as it runs into excess in proportion to the wants of the community, must be a general and national loss. As with the farmer, the first and particular loss falls on the landowner, but the general loss reaches the whole community, not only by the depreciation of the income which it involves, but also in the high range of prices which must succeed such depreciation.

So exactly as was the case with the farmer in 1817 and 1818, and in 1828 and 1829, when the landowner was promised, by all apparent causes, and by the most binding contracts, a long range of high rents, he very soon discovered that, from some secret cause, his reasonable expectations were disappointed, and his contracts of no avail. The interests of his tenants were drooping so fast, and their means of fulfilling their engagements vanishing so rapidly, that to have insisted, in the years which followed the above periods of promise, on the full payment of rent would have been to have untenanted his whole estate, become the cultivator himself, and thus put himself in the same unfavourable position as the departed tenant, or allow his lands to run into barren waste. It became as much a necessity for the landowner to accept a greatly diminished rent in one form or another, as for the farmer in the same years to accept a price for his produce far below the cost of cultivation; and thus the landowner is obliged, like the farmer, to accept a low price in the very years of the greatest productiveness, which ought to yield the highest rent, only because by false hopes and promises this productiveness is pressed too far, so as to supply not only the wants of the present, but to anticipate those of the future, in the ruinous consequences of which, already pointed out, he is thus compelled to share.

The new and reduced value which his property now assumes continues for a number of years, as has been shown by its depreciated productiveness; and so as the times of high prices arrive in 1828-29 and 1838-39, which alone could afford him the high rent for which he had originally stipulated, he reaps none of the advantages to which such prices would appear to entitle him; for the same reason that his tenants reap so little of the advantage of these prices: his lands at this period can only bear a value corresponding with their productiveness, which by the necessary consequences of these fluctuations is now at the lowest ebb; and then the interest of the Continental landowner, which has been most carefully excluded during the whole period of depression, is introduced in the accumulated form which its surplus produce for many years has acquired, and a large portion of the advantages of the high prices paid by the community is thus contributed, as before shown, to this interest. As the farmer partially, and to a small extent, participates in the advantages of the high prices, so now the landowner participates likewise by a fresh promise of high rents, which he will receive as long as the farmer can pay them, but which he will soon find is no less delusive than the similar hope he formerly entertained, and which, if the same causes continue, will end in the same disappointment.

It is, therefore, clear that all the causes which influence the prosperity of the farmer must correspondingly apply to the landowner, and we must for ever dismiss from our considerations the notion that a policy which can be detrimental to one can be beneficial to the other.

If, therefore, the landowner has the merit of making these protective laws, it is curious with what ingenuity he has discovered a principle which secures to himself only the rents yielded by the *lowest* prices, and by the lowest or most depreciated state of cultivation and consequent productiveness, while he secures to the foreign grower a full participation in the highest prices, and thus affords him, or the intermediate speculator, a high remuneration for holding his surplus produce of the years of low prices here until the arrival of high prices.

It would be satisfactory could we arrive at any accurate mode of ascertaining the loss to which these fluctuations have thus subjected this country. In the absence of correct information as to the exact produce of each year, and the whole quantity entering into consumption in each year, this is impossible; but we can arrive at an approximate estimate of it by using as a criterion the operations of Mark Lane; and we see every reason for thinking that the result of this test must bear a close comparative relation to the whole kingdom.

As we shall afterwards show, we take 52*s*. 2*d*. to be the proper price for wheat, at which an exactly sufficient amount of production would be kept up, it having been the average price for the last seven years: we therefore take it as the standard price at which wheat can be sold to the consumer. It must be clear that whatever average annual price the farmer receives in any year above that price, he obtains so much profit beyond the average rate; and that whatever average annual price he receives in any year less than that standard price, he makes so much distinct loss; and therefore the difference between the profit derived from the higher prices and the loss from the lower prices must show the balance in favour or against the home grower. We therefore present the following tables, showing these results for the last seven years:—

Years in the last Seven when Wheat sold above the Average Price of the period.

Years.	Quantity brought to Mark Lane.	Price sold for.	Average Price.	Gain.	—		
	Qrs.				£.	s.	d.
1832	300,073	58/8	52/2	6/6	97,523	14	6
1833	388,171	52/11	. .	/9	14,556	8	3
1837	321,735	55/10	. .	3/8	58,984	15	0
1838	296,500	64/7	. .	12/5	184,077	1	8
Total Gain of these Years.........					£355,141	19	5

Years in the last Seven when Wheat sold below the Average Price of the period.

Years.	Quantity brought to Mark Lane.	Price sold for.	Average Price.	Loss.	—		
	Qrs.				£.	s.	d.
1834	418,431	46/2	52/2	6/0	125,529	6	0
1835	468,348	39/4	. .	12/10	300,516	17	8
1836	414,145	48/6	. .	3/8	75,926	11	8
Total Loss of these Years..........					£501,972	15	4

Amount of loss in three years, when wheat sold below the average price..............................	£501,972	15	4
Amount of gain in four years, when wheat sold above the average price..............................	355,141	19	5
Balance of loss...........	£146,830	15	11

These tables show a clear balance of loss against the landed interest of nearly 150,000*l.* on the operations of Mark Lane alone. Now, when it is considered that the average quantity included in these calculations is only 372,486 quarters annually, to what a fearful amount does this balance of loss point, when taken in relation to the whole kingdom,—the annual consumption of which cannot be estimated below 16,000,000 quarters! And it must be borne in mind that, whatever this loss may be, huge as it may appear, the whole of it must first attach to the landed interest, and through them to the community at large.

At the hazard of being very tedious, we have dwelt thus long on the influences exerted by these laws on the agricultural interests, because we believe them to be chiefly interested therein, if not wholly so, speaking particularly of different sections of the community:—though nothing can possibly injure one portion without injuring the whole, as nothing can benefit one part without benefiting the whole.

In this view chiefly we are to consider it in relation to the mercantile and manufacturing interests: we are only to consider them in this place as generally interested, as we shall hereafter treat of their supposed personal or particular interest therein. Nothing can be more clear than that the manufacturing industry of the country depends entirely on the ability of our home population to consume, and of our merchants to export, and that the latter ability must greatly depend on the home demand for the products of foreign countries. Any cause, therefore, which diminishes our internal ability to consume either the manufactured products of this country, or the imported products of others, cannot fail to operate in a double capacity on the manufacturing interests, and in the same double capacity on the mercantile interests: for with regard to the former, our own immediate consumption being lessened, as well as the consumption of those articles of foreign produce, by the importation of which alone we enable many distant countries to consume our manufacturing products, must act, not only on the home demand immediately, but also on the foreign demand ultimately: and, with regard to the latter, their ability or interposition to import for the home consumer of foreign products, and export for the producer of our manufactures, must greatly depend on our internal means of consumption. In short, the whole chain of mutual interests is so perfect and so complete, that one single link cannot break without injuring the entire frame; that a loss, however trifling, can be experienced nowhere without reaching the whole, and nothing can give gain to one without advantage to the whole.

Any system, therefore, by which a huge and important portion of the community is impoverished, and that only by sinking and waste, by which so fearful a sum as we have shown is annually lost to themselves first, and the community secondly, in the unproductive application of capital and labour, in the creation and feeding of vermin, and in the natural decay of time, cannot fail to produce a most important restriction on the ability of this portion of the community to consume not only the articles manufactured here, but the articles imported in exchange for our manufactures; and so likewise on the mercantile interests, by restricting the amount both of exports and imports comparatively.

There is, however, one view in which we may consider

the result of these laws in this place as bearing materially on the mercantile interests. In consequence of our demand for foreign supplies of grain being only occasional and accidental, no regular mode of exchange exists by which the payments can be made, and it therefore becomes necessary to send the amount in bullion for whatever we take.

Strong cases are justifiable to elucidate principles.—Suppose that the wheat crisis of 1828-29 had been simultaneous with the money crisis of 1825-6, or that the late money crisis of 1836-37 had been simultaneous with the present condition of wheat;—and there is no reason why such corresponding similar circumstances should not occur at the same time; on the contrary, there are many reasons why they should so occur simultaneously: for if, from its own position, the money-market at any time had a tendency to derangement and pressure, it is clear that the demand for bullion to import wheat at such a moment could not fail to accelerate the difficulties of such derangement. Well, then, suppose that in (the winter) 1836-37 we had required to import two millions of quarters of wheat, as we are doing at this time, at a prime cost of upwards of 60*s.* per quarter, landed on our shores, which would have therefore involved a sum of six millions of pounds sterling for the payment,—in what position would the Bank of England have found itself, with its stock of bullion already reduced from other causes to an amount far below that sum? Under such circumstances, to have derived such a supply had been an impossibility; and the distress which must have ensued from the money crisis and the scarcity of wheat at the same moment must have been of a most fearful and alarming description.

Those who are familiar with these subjects can well suppose what the condition of this country would have been, had we been called upon for such a sum at that time.

Fortunately, however, the present difficulty has not arisen until just a sufficient time had elapsed to bring about the effects of the reaction of the crisis of 1836-37, and to fill the coffers of the Bank fuller than she could profitably retain them; and therefore this evil has assumed the most mitigated form it could have done. We may not always be so fortunate; and, if these two circumstances should ever occur together, in such forms as they have individually assumed in the two periods alluded to, that moment would indeed long continue a marked and mournful page in England's history.

There remains one more effect of these fluctuations to which we must briefly allude: that is, upon the moral and political condition of the labouring population of all kinds—particularly the agricultural.

It must be obvious that the tendencies experienced by the farmer must immediately influence the labourers he employs. In his successful or advancing years, a good demand exists for labour, and either attracts or retains more to this pursuit than on an average it is capable of maintaining; and thus we find, when the period of diminished cultivation arrives, the strongest evidences of surplus labour, as of surplus stock; distress to a painful degree becomes the lot of the hard-working tiller of the ground, whose only desire is for "*leave to toil;*" but, like his master, he has already toiled too much, and too unprofitably. Ignorant of the real causes of his distress, driven to pinch and want, he becomes too readily the victim of vicious and designing men, and has recourse to many acts of violence and injustice, which, instead of mending his case, can only tend to make it still worse.

No one can have forgot the terror and dismay which, from this cause, spread through our usually quiet and peaceful rural districts a few years ago, when the agricultural interest was severely depressed; the awful and mysterious midnight fires, which frequently lighted up a whole district at the same moment, consuming the very means of subsistence; anonymous letters followed up by all their threatenings; secret societies to fan and inflame the worst passions; highway robberies and personal attacks; outrages of every description; and all perpetrated by men whose ignorance and misery (from causes over which they had no control) were really much more apt to excite our pity than our blame. But how insensibly all these evidences have vanished with a return to prosperity, although it is impossible that they have not left behind a population of a lower and more debased standard of morals! They are now as quiet as ever, but the return of distress to their employers will not fail to reduce them once more to a similar condition.

It should also be remarked that this distress cannot fail materially to increase the poor-rates, and the charges of maintaining good order, which must act as a distinct cause of reducing the rents and income of both farmer and landlord. In some instances these charges have pressed so heavily at particular times as to consume the whole rent, and to render land of little or no value, which would otherwise have let at a fair average rate.

With the manufacturing labouring classes similar effects occur at opposite periods, when the necessaries of life are pressed to the highest point: they are introduced in the years of ruinous cheapness to habits of comparative luxury, and consumption which their labour cannot on an average command; and they therefore feel much more the want occasioned by extreme high prices, when they cannot command so much as their labour should produce to them. So the effect is that in cheap years his labour commands too much agricultural labour, and he then anticipates a part of what should be the consumption of a future day; and in dear years his labour commands too little agricultural labour, and he is obliged to receive proportionally as much too little as before he received too much. It is, however, no answer to a half-fed and distressed population, that they must be patient under the cravings of nature now, because two or three years ago they had more than was necessary. It cannot, therefore, be a matter of surprise, that the worst consequences should often result from this distress: there can be no doubt that to this alone may be traced many of the riotous and often murderous scenes which have disgraced our manufacturing districts, which are otherwise distinguished for their patient, persevering industry and ingenuity, and which have won for England' triumphs more glorious, territories more extended, and influence more respected, than she ever obtained by her most glittering and dazzling military achievements.

PROPOSITION THE SECOND.

That the Agricultural Interest has derived no benefit, but great injury, from the existing laws;—and that the fears and apprehensions of the ruinous consequences which would result to this interest by the adoption of a free and liberal policy with respect to the trade in corn, are without any foundation.—That the value of this property, instead of being depreciated, on the aggregate would be rather enhanced, and the general interests of the owners most decidedly benefited thereby.

It is not without having very carefully considered the subject, and having most minutely investigated the facts bearing upon it, that we venture to undertake the support of a proposition so widely differing from the general sentiments of the combatants on both sides of this most important subject. What the landed interest claims to preserve as a privilege to which it is entitled by its position in the state, and by the important influence which its well-being must exercise over the whole community; and what the opposite interest seeks to be given up as an acknowledged sacrifice on the part of the landowner, in common justice to them and the whole,—we seek chiefly, and first, as the greatest boon to those who are called upon to make the supposed sacrifice, and only through them as an untellable advantage to the general mass. We adhere closely to what we believe the only true theory on national interests:—That nothing can possibly be favourable to the whole that is detrimental to a part, and that nothing can be detrimental to one portion that is favourable to another portion; that the whole mass being made up only of parts, and as each part can only be interested through the medium of some or all of the other parts, it follows that any one part can only prosper in proportion to all the others from which it derives its support; and that the whole of these parts are so linked together, that no weight or pressure can apply at any one point without bearing less or more on the whole chain of connexion.

We shall now proceed, and endeavour, by fair reasoning supported by undeniable facts, to reconcile our proposition and our theory with the interests in question, as proved by the experience of the past.

One part of the present proposition, that the agricultural interests derive great injury from the operation of the present Corn Laws, or from any prohibitory law for their protection, has been sufficiently considered already to require any further notice; but it remains to be considered whether or not they have derived any benefit from the working of these laws in any way to compensate for the great injury sustained.

The professed object of these laws has always been to secure to the agricultural interests of this country high prices, high rents, and a high value of property, by granting them the monopoly of solely supplying the whole food necessary for the support of its population, by excluding all foreign agricultural produce, except at such periods as might arrive from any cause whatever, when the home supply should prove inadequate thereto.

Without, in this place, entering into any consideration of the justice or policy of such an attempt, had it proved of any practical effect, we will at once proceed to consider how far the intended object has been accomplished in the past, or is likely to be in the future.

In order to determine this question, it is necessary to ascertain what really have been the effects produced on prices by these acts, what effects would have been experienced had they not existed, and what effects are likely to be produced in the future, should they be entirely abandoned.

Some of the most important effects having been already fully considered, which went to prove the necessary existence of great fluctuations, we must now determine what has been the average price which, for a period of high and low years, has been received by the grower.

By taking the quantities sold at Mark Lane in each year from 1829 to 1835 inclusive, which includes a whole period from the highest to the lowest years, we find that the average price at which each quarter of wheat sold was 53*s.* per quarter; and we find, by the official return issued from the Board of Trade on the 3rd of January last, that the average price of wheat for the whole kingdom, for the last seven years, had been 52*s.* 2*d.* per quarter.

It must be clear that, however small this price may appear, a very large diminution from it is required to show what really the grower received. This average price necessarily includes all expenses, of whatever nature, arising between the grower and purchaser—of all carriage, whether by land or by water, all freights by sea, all commissions, intermediate profits, market dues, and all other charges attending the sale; of all interest of capital, of granary-rent and waste, and whatever else may attach by keeping the surplus of one year to secure a higher price in another: what all these charges may amount to it is impossible to calculate, but it is certain they must constitute a very considerable total charge; and, however large it may appear, it must form a necessary deduction from the average price of 52*s.* 2*d.*, to arrive at what the British farmer has obtained, during the last seven years, for his wheat when put into sacks and ready for market.

It must however be admitted, that, whatever may be the rate to which this necessary deduction would reduce the actual price obtained by the grower, it must have proved a sufficient price, on this average, to support the whole of the landed interests in their various connexions, in the actual amount of profit or income which they have derived from their property and pursuits; and that, whatever this real interest may be, it is the exact amount which can be secured to them by the existence of such protection; or, in other words, this price of 52*s.* 2*d.*, reduced by the whole amount of the specified charges paid annually to the grower, would have been exactly equivalent to all the varying prices which he has actually received, but, nevertheless, subject to all the sacrifices and misery pointed out in a former part of these remarks, as the necessary attendants of the fluctuating manner in which he has received thus much.

We are the more convinced that even this diminished rate has been sufficient to remunerate all parties to the present extent of their interests, by the facts, that, while the population of Great Britain increased upwards of two millions from 1821 to 1831, and there can be no doubt has since that time increased in an equal ratio; the general condition of the whole population has much improved, and the aggregate consumption much increased, without any increased supplies from abroad as compared with former years, and with an average price for the last seven years lower than that of any former seven years for the last half-century; which proves, without the possibility of doubt, that the rates obtained have not only served to sustain the former amount of production, but to increase it in a proportion equivalent not only to the increased rate of consumption, but also to the increased number of consumers.

This may, therefore, be called the rate which is fixed by our own internal competition and resources: 52*s*. 2*d*. per quarter may be called the prime cost of wheat to the consumer, and that sum, reduced by the charges enumerated, may be called the remunerating price to the landed interest, to the exact extent to which they have been remunerated.

We believe there has been no source of error and misconception on the subject of our inquiry generally so great as the exaggerated belief, entertained and admitted by all, of the ability of the Continent to supply wheat, whether taken in relation to the prime cost of production, or as to the quantity capable of being produced. When, however, we consider that on this very point hung the argument of all parties, and to sustain which it was necessary to make it appear that this ability was almost without limit; when, on the one hand, the agriculturist claimed protection from a formidable and unconquerable competitor, who, if allowed to stand on the same ground, would annihilate his pursuits, the greater, therefore, he could exaggerate the ability of the antagonist, the more he considered he made out his case for protection. On the other hand, the manufacturer opposed the claims of the agriculturist by insisting exactly upon the same Continental ability. He complained of the competition which resulted to himself by the extreme low prices of labour on the Continent, and demanded a participation for his labourers in the cheap and abundant products of those countries. The cheaper, therefore, and the more abundant, he could make them appear, the more he showed that his interests would be consulted by obtaining them; the more he proved that these prohibitory laws were made as a protection to the landowner at his cost, the more he proved that the manufacturing interests of the country were sacrificed to the landed interests.

All parties were therefore equally interested in insisting upon and exaggerating this point,—the question had never fair play; there was no motive, no disposition for one side to discover or point out the fallacies or extravagant statements of the other: on the contrary, they were only taken as admitted facts, and, if possible, still more exaggerated, to be used by each party in its turn, only differently applied. We thus find that, with these long accumulating extravagances incorporated into the opinions and sentiments of all, a universal impression prevails, that the Continental countries have the power of producing an unlimited quantity of wheat, and of supplying this country at prices less than one-half of the British cost of production;—that to open the door for the free admission of foreign grain would, on the one side, throw half our home-lands out of cultivation, ruin the farmers and landowners, and, on the other hand, lower the price of provisions to half their present rate, and the price of labour in the same proportion. Such are the extravagant notions entertained on this subject, that we might suppose we inhabited only a barren rock, without skill, industry, or capital, while our neighbours, whom we feared, possessed a soil which required no tilling, yielding spontaneously, year after year, the richest harvests. We never could dream that, co-existent with these fears, we possessed the finest climate, the finest and best-cultivated soils, the greatest amount of skill, industry and capital, of any country in the world, taken as a whole; while many of the countries whose competition we fear are sunk in the most abject poverty and ignorance. What are the elements of cheap production? Fertility of soil, climate, skill, and capital. What country possesses the whole to the same extent as this? But it may be said that our population is so large that it presses on the produce of the land, and that these elements have not fair and extended application. We can only reply that, were it so, or when it shall be so, then a stronger reason will never be made out for encouraging the growth of wheat for our consumption elsewhere; but it is not so, for it has already been shown that at two distinct periods within the last 20 years, and the last only four years ago, the production of this country had been pressed so far as to force prices much below the cost of production, and this was accomplished altogether by the efforts of our own growers, without the aid of any foreign supplies worthy of notice.

Our belief is, that the whole of these generally received opinions are erroneous; that, if we had had a free trade in corn since 1815, the average price of the whole period, actually received by the British grower, would have been higher than it has been; that little or no more foreign grain would have been imported; and that if, for the next twenty years, the whole protective system shall be abandoned, the average price of wheat will be higher than it has been for the last seven years, or than it would be in the future with a continuance of the present system: but with this great difference,—that prices would be nearly uniform and unaltering from year to year; that the disastrous fluctuations would be greatly avoided, which we have shown in the first proposition to be so ruinous under the present system.

When we say that we believe the price will be higher, we mean relatively with the cost of production, and that it will give, on an average of years, a better profit to the farmer, and a higher rent to the landlord. We know it to be an opinion held by many most intelligent men on this subject, and in which we cordially join, that, by the improvements in agriculture and the economy of labour by the introduction of machinery, the cost of production has been much less of late years than formerly, (which opinion is fully sustained by the fact noticed in another part of this proposition, that, notwithstanding the great increase of our population of late years, the increased productiveness of the soil has supplied a sufficient quantity for our greatly increased consumption, at a lower average price than at any former period, without any additional foreign supplies;) and that continued improvements and application of machinery in the future will more than keep pace with our increasing consumption, and thus, by abridging the cost, will lower, by our internal competition only, the general price of all commodities. By this operation the condition of the landed interest cannot fail to be improved, especially the landowner (as a great proportion of the increased productiveness would enter into rent), by a more extended consumption and general business; and in this case the more effectually must all foreign competition be shut out.

There are two modes by which supplies of any article may be materially increased: first, by an attempted protection and monopoly; and, secondly, by a free and open competition. In the former instance the increase is caused by a feeling of security against competition, and of the command, on the most advantageous terms, of the whole supply: the increase therefore which is thus produced, is only done by greatly increased expense and generally enhanced cost; so that, as soon as a surplus is felt, the inability of the producer to sell at a price to induce the consumption of the increased quantity renders it imperative that he should sell at a loss, and a consequent reaction takes place in the supply:—this has been the case with wheat. In the latter case, the increased supply will only be brought about by the application of more ingenuity, labour, and economy, causing altogether so much lessened a cost, that the lower price at which the article can be profitably sold will always cause consumption to keep pace with production; and in this case, as the article still yields a profit at the low price, no reaction will ensue. This has been the case with all our manufactured goods. While cotton goods have been reduced to less than half the price they were a few years ago, no reaction has taken place in their supply; but, on the contrary, a steady onward course of increased production has been observable; because that diminution of price has only taken place in consequence of the greatly diminished cost by the introduction of more perfect machinery, and other improvements, which have greatly improved the interests of all concerned in such pursuits by enlarging the field of their enterprise.

In this way alone can we ever expect the prices of provisions to be cheaper, and in this way they would only be cheapened, by a general improvement of the landed interest; and it must be obvious to every one how great are the advantages which the British corn-grower has over any other in the world, in accomplishing this great and desirable end, as found in the great amount of chemical and mechanical skill, in the great command of capital, and in the congeniality of soil and climate to his pursuits, which this country possesses in so superior a degree to any other.

We shall now proceed to institute a comparison between the present ability of the Continent and that of Great Britain to supply the population of this country with wheat, both in quantity and price, taking the cost price of the last seven years as the remunerating price in this country.

To arrive at what is the cost of raising wheat on the Continent is rather difficult, as it would be in this country, if we were only to rely on the calculations of producers for our information: for it is obvious that many circumstances may make it very variable; and we are only able to do so by seeing what average price has been sufficient to sustain the average rate of production.

With regard to the Continent, circumstances are still more variable; but we have sufficient data, which enable us to discover near enough for any useful purpose, what price would be sufficient to maintain the present state and extent of cultivation in these countries.

The chief and best official information that we have on the cost and extent of cultivation on the Continent is to be found in Mr. Jacob's report, presented to the Board of Trade in 1828, subsequent to his official tour on the Continent for inquiry into these subjects in 1827.

We will consider this question under two distinct heads: first, the cost at which the Continental countries could supply their surplus produce; and, secondly, the extent to which this supply could be furnished.

Mr. Jacob appears to have made great exertion to obtain from the cultivators the actual cost of wheat; and in many instances they appear to have bestowed extraordinary pains in the attempt to furnish them; but it is quite clear that, however correct any calculation may be made for any one estate, it may be very different from the general cost of the whole country: much will depend on the fertility of the soil, where, in consequence of the cultivator being generally the owner, he calculates no rent; much again will depend on the skill with which the whole arrangements and culture are carried on; and again much will depend on the relative cost at which different men may estimate the value of the other portions of their produce.

It may, however, be useful to quote these calculations, as they appear to be near the actual general cost as deducible from other circumstances. Mr. Jacob dwells very much on the capabilities of Mecklenburg, as being, from its geographical situation and other circumstances, capable of furnishing wheat to this country cheaper than any other.

In the appendix to his report, Mr. Jacob furnishes a copy of a most elaborate and intelligent letter from J. H. Van Thuenen of Tellow, the proprietor and cultivator of one of the finest estates in Mecklenburg. This letter indicates sufficiently how superior this individual must be to the great mass of Continental cultivators, and so far shows how little his estimate can be depended upon as a criterion for the whole.

The price at which he estimates the prime cost of his wheat is 26*s.* per quarter, allowing no profit to the farmer beyond the interest on live stock and implements, or income to the proprietor beyond the interest on the value of the buildings. And then he adds that, in consequence of the general inferior cultivation, the average cost of all the wheat grown in Mecklenburg is fully 5*s.* per quarter higher than this calculation, and that the average quality is 3*s.* per quarter worse; and that the produce of Tellow is in point of quality 5*s.* per quarter worse than the average produce of Great Britain. To this must be added the profit of the farmer, the rent of land, the price of conveying to the port, and then 1*s.* per quarter for skreening, besides the merchant's profit and expenses, to arrive at the price at which it could be put *free* on board a ship.

Mr. Jacob gives another very elaborate statement of the actual cost for an average of years on another estate, furnished by Mr. Canning, Consul General at Hamburg, which shows that, in order to pay a profit of 5 per cent. on the capital invested, to be divided between the farmer and the landowner, 40*s.* per quarter must be obtained for wheat: this price, we suppose, includes the cost of taking it to the shipping port, which rises very rapidly in proportion to the distance.

In Holstein and Sleswick, Sir C. Echard and Mr. Iverson estimate the net cost of growth at about the same as Mr. Van Thuenen; but here the quality is still worse, the best being estimated at least 6*s.* per quarter worse than the average of British wheat. The expense of conveying wheat to market must depend entirely upon the distance; on this point Mr. Jacob furnishes a very interesting table, founded on the experience of an intelligent and extensive cultivator in Mecklenburg, by which it is shown that the cost of land-carriage of grain is —

For 24	English Miles	3*s.*	0*d.*	per quarter.
48	„	„	5	10½	„
72	„	„	8	6	„
96	„	„	11	0	„

And so on in the same proportion, until the expenses incurred in moving this bulky article two hundred and forty miles would absorb its whole value.

We prefer, however, to go more fully into this consideration, by taking the well-authenticated average rates which in these countries have proved sufficient to sustain the actual extent of cultivation which has of late years existed, as on this result we are inclined to place much greater reliance than on any private calculations.

In this inquiry our chief attention shall be directed to the extended territory of Prussia, including Poland, because the exports of grain from that country are three times larger than any other country in Europe.

Fortunately for our subject, this country has a government which has had the wisdom not only to be furnished itself, but also to furnish its whole population, with a more accurate knowledge of their internal resources and condition from time to time than any other country in Europe, by carefully collecting and publishing periodically a statistical view of the progress making in their different internal interests.

Since the year 1816 the Prussian government has watched with great care the average prices of grain.

They are published in the Official Gazette at the end of each month, from the returns made by proper people appointed for the purpose throughout the different provinces. From these returns monthly averages are calculated for each province; and from these the annual average is ultimately derived. They then calculate the average price of each last fourteen years, in the same way as we calculate the averages of each last six weeks; by every year dropping the first year, and adding the newly-expired year in its place.

This appears so perfect a mode of arriving at the average price for a long period, that we adopt it with the greatest confidence of its accuracy. We feel that any little deviations from precise accuracy, which can ever occur in returns and calculations of this kind, must be so equally balanced on each side, and be spread in this mode of calculation over so extended a surface and quantity, that they can be of no importance in the general result. We therefore present the following tables, containing the above official returns for all Prussia from 1816 to 1837 inclusive.*

* These tables, extracted from the official accounts, were published (along with a very intelligent article on this subject translated from the "Allgemeine Preussische Staatszeitung." Nos. 85 und 86, 1838) in the Journal of the Statistical Society of London, No. VIII., December, 1838.

Table, No. 1.

Showing the Annual Average Prices of Wheat per Scheffel, in each Province, for each year from 1816 to 1837 inclusive, in Silver Groschen.

WHEAT.							
Periods.	Prussia Proper.	Posen.	Branden-burg and Pomerania.	Silesia.	Saxony.	West-phalia.	Rhenish Provinces.
	Sil. gr. pf.	Sil. gr. pf.	Sil. gr. pf.	Sil. gr. pf.	Sil. gr. pf.	Sil. gr. pf.	Sil. gr. pf.
1816	70 1	78 10	84 9	94 11	96 10	110 7	112 2
1817	100 5	96 10	115 11	106 0	122 6	152 0	165 0
1818	94 3	78 4	101 8	80 7	92 4	103 1	105 9
1819	65 5	60 5	72 11	61 10	61 5	77 10	72 1
1820	51 10	52 1	56 9	55 1	52 3	59 7	65 1
1821	48 8	54 7	54 7	67 5	48 8	62 1	56 10
1822	49 5	54 2	50 9	62 8	50 7	60 4	55 8
1823	46 0	52 2	50 10	57 0	51 10	54 2	58 4
1824	34 9	35 11	38 1	39 10	39 9	36 4	39 9
1825	32 5	32 2	33 10	35 2	33 10	35 0	40 11
1826	35 5	36 0	40 0	39 5	33 5	38 3	44 2
1827	42 4	44 1	49 1	47 10	41 11	55 1	56 7
1828	51 8	51 0	54 6	56 9	56 8	62 7	72 6
1829	61 5	60 1	66 8	58 11	65 8	75 3	78 7
1830	56 3	55 9	64 8	53 9	60 8	77 7	75 11
1831	75 5	78 2	74 9	71 9	67 0	92 11	91 2
1832	64 9	59 8	63 7	51 4	56 10	71 11	83 8
1833	47 6	44 3	44 9	41 2	41 11	50 7	57 2
1834	45 1	43 10	43 9	43 2	39 1	43 8	49 1
1835	43 7	46 9	45 4	49 9	42 1	44 7	49 4
1836	39 8	39 10	43 6	39 9	44 2	46 7	52 0
1837	42 8	44 7	49 3	41 1	47 0	50 11	58 0

Table, No. 2.

Showing the Average of nine Periods of fourteen years each, and for the whole Period of twenty-two years, from 1816 to 1837 inclusive, in each Province.

WHEAT.							
Periods.	Prussia Proper.	Posen.	Branden-burg and Pomerania.	Silesia.	Saxony.	West-phalia.	Rhenish Provinces.
Average of	Sil. gr. pf.	Sil. gr. pf.	Sil. gr. pf.	Sil. gr. pf.	Sil. gr. pf.	Sil. gr. pf.	Sil. gr. pf.
1816–29	52 3	54 3	58 1	58 9	56 1	64 10	66 7
1817–30	50 10	52 0	56 1	56 1	52 11	62 3	63 7
1818–31	50 10	52 0	56 1	56 1	52 11	62 3	63 7
1819–32	50 9	51 11	55 2	54 6	52 1	61 8	63 7
1820–33	49 1	50 4	52 11	52 5	50 1	59 0	62 1
1821–34	48 4	49 7	51 8	51 3	48 9	57 5	60 6
1822–35	47 10	48 9	50 9	49 11	48 2	55 8	59 9
1823–36	46 11	47 4	50 0	48 0	47 6	54 3	59 4
1824–37	46 7	46 7	49 10	46 5	47 0	53 11	59 4
Average of the whole Period...	49· 3	50. 4	53· 5	52· 7	50· 7	59· 0	62· 0

Table, No. 3.

Showing the Average of each of the Provinces for the nine Periods of fourteen years each, as shown in Table No. 2; and the whole Average of the whole Period. To this and the following Table we have added Rye, Barley, and Oats, for the information of those who may wish it —calculated exactly in the same way as Wheat.

Provinces.	Wheat.	Rye.	Barley.	Oats.
	Sil. gr. pf.	Sil. gr. pf.	Sil. gr. pf.	Sil. gr. pf.
Prussia Proper . . .	49 3	30 2	21 10	16 3
Posen	50 4	33 1	25 4	19 5
Brandenburg and Pomerania.	53 5	36 2	26 10	21 3
Silesia	52 7	38 0	29 2	21 7
Saxony	50 7	38 3	28 11	21 7
Westphalia	59 0	44 9	33 4	23 9
Rhenish Provinces . .	62 0	46 6	35 5	23 3
Average . .	53·11	38· 1	28· 8	21· 0

Table, No. 4.

Showing the Average Prices in each of the nine Periods for the whole Provinces, and arriving at the same Annual Average Price for the whole Country during the whole Period, as shown in Table No. 3.

Periods.	Wheat.		Rye.		Barley.		Oats.	
	Sil. gr.	pf.	Sil. gr.	pf.	Sil. gr.	pf.	Sil. gr.	pf.
1816–29	58	5	41	3	31	1	22	8
1817–30	56	3	39	3	29	7	21	9
1818–31	56	3	39	3	29	4	21	5
1819–32	55	9	38	11	29	2	21	3
1820–33	53	9	37	8	28	2	20	8
1821–34	52	6	37	2	27	8	20	4
1822–35	51	7	37	4	28	1	20	8
1823–36	50	6	36	7	27	8	20	6
1824–37	49	11	35	9	27	4	20	0
Average	53·	11	38·	1	28·	8	21·	0

It thus appears that the average price, which has been just sufficient to maintain the cultivation in Prussia in its present extent, and in all the necessary ramifications of *landowner, tenant, labourer or serf,* and whatever arrangements they may have peculiar to the country in their mode of cultivation, is for

	Sil. gr.	pf.	
Wheat...........	53	11	per scheffel.
Rye.............	38	1	,,
Barley...........	28	8	,,
Oats.............	21	0	,,

To enable us to pursue our comparison, we will reduce these rates into sterling money per English quarter. The average rate of exchange on London at Dantzig, for the last few years, has been 203½ sil. gr. per pound sterling.

Then, if 203½ sil. gr. equal 20*s.* sterling, 53 gr. 11 pf. will be 5*s.* 3⅝*d.* sterling per scheffel for wheat.

Again, if 203½ sil. gr. equal 20*s.* sterling, 38 gr. 1 pf. will be 3*s.* 8⅞*d.* per scheffel for rye.

Again, if 203½ sil. gr. equal 20*s.* sterling, 28 gr. 8 pf. will be 2*s.* 9¾*d.* per scheffel for barley.

And again, if 203½ sil. gr. equal 20*s.* sterling, 21 gr. will be 2*s.* 0¾*d.* per scheffel for oats.

An English imperial quarter is equal exactly to 5⅓ scheffel, so that the average in imperial quarters will be —for

Wheat...5⅓	scheffel, at	5*s.*	3⅝*d.*,	is	28*s.*	3*d.*	per imp. quarter.
Rye.....5⅓	,,	3	8⅞	,,	19	11½	,,
Barley ..5⅓	,,	2	9¾	,,	15	1½	,,
Oats....5⅓	,,	2	0¾	,,	11	1½	,,

These are the average prices thus obtained in a series of years throughout the huge territory of Prussia and Prussian Poland; but, in looking at them in reference to prices in other countries, we must bear in mind that beyond these prices must be added considerable charges, before we arrive at the prime cost on board the ship in any port. The great bulk of the grain grown, especially in Poland, is purchased from the growers, either on their own farms or at their local markets, by the merchants from Dantzig, who not unfrequently make advances on the crops while yet growing on the ground. It is therefore clear that the merchant's profit, as well as all the charges of conveying it, first from the spot of purchase to the nearest navigable river, of loading into craft, of freight and dues in descending the rivers, of landing and warehousing at the seaport, must, in most cases, require to be added to these averages. Making a sufficient allowance for the fact that a portion of the returns of sales which constitute these averages include some of these charges, it is considered that the smallest calculation on this account must be at least 6*s*. per quarter on wheat, 5*s*. per quarter on barley and rye and 4*s*. per quarter on oats. We believe that this calculation is extremely near the correct amount, because we find that the average price of wheat in the port of Dantzig from 1817 to 1837 inclusive is 34*s*. 4*d*., which nearly corresponds with this additional charge of 6*s*. per quarter, added to 28*s*. 3*d*., the average of the whole kingdom.—Thus the average prices in Dantzig, in the following years, were

1817 . .	75*s*.	8*d*.	per quarter.	1828 . .	24*s*.	4*d*.	per quarter.
1818 . .	64	7	"	1829 . .	36	10	"
1819 . .	43	9	"	1830 . .	34	3	"
1820 . .	33	3	"	1831 . .	37	3	"
1821 . .	31	7	"	1832 . .	37	7	"
1822 . .	29	1	"	1833 . .	29	4	"
1823 . .	26	8	"	1834 . .	25	5	"
1824 . .	22	9	"	1835 . .	23	0	"
1825 . .	23	3	"	1836 . .	33	6	"
1826 . .	23	1	"	1837 . .	29	4	"
1827 . .	22	5	"	1838 . .	48	1 *	"

Average of the whole period, 34*s*. 4*d*. per quarter.

We thus show that the prime cost, when arrived at the port, before any steps are taken for shipment, is—for

Wheat	34*s*.	3*d*.
Rye	24	11½
Barley	20	1½
Oats	15	1½

There is another feature in these averages which must

* As near as has been ascertained.

not be lost sight of.—In Prussia and in all parts of the Continent, the quality of wheat and grain generally varies much more than it does in this country, so much so of wheat, that at Danzig one quality frequently is worth 50 to 75 per cent. more than others sold at the same time;—thus in the first three months of 1837 the prices were—

1st week	in January	27*s.*	4*d.*	to	40*s.*	0*d.*	per quarter.
2nd ,,	,,	27	6	,,	40	4	,,
3rd ,,	,,	27	5	,,	40	3	,,
4th ,,	,,	25	7	,,	40	3	,,
1st ,,	February	25	7	,,	39	9	,,
2nd ,,	,,	23	9	,,	38	5	,,
3rd ,,	,,	22	10	,,	38	5	,,
4th ,,	,,	23	9	,,	38	5	,,
1st ,,	March	23	9	,,	38	4	,,
2nd ,,	,,	23	9	,,	38	4	,,
3rd ,,	,,	22	0	,,	36	8	,,
4th ,,	,,	22	11	,,	35	9	,,

And this is only a fair example of the usual difference which exists in this respect at all periods.

It is therefore clear that these general averages include a large portion of extremely bad quality and low-priced wheat, altogether unfit under usual circumstances for shipment. If therefore the average price of that quality could be obtained which is fit for shipment, but especially to Great Britain, where the average quality is so vastly superior to that of any other country, we should find a large addition would require to be made to 34*s.* 3*d.*; but, however, without taking any advantage of this obvious cause of additional price for such quality, we will consider that we have now arrived at such prime cost of wheat, ready for shipment in a port in Prussia, as will enable that country to sustain its cultivation exactly in the condition in which it is, both in respect to quantity, quality, and the advantages derived by all those connected with its production. As 52*s*. 2*d*. per quarter has proved sufficient in England to bring the quantity of wheat which has been produced to the consumer, so 34*s*. 3*d*. in Prussia has proved to be the exact price to place the average quality of produce of that country in her seaports ready for shipment.

The former is, therefore, the prime cost to the consumer in England, while the latter is the prime cost to the shipper at Dantzig. In order to determine how far the latter could be brought into competition with the former, in case we should have a free trade in corn, without any duty whatever, we will now examine what must be the necessary charges to bring it from Dantzig to the market in England.

In this respect, we have bestowed great care, and derived our information both from Dantzig and London; and, also, have calculated the precise actual charges which many real shipments have shown:—

	Per Qr. *s.*	*d.*
Unhousing, shipping, and export-dues, at Dantzig, paid by the shipper there	1	9
Freight and primage	6	0
Sound-dues	0	6
Insurance in winter £5 5 per cent.		
Ditto spring 1 5 . .		
Average . 6 10		
£3 5 . . at 50*s*. per quarter to cover all charges. £100 would be 40 quarters, or	1	7½
Carried forward	9	10½

	Per Qr. s.	d.
Brought forward	9	10½
Entry and lighterage	0	6
Metage inwards	0	6
Landing	0	4
Warehouse-rent, and insurance against fire for six months, at 5*s*. per 100 quarters per week, or .	1	3
Turning for six months, at 1*s*. 6*d*. per 100 quarters per week, or	0	4
Loss in quantity, and damage from the time of shipment at Dantzig, until sold after lying six months in granary, 3 per cent., at 50*s*. per quarter, is	1	6
Factorage for sale, and *dilcredere*, 1*s*. per quarter, and 1 per cent. on the sale, at 50*s*. per quarter, is 6*d*.	1	6
Metage, portion paid by seller	0	4
Delivering	0	3
Interest of money for nine months, including the voyage, and the customary credit given on wheat, at 50*s*. per quarter, at 5 per cent. per annum . .	1	10½
	18	3

	s.	d.
Of which is paid by the shipper	1	9
And by the purchaser . . .	16	6
	18	3

In this calculation we have assumed that the wheat shall lie six months in warehouse on an average, which must be considered a very moderate time, in the case a regular trade should be carried on between the Continent and this country, free at all times. We believe the average would be much longer, but will rather err in being too moderate than in being extravagant. These charges are the *nett* cost without any profit to the *merchant* shipping from Dantzig, or without any commission to the merchant in London, to whom it might be consigned, without which, it is quite clear, no trade would continue to be carried forward.

If between the house at Dantzig and the house in London, to cover their necessary expenses, and to yield them a remunerating profit, we allow 5 per cent. on the amount, we think we shall not be blamed for extravagance in this respect; and those who know the risk, trouble, and advance of capital, needed to conduct such a business, will be convinced that, at this rate, the trade would be neglected. So that, if we add to the prime cost these charges, we shall bring the Prussian wheat into the posture of competition with British-grown at a seaport, thus:—

	s.	*d.*	
Prime cost	34	3	per qr.
Shipping, landing, warehousing for 6 mo., and selling	18	3	,,
5 per cent. profit or commission on 50*s.* per quarter, between the merchant in Dantzig and in England	2	6	,,
	55	0	,,

The quality of the wheat shipped from Dantzig to this country may be considered as about equal in value to the average quality of our home-grown wheats; but the average quality at Dantzig of all the wheat, of which 34*s.* 3*d.* is the average price, must be at least 6*s.* to 8*s.*

per quarter worse than the average of British wheats; for it must be borne in mind, that only the better qualities are shipped to this country in general, and when the inferior qualities are shipped, by a great pressure for the article, they are not only worth much less here, but they entail much greater expense, in skreening, kiln-drying, &c.; and they are subject to much greater decay and loss. It may be remarked, perhaps, that a great number of the charges to which we have submitted Dantzig wheat, included in the 18*s*. 3*d*., must also be borne by home-grown wheat: true, they must; but it must be kept in mind, as we have before shown, that the average price of 52*s*. 2*d*., obtained for English wheat during the last seven years, not only includes all these charges, but an immense train of other charges, having their origin only in the existence of a prohibitory and protective law.

After all the fear and apprehensions of the ruinous low prices which an admittance of Continental wheat would entail on this country, we find, on the average of years, that the prime cost of importing it from the richest, cheapest, and most extensive wheat-growing country on the Continent, would have been at least 2*s*. 10*d*. per quarter higher than the actual average price obtained in this country, with the strictest prohibitory law. But we have only brought the two into competition at the port of arrival. As we recede from the port into the country, with English wheat, the charges become smaller and smaller, but, as the foreign competitor would advance from the port into the interior, his charges would become greater and greater, and his ability to compete sensibly decline.

If this be true with respect to wheat, which we submit we have clearly proved, then, with respect to all the inferior articles of produce, it must be much more true: the high charges which we have pointed out would bear more heavily on all the others just in proportion as they are of lower value. If any article of agricultural produce could support such *taxes*, wheat is that article, as bearing, in a given weight and bulk, a higher value than any other. It would, therefore, only be tedious to go through the same calculations with rye, barley, and oats.

Thus it becomes an indisputable fact, that, had the state of our laws for the last twenty years been such as to have maintained the price of wheat at the actual average price of 52*s*. 2*d*. which has been received, no wheat could have been grown in Prussia for this country; either must the prices have risen here above 55*s*., or must the cost of production have been materially curtailed in Prussia. This, perhaps, might have been done to a small extent by throwing out the worst portions of land in cultivation, and retaining only a small portion of the best; but this would have curtailed their surplus quantity produced, which at most is very trifling. The difference of the two prices of 2*s*. 10*d*. in London, although not so large apparently on 52*s*. per quarter, yet is very large on 28*s*. 2*d*., the original cost in the country, and, as it would require to be all saved in the act of production, it would be all chargeable on that low price, or even a lower one,—viz. the actual price received by the farmer.

The result of this investigation differs so widely from the generally-received opinions, that it appears needful to bring not only all the facts and arguments immediately connected therewith to reconcile the common prejudices with the truth, but, also, whatever may remotely tend to confirm our propositions so far proven,—viz., that no part of the Continent of Europe can carry on a successful competition with England in the growth of wheat for her own home consumption, supposing the relative condition and value of property, in both cases, to continue exactly as they have been for some years past, fixed by the combination of the laws and circumstances which have existed.

Fortunately this is not an untried question: the history of the past century furnishes some very satisfactory experience on this head.

During the first seventy-three years of the last century a bounty of 5*s*. per quarter was given by law on all wheat exported whenever the average price was at or below 48*s*. per quarter, and importation almost prohibited.

It must be admitted that this bounty could not be sufficient to pay the charges of taking wheat from this country to the Continent, but still we find that during this period England was the largest wheat-exporting country in Europe.

The following table will show the exports from Great Britain and Dantzig during this period, by which it will be seen how much the former exceed the latter.

	Years.	Exported from Dantzig.	Exported from Great Britain.	
		Wheat.	Wheat.	Barley.
		Qrs.	Qrs.	Qrs.
War.	1700	33,316	49,056	25,896
	1701	34,626	98,323	21,953
	1702	43,892	90,230	16,280
	1703	33,895	106,615	71,523
	1704	52,148	90,813	30,729
	1705	64,532	96,185	21,386
	1706	73,981	188,332	10,221
	1707	65,521	74,155	4,771
	1708	98,180	83,406	29,937
	1709	83,173	169,679	40,512
	1710	38,119	13,924	5,714
	1711	46,429	76,949	8,412
	1712	79,238	145,100	19,838
Peace.	1713	130,698	176,227	52,542
	1714	48,816	174,821	18,579
	1715	10,900	166,490	5,079
	1716	19,543	74,926	14,857
	1717	87,066	22,953	18,435
	1718	23,822	71,800	71,139
	1719	54,728	127,762	9,649
	1720	37,496	83,484	4,505
	1721	59,824	81,432	11,607
	1722	67,757	178,880	37,528
	1723	98,846	157,719	45,780
	1724	96,804	245,865	10,298
	1725	123,270	204,418	13,782
	1726	98,018	142,183	20,017
	1727	41,764	30,317	8,683
	1728	92,998	70,757	11,547
	1729	204,142	21,332	12,551
	1730	113,455	93,970	14,982
	1731	116,315	130,025	13,562
	1732	74,476	202,058	13,874
	1733	115,218	427,199	37,598
	1734	103,318	498,196	70,224
	1735	86,409	153,333	57,520
	1736	25,187	118,170	6,860

	Years.	Exported from Dantzig.	Exported from Great Britain.		
		Wheat.	Wheat.	Barley.	
		Qrs.	Qrs.	Qrs.	
Peace.	1737	20,500	461,602	23,669	
	1738	49,901	580,599	70,689	
	1739	92,192	279,542	54,447	
War.	1740	164,131	54,390	24,086	
	1741	93,224	45,416	6,618	
	1742	56,330	293,259	11,482	
	1743	53,212	371,431	34,995	
	1744	53,879	231,984	20,090	
	1745	24,886	324,839	95,878	
	1746	24,037	130,646	158,719	
	1747	47,762	266,906	103,143	
	1748	98,943	543,387	73,857	
Peace.	1749	113,789	629,019	52,621	
	1750	99,502	947,603	224,500	
	1751	202,588	661,416	38,698	
	1752	191,307	429,279	106,333	
	1753	147,986	299,608	67,049	
	1751	131,118	356,270	47,776	
War.	1755		237,466	381,659	Barley and Malt.
	1756	82,581	102,752	269,949	
	1757	183,094	130,017	57,511	
	1758	87,451	11,119	1,504	
	1759	87,612	227,367	208,797	
	1760	116,619	303,614	291,150	
	1761	68,230	441,956	413,891	
	1762	55,911	295,385	423,064	
	1763	127,258	429,537	215,681	
	1764	181,299	396,858	246,891	
	1765	190,393	167,126	251,927	
	1766	145,619	164,939	95,115	
	1767	151,424	5,071	18,700	
	1768	197,789	7,433	6,587	
	1769	124,775	49,892	39,825	
	1770	269,158	75,449	170,409	
	1771	181,417	10,069	34,193	
	1772	159,917	6,959	11,031	

With this trifling encouragement, we exported more wheat than we ever imported on an average of years. There is no doubt that the bounty on export gave a great and perhaps unprofitable stimulant to production, but, still, during the whole period of its existence, our farmers continued to be large exporters; now, if this bounty was not sufficient to pay the charges of export, it is clear that, when the British wheat arrived on the Continent, it had even to encounter the disadvantage of bearing a considerable charge above the bounty given; and, if it was able to bear this charge and compete with the growth of the Continent, how much more could the former compete with the latter if retained at home, without any additional charge, while the foreign would have to come here at a considerable cost.

From 1697 to 1773 only seven years occurred in which England did not export more wheat than she imported, by the aid of this small bounty. In four years the average annual export was 1,200,000 quarters, and in one year (1750) it amounted to 1,667,000 quarters; for the whole period the average annual exports exceeded the imports by rather more than 200,000 quarters.

But the experiment was carried still further in aid of our argument. In 1773 an act was passed abolishing the bounty on export, except when wheat was under 44*s*. per quarter, and allowing imports on the most liberal terms ever acknowledged by the English law,—viz., at 6*d*. per quarter duty when wheat should be 48*s*. per quarter or higher.

The result of this was that Great Britain was still enabled to export wheat. In ten years out of the next twenty years following the enactment, our exports still exceeded our imports,—the following being the quantities of wheat and flour exported and imported in each of these years:—

Years.	Wheat and Flour. Great Britain.		Barley and Malt. Great Britain.	
	Imported.	Exported.	Imported.	Exported.
	Quarters.	Quarters.	Quarters.	Quarters.
1773	56,857	7,637	63,916	2,475
1774	289,149	15,928	171,508	2,911
1775	560,988	91,037	139,451	51,414
1776	20,578	210,664	8,499	136,114
1777	233,323	87,686	7,981	142,725
1778	106,394	141,070	42,714	103,930
1779	5,039	222,261	7,085	85,777
1780	3,915	224,059	352	191,563
1781	159,866	103,021	56	150,468
1782	80,695	145,152	13,592	127,744
1783	584,183	51,943	144,926	54,065
1784	216,947	89,288	77,182	66,889
1785	110,863	132,685	67,212	166,448
1786	51,463	205,466	62,374	111,598
1787	59,339	120,536	43,244	135,089
1788	148,710	82,971	11,479	212,811
1789	112,656	140,014	11,128	345,685
1790	222,557	30,892	29,718	50,966
1791	469,056	70,626	61,134	41,590
1792	22,417	300.278	118,526	49,131

It will be observed that both these laws failed in the effect intended by the framers—the object of the former being evidently to maintain a high range of prices, by not only securing the entire home consumption to the British grower, but by affording him the assistance of a bounty to export his surplus stock: the object of the latter was as evidently intended to admit a more free supply, which it was naturally expected would reduce the prices; and by the opponents of the measure it was strongly urged that by its operation this country would be deluged with Continental wheat: but, like almost every effort of government to control and influence such matters, the result was, in both cases, the reverse of what was intended. By the encouragement of the bounty production was stimulated so much, that in one year, 1743, the whole average price of wheat was only 24*s*. 10*d*. per quarter, and in several years it did not reach 30*s*. Complaints at that period were greater than at any other from the landed interest, and, perhaps, with better reason. When this encouragement was withdrawn, and the English market opened to a free competition with the Continent, a more prudent cultivation appears to have been adopted; prices, instead of being lowered, gradually advanced, but it was not until that advance had become considerable that the Continental grower was enabled to send any very important quantity of wheat to this country.

It is extremely worthy of remark, that the average price during the thirty-two years that this law continued in operation* is shown to be 2*s*. 2*d*. per quarter higher than the average of the last seven years, and 11*s*. 11*d*. per quarter higher than the average of the thirty-two preceding, with the assistance of the bounty on exports and prohibited imports. The following table shows a comparative view of the range of prices during these two periods.

* By a slight alteration in the law, in 1791, the price of admission at 6*d*. per quarter was raised from 48*s*. to 54*s*. per quarter.

Average, No. 1.			Average, No. 2.		
Years.	s.	d.	Years.	s.	d.
1772	50	8	1773	51	0
1771	47	2	1774	52	8
1770	41	4	1775	48	4
1769	45	8	1776	38	2
1768	60	6	1777	45	6
1767	64	6	1778	42	0
1766	43	1	1779	33	8
1765	52	0	1780	35	8
1764	46	9	1781	44	8
1763	40	9	1782	47	10
1762	39	0	1783	52	8
1761	30	3	1784	48	10
1760	36	6	1785	51	10
1759	39	10	1786	38	10
1758	70	0	1787	41	2
1757	60	0	1788	45	0
1756	45	3	1789	51	2
1755	33	10	1790	53	2
1754	34	8	1791	47	2
1753	44	8	1792	41	9
1752	41	10	1793	47	10
1751	38	6	1794	50	8
1750	32	6	1795	72	11
1749	0	0	1796	76	3
1748	27	0	1797	52	2
1747	34	10	1798	50	4
1746	39	0	1799	66	11
1745	27	6	1800	110	5
1744	0	0	1801	115	11
1743	24	10	1802	67	9
1742	34	0	1803	57	1
1741	46	8	1804	60	5
Average of the whole period, 42s. 5d.			Average of the whole period, 54s. 4d.		

1.—Average price of wheat in Great Britain in each year of the thirty-two years preceding 1773, when a bounty was given on exports and strict prohibition against imports.

2.—Average price of wheat in Great Britain in each year from 1773 to 1804, when the bounty was repealed, and importation allowed at 6*d.* per quarter duty, when the average price should not be below 48*s.*, and, from 1791, 54*s.* per quarter.

The experience of these two periods proves not only the total inefficacy of any government interference to control or influence production or prices, but it also proves again that the landed interest of this country has no competition to fear, except that of its own over-excited and stimulated power put forth to an extravagant extent to catch the phantom advantages held out by protective laws. There never was a time of surplus stock and low prices which proceeded from any other cause. During the thirty-two years that our trade was free, there was surely abundance of time for the continental countries to take all the advantage of the privilege, if it had proved really a profitable one. The prices in Dantzig during this period were not higher, relatively with those in England, than they have been during the last twenty years. A comparison of these prices may be very useful to show what really is the great difference which the mere charges of transport must ever entail, and for some difference of quality; and we have every reason to believe that in the case of a free trade now, the same, if not a greater difference, would continue to exist between the prices in England and Dantzig; for the average quality of English wheat has improved during the period that has elapsed since 1804, much more than the produce of Prussia. This is an additional evidence of what we think we have already successfully proved, that with wheat in England at the average price of the last seven years, viz. 52*s*. 2*d*. per quarter, and wheat in Dantzig at the average price that has ruled there of late years, no trade could be profitably carried on between the two places; no continental supply could to any extent come to this country.

The following are the average prices of wheat in England and Dantzig, during this period of free trade:—

Average price of wheat 1773 to 1804.	In Engla	At Dantzig.	Average prices of wheat 1773 to 1804.	In England.	At Dantzig.
1773	51*s.* 0*d.*	35*s.* 8*d.*	1789	51*s.* 2*d.*	43*s.* 8*d.*
1774	52 8	32 1	1790	53 2	40 4
1775	48 4	33 11	1791	47 2	00 0
1776	38 2	27 6	1792	41 9	29 0
1777	45 6	22 4	1793	47 10	32 0
1778	42 0	23 9	1794	50 8	36 0
1779	33 8	21 10	1795	72 11	57 9
1780	35 8	19 4	1796	76 3	54 3
1781	44 8	24 9	1797	52 2	33 1
1782	47 10	26 3	1798	50 4	32 10
1783	52 8	27 5	1799	66 11	46 10
1784	48 10	28 10	1800	110 5	73 9
1785	51 10	30 2	1801	115 11	78 11
1786	38 10	29 2	1802	67 9	53 5
1787	41 2	29 2	1803	57 1	46 3
1788	45 0	29 1	1804	60 5	53 3
Average of the whole period				54*s.* 4*d.*	37*s.* 2*d.*

There therefore existed during this period of free importation an average difference of price between England and Dantzig of 17*s.* 2*d.* per quarter; and we have already shown that of late years, with the strictest attempt ever made to exclude continental wheat, the average difference has only been 17*s.* 10*d.* per quarter.

If any farther evidence were required to prove that the continent of Europe cannot supplant our home-growers in the supply of grain for the consumption of this country, we must claim attention to a case exactly in point existing at the present time, and which may be fairly cited as an experiment of a free trade in corn for the whole of Great Britain.

The islands of Guernsey and Jersey, ever since they belonged to this country, have had the privilege of exporting their produce, of whatever kind, to the English market at all times free of any duty, and at the same time of importing whatever they please, from wherever they please, free of any duty whatever, except a small local duty levied chiefly on spirits.

These islands, although very fertile, and producing a large quantity of the finest grain, do not grow sufficient for their whole consumption, and they are obliged at all times to import largely of continental grain. Now if the general impression had any foundation in truth, that wheat could be imported so much cheaper from the continent than the prices paid in this country, it would follow as a matter of certainty, that the sharp and intelligent merchants of these islands would send every bushel of home-grown corn, to secure the high prices of the London market, and import from the Baltic as much more as would make up this quantity. The expense of sending wheat from these islands is not greater than from Lincolnshire, Yorkshire, or Northumberland; but if to either of these counties this privilege was given, with the present opinions on the subject, the imaginary value of land would be greatly increased; the whole of the grain would be sent to London, or other parts of England not possessing such privilege, and whatever was required for the consumption of the county would be brought from the continent:—What would be the profit? We will consult those who have long had the experience, and we will consult them by the surest test; their actions, dictated by a free exercise of their own will to direct their own interests.

It may perhaps be remembered that during the extreme depression of the agricultural interests in the winter 1833-34, when the accumulating surplus stock of home-grown wheat pressed with great severity on the markets, those interested in its growth could with difficulty believe that the home production alone could have had such an influence: this gave rise to many rumours and surmises that foreign grain had been introduced in large quantities through the Channel Islands under an abuse of this privilege. For political purposes this surmise was encouraged by many, and a charge preferred against the government of the day, of having encouraged such illicit imports. During the short period that the present government were out of office, in that winter the charge was again and again repeated by their opponents in the agricultural districts; so much so, that as soon as parliament met the matter became a subject of investigation, and the necessary returns were ordered which could throw any light on the matter.

What was the result? These fine islands, with all their privileges, had shipped between them in *three* years, 1831, 1832, and 1833, eight thousand six hundred and thirty-three quarters of wheat to all England: viz.

	Guernsey and Sark.	Jersey.	Total.
	Qrs.	*Qrs.*	*Qrs.*
1831	185	1233	1418
1832	32	1873	1905
1833	1326	3984	5310
	1543	7090	8633

or an annual quantity of 2877 quarters; and by reference to the first table, it will be seen that the difference between the prices in England and at Dantzig during these years, were more than usually encouraging for such an operation; but the enormous expenses attending the movement of this bulky article always has, and always will continue to render this privilege a dead letter as far as grain is concerned, and so it would in England if the same privileges were possessed, and an entirely free trade in corn adopted. It may just be observed, that notwithstanding the free introduction of all continental produce, the value of land is higher in these islands than in any part of England, the average rent being 2*l.* to 2*l.* 10*s.* per *vergee*, or 4*l.* 10*s.* to 5*l.* 12*s.* 6*d.* per English acre.

It has therefore only been the mere accidental chances which the fluctuating effects of our Corn Laws have produced, that the continental countries have been enabled to send their accumulated surplus produce to this country at moments of extreme high prices,* and therefore what

* "The hope of admission to the English market at extreme high prices induces the continental farmer to raise a greater quantity than he would do."—*Von Theunen's Letter to Mr. Jacob.*

little competition the home-grower has felt with the continental grower may be fairly said to have resulted only from the operation of the law intended for his entire exclusion.

Having thus fully examined the price at which the continental grower could come into competition with the home-grower, we shall now, as proposed, consider the extent to which he could do so, even though the present relative cost of production enabled him. On this point, as we have already seen with regard to price, the most extraordinary exaggerations have been circulated. In order to support the exaggeration of low prices, exaggerated quantity was quite needful, both parties to the question have agreed thereon; the agriculturist insisted that the weight would be intolerable and crushing, the quantity inexhaustible. The opposite party saw the field of plenty through an equally magnified vision: what one dreaded for its abundance the other courted and sighed for, as having only that quality to recommend it. Every inducement which tended on both sides to diminish the cost of production, tended at the same time to exaggerate the quantity produced, for exactly in this proportion was it to be feared by the one party or sought for by the other. We shall now endeavour to arrive at the real facts of this most important part of our consideration.

On this subject Mr. Jacob, in his Report before alluded to, gives much valuable information.

In page 80 he shows that the whole export for the preceding ten years, from Hamburg, had amounted to

675,774 quarters, and that of this quantity there had been imported into Hamburg—

	Quarters.
By sea	51,766
By craft ascending the Elbe . . .	116,754
By land from Holstein	73,062
	241,582

leaving 434,192 quarters as the surplus of the wheat on both banks of the far-stretching Elbe above Hamburg, after deducting the consumption of the city for ten years, or 43,419 quarters annually.

With respect to Prussia, in page 99, it appears that, independent of what is sent from the Rhenish provinces to the Netherlands and there consumed, and the produce of Magdeburg and the provinces adjacent to the Elbe, which is sent down that river to Hamburg, and forms part of the supply of that city, the whole exports of Prussia in nine years amounted to 1,971,577 quarters, or to 219,064 quarters annually. He says, "this amount comprehends the whole of that which descends by the several rivers from Poland;" which quantity he estimates at 140,000 to 150,000 quarters annually, as part of the 219,064.

From the duchies of Mecklenburg the annual exports in twelve years had been 66,456 quarters, through the ports of Rostock, Wismar, and Boitzenburg.

From Denmark, including Holstein and Sleswick,

the annual exports for seven years had been 104,768 quarters.

The exports from Bremen appear to be very trifling, being only estimated at 1850 quarters annually. So that the annual rate of exportation, or, in other words, of *surplus produce*, is thus shown to be, from

	Quarters.
Hamburg	43,419
Prussia	219,064
Mecklenburg	66,456
Denmark	104,768
Bremen	1,850
Total . . .	435,557

This shows the total annual amount which these countries had furnished to all parts of the world during those respective periods. It must be borne in mind that the surplus produce of these countries, whatever it may be, is occasionally taken for every country where from any cause a scarcity prevails. Spain, and the south of France, take less or more every year; Holland also takes annually a portion of the shipments from the Baltic ports, independent of what she takes from the Rhenish provinces of Prussia. The United States and British America two years ago took very largely from these and other continental countries to make up the deficiency of bad harvests and neglected cultivation. The West India islands, the Brazils, and a large portion of the rest of the South American continent, are dependent on these countries less or more, especially in years when a deficiency exists in the United States, which generally, when they are well supplied, furnish these countries with flour. When all these claims are considered as bearing on so small a quantity, what portion could annually be allotted to England?

As with regard to price, so with regard to quantity, Prussia is by far the most important country for our consideration.

The following table, derived from the best official sources of the whole exports of wheat from all the Baltic ports of Prussia, in each of the following years, may be relied upon as perfectly accurate:—

1819	155,055	quarters	Report on foreign corn, ordered to be printed by the House of Commons, 14th March, 1826.
1820	464,744	,,	
1821	194,840	,,	
1822	78,316	,,	
1823	121,692	,,	
1824	93,630	,,	Officially communicated from Berlin to His Excellency Baron Bulow.
1825	219,290	,,	
1826	373,444	,,	
1827	270,576	,,	
1828	614,453	,,	Page 570. Part 3d of the Tables compiled by the Board of Trade from official documents.
1829	553,933	,,	
1830	707,100	,,	
1831	380,731	,,	
1832	362,177	,,	
1833			
1834	107,341	,,	Official reports from Dantzig, Koningsburg, and Stetin.
1835	62,841	,,	
16 years	4,760,163		

297,510 quarters annually.

This quantity comprehends the whole of the surplus produce of Prussia and Prussian Poland. The Prussian wheat generally is inferior in quality to the English, and forms about one-third of the whole quantity. The Polish wheat may therefore be estimated at about 200,000 quarters annually, of which about 150,000 quarters are of the finest white quality, and which alone, of all the wheats produced on the Continent, is equal to our best English produce. These proportions agree nearly with Mr. Jacob's statement in his Report, and also with all the information we can collect from practical men.

It remains that we should notice Russia as having contributed in some years of scarcity to supply our markets. Very little is known of the extent of cultivation, except that a large quantity of very inferior wheat is grown, which in usual times is quite excluded from the English market, for two reasons: first, on account of its inferiority in quality; and secondly, on account of the great expense of bringing it to England. These remarks apply with greatest effect to the shipments from the ports in the Black Sea. We find that for ten years, 1820 to 1829 inclusive, the whole quantity of wheat furnished from all Russia to this country was 535,687 quarters, or on an average annually 53,568 quarters.*

In endeavouring to form a careful estimate of the exact available surplus produce of wheat in the present state of European agriculture, it is needful to guard against an error of confusing the amount of produce raised in the countries from which the shipments are made with the produce of other countries, which has been imported and

* See Note II. at the end.

then re-shipped to this country. For example, considerable portions of the exports of Hamburg, Antwerp, &c. are first imported from the Baltic and Black Seas, and consequently enter into the computation of the respective countries from which they are originally brought.

There is still a more important feature in this consideration which claims our particular notice. We have already sufficiently noticed the fluctuations in our prices for the last twenty years, by which the foreign grower has been enabled to send his produce to this country at the high periods. At these periods prices have ranged from 70*s.* to 80*s.* per quarter, and these high prices have enabled us to import wheat profitably from a much more extended radius of country than could possibly be the case if the price of wheat were at the real average price of a range of years, 52*s.* 2*d.* per quarter. We have already shown that it would be with great difficulty that the nearest and most productive countries could send their produce to this market at this average price, much less could the many distant countries from which we derive large supplies at these extreme high prices. At a period like the present, the demand for this country raises the prices to such an unusual rate in the continental ports, that supplies are procured from very distant inland places, which in usual years, at usual prices, could furnish nothing; the expense of transport would absorb the whole price in ordinary times. Except at these extreme high prices it would, for example, be impossible to import wheat from the ports in the Mediterranean or Black Seas; and even from the Baltic ports the quantities are much increased by the same cause. It must be quite clear, that just in proportion to the highness of the price, must the radius of country from the ports be extended which can furnish supplies; and as the price diminishes this radius must also diminish.

By the present system our prices are for a period so low as to admit no foreign wheat at all; then they are so high as to admit the whole accumulated surplus from an immensely extended surface. If they were uniform we might take annually, in regular proportions, a part of the finest quality (which alone could bear the cost of transport) of the produce of a limited surface, which at present we take irregularly in an accumulated form, and in addition thereto the produce of distant districts which could otherwise never reach us. As these distant supplies enter, at present, into the general average consumption of this country, one of the effects of the present Corn Laws may, therefore, be said to bring much more extended and distant countries into competition with the British farmer than could otherwise be the case.

But even taking all the advantages which these high prices afford to very distant places to add to the quantity available for this country, it is quite impossible to show that the total quantity of continental surplus has reached on an average 700,000 quarters annually.

If we estimate the outside average capabilities at present of each country as follows—say

Prussia . . .	300,000	quarters.
Mecklenburg .	80,000	„
Denmark . .	100,000	„
Russia . . .	100,000	„
Hamburg . .	80,000	„
	660,000	

we considerably exceed what all the official accounts show them to be, and yet the aggregate amount, suppose it all sent to this country, would not exceed four per cent. of our annual consumption, or about the entire supply of two weeks in each year. The actual average annual quantity of foreign wheat and flour taken into consumption in Great Britain for nineteen years, from 1817 to 1835 inclusive, and which embraces the five most extensive years of import that have occurred in the present century, was only 532,237 quarters, and this includes the whole imports from our own colonies.

These facts cannot fail to show how exaggerated have been the representations as to the capability of the continent to supply wheat, as well in price as in quantity. Suppose the whole of the above quantity were annually brought to this country, it could not in any sensible way affect the general price of sixteen or seventeen millions of quarters. If any difference did exist in the rate at which this quantity could be brought to this market favourable to the continental grower, (which we have sufficiently shown does not) even then his small quantity could not make the price for our large quantity, but our large quantity would make the price for his small quantity.

It will appear by the whole of these arguments that, compared with any other country, Great Britain is not more extensively and strikingly a manufacturing than a corn-growing country; and that the advantages which we possess in securing higher prices arise from natural causes, the result of our peculiar condition, and not from the attempted interference of the law. In the next proposition we shall have to examine how these two leading interests co-operate in favour of each other.

But it may be urged that had we a free trade in wheat the small surplus quantities at present produced on the continent might be increased so as to become a formidable quantity. On this point exaggeration has done as much as in the two points already discussed.

In examining the price at which continental wheat could be furnished to this country, we have taken it in the exact state in which production has existed in every respect of late years, and we have taken the price which they have actually received, as the best possible evidence of the exact price which, on the average of years, has enabled them to produce the exact quantity which they have done: nothing can be more plain than that the amount of production must in every country be determined by the price received for the produce. If prices rise, an increased production must follow; if they fall, a diminished production must be the consequence.

If therefore we have shown that in the event of such an alteration taking place in the English Corn Laws as would by free and natural competition keep prices steady at the average rate of late years, 52*s*. 2*d*. per quarter, the continental growers could not send their produce to this country at a profit on the average prices, which they have received, and which average prices have determined the extent of their production; then, as before shown, the surplus produce would necessarily be diminished instead of increased. The large portion which under the present mode is held by speculators for the moment when 60*s.* to 70*s.* per quarter is paid for it to supply a case of exigency, could not be raised to be sold at a price below 34*s.* 3*d.* per quarter; which we have shown would be needful to enable them to send it to England, even free of duty, to compete with our average price. Either must it be shown that, with our average price, the price obtained on the Continent would be higher than it has been, or it is evident that production could not increase. It cannot, for one moment, be supposed that all the lands best suited both in quality and local position for raising wheat for shipment, are not at this moment in cultivation; there are therefore only two modes by which the cultivation can be increased; first, by the application of more capital and labour to force the production of the lands at present in cultivation, or by taking into cultivation inferior lands, either in point of quality of soil, or more distant points from the shipping ports or markets: but in which ever case this might be accomplished it could only be done at an increased cost of production. If, therefore, an increased price was not obtained, it is quite evident the attempt could only be momentary. If, we again repeat, the average price in England is too low to admit the continental grower, even though free of duty, to pay him at his present cost of production, it requires no argument to show that, if he attempted to increase his production in the only way he could by increasing his cost, he would be still farther disabled for competition with the grower in this country.

The only case, therefore, in which we can suppose it possible that an increased production would take place on the Continent, is by supposing that their prices would improve, which might be effected either by a material general advance on the prices in this country, or by the more likely cause, an increased prosperity and consumption amongst themselves.

The former cause could not exist without first and most particularly benefiting the English grower: nor could the latter cause exist without benefiting him in an indirect manner in common with the whole community.

It must also be borne in mind, that even though an attempt should be made to increase the production of the continent, it could only be the surplus of that production which could, at *any price*, be available for exportation. For example; in order to double the quantity of grain available for exportation, it would require that the whole cultivation should be doubled, or even more: for, in the first place, the labour of production must be sustained, which would consume as large a portion of the increased produce as it does of the present quantity, and in all probability a larger proportion, for such an increased demand for labour which would necessarily be called into existence by such an attempt, could not fail to advance wages so much, that not only would the labourers be multiplied in proportion to the increase, but their condition so much improved that their individual consumption would be greater in proportion than it now is; and this circumstance in its turn could not fail again to add to the general cost of production, and render it still more difficult for the grower to send even the surplus to this market.

In the former proposition we sufficiently discussed the whole train of evils which attend the landed interest, by the operation of the present corn laws, and we think it must be admitted that we have discovered no counteracting benefit in the second proposition. We have discovered no real advantage or protection which has been conferred beyond what the local position of the English agriculturist will ever secure to him; beyond which it is utterly impossible for the law to afford him any advantage whatever, as long as the internal resources of the country are able by internal competition to supply the whole wants of the nation. Let the imaginary price be fixed by law at whatever rate it may, be it 72*s*., 80*s*., or 100*s*. per quarter, it could have no effect in securing one shilling more than the free internal competition of the home-growers found to be the remunerating rate of production; to that extent it would be pushed, and by an unerring law, the average price would be just sufficient to produce the required quantity, but with the enormous disadvantages attendant on fluctuation. The great and general advantages of equal prices will only be secured by a free and unrestrained trade; when a confidence can be felt by the parties interested therein, that any slight fluctuations which momentary and temporary causes might create, would soon pass away, and thus confidence would become general to maintain an equality of price by fair and legitimate support, and speculative purchases by the regular dealers, of which, in the present uncertain state, the trade is entirely deprived.

The only circumstance which can ever drive wheat out of cultivation in this country, will be when land shall become too valuable for this purpose. As, for example, in the immediate neighbourhood of London, Manchester, &c. land is at present too valuable for growing wheat, so a time may arrive when, by the increased prosperity and population of the country, a larger portion may be similarly circumstanced.

Although we have seen how expensive the transport of wheat is from one place to another, yet it is the least expensive of any article of agricultural produce, because it contains in a given weight and bulk a greater value than any other article. It will therefore always be more profitable to remove wheat from a distance, to supply a neighbourhood or district, than barley, oats, hay, or turnips, or the first produce of the dairy. In consequence of this fact, we find that while hay fields and pasture fields continue round large towns, the cultivation of wheat is moved to a distance.

As this movement could only take place by greatly increasing the value of land, and more especially the *rents*, it is one to which the landed interest could never be averse, and with which the whole community could only be well satisfied, as the result of its general and extended prosperity.

We have not considered it needful to allude in particular to the interest of the land-owners in this proposition, it being so inseparably mixed up with the general consideration of the agricultural interest. With respect to rent, we would, however, just remark, that if the farmer is protected by natural causes and local situation alone, to the extent of 18*s*. 3*d*. per quarter for wheat, and if an acre of land produces three quarters of wheat, then must the landlord's interest, in point of rent per acre, be very largely protected from the same cause.

PROPOSITION THE THIRD.

That while incalculable benefit would arise to the manufacturing interest, and the working population generally, in common with all classes of the community from the adoption of such policy (a free trade in corn), nothing can be more erroneous than the belief that the price of provisions or labour would, on the average, be cheapened thereby, but that on the contrary, the tendency would rather be to produce by a state of general increased prosperity a higher average rate of each.

MOST of the considerations which arise out of this proposition have been directly or indirectly referred to already. In the first proposition, the baneful influence of the present system has been alluded to; and, in the second proposition, the question of cheaper provisions being the result of an alteration in the system, has been set at rest.

As far as the distinct benefits which would result to these interests in such case are to be considered, we will divide them into two heads:—first, that which would be derived from a uniformity in the prices of provisions as particularly affecting the labouring classes; and, secondly, the general advantages which would result from an improvement, so great in the condition and interests of so large and important a portion of their customers as the landed interest constitutes. But before proceeding to these considerations, it will be necessary to notice a popular and general error, to which the exaggerated notions respecting the price at which wheat could be furnished by the continent in case of a free trade, have necessarily led the public.

By the whole tenour of the arguments urged by the manufacturing interest against these impolitic laws, it appears that they consider, first, that the high price of labour in this country, as compared with the continent, is only the result of a higher price of provisions; and that the lower price of labour on the continent, consequent on a lower price of provisions, is the chief cause of whatever progress these countries have made in the arts and manufactures. These opinions we believe to be wrong, both as regards the facts and the principles deduced.

If we have proved anything in the second proposition, it is that, on the average, provisions would not be cheaper if we had a free trade than the internal competition of our own resources and means has furnished them, and therefore, though their price did regulate the price of labour, that commodity could not be cheaper.

But while we must admit that, in all cases, the price of provisions enters as one of the measures of the price of labour, and in some cases as the chief measure—yet it is by no means the only measure; and in respect to the particular description of labour of which we now treat, we believe it to constitute a most unimportant and trivial portion.

If the price of provisions were the sole or chief measure of the value of labour in all cases, then it would necessarily follow that its price would vary in different places, just in proportion as the price of provisions varied. That in the same place, at the same time, the price of all kinds of labour would be exactly the same; and that everywhere the real condition of the labourer, in respect to the amount of the necessaries, or comforts of life, which he could command, would be exactly equal; that he would everywhere receive exactly the sum of money which would purchase a given uniform quantity of provisions for the same number of hours' labour. Now not one of these consequences accord with the facts. The reverse will be found to exist in most cases, especially in this country. Wherever provisions are dearest the condition of the bulk of labourers is decidedly best, and their ability to command the necessaries, comforts, and even elegancies of life, form a striking contrast with the extreme difficulty with which even the barest necessaries are obtained where they are cheapest.

Compare the condition of the working population of London, Manchester, and the manufacturing districts, their ability to consume articles of comparative luxury, their expenditure, unfortunately sometimes of the most profuse character, and the comfort of their dwellings, with the mean style of diet, clothing, and habitations in most of the rural districts in England where provisions are so much cheaper—with the mud cottage, the tattered and patched dress, and the mean fare of the labourers in Ireland, where provisions are cheaper than anywhere else in this country.

Compare the general condition of the whole labourers of this country with that of any of the countries on the continent where provisions are at the lowest prices: compare their *diet, clothing*, and *habitations*, with what are allotted to the labouring classes in Prussia, Poland, or France, and see how superior the worst classes are in these respects in this country compared with the very best in these lands of supposed abundance and cheapness.

These considerations suggest to us a principle which appears better to reconcile these facts, and to be more applicable to the solution of the relative value of labour and provisions in most cases in the present state of society, viz. that the high price of provisions is rather the *effect* than the cause of high and well-paid labour; and that low prices of provisions is, on the contrary, the effect of ill-paid labour, and the consequent inability to consume proportionably with the production.

Thus, for example, it can never be said that the price of labour is high in Manchester or the manufacturing districts, because provisions are dear. Labour does not there exist in order to consume the provisions, but the provisions are brought from great distances in order to supply the demand created by a given quantity of labour paid at a given rate. In proportion, therefore, to this rate must be the consumption, and, in proportion to the consumption, must be the distance from which the supply must be drawn, and consequently its price; and as the produce of the land in the immediate vicinity is of equal value to that grown at the greatest distance of supply, its price must increase exactly in proportion to the extended radius of country necessary to supply the neighbourhood; that is, it must be worth the general prime cost, and the cost of conveying the distant produce to the spot of consumption.* The price, therefore, paid for labour, and the quantity of it employed in particular spots, are evidently the cause and not the effect of the high prices paid for provisions.

So, on the contrary, the low price of provisions in Cumberland is not so much the cause of the low price of labour as its effect. The demand for the labour of that part of the country being much less, and its price much lower, the ability of the neighbourhood is not sufficient to consume the whole of its products, a considerable portion of which must, therefore, be sent to a great distance to be used, and the expense of which must be deducted from the price ultimately obtained, which diminished price of the portion removed to a great distance must fix the price of the portion consumed in the neighbourhood; and just in proportion to the distance and consequent expenses thus incurred to consume the surplus produce of the country, must the nett value of the produce on the spot, and of the land on which it is reared be reduced. If the quantity of labour or its price should be increased in the neighbourhood, then the surplus produce would diminish and be consumed in a narrower radius, at less expense, and the general price would advance; and, on the contrary, should the means to consume be diminished, the surplus would increase, and the general price diminish. This principle must apply in all

* See Note III. at the end.

countries where there is a mixture of manufacturing and agricultural labour and pursuits.

It becomes, therefore, quite clear that some other more important causes must exist to determine the different value of different kinds of labour, and of the labour of different countries; which, we believe, will be found to consist in the amount of skill, intelligence, and ability; in the assistance which physical exertions have received from mechanical discoveries, and in the proportion of supply and demand, as existing in different places or in different countries.

For the same reason that the skill and intelligence of the physician or lawyer, and the capital or labour invested in his acquirements, entitle him to a high reward for his labour, the English mechanic is entitled to a higher reward than the labourer elsewhere: for the reason, that by the ingenuity of this country his physical ability to produce for other countries at very low prices is increased by the aid of the most perfect mechanical assistance, his labour becomes more valuable; for the reason, that the country in which he lives possesses unbounded capital, enterprise, and mercantile resources of every description, which necessarily create a greater demand for manufacturing and mechanical labour than is to be found in any other country; the value thereof must be higher here than elsewhere.

As is the case with the physician and lawyer, the English manufacturing labour generally, of which we now speak, is of a higher quality than the common labour of this country, or the labour of any other country, and, as such, commands a higher price, just in the same way that the fine white wheat of Essex commands a higher price than the miserably shrivelled grain imported from the Black Sea. As with the learned professions, the remuneration is not only for the bare labour of the moment, but for a large amount of accumulated labour and ingenuity previously spent in acquiring the skill and intelligence necessary for its exercise.

The price of this labour is one of the distinct modes in which a nation becomes benefited by ingenious mechanical discoveries, which tend so much to abridge the total quantity of labour necessary to produce a given article, and renders the portion still employed of much greater value, by the increased demand and consumption which the entire lower price secures to the article.

The price of this labour is one of the distinct modes by which a nation becomes benefited by the possession of a large capital, industry, and mercantile enterprise, which seek for profitable employment, by the exchange of the skill and ingenuity of this country for the simpler products of distant and different climates.

Such is the value and quality of English labour of this class, that there is no country in the world, not even the cheapest corn-growing countries of the continent, in which it does not command a higher price than in this country, notwithstanding the low general rate of labour. An English mechanic will command very much higher wages in Petersburg, Berlin, Brussels, or Paris, than he usually obtains here.

From all these considerations we are induced to consider, that there is no better evidence of a prosperous community or country than the existence of a high average price of provisions, when the condition of the labourer, as is the case in this country, is relatively better than in other countries; and that, on the contrary, there is no stronger evidence of a miserable and impoverished country than the existence of low prices of provisions, where the condition of the labourer is comparatively and infinitely worse than in other countries where prices are higher.

We are therefore of opinion, that in the event of a free trade in corn, the price of labour in this country would be rather increased than diminished, by the operation of the distinct benefits which to the whole community would result from such principles.

We will now glance at the two proposed ways in which the manufacturing and mercantile interest would be benefited by such a policy.

First,—That which would result from a uniformity of the prices of provisions, as particularly affecting the labouring classes. In the first proposition we alluded to the evils which afflict this class in consequence of the present fluctuation of prices, which would be entirely removed by an equality of price. We cannot hold out any prospect that, on the average, he would have his provisions cheaper, but that, instead of being lavishly supplied at one period, which leads to habits of luxury and indulgence, and the more unfit him for the period of comparative scarcity and want, his condition would be nearly uniform.

We have already shown that his wages are determined by principles which do not necessarily fluctuate with provisions, and it is therefore most desirable to him, that as his wages are comparatively uniform, the amount of the comforts and necessaries of life which they can procure should also be uniform. It is a cruel policy which introduces a working population into the temporary possession of comforts and luxuries far beyond what their average condition will enable them to support, and which, by a reaction, reduces their means before long as much below what that average should be as it had before been above it. Great complaints at present prevail, that the present high price of provisions is more severely felt in many places where, previous to the *low* prices and lavish consumption of 1834, 1835, and 1836, a very inferior scale of food and general comforts prevailed, than became common in those years: but sweets once tasted, advantages once enjoyed, are not easily relinquished. In many districts, where oat meal or barley meal formed a wholesome and considerable portion of diet before those years, wheat-flour was substituted, as being at the moment from unnatural causes as cheap. In such cases, the necessary return to inferior diet, and even to a more limited quantity of it than on the average they are entitled to, cannot but be considered a great evil and hardship.

But these fluctuations are apt to exercise another influence, in which the labouring classes, in common with their employers, are deeply interested. The supply of the first necessaries of life in this country has become a matter of such huge extent, that any little derangement therein becomes a question of much more serious extent than is generally imagined, in its indirect influences on commerce, by deranging the currency of this country, and the courses of exchange with others. As before stated, there have been, and of very late years, times when the whole amount of bullion in the Bank of England would not have purchased the wheat required this year to make up the deficiency, which is estimated at only *one-sixth* of the annual consumption.

To examine these influences minutely would require more time and space than we can here afford, but this one fact may lead to a consideration of the extent to which they may be indirectly felt.

The manufacturing and mercantile interests are, however, more directly interested by the second mode in which we propose to consider their distinct benefits, viz.—In the general advantages which would result from an improvement so great, in the condition and interests of so large and important a portion of their consumers, as the landed interests constitute.

If we have shown that the landed interests suffer, by the present state of the law, great and fearful losses in our first proposition, and if in our second proposition we have shown sufficient to prove that a free trade in corn would avoid these losses, and not submit them to any other; — then have we shown that the whole wealth of the country, both in income and capital, would be much increased; that immense sums which are at present expended in unprofitable labour would become applicable to general and useful consumption; that large amounts of capital which lie dormant until wasted and decayed, would be available for the employment of useful and beneficial production.

The connexion between the manufacturer and the landed interest in this country is much closer than is generally admitted or believed; not only is the manufacturer dependent on the landed interest for the large portion of his goods which they immediately consume, but also for a very large portion of what he exports to the most distant countries. All commerce is, either directly or indirectly, a simple exchange of the surplus products of one country for those of another. It is therefore a first essential that we should be able to take the cotton of America, the sugar and coffee of India, the silk and teas of China, before they can take our manufactures; and if this be necessary, then must it follow that in proportion to the extent to which we can take their produce, will they be enabled to take our manufactures. Therefore whatever portion of these products is consumed in this country by the landed interest, must to that extent enable the manufacturer to export his goods in return; and thus any causes which increase this ability on the part of the landed interest to consume, must give a corresponding additional ability to the manufacturer to export. Every pound of coffee or sugar, every ounce of tea, every article of luxury, the produce of foreign climes, whether consumed within the castles and halls of our wealthiest landowners, or in the humble cottages of our lowliest peasantry, alike represent some portion of the exports of this country.

On the other hand the dependence of the landowner is no less twofold on the manufacturer and merchant. He is not only dependent upon them for their own immediate consumption, but also for the consumption of whatever food enters into the cost price of their goods. Although the English farmer does not export his *corn* or his other produce in the exact shape and form in which he produces them, they constitute not the less on that account a distinct portion of the exports of this country, and that in the best of all possible forms.

Just as much as the manufacturer exports the wool or the silk which enters into the fabrics of those materials, does he export the corn which paid for the labour of spinning and weaving them. It would be an utter impossibility that this country could consume its agricultural produce but for our extensive manufacturing population; or that the value of what would be consumed could be near its present rate. If without this aid our agricultural produce were as great as it now is, a large portion would have to seek a market in distant countries: it would then have to be exported in the exact form in which it is produced; the expenses of which being so large would reduce very greatly from its value and nett price, and the landed interest would be immediately effected thereby. But, as it is, the produce of the land is exported in the condensed form of manufactured goods, at a comparatively trifling expense, which secures a high value to it here. Thus, for example, a few bales of silk or woollen goods may contain as much wheat in their value as would freight a whole ship.

To this advantage the landed interest is indebted, exclusively, for the very superior value of property and produce in this country to any other; because, by our great manufacturing superiority, a market is found for our produce over the whole world, conveyed in the cheapest and most condensed form.

While the Chinese, or Indians, buy our cottons, our silks, or our woollens, they buy a portion of the grain and other produce of the land of this country; and therefore the producer here, while indulging in the delicacies or luxuries of oriental climes, may only be consuming a portion of the golden heads of wheat which had gracefully waved in his own fields at a former day.

Is it not, therefore, sufficiently clear that no circumstance whatever can either improve or injure one of these interests without immediately in the same way affecting the other? The connexion is so close that it is impossible to separate or distinguish them. Any circumstance which limits our commerce must limit our market for agricultural produce; and any possible circumstance which deteriorates the condition of our agriculturists must deteriorate our commerce, by limiting our imports, and consequently our exports. These are general principles, and are capable of extension to the whole world, in all places, and at all times; and the same principle as is thus shown to connect and combine the different interests of any one country, just as certainly operates in producing a similar effect between different countries; and we ardently hope, ere long, to find not only the petty jealousies between different portions of the same community entirely removed, but that all countries will learn, that a free and unrestricted co-operation with each other in matters of commerce can only tend to the general benefit and welfare of all.

PROPOSITION THE FOURTH.

PART FIRST.

A consideration of what change in the present laws would best suit the interest of all parties at this particular time.

Every change of an extensive or important character, however beneficial it may be in its ultimate operation, is apt to be attended with considerable inconvenience and partial evil in its first consequences, and it is therefore an incumbent duty on the part of governments to introduce any change with the greatest care and circumspection; and in this particular case this precaution is more than usually needed, to avoid the evil consequences which might arise from the deeply-rooted prejudices and ignorance so common with respect to the subject.

We have already sufficiently noticed all the different fluctuations in the extent of our cultivation and supply; and it will easily be seen, that although the same one ultimate principle can alone be a cure to the whole evil, yet that the particular mode in which it should be resorted to may fairly differ, according to the particular period in these fluctuations selected for the change.

The great object which is to be accomplished is to get wheat fixed at the fair average price at which it can be produced ; and in endeavouring to do this we must bear in mind, that though we may be correct in every deduction throughout these pages, yet that the generally prevailing prejudices, both in this country and on the continent, will not fail to have a considerable influence in the first instance. Thus, in the event of an immediate free trade in corn, the deeply-rooted prejudices of the cultivators in this country would not fail to discourage and limit their efforts of cultivation, until experience had sufficiently proved the real effects of this change ; and, in like manner, the same cause would no doubt influence the growers on the continent to exceed the bounds of prudence in their efforts to avail themselves of this privilege, which when they have ever possessed it of late has been only when prices have been unusually high, and which has led them to form a very exaggerated notion of the profit they could derive from a constant trade with us. As, however, we have already shown that the whole quantity which the continent could supply is, when compared with our home production, so absolutely insignificant, we will look at these influences chiefly in reference to the latter.

In looking at the fluctuations which have occurred it must be clear that there have been times when it would have been useful to all that cultivation had been checked, and other times when it would have been as useful that it had been encouraged. If in 1832, 1833, or 1834, when cultivation was extending to an unprofitable degree, any change in the law had been proposed, then it might safely have been introduced in such a way as would have tended immediately to check cultivation and supplies; because such an effect at that time would have prevented the surplus being so great, and have maintained the price nearer the proper average. But if such a change had been proposed in 1837, 1838, or at the present time, then we think that it should be introduced in such a way as to avoid checking an increase of cultivation, when such is actually required to bring the supply and price to the proper average.

Considering the first influence of such a change on the fears of the home cultivators, we should have expected that if, at the former period, a free and unrestricted trade had been instantly introduced, the effect would have been a general curtailment of cultivation, which at the time would have been beneficial: and at that time prices being moderate, the cultivator on the continent would not have had such a great inducement to enter into a competition which might afterwards prove ruinous to him; and therefore, at that period of the fluctuation, the best mode of introducing the change would have been in an instantaneous manner.

In like regard to the first influence of such a change, we should expect that at this moment a similar effect would be exerted over the home cultivator, which we are of opinion would operate very badly for all parties to the question.

Our stocks are exhausted, and even with a cultivation equivalent to our annual consumption, it would be a long time before prices assumed their fair average rate. It could not be until such a convenient stock existed as enabled the trade to be carried on easily without pressing too much on the supply.

If, therefore, our home production were checked at this moment, the tendency would be to keep a very badly supplied market for a long time, and consequently high prices, and it would be much longer before the price and supply arrived at the proper average.

This could not fail to be injurious to all parties. To the cultivator, who, though he received a higher price, would only do so on an inferior cultivation. To the general community, by being obliged to pay much higher prices than the fair average at which production can be profitably conducted; and from the longer maintenance of high prices which would ultimately give way, the continental growers would be induced to embark in a competition with our home-growers to an extent which would ultimately prove very injurious to them, as well as to our farmers for a time. In this case it would be much longer before that desirable equality of price was arrived at, which should secure a regular and just sufficient cultivation.

It may, however, be said, that though an immediate repeal of the present restrictions tended to curtail the home growth, it would tend to give additional stimulus to foreign supplies, and that thus the desirable point would be only in another way arrived at. Such an effect would not only fail to accomplish the object, but even though it did, would do it in a manner which would ultimately be prejudicial to all concerned. It would fail to accomplish the object, because no increase which could take place on the continent, with its extremely limited means, could for many years be equivalent even to an inconsiderable curtailment of the huge production of this extraordinary country; but even if it should prove equivalent, it would be injurious to our growers in the first instance, by inducing them to throw the lands out of cultivation when they could have been profitably retained, and to the continental grower by giving a momentary and unnatural impulse to his productive powers, which could not be maintained when our own level of cultivation was again restored.

It therefore appears clear, that while such an exaggerated inducement to extend cultivation in this country as was given by the Corn Law of 1815 or 1828, could not fail to produce the same baneful effects that they did at those times; yet that this is not the moment to induce a curtailment of cultivation—on the contrary, rather a gentle impulse to extension. The high prices of the past and present year have partly had that influence already, but it should not be suddenly stopped.

Under these considerations, although we are most decidedly of opinion, and if our arguments have proved anything, it has been, that the evils resulting from the present Corn Laws can only be altogether removed by a total and entire repeal of all protective and prohibitory laws; yet for the reasons that we have stated, we think it for the interest of all, the producer and consumer alike, that this should not be, under present circumstances, an instantaneous measure. We should suggest that a specific duty of 10*s.* per quarter should be fixed on wheat in the first place, and that it should be reduced 1*s*. in each year for the first five years; and that it should remain fixed at 5*s*. for three years longer, and then be finally and for ever abolished.

We believe that by such a measure the prices of grain would not only more easily find their proper and natural level, but that they would be actually considerably lower during the next few years than if the present protective system were instantaneously abolished: for in the latter case the fears of the growers could not fail to abridge their efforts to produce in the first instance; and as we have before stated, we have no confidence whatever in the ability of the continent to supply the deficiency of even a very insignificant reduction of the cultivation of this country. The experience of the present year proves how well founded is our want of confidence on this point; we have felt with what difficulty the deficiency of the last year (estimated at only one-sixth) has been made up, not from the surplus of *one* year, but from the accumulated surplus of many years; and not from the moderate range of country which ordinary prices would permit wheat to be brought, but from the very extended range, which a long continuance of extreme high prices has induced to contribute to our supply. The whole that was accumulated in bond here, and the whole of our new imports, have scarcely had a perceptible effect on prices, though all admitted to consumption. Does this not sufficiently prove how perfectly insignificant any competition could ever be between the continental and the home-grower?

PART SECOND.

An examination of the benefit which would be derived by the establishment of a government institution for the purpose of collecting and furnishing periodically to the agricultural interests all the statistical facts connected with their pursuits.

Although we have sufficiently proved, that the great and leading cause of the extraordinary and unnatural fluctuations in the price of wheat is to be attributed to the necessary operation of protective laws, yet there can be no doubt that fluctuations to a small extent, comparatively, would ever continue to be experienced, as long as the landed interest remains in its present state of ignorance and uncertainty from time to time as to the real extent of cultivation which is going forward, of the comparative result of different harvests, or of the stocks remaining on hand from time to time.

The interests of the agricultural community in particular, and the public in general, have been injured in an incalculable degree from the absence of this important knowledge; which, had it been accurately possessed, would in some degree have modified the evils which have attended, and must ever attend the present principle of protective laws.

The statistical information acquired and collected chiefly from the custom-house regulations of different countries, affords to the merchant in all his transactions a guide and a beacon, without which the future would ever remain enveloped in mist and obscurity. They teach him the average amount of supply, or the supply in any given time; they teach him the rate of consumption; they teach him what amount of stock is needful for the safe and easy supply of the demand. By them he can see when the supply is increasing or diminishing as compared with the past; by them he can determine the exact progress of consumption; by them he is informed from day to day whether the whole stock is increasing or diminishing.

The information which he is thus acquiring afresh every day as the facts arise, enables him not only to fix the prices of his merchandise at the time, in some degree in relation to the movement the article may be making either towards a lower or higher value, and thus to anticipate alike a period of abundance or scarcity, (by which anticipation the more serious effects of either the one or the other are materially prevented,) but, besides this, he is enabled to direct his future transactions.

The merchant who is trading to distant parts of the earth must be able to look forward a long way in advance, in order to direct with success operations which can only be developed at a remote period. The distance and time occupied in such transactions render this imperative. It is only by a great amount of statistical information carefully collected from day to day, by narrowly watching the progress of supply and demand, and by general observation of the circumstances passing around him which are likely to influence the future, that he can approximate to a correct estimate of the future, for his guidance.

A knowledge of the future is so essential to the success of the merchant, every act of his life being less or more one of anticipation, that the extraordinary alacrity and ardour with which information is sought after is easily understood, as well as the deep interest felt in rapid modes of communication from distant places. The extensive engines which are put in operation,—the pains which are taken to possess early and good information, and the consequent knowledge of the most trivial circumstances passing in the most remote corners of the globe, are truly interesting and astonishing.

However necessary such knowledge may be for the merchant, we are of opinion that it is not more so to him than to the agriculturist. The result of his operations are in like manner all dependent on a future time. The routine of his cultivation may require one, two, or three years to complete it. There is not one reason which can be supposed to interest the merchant in the future, that does not equally or even more affect the agriculturist; but the degree of advance and perfection to which the former has arrived in this respect, is not nearly so astonishing as the entire neglect and absence of such advantages which exist with the interests of the latter. The surprise at this entire neglect is much increased by the fact, that the whole of the elements of information are so near at hand, and, as compared with any other pursuit, of such immense importance.

It appears extraordinary that, with all the institutions with which this country abounds, both public and private, no attempt has ever been made to accomplish this object. When we consider the practical inconvenience which has ever been acknowledged to arise from the imperfect and vague conjectures (for we have never advanced beyond this) as to the extent of cultivation of the different articles of agricultural produce needed to supply the average demand;—how far this has from year to year existed;—what the actual average consumption has been, and what progress the existing stocks have been making towards a glut or a scarcity;—when we consider that the absence of all perfect knowledge of these heads has alike bewildered the legislature, the cultivator, and the dealer, it is a matter of great surprise that no attempt has been made to remove so great an amount of ignorance.

An attention to this subject is absolutely needful to conduct the pursuits of agriculture to a state of perfection, both for the interest of those immediately concerned and the public,—to secure a more perfect equilibrium of supply and demand, and to protect the public against the evil of partially varying crops, which will, to a certain extent, exist in the most perfect and equal state of cultivation.

Let us examine what would be the effects of such knowledge. Suppose there were means of ascertaining exactly how many acres of wheat and different other grain were in cultivation in each year; at the end of each year what the yield per acre had been; on the 1st of each month what stocks remained in granary, and what stocks remained in the stack yard: all those interested in these matters would watch, as narrowly as does the merchant, these beacons of his future course.

It would be ascertained sufficiently near for all useful purposes, how many acres were required to be cultivated with each kind of grain, to furnish our average consumption, which would also soon be clearly determined. The farmer would be governed by the facts thus disclosed to him, of the progress the whole nation was making, and any very important deviation from the correct relative proportions would be thus obviated in good time. It would soon be ascertained, by comparing year after year, what amount of stock should appear on the first of each different month to supply the consumption of the remainder of the year, and, in proportion as any deviation appeared between the corresponding periods of one year and another, influences would immediately be produced on prices as the case might be, and by anticipation, avoid such extreme effects, either of a superabundance or scarcity, as must occur, if the public remain in ignorance until the crisis comes unexpectedly upon them. These monthly and periodical statements would be consulted with as much interest and profit by the farmer, the corn-merchant, and the miller, as the periodical publications of the stocks, arrivals, and deliveries of all articles of foreign produce, are by those interested in them, and could not fail to direct these extensive interests in a way most convenient and profitable to themselves and the public, by producing and maintaining the greatest possible equality of prices. If the stocks showed a diminution, then dealers would anticipate their wants by speculative purchases: prices would be a little advanced by this action on the market; a wholesome stimulant would be given to supply from a greater distance, and to a more careful consumption. If, on the contrary, the stocks showed a material increase, prices would decline a little; a check would be given to supplies from such a distance as would be unprofitable, a little increased stimulus would be given to consumption, and, in both instances, the fluctuations would be limited to a much narrower compass, than could be the case without such timeous warning.

At first sight it may appear to many a matter of some difficulty to arrive at such information, with any degree of accuracy that could be relied upon. Nothing, however, would be more easy to accomplish, at least with sufficient accuracy for all practical purposes.

Many of the continental countries, but particularly Prussia, Holland, and Belgium, have set us an example in the care with which they furnish information to their respective countries, on all matters connected with the progress of their internal interests, and amongst others on agriculture; the beneficial influence of which is much acknowledged by the different interests in these countries, where, instead of groping in the dark, as every man does who is engaged in any of the internal productive resources of this country, whether it be in raising wheat, iron, lead, or coals, the producer has always before his eyes an exact statement of the progress of production and consumption to regulate his acts.

When we consider with what a degree of accuracy the productions, from year to year, of our most distant colonies are estimated, not only before shipment, but even while growing—productions extending over immense and half-civilized countries, many of them difficult of access—throughout our Indian territory—along the banks of the Ganges, stretching through the vales of Dacca and

Jessore—in the far-west dominions of the King of Oude, in the hills and valleys of Tirhoot, or the wide plains of Kishnagur—we ought to find no difficulty in arriving with much greater accuracy at every possible information, relating to the cultivation and production of fields comparatively around our own dwellings.

When we consider with what accuracy the Government can collect all the statistical information required to protect the revenue, how well defined is the extent of cultivation of hops, for that reason, it must at once be clear that it only requires to be considered of sufficient national importance, to enable us to collect, and publish accurate statistical periodical statements on the whole of the leading branches of internal industry.

Any one who has watched for some years the progress of those interests cannot but have remarked how subject they have been to extreme changes—to depression and the reverse; particularly the great leading articles of iron, lead, and coal, which would, no doubt, have been greatly alleviated by a better knowledge of the true relation of supply and demand at particular periods.

With respect to agriculture alone, we conceive that the country would be so greatly benefited, that no portion of the public expenditure would be more usefully applied than what would be spent to procure this information.

We would propose, to effect this great object, some plan similar to the following:—

That a Board of Internal Industry should be established, which should procure and publish periodically all information interesting to these objects. For example, with respect to agriculture: at the most convenient periods in each year, returns of the exact quantity of land sown with wheat, with the different spring grain crops, and green crops; of the yield of different kinds of grain in the preceding year; of the quantity of sheep slaughtered and shorn (to arrive at the product of wool); of the stocks of grain of all kinds in granary and stack, at fixed periods; and any other information, which, on proper consideration, might appear desirable, respecting these objects of overwhelming importance. Many regulations would be necessary to carry such a plan into operation, but it is believed they would neither be very expensive nor troublesome to the parties interested, who would soon find their benefit so great in their existence, that what attention was needed would be cheerfully given to secure accurate returns.

A difficulty with regard to ascertaining the existing stocks has been suggested; if however all grain was required to be warehoused in licensed granaries, which licence should be granted to every applicant at a mere nominal charge, and such granaries all registered, and obliged to make periodical returns of their stocks; and uniform sizes fixed for stacks, the number of which could easily be returned, very little difficulty would arise in gaining such approximate estimates of the actual stocks as would answer every useful purpose;—and even though, from any possible reason, some parties might wilfully or carelessly make erroneous returns, yet on the whole country these differences would so nearly be the same in different years, and perhaps on the whole bulk would so nearly balance each other, that no practical inconvenience could arise from them;—in a very little time experience would teach those interested in the different objects to make an exact allowance for such necessary deviations from exact accuracy.

We believe that such an institution would confer an incalculable advantage on this country, the internal resources and productive industry of which so far exceed those of any other country on the globe, and that its operation and effects would be watched by all with more intense interest than perhaps any institution which at present exists in these kingdoms.*

* See Note IV.

NOTE I.

The impression that the changes in the price of grain have arisen from the characters of the seasons is almost universal; and it has often been noticed as a curious circumstance, that a number of good seasons and bad seasons followed in succession.* It is impossible to reconcile our mind to a belief that the seasons move in these uniform cycles; but we think the circumstance capable of the most satisfactory solution by the fluctuations of cultivation. We find, for example, that 1820-21-22-23 were extremely productive seasons: by the principle we have laid down, the influence which the high prices of 1817 and 1818 had, in stimulating production in every way, ought to have produced this effect. Then the years 1827-28-29 were remarked as very unproductive years: the reaction of the previous period of abundance and low prices was in these years experienced in its strongest effects. Again, 1832-33-34 were noticed as being most prolific and abundant seasons: here we once more find the result of stimulated cultivation in producing extensive crops. The reaction which followed the low prices again brings us to the comparatively short crops of the three last years. It will be therefore observable that the cycles of productive and unproductive seasons correspond exactly with the necessary influences of the fluctuations pointed out in cultivation. How far the increased or curtailed, the

* The history of the last half-century shows that several productive and unproductive seasons have generally followed in succession.—*J. and G. Sturge's Report for January*, 1839.

high or low state of cultivation, may influence the character of the season, as far as the weather is concerned, it is difficult to say; but as it is an admitted and ascertained fact, that the general state of the cultivation of a country has a material influence on the climate and weather, it is not impossible that even slight fluctuations, such as we have pointed out, may have some influence. At all events there is one thing certain,—that in years of high and rich cultivation the crops are stronger and generally earlier, and much better able to resist or throw off the influence of bad weather; and that, in years of weak and impoverished cultivation, the crops must be more easily influenced by adverse weather.

The evidence given before the Committee of the House of Commons on agriculture in 1836 sufficiently explains the true cause of the enormously increased supplies of the four preceding years which had so depressing an effect on prices. We strongly recommend a perusal of this evidence.

NOTE II.

The great bulk of the wheat shipped from Odessa is not the produce of Russia, but of Poland. It is through this port chiefly that the Mediterranean islands and ports are supplied with wheat. A regular and extensive trade is carried on between *Odessa* and Malta, Leghorn, Trieste, Marseilles, and other places, in this article; and in usual years, at usual prices, it requires the whole quantity which finds its way to Odessa to supply these places, chiefly or entirely dependent thereon.

Although considerable shipments have been made this season from Leghorn, Trieste, &c., to this country, it by no means follows that they can spare from their own consumption the quantities thus shipped. Being so much nearer to this country than Odessa, they have shipped their own natural supplies to reach this country while yet the duty is low and the prices high, relying upon the stocks behind them at Odessa to replace the same.

The shipments from Odessa up to the 5th of January from last harvest had only reached 62,857 quarters of wheat, and there then remained in stock about 500,000 chetwarts, or 365,000 quarters, to supply the whole consumption and exhausted stocks of the Mediterranean.

NOTE III.

The claim which property has, and must ever continue to have (as long as this country maintains its present condition of prosperity), to a higher value in this country than in the Continental countries, results chiefly from the same reason that property in the neighbourhood of London, Manchester, &c., has a much higher value than in Cumberland, or throughout the rural districts of Ireland.

We have already considered sufficiently the cause of the difference of the price of provisions and land in the latter relative circumstances, and we do not find that the freest and most unrestricted intercourse has had any tendency to lessen this difference. From what we have already said it is obvious that local situation, in the precincts of populations differing in their ability to consume the produce of the land, by which, in the one case, food has to be brought from a greater distance, and consequently at an enhanced price, and, in the other case, the surplus produce has to find a market at a great distance, and therefore subject to considerable deductions for charges, may be called the natural causes of this difference.

In the one case, if the prosperity, and consequent ability to consume, should diminish, the value of property and food must fall. In the other case, if the means of consumption should increase, their value must rise.

It would also appear as a law, that as greater and cheaper facilities were afforded of conveying the surplus produce from the one point to the other, a higher price in the place of production, and a lower one in the place of consumption, would be the result. But this has not altogether proved to be the case. Of late years the facilities of steam-navigation have enabled the producers in Ireland, Cumberland, and elsewhere, to send the fruits of their industry at cheaper and easier rates to Liverpool, Manchester, &c.; but, while we find that in the former places these facilities have tended to improve the value of property and general condition of the producer, yet they have in no way tended to reduce the value of property or the condition of the producer in the neighbourhoods of the latter places.

Without these additional supplies the consuming ability of the large towns would have been abridged to a smaller quantity of food; but with such additional supplies of such articles as can be best brought from a distance, at a cheaper rate, a larger ability to consume other articles which are not so easily transported is obtained by the community, in the production of which the immediate producers find an occupation as profitable as before; and thus the whole community of producers and consumers is equally benefited.

In such relative position may we fairly consider the Continental countries generally, and this country in their present respective conditions. The value of property is higher here than on the Continent, for the same cause that it is higher round Manchester than in Ireland.

The distance between those countries and Great Britain will be found to be sufficient ever to maintain, as far as we are concerned, the whole difference which at present exists; or, if this difference should ever be altered, it will be by a diminishing prosperity and ability to consume in this country, or by an increasing ability on the part of the Continent to consume their own products. To avoid the former cause we cannot give too free and full an encouragement to our manufacturers; and as to the latter cause, if it did not arise from our own decline, we could not too much rejoice at its existence.

There is no more reason why the consumer in Great Britain should not be benefited by the producer of the Continent, without injury to our own property, than that the consumers in Liverpool and Manchester should be benefited by the producers in Ireland and Cumberland, as has been shown, without lowering the value of the immediate neighbourhood.

NOTE IV.

It was intended to have followed up these observations by an inquiry into the competition, of which we have heard so much of late, which has manifested itself on the Continent, with the manufacturing pursuits of this country; a consideration of the causes by which it had been produced; and an investigation of the influences which are likely thereby to be exerted on these interests in this country, as having been generally associated with the subject of these pages.

It has however been found, that to do justice to this most important and interesting inquiry, much more time would be required to collect the necessary facts in proper form to prove the reasoning than was at first anticipated, and therefore, for the present at least, this intention has been necessarily postponed, though not entirely abandoned.

APPENDIX.

The following two objections having been raised to the views and principles contained in this work :—first, that the extreme low price at which continental wheat has sometimes been sold in this market appears incompatible with the estimate given of the charges necessarily incurred in importing it; and, secondly, that, from the admitted and well-ascertained fact, that the prices of wheat have fluctuated even more in the Continental countries where there are no corn-laws, and on the Continent generally, than in England, the fluctuations here cannot be attributed to the existing corn-laws;—the following observations, contained in a letter from the author, in reply to these objections, will sufficiently reconcile these facts to his general principles, and prove them to be part of the necessary consequences resulting from the present laws :—

" It is a matter of great satisfaction for me that these points are capable, in my views, of being made very clear, and of advancing the general tendency of my arguments, instead of in any way interfering with them.

" With respect to the objection, that the charges attendant on the import of grain from the Continent to this country, being put very high, the same objection has frequently been urged to me even by men engaged in that trade; but when I requested them to point out in what respect, they have always failed to discover one point of exaggeration when fairly looked into; but many are misled at the first sight at the rates I give, by their not sufficiently attending to the numerous and various items which are introduced into the sum, but which are nevertheless quite indispensable to the operation. Of the 18*s*. 3*d*. given as the total of these charges, only 6*s*. is put down as freight, but all the other charges are not less necessary to complete the importation.

"The fact to which you refer, of wheat having been delivered in London at 23*s*. per quarter, in no way interferes with the above calculations, if, as I believe must have been the case, the wheat alluded to was already in London, and not imported purposely to sell at that price. Although as a general principle the cost of an article must regulate its selling price, yet the exceptions are very numerous in mercantile experience, in which the cost has no influence whatever over the price: and the present is one of these cases, the causes of which are easily explained.

"In the years 1829, 1830, and 1831, extensive importations of wheat took place, a large portion of which, owing to the high prices of those years, was cleared for consumption; but towards the end of 1831 the average prices in this country fell very much, and the duty increased so much that it was no longer possible to introduce the shipments then arriving, and to arrive, for the consumption of this country; the consequence was, that in 1832 a very large quantity of wheat, little less than *two* millions of quarters, existed in our bonded warehouses, while our average prices were regularly falling for three or four years after that period, and the rates of duty consequently so high, that in some of these years the duty alone was greater than the market-price of the wheat: much of this wheat, therefore, which had cost the importer 50*s*. or 60*s*. per quarter, laid down in London, became actually worth less than nothing, as far as its application for English consumption was concerned; for not only was it chargeable with heavy granary-rent, &c., but the duty which must have been paid on its being introduced into consumption, was greater by far than the price which could have been obtained for it duty paid. Thus the average price of wheat in Great Britain, in 1835, was 39*s*. 4*d*., at which, according to the present laws, the duty is 47*s*. 8*d*.

"At this time much wheat was sold to pay the charges of rent, &c., incurred upon it, and many, wearied of holding any longer with so little prospect of relief, were desirous of getting quit of so ruinous a bargain; but it is quite clear, if they got anything for it at all, it could not be given in reference to British consumption, the duty being then higher than the whole price if cleared from bond. There could, at this time, be only two motives in buying such wheat:—first, as a speculation, to hold it an indefinite number of years, till a chance occurred of getting it into consumption at a low duty, which being very remote and doubtful would only be purchased at a *very* low price; or, secondly, for exportation to other countries requiring supplies, such as the West India islands, the Brazils, &c. If a merchant required a cargo of wheat for the latter purpose, it can be easily understood that he would first inquire in what market he could most profitably purchase it, as it would be a matter of indifference to him whether he shipped it from Dantzig or London.

"In the year 1835 the average price in Dantzig was 23*s*. per quarter, and in Sweden and Denmark, where the quality is worse, it was even below that price. It is therefore evident that no man would give above that price for the same article in London, when it would answer his object as well to buy it in Dantzig. I find, therefore, on inquiry and reference, that 23*s*. per quarter was a common price in 1835 for fine wheat in bond: and we can easily conceive that the holders here, whether compelled to sell by their circumstances, or willing to get rid of such a losing affair, would be glad to accept that price *in bond* when, for the purpose of introducing it for consumption, it was worth less than nothing. Yet this wheat had cost, when landed in 1831 or 1832, 50*s*. to 60*s*. per quarter, besides all the charges from that time, which would, in many instances, be more than the price obtained. I am told by many keepers of granaries that they have frequently sold grain, the price of which has not paid their charges. You will therefore see that the effect of the corn-laws renders the price of wheat in bond quite independent of its cost. I may just add, that a large portion of the wheat which was cleared for consumption in the autumn of last year had remained in the warehouses since 1831 and 1832, and that, if even double the high price of the time had been obtained, it would not have paid the original importers a profit. These circumstances constitute the corn-trade into the character of the most desperate gambling.

" With respect to the other objection to which you allude, viz., that, while I attribute the great fluctuations of prices in this country to the effects of our corn-laws, yet in many Continental countries, where there are no corn-laws, the fluctuations are as great, I believe will be most satisfactorily explained by the necessary influence which our laws exert over the whole of Europe. I admit, indeed, as a necessary consequence, that the fluctuations on the Continent must be much greater than even here. Thus, for example, in 1834, 1835, and the beginning of 1836, the prices of wheat were so low in this country as to hold out no hope, for many years, of any foreign supplies being admitted. The prices on the Continent were, therefore, only established in relation to their own consumption, with a larger supply than they naturally required, the production having been artificially stimulated by the demand for England two or three years before. In the end of 1836 some suspicion existed that, owing to the bad weather during harvest, we should require a foreign supply. This feeling caused a much greater advance in foreign wheat than British. If the market-price of British wheat rises 1*s*. per quarter, the price of foreign, with such a prospect, will rise 2*s*.; for, while the intrinsic value of the article rises 1*s*., the duty for its admission falls 1*s*., and makes the latter 2*s*. more valuable. Thus, if English wheat in London were worth 60*s*. per quarter, and foreign wheat at 40*s*., at which the duty would be 26*s*. 8*d*., if the former rises 1*s*., to 61*s*. per quarter, at which the duty would be only 25*s*. 8*d*., there is then on the foreign 1*s*. advance in intrinsic value, and, being then subject to 1*s*. less duty, would be equal to 42*s*. of a market value.

"As the price of foreign wheat advances in our market, orders are sent to the Continent to buy at comparatively high prices: it is therefore clear that, while we advance here, the prices on the Continent must be advancing at a double rate compared with British wheat, if it is expected that wheat will come in duty free. In the spring of 1837 it was discovered that, instead of any deficiency, the harvest of 1836 was the largest ever known: the prices of English wheat receded; but, for every 1*s*. it fell back, the price of foreign here, and consequently abroad, fell back much more.

"The average price of wheat in this country is about 52*s*. per quarter; during the last year it has been about 70*s*. to 72*s*. —say 40 per cent. above the average. The average price in many parts of the Continent is 30*s*. per quarter, where this year, owing to the high prices here, by which it is not only admitted free of duty, but also at the very time our prices are at the extreme point, the average prices have been about 50*s*. to 60*s*.—nearly 100 per cent higher.

"Our duties being high, when our prices are low, excludes the Continent from our market at that time, and depresses them to a most unnatural extent. But our duties being only nominal, when our prices are double the lowest point, gives them a full participation of these high rates. Thus when wheat is 39*s.* the duty 47*s.* 8*d.*, and freight, &c., about 18*s.*, no operation takes place with foreign wheat at all. The English price rises to 72*s.*; the duty is 1*s.*, freight, &c., 18*s.* or 19*s.*: if, therefore, wheat can be bought at 53*s.* per quarter on the Continent, it will then pay to import; whereas, if it had been got as a gift two years before, it would have been a serious loss, if introduced into English consumption. It is, therefore, evident that our own laws render the prices more fluctuating on the Continent than even here.

"It is not surprising, after considering these reasons, that the high prices of the present year are producing a much more baneful and serious effect on the general interests on the Continent than even in this country.

"Here the price of bread is 40 per cent. higher than our average; there, 80 to 100 per cent. higher: the calls, therefore, on the means of the Continental population to provide food, are found to be abridging their ability to consume manufactured goods and colonial produce at the present time even more than here; their trade is, therefore, languishing as much or more than ours from this cause. Hence the disturbances and distress in France, in Ghent, and many other places."

THE END.

London: Printed by W. Clowes and Sons, Duke-street, Stamford-street.

FLUCTUATIONS

OF

CURRENCY, COMMERCE,

AND

MANUFACTURES;

REFERABLE TO

THE CORN LAWS.

BY

JAMES WILSON, Esq.

LONDON:
PUBLISHED BY LONGMAN, ORME, BROWN, GREEN, AND LONGMANS.

1840.

James Wilson (1805–60)

Wilson's published works include:

Influences of the Corn Laws, as affecting all classes of the community, and particularly the landed interests, London: Longman, 1839.

Fluctuations of currency, commerce and manufactures referable to corn laws, London: Longman, 1840.

The revenue: or, what should the chancellor do?, London: Hooper, 1841.

The cause of the present commercial distress, and its bearings on the interests of ship-owners; a speech delivered by James Wilson ... at the free trade banquet, held in the Amphitheater, Liverpool, on Tuesday, 31st January, 1843, Liverpool: Anti Monopoly Association, 1843.

Capital, currency, and banking; being a collection of a series of articles published in the Economist in 1845, on the principles of the Bank act of 1844, and in 1847, on recent monetarial and commercial crisis; concluding with a plan for a secure and economical currency, London: The Office of the Economist, 1847. 2nd edition with an appendix, containing the weekly and monthly accounts of the Bank of England, and of the general circulation of the United Kingdom, since the passing of the acts of 1844 and 1845; also, extracts from the evidence taken before the late banking committee, bearing upon the points discussed, London: D. M. Aird, 1853.

Speech of the navigation laws, delivered on the 9th March, 1849, London: D. M. Aird, [1849].

Financial measures for India. Speech ... delivered before the Legislative Council of Calcutta on the 18th February, 1860, London: Wm. H. Allen, 1860.

March 3rd. Legislative Council, Calcutta. Speech on paper Currency for India (Corrected and revised), Calcutta: G. A. Savielle, 1860.

INTRODUCTION.

THE frequent recurrence of periods of excitement and depression in the monetarial and commercial interests of the country, and the serious evils which have thereby been inflicted on all classes of society, have become matters of the gravest interest.

In the numerous inquiries which have been made as to the cause thereof, with a view to remedial measures, attention has been directed almost exclusively to the operation and management of the currency and banking system of the country; so much so, that it appears to be almost implicitly admitted, that somewhere within the range of these subjects the true cause is to be found; and in consequence, the inquiry appears in a great measure to have been narrowed into a consideration of the principles upon which they are and ought to be conducted.

As yet, however, no satisfactory result has attended these inquiries, and the further they proceed, the more it appears that these influences are too much themselves under the control of the public feeling, and to be regarded as the cause of these constant fluctuations.

In the discussions which have recently taken place on the effects of the present Corn Laws, many circumstances have tended to associate their operations upon prices and the general condition of the country with these periodical derangements. We have long thought that they were most intimately connected, and that the influences produced on society by the fluctuating character of the price of the first necessaries of life have been sufficiently powerful in themselves to create derangements in all interests and classes of the greatest magnitude.

With a view to ascertain how far facts and circumstances, as to time and otherwise, agree with the strong conviction we entertained on this subject, the following investigation has been undertaken: and we trust that this attempt may lead others to a further inquiry on this important subject, as we are now more than ever convinced, both by principle and by facts, that the fluctuating character of the cost of the first and imperative necessaries of life is the chief cause of the whole derangements of the monetarial and commercial interests of this great country, which have been attended with so much *distress, disappointment,* and *ruin.*

London, March 20, 1840.

FLUCTUATIONS

OF

CURRENCY, COMMERCE,

AND

MANUFACTURES, ETC.

In the "Influences of the Corn Laws" our attention was confined to those exerted over the agricultural interests; not only because we consider that class particularly interested therein, but because the primary effects produced on them become the second causes which are productive of all the baneful consequences resulting from these laws to the remaining parts of society.

We then only glanced at some of the effects produced on the commerce, industry, and morals of the country, as far as they were intimately associated with the agricultural interests, and as far as they appeared necessary to illustrate the influences exerted over this class.

It is our intention now to direct our attention more exclusively to the influences which these laws ultimately exert over the currency, commerce, industry, and morals of this country, and of the continental countries. merely glancing as we go along at some of the retributive effects (if we may use the term) which these influences in their turn produce upon the agricultural interests.

We are the more induced to turn our attention to this part of the subject at this moment, from a conviction that the present derangement of national prosperity can be fairly traced to these influences as its exclusive cause.

In proceeding to this argument, we take it for granted that the considerations in the "Influences of the Corn Laws" have been carefully perused and understood; and more especially the most important feature of the whole matter, viz., the necessary tendency which these laws have of creating great fluctuations in the supply and price of the first necessaries of life.

PART I.

FLUCTUATIONS OF THE CURRENCY, &c.

It is not our intention to detain the reader by entering into any evidence of the rapid and extensive fluctuations which for some years have been continually taking place in this country in the amount of the *floating capital, disengaged money*, and *currency*, which from time to time have been available for carrying on and conducting the ordinary business and commerce of the country.

These facts are so generally known, and have excited so much of the public attention, that we shall content ourselves with merely referring the reader to the table at page 41, showing the amount of bullion and deposits possessed by the Bank of England by the returns from 1828 to the present time, as exhibiting an index of the proportions in which these fluctuations have taken place, as well as the periods.

The fluctuations shown in this table, however great, are less than those which have actually taken place, owing to the mode in which the Bank's returns are made; being made once in each month, of the average of the three preceding months. In the case of a diminishing amount, it is evident that at the moment when it is at the lowest point, that month has the advantage of being mingled with the two preceding months of larger amounts, and therefore showing a larger stock than is actually on hand; and so also in the case of an increasing stock, it is equally evident that at the moment when it is at the highest point, that month being averaged with the two preceding of smaller amounts, must show a smaller sum than is actually possessed. Thus the smallest and largest amounts of bullion in possession of the Bank is never shown; and thus the fluctuations are even greater than displayed by these returns.

This table furnishes only an index of the *proportions* in which these fluctuations have taken place, and has little or no reference to the *actual amount* of the fluctuations of available capital in the whole community.

We must disclaim any intention of entering into the general question of the currency, or of the constitution and management of the Bank of England, further than is necessary to elucidate the causes of these fluctuations, and to show what influence the Corn Laws can fairly be said to have exercised over them, or how far they can be proved to have been the chief causes thereof.

For some years past, during the exciting and ruinous changes which have taken place in the *money market*, as it is termed, men have eagerly sought for reasons and cures; but, as is too frequently the case, mistaking effect for cause, mere symptoms for the disease, the extent of that inquiry has seldom proceeded further than all agreeing in denouncing the

Bank of England and the caprice of its management (expanding and contracting the currency at pleasure) as the groundwork and base of all the mischief: nor is this a matter of surprise when we consider that these fluctuations and changes must first be made visible to the public eye by the policy of that establishment, however little control it can exercise over them.

There is no greater danger to society than arriving at and resting satisfied with an erroneous cause for an existing evil. In the first place, it is apt to preclude further investigation; and in the second place, a cure to such evils is difficult to effect, when opposed on untrue grounds: there are always some parties who are more or less interested in existing evils; and to them it is no difficult task to oppose arguments which have not as their base the strength and symmetry which truth alone can afford them: to this reason, we think, may be attributed the continued existence of many of the most glaring evils long after they have been almost universally acknowledged as such.

Whatever are the defects of the constitution of the Bank of England, and however inefficient that establishment may be for the supposed position which it holds as the head of the monetarial system and arrangements of the great commercial country, it is no difficult task to prove that the charge here brought against it *cannot* be true, that it must indeed be *too innocent* of any charge of exercising a control over the currency, and that, therefore, the general reasons assigned for the changes in the money market are equally erroneous.

The Bank of England is an establishment possessed of an enormous capital; but that capital is more than absorbed by loans to the Government, and therefore not available for the general purposes of business; but it communicates to it all the credit and security which could be afforded by the government; which, with a certain degree of publicity given to its actions, secures to it an extent of confidence greater than is enjoyed by an other such establishment in the world.

In respect of credit, therefore, while the Bank of England ranks highest, in respect of real available, independent means of conducting its usual business it must rank on the lowest scale of solvent establishments. It, therefore, necessarily follows, that when money is everywhere abundant and prosperity general, the resources of the Bank of England must be very great: at such times the surplus of every man throughout the country finds its way to his banker; a portion of the surplus of the bankers throughout the country finds its way to their agents in London for employment; and the surplus of these agents, as well as all the London bankers, finds its way to the coffers of the Bank of England, as the most accredited place of safety; and thus constitutes an index not of the wealth and capital of the Bank of England, but of the extent of surplus capital possessed at any given moment by the whole country: at this moment the Bank of England has no power to prevent money being cheap, as it is termed, because it is universally abundant; and being obliged to employ its deposits and circulation for the benefit of its proprietory (we speak of the Bank of

England as it is), it must do so at the rate established by the law of supply and demand, or leave all the business to be done by other establishments.

In like manner it follows as necessarily that when money is everywhere becoming scarce, the surplus balances of money must be everywhere diminishing; individuals throughout the country draw a larger portion from their bankers, who, in their turn, retain a smaller amount with their agents in London, and who, with all the London bankers, have less to employ in loans and discounts and smaller balances with the Bank of England. If, then, the cause which has rendered money scarce, has proceeded from a demand to send money abroad either to purchase some necessary such as corn, or to conduct some huge speculations into which the public has been tempted, or to carry on an expensive war, the unusual transfer of this capital from this to another country can only be accomplished by the means of bullion as having a common and well ascertained value everywhere: the Bank of England is, then, not only called upon to give up a large portion of her deposits, but also to redeem a portion of her notes for gold; and thus, without any independent resources of her own to fall back upon, she becomes the more seriously and dangerously affected by the pressing scarcity than any other solvent establishment in the country. The situation of the Bank of England is, then, not an index of any diminution of its own wealth or means, which remain as safely locked up as before, but of the general diminution of the floating money of the whole country available for trading purposes.

The Bank of England is now competent to conduct its transactions as before only in reference to supply and demand; and in the rates of interest to be governed by the general market value, having no control whatever over them at either period. If, at the former period of plenty, the Bank of England were to attempt to charge more than the market value, in order to make money scarce, the consequence would merely be that all the business would be done by other establishments; or if the Bank of England were to attempt to charge less at the latter period than the market rate, in order to make money abundant when it really was not so, two days would exhaust her reduced means; and in neither case would she be able to pay any dividends to her proprietors.

It must, however, be admitted that there are many circumstances connected with the movements of the Bank, which naturally give rise to the erroneous opinion that these movements are the causes which induce fluctuations. From the position which we have just explained the Bank to hold, it is evident that the directors of that establishment must be the first to notice, by their own internal index, any movement which is going on either to render money scarce or abundant; they must be the first to observe either the efflux or influx of bullion; they must first feel either an increasing or decreasing demand for money. And from their own dependent state on these events, requiring always the greatest watchfulness to look before them for their own safety and protection, or profit, they are forced into a line of policy, the reasons for which are not visible to the public eye at the moment, and which, as they afterwards become developed, are often mistaken as the effects instead of the inducing causes of the policy of the Bank.

These are the simple facts which must ever influence this establishment as at present constituted. however different circumstances, political and civil, are continually occurring to render them intricate and difficult to understand, however a season of prosperity gives rise to speculation and excitement, and however a season of alarm and scarcity creates fears and distrust, which alike aggravate the natural consequences of such occurrences.

It must, therefore, appear clear that the conduct of the Bank of England as connected with the fluctuations complained of has been merely part of the *effects* and *symptoms*, not the *cause* of the disease—that it is utterly innocent of causing these changes, and as utterly weak and powerless to control them. It would be far different if it traded upon its own real substantial capital, instead of only upon a credit, however good, or privileges, however valuable, purchased at the cost of locking up that real strength.

We must look to some wider and more extensive first cause for these fluctuations and changes in the condition of a nation the most uniformly industrious, persevering, and enterprising that has ever existed, and we believe that we shall find some more satisfactory result in attributing them to the huge fluctuations in the amount of its means which, from time to time, have been required to pay for the necessary subsistence of life; or, in other words, to the fluctuations of the price of food, which we have shown in a former work to be the necessary consequence of a restriction of the supply of that first great necessary.

It may be here useful to examine what is the amount of the national income which is on an average absorbed in the price of wheat; fluctuations being much more apparent in this than in any other of the great necessaries of existence, we shall confine our attention to it, merely inferring from the result, the aggravation of the consequences shown, if the consideration had extended over every article. The nearest estimate of the annual production of wheat which we have been able to arrive at is as follows. It is estimated that there are, in average years, in the united kingdom five millions of acres cultivated with wheat, producing on an average three quarters and a half per acre. The following will, therefore, be the annual cost of wheat to the country:—

5,000,000 acres, 3½ quarters per acre, will give 17,500,000 quarters; from which deduct 1,500,000 quarters for seed, &c.; will leave 16,000,000 quarters to be consumed by the country, which, at the average price of the last seven years, 52*s*. per quarter, will amount to the annual sum of £41,600,000.

It thus appears that the annual average value of the wheat consumed in this country is £41,600,000. In the absence of any accurate and authenticated statistical accounts, this apparently enormous sum is the nearest we can arrive at; and although it may not be perfectly accurate, it is sufficiently so to elucidate our theory and argument.

This amount, then, we say, is absorbed annually from the national income to pay for this first great necessary, calculating the price at the average prices of the last seven years, which, including high and low, may be taken as a fair average price over a longer space. It will, however, be sufficiently evident, that in proportion as the price rises above or falls below the given average, that the amount of the national income and wealth which is then thereby absorbed in this great first necessary, must increase or diminish accordingly, and thus altering in the same proportion the amount left for all other purposes.

Thus, in the event of a number of cheap years following each other, when prices are below the average rate, the diminished amount of money absorbed in this way, accumulating year after year, cannot fail to give to the community a very greatly increased command of wealth, and to render more abundant the means of employing it in all other ways; and that, on the contrary, when a number of years occur when prices are above these average rates, the increased amount of money absorbed in this way, year after year, cannot fail to diminish the general amount of wealth, to be employed for other purposes.

It may here be remarked, that the facility with which money is removed from one country to another by investments in public securities, altogether independent of commerce, and that the periods of low prices and high prices, above referred to, having occurred simultaneously throughout Europe, has tended materially to aggravate the effects of the greater amount of capital let loose in the former, and absorbed in the latter periods. Another serious aggravation of these changes in this country has arisen from the fact that, in dear years, not only is the sum absorbed much above the average, but a large amount is sent out of the country in the shape of bullion to purchase supplies abroad; while in cheap years, not only is the sum thus absorbed much less, but the country is in such years deprived of nothing for foreign purchases. In order to show the great fluctuations in the amount of money absorbed in the article of wheat alone, we present the following table, showing the sum in each year which must have been paid for wheat at the average price of the year, calculating the consumption at 16,000,000 quarters, which, whether correct or not, displays with equal truth the proportion of these fluctuations:—also showing the amount in each year paid for foreign wheat; which will be found to be important in the dear years, when we could least afford it, and most trivial in the cheap years, when the redundancy of means could best afford it.

Years.	Quantity consumed.	Average price.	Total amount of Cost.	Quantity of Foreign Wheat taken into Consumption.	Cost of Foreign Wheat at 15s. per Qr less than British Average.
	Quarters.		£	*Quarters.*	£
1817	16,000,000	94/0	75,200,000	1,020,949	4,032,748
1818	,,	83/8	66,933,333	1,593,518	5,471,018
1819	,,	72/3	57,800,000	122,133	349,605
1820	,,	65/10	52,666,666	34,274	87,113
1821	,	54/5	43,450,000	2	5
1822	,,	43/3	33,600,000	. . . .	. . . .
1823	,,	51/9	41,400,000	12,137	22,301
1824	,,	62/0	49,600,000	15,777	31,075
1825	,,	66/6	53,200,000	525,231	1,352,469
1826	,,	56/11	45,533,333	315,892	662,056
1827	,,	56/9	45,400,000	572,733	1,195,580
1828	,,	60/5	48,250,000	842,052	1,912,159
1829	,,	66/3	53,000,000	1,364,220	3,495,813
1830	,,	64/3	51,400,000	1,701,885	4,190,891
1831	,,	66/4	53,066,666	1,491,631	3,828,519
1832	,,	58/8	46,916,666	325,435	710,533
1833	,,	52/11	42,316,666	82,346	156,114
1834	,,	46/2	36,933,333	64,653	101,750
1835	,,	39/4	31,400,000	28,183	34,654
1836	,,	48/6	38,800,000	30,554	51,177
1837	,,	55/10	44,666,666	244,619	499,430
1838	,,	64/7	51,666,666	1,853,048	1,594,014
1839	,,	70/8	56,533,333	2,700,131	7,515,864*

* It is necessary to remark, with respect to this table, that the quantity of sixteen millions of quarters, being taken as the annual consumption, in the absence of any statistical information that can be relied upon, is the nearest approximation to the truth to which we can arrive, as the average consumption of the last few years:—but there is not the slightest doubt that it exceeds the real quantity consumed in the early period embraced in the table, and perhaps falls short of the quantity consumed in the last three

The facts which are brought to view in this table demand the most minute attention and the gravest consideration. We find the entire cost of the wheat consumed in this country representing in one year. 1817, upwards of seventy-five millions of pounds sterling:—with a payment for foreign-grown wheat, in the same year, of four millions sterling, gradually falling, for five years, to thirty-three million pounds sterling in 1822, without any expenditure for foreign wheat; then again gradually advancing until, in 1829, fifty-

or four years; but still it serves the purpose of comparing the fluctuations of the amount of national means absorbed in this article, better than if we had been able to ascertain the actual quantities consumed in each year, and calculated accordingly: for although the whole quantity annually consumed has gradually increased during that time with the increase of population, yet it is assumed that the consumption of wheat, the first necessary of life, not an article of fashion, luxury, or caprice, has always borne the same relative proportion to the population and its means:—and that, therefore, the fluctuations in the total annual price of it, whether the consumption were larger or smaller, but still bearing the same proportion to the wealth of the community, would have the same influence in increasing or diminishing proportionably the general wealth of the country available for other purposes. As has been already remarked, the fluctuations in the price of wheat having been simultaneous in every part of Europe with those in England, it becomes a difficult task to compute the stupendous amount of capital let loose at one period, and absorbed at another, in this article alone. In France, where *bread* forms so large a portion of the diet, and the population is one-third greater than in this kingdom, it would appear a moderate estimate to state the capital thus fluctuating at the same amount as in this country: in other parts of Europe the fluctuations of price have been as great as in this country, but the consumption of wheat-bread is comparatively three millions sterling is the entire cost, with a sum of nearly three millions and a half paid for foreign-grown wheat; then declining gradually until, in 1835, thirty-one millions is the whole cost, with the insignificant sum of thirty-four thousand pounds paid for wheat of foreign growth; and, lastly, gradually advancing until, in 1839, the entire cost to the community for wheat is fifty-six millions and a half sterling, with no less a sum than seven millions and a half paid to foreign growers, chiefly in bullion. These extreme points will stand thus:—(*See next page.*)

---

limited. The following table will show the uniformity, in regard to time, which has prevailed in different parts of Europe, in the changes of price:—

Years.	Average price in Great Britain.	Average price in France.	Average price in Danzig.
1817	94/0	....	75/8
1818	83/8	....	64/7
1819	72/3	34/1	43/9
1820	65/10	45/7	33/3
1821	54/5	31/3	31/7
1822	43/3	36/9	29/1
1823	51/9	35/10	26/8
1824	62/0	34/4	22/9
1825	66/6	35/6	23/3
1826	56/11	36/5	23/1
1827	56/9	49/7	22/5
1828	60/5	52/6	24/4
1829	66/3	48/2	36/10
1830	64/3	51/0	34/3
1831	66/4	50/10	37/3
1832	55/8	41/3	37/7
1833	52/11	34/1	29/4
1834	46/2	35/9	25/5
1835	39/4	33/8	23/0
1836	48/6	39/8	28/7
1837	55/10	41/0	29/0
1838	64/7	51/6	45/0
1839	70/8	....	....

	Whole cost of Wheat.	Cost of Foreign Wheat consumed.
1817 . .	£75,200,000 . .	£4,032,748
1822 . .	33,600,000 . .	nothing.
1829 . .	53,000,000 . .	3,495,813
1835 . .	31,400,000 . .	34,654
1839 . .	56,533,333 . .	7,515,864

It is impossible to look at these facts—to consider that the sum absorbed in the consumption of wheat alone, in this country only, has been more than twenty-one millions of pounds sterling greater, during the last year, than it was only four years ago; that in France the increase must be in the same proportion; that independent of this additional absorption for our own purposes that upwards of seven millions of it has actually gone out of the country for the purchase of foreign wheat, while, in the former year, only about thirty-four thousand pounds was required on this account:—it is impossible, we say, to have these facts placed before our eyes without feeling at once the strongest conviction that they are sufficient to produce enormous fluctuations in the currency, in the wealth and prosperity of the country.

It shall now be our task to endeavour to trace the influences exerted by such striking causes, to endeavour to discover, by fair and close investigation, how far the facts which have occurred, during the last few years, agree with and corroborate the conviction which has been produced by the simple details before us; and if, in the course of this investigation, we may have occasion to allude to the policy pursued by any of the different classes of banking establishments, it shall only be, as far as is necessary, for elucidating our principles; as we again disclaim any intention, in our present inquiry, to mingle with it the general question of currency or banking, as they exist or have existed.

We have already intimated that it is not to high prices or to low prices that we attribute the evils complained of; but to a constant and incessant changeableness; to periodical fluctuations; to a series of years of great cheapness, followed by years of very high prices. There is no more striking truth in political, mercantile, and social existence than there is in human nature a strong tendency to adaptation; to conform every arrangement and plan, as well for the present as the future, in reference to existing circumstances; to enact laws, to enter into engagements, and to contract habits consonant with the wants and the means of the present: for, however the mind may indulge in the retrospective, or delight in speculative views of the future, it is the *present* only which has sufficient substantiality and form to constitute the great cause of all our actions. If, then, that *present* has no endurance; if great and important changes are ever going forward, it follows that there is no security in the most prudent calculations for the future; that circumstances, over which persons have no control, may interfere with engagements and habits contracted with the most justifiable reasons; and thus, by constant fluctuations, *security in the future*, the greatest moral tie which Providence has pleased to link to the human constitution, is materially weakened.

From these remarks it will naturally follow, that we regard the seasons of extreme low prices as productive of as much mischief, of being accessory to as great an amount of evil, as we do the seasons of extreme high prices: the two are naturally and necessarily linked together as cause and effect; and although distress and disappointment are more apparent in the latter than the former period, yet it remains to be seen how far the former period has been accessory to the necessary cause of the great evils experienced in the latter period; and if the causes of the mischief are equally identified in the two periods, they must equally share the blame.

It may be imagined by many who have not well considered the subject, that as far as the fluctuations which we have shown to exist in the amount of money absorbed in payment of the necessaries of life are of an internal nature; that is, as far as the additional amount paid by the community in a series of years goes only from one portion of the community to another; from the general consumers to the agriculturists, that there should be little or no interruption of national prosperity—that there should be little or no derangement of the currency: this point deserves and will obtain our close attention as we go forward with the investigation in this and the following propositions. Every person, however, easily understands that inasmuch as these fluctuations have called for only £34,654 in one year, and for £7,515,864 * in another

* Although the sum of £7,515,864 is put down as paid for

year, only four years apart, to be remitted to foreign countries for our consumption of bread, great and important evils must ensue.

In order to go into the investigation proposed, it is obvious that we must discover, that we must condescend to some given sum which, could it be maintained steadily, would be the correct amount of the means of the country absorbed for this particular purpose annually, namely, for the purchase of wheat; in order that we may determine what the fluctuations really have been; how much too cheaply the community have been served at one time, and how much too dearly at another time. Now we know of no principle so accurate to determine this point, and, at all events, it is sufficient for a fair and full consideration of our case, as to take the actual average price which has been obtained in a currency of years amidst all these oscillations and fluctuations. Relying as we do upon the excitement being in exact proportion to the depression, and the depression, in its turn, being in exact proportion to the excitement; to the vibration of the pendulum being to the left in the same proportion that it was to the right, and on the right that it obtained on the left, we take the average price of the whole period as a fair and just point from which

---

foreign wheat in 1839, yet from Oct. 10, 1838, to Oct. 10, 1839, one year, the sum of £12,126,369 was paid: this large amount, crowded into the short space of twelve months, and not as it appears diffused over two years, is an important feature in reference to the effects produced on the currency.

to date all our calculations in elucidation of the principles we advocate.

It has already, in a former work, been shown that the average price of seven years, from 1832 to 1839, was 52*s*. 2*d*. per quarter for wheat, and that price is, therefore, without hesitation, taken as a fair average on which to ground our calculations.

At this rate the average amount of the national means absorbed in wheat will be £41,600,000 sterling, and, therefore, as the actual sum paid in each year differs from this, either in excess or diminution, must we regard it as a fluctuation of the general wealth or means of the community, whether the difference may be felt in the increased or diminished amount of deposits in bankers hands, the increased or diminished demand for manufactured goods or other luxuries, or in any other way.

By way of illustrating these principles, we would claim especial attention to the occurrences since the year 1831, in relation to the points under consideration.

On referring to the table, page 13, it will be seen that 1828, 1829, 1830, and 1831, were years of very high prices of wheat, in which large importations took place, at an enormous cost to the country: during these four years, it must be obvious that the means of the country must have been absorbed to a great extent as compared with previous years; and there is no difficulty in reconciling, with such state of matters, the great scarcity of money which was felt during these years, the contraction of circulation especially felt in 1829, and the languishing condition of the general pursuits of industry and commerce at this period.

It may be imagined that as far as the excess of national income paid in these years went chiefly to enrich the agriculturist, no derangement of the currency, of the means of conducting the great commercial operations of the country, should have been experienced, as the amount only passed from one part of the community to another, from one kind of industry to another; this notion, however, is false; and we will show that this excess, as well as the three to four millions sterling annually transmitted to the continent during these years, could not fail to impair the general active capital of the country. At the commencement of this period there was a given distribution of the entire capital of the country; so much in mercantile operations—so much in manufacturing establishments—so much in government securities—so much in agricultural property and industry, &c., &c.; and, for the sake of illustration, let us suppose that the capital thus sunk in these various ways bore the exactly proper proportion to each other to supply the wants of the community—that all at once an unusual proportion of the income of the country begins to flow into the agricultural interests, in consequence of very high prices. What follows?—some one or all of the other public interests must suffer an abstraction of their previous share of the annual expenditure in the like proportion; the demand for their products must become more limited, and their ability of production too great for the wants of the country; and as far as this ability is in excess does it show a portion of the general capital unprofitably and idly invested – in fact, so much abstraction from the national wealth while it remains unemployed. Well, but how is the currency affected?—if there is, in reality, nearly the same amount of annual income—if all the excess of expenditure which flowed into the agricultural interest remained in circulation, the currency would not be much curtailed, although it would experience a different distribution. But what is the fact?—high prices and high profits in every pursuit stimulate extended production, and we consequently find that the excess of the nation's income, which in the three years went into the agricultural interest, was invested in improved and extended cultivation; and thus went to increase the entire amount of the whole capital stock embarked in this industry, while it diminished, as has already been explained, the value of the capital stock previously invested in other interests; inasmuch as it absorbed, for the creation of its new capital stock, the portion of the national income which alone gave the previous existing value to all the other invested capitals.

During the four years at present under review, it is evident, from these principles, that the amount of capital employed both in extending and improving the cultivation of the land must have been materially increased, and that in nearly the same proportion must have been the tendency of the currency to diminish, but for the following reason. The increased absorption of national income in agricultural produce had two obvious tendencies; first, to reduce the demand for the produce of all other capital and industry, and consequently the profits; and, secondly, to diminish the amount of the circulation, or money, by increasing the amount of its fixed capital stock, and thus to cause a rise in the rate of interest at the moment of the greatest depression of commerce. A higher rate of interest, and a greater reduction of profits would then, no doubt, have a tendency, in the course of time, to cause an abstraction of capital from such pursuits, where an abstraction was practicable, to fill up the blank created in the currency. But such abstraction is only practicable to a certain extent, while in many of the chief objects of investment it is quite impracticable; for example, in the capital represented by manufactories, machines, mines, ships, &c., &c., which must all at such periods assume a deteriorated value. The floating capital, or currency, of the whole country must, under such circumstances, have very materially diminished; or, in other words, at this period our means must have become very much contracted for commercial enterprise, and the value of property must have assumed a very reduced rate. Let any one ask himself what was the fact, and how far our theory agrees with it?

But four years is a period sufficiently long for a community in a considerable degree to adapt itself to existing circumstances, however they might have changed for the worse; and, having suffered a great diminution of its capital, to turn to the best account what still remained. But let us now narrowly watch what occurred, and how these occurrences (the natural offspring of cause and effect, and therefore not peculiar to this period, but alike applicable to every recurrence of similar causes) acted on the currency. At this time, when it might have been expected that much of the evil of such a change of national wealth had passed away, by the aptness of adaptation to circumstances, it proved that we were on the eve of an era, of greater and more sudden expansion of available floating capital than we had for the four previous years suffered its contraction.

The immense increase of fixed capital which had become absorbed by the agricultural interest had stimulated production so much, that in 1832 the amount of national income absorbed in the price of wheat was reduced upwards of six millions sterling, as compared with 1831; and instead of nearly four millions being sent abroad for this article in the latter year, only seven hundred thousand pounds were required in the former.

Such an amount of the national income (accompanied by such a diminution of the export of our means for this purpose) becoming available for all other purposes, could not fail to give a fuller currency, part of which would remain available as currency, and part would be absorbed in the products of other industrial pursuits, which, in their turn, would give a stimulus to industry and credit, and ultimately to a further extension of the currency.

It appears here necessary to show why the reaction in the price of wheat, and a lesser amount of income thereby absorbed and thrown into other industry, acts differently on the currency than when a larger portion of income is taken from other pursuits and thrown into the price of wheat.

Wheat is the *first* necessary of life, and, whatever may be its price. differs less than any other article in the quantity consumed. The variations in price. therefore, may be considered only owing to the variations in quantity produced, and not in any material variation in consumption. We always consider that wheat has the first and imperative claim on our income, to which all other productions must yield; it is, therefore, a scarcity of wheat which *drags* capital from all other uses, and an abundance which again gives it back: therefore, when capital is flowing into the agricultural interest in a greater than average proportion, it is owing to great scarcity, and an absorption immediately takes place to stimulate a larger production, and the currency is thereby contracted; whereas, when capital is again flowing back by a reaction in the price of wheat, it is caused by a redundant supply of that article, and not by a too limited supply of the results of other industrious pursuits: they only ultimately become stimulated by the expanded currency which is thus effected, and a consequent greater ability to consume their products on the part of the community; but the first influence is to enlarge the currency or available capital of the country.

We may consider 1832 as the beginning of a new era—as the change in the tide when the excess of capital which had, under an artificial stimulus of high prices and a legal promise of their continuance, began to flow back into all the channels from which it had been absorbed. It is not here our place to inquire how much was actually wasted in the operation; we will confine our attention to its necessary influence on the currency, or floating available capital of the country. As we have already remarked, upwards of six millions sterling was required less of the national expenditure this year than the previous to pay for the consumption of bread alone; and more than three millions sterling, which had been the year before sent abroad for wheat, was retained at home; so great a difference could not fail sensibly to affect the amount of surplus money at the end of that year, and to render that commodity more abundant.

The same causes still acting, the following year, 1833, another reduction took place of more than four millions and a half sterling in the total cost of bread, with another reduction of more than half a million sterling in the sum remitted for foreign supplies: towards the close of this year we consequently find that the currency became very full—money very abundant; for as yet commerce had not shown sufficient symptoms of recovery to induce an extension of operations equal to the disengaged capital. In the following year, 1834, we find another reduction of nearly five millions and a half sterling; and again, in 1835, another reduction of upwards of five millions and a half sterling took place in the cost price of this one first necessary of life. Thus we find that in the short space of four years the portion of the national expenditure absorbed in this way was reduced from fifty-three million pounds sterling, with an import at the cost of three millions eight hundred thousand pounds sterling, in 1831, to thirty-one millions four hundred thousand pounds sterling, with an import at the cost of only thirty-four thousand pounds, in 1835; making a difference of upwards of twenty-one millions of pounds sterling in the cost of wheat in these two years. But the following table will show still more the accumulated effects of the two different periods of years, viz., the four years from 1828 to 1831 both inclusive, and the four succeeding years:—

Years.	Total Cost of Wheat.	Total Cost of Foreign Wheat.	Years	Total Cost of Wheat.	Total Cost of Foreign Wheat.
	£	£		£	£
1828	48,250,000	1,912,154	1832	46,916,666	710,533
1829	53,000,000	3,495,813	1833	42,316,666	156,114
1830	51,400,000	4,190,891	1834	36,933,333	101,750
1831	53,066,666	3,828,519	1835	31,400,000	34,654
Total, 4 years	205,716,666	13,427,377		157,566,655	1,003,326
			difference	48,150,001	12,424,326
				205,716,666	13,427,652

This table shows that during the first four years the huge sum of forty-eight millions sterling was paid for wheat more than in the same period next succeeding; and in the former period twelve millions sterling was paid for the foreign wheat which was taken into consumption more than in the latter years. It will be seen, by a further examination as we go along, that the sum paid in the latter period was as much too little as that in the former period was too much: judging by what should be the annual sum spent according to the average of a number of years, by which the different interests have been sustained amidst all these changes. Can it. then, be a matter of surprise that extraordinary changes and fluctuations were visible in the currency with such facts before us—that the increasing abundance of money which every year was experienced from 1832 to 1835 should have given rise to all manners of speculations, many of which tended only still more to increase the already surcharged currency, especially the establishment of joint-stock banks, one of the favourite schemes of the times, all eager in the pursuit of business? But it is evident that this state of the currency had in itself the principles of its own cure. The abundance of money reduced its value so much, with a growing eagerness to invest, that not only were all the usual channels of absorption and occupation greatly expanded—not only were new and extensive internal improvements undertaken, especially in railways—but speculators in foreign countries. particularly in America, attracted by the facility of obtaining loans in this country at a low rate of interest. were induced to embark in the wildest undertakings. In short, at home and abroad, the plethora of money in this country, at the period we now speak of, produced a spirit of speculation, in every possible way so formidable in its extent and ramifications, that by the middle of 1836 there were symptoms of a reaction, by an unfavourable turn in the foreign exchanges, a decrease of bullion, and a growing scarcity of money, which ended in the *panic* of the autumn and winter of that year. The derangement which then occurred in the currency can be regarded in no other light than the mere reaction of the unnatural abundance of money and credit which had existed for the two or three previous years, and the necessary consequences arising therefrom. We term it an unnatural abundance, because it was created by a price of wheat, which could not possibly be sustained as it was below the cost of production. The influences of this panic were chiefly felt, as was to be expected, by the highest monetarial interests; the channels through which foreign loans had been negotiated; by those who bore the enormous responsibilities arising out of the overheated and excited engagements called into existence between this country and America; by the great abundance and cheapness of money here, and by the spirit of speculation which was fostered in that country by the facilities afforded in raising money on their securities in this market.

At this period it was evident that a great part of the rapidly accumulating surplus capital of the few previous years had been absorbed by the extension of private enterprise, by the huge number of public undertakings at home, and by investments in foreign securities: and that thus the actual available currency of the country had become much contracted. We find, however, that a few months' caution and quietude gradually restored confidence; the price of wheat and other provisions was still comparatively low in 1836 and 1837; and by the end of the latter year, a sufficient abundance of money, for all useful purposes, was found to be in circulation; we were then, as nearly as possible, the proper medium condition of relative prices and expenditure, which the experience of a number of years has shown to be the correct average price at which the different interests of this great community could be sustained in these different postures and advantages which on an average of years they have enjoyed.

We consequently find that from the autumn of 1837 to that of 1838 every circumstance indicated a stationary, but healthy condition of the currency, whether we regard the character of the business of that year—the absence of all speculation—of any depression or complaints from the numerous interests of the community—of the uniformity of the amount of bullion held by the Bank of England: all concur in giving the strongest evidence that the currency was more equally proportioned to all the wants of the community than had been experienced for many years.

But just at this moment we discover that the apparent calm and healthy equanimity which was then enjoyed was only leading to another great, but natural and imperative reaction. We have seen that from 1833 up to 1837 capital to an enormous amount had annually been flowing from the agricultural interests; and, while it left that interest, year after year, more and more weakened and impoverished, had, by its unnatural abundance in other channels, produced much evil. The advance of the price of wheat in 1837, although only to what may be deemed the correct average, showed that the low prices of previous years had produced an effect on the productive powers of the land; and the harvest of 1838 being not only backward, but deficient, found us with an exhausted stock of the first great necessary of life.

This is a moment which demands the most attentive consideration. In the whole range of society there was not one evidence of a disturbing cause to the currency; a year more void of speculation never expired; a year of more healthy and legitimate business was never enjoyed, when all the industrial classes, of whatever denomination, had a full and satisfactory share of prosperity; or when the monetarial engines of commerce maintained so much equality and uniformity of action: a year in which nothing disturbed our prospects of peace abroad; in which the uniform and prosperous condition of the working classes gave the greatest guarantee for contentment and quiet at home.

But, notwithstanding all these securities, we find that we are once more on the eve of a great convulsion of the currency. As the harvest of 1838 approached, its lateness and supposed deficiency began to excite some alarms; the diminished stock of wheat caused prices to advance rapidly; and the exhausting influence of the prices of 1834, 1835, and 1836, on the productive ability of the soil was now seen as the inevitable consequence of prices having been pressed below the cost of production. In the end of 1837 and the early part of 1838 the average price of wheat was maintained about 52*s*. (the actual average price of a number of years); towards the autumn of 1838 it rose until it reached in August 75*s*., and, with some fluctuations, ranged nearly that rate until the middle of last year.

It therefore follows that, calculating the national consumption at sixteen millions of quarters annually, or upwards of three hundred thousand quarters weekly, that, in the autumn of 1838, we commenced an absorption of the national income of more than 300,000*l* weekly, in addition to the fair average price of wheat: and, as compared with the expenditure of 1835, the additional weekly sum now required to pay for wheat, was upwards of 450,000*l*., or nearly half a million sterling.

This cause, sufficient as it may appear to account for any amount of derangement in the currency—the abstraction of 300,000*l*. weekly from the channels in which, by all the existing arrangements of society and commerce, it was at this moment finding useful and convenient employment—was accompanied by the usual attendants on high prices, a large foreign importation.

For some years a most trivial portion of the resources of the country had been abstracted for the purpose of importing wheat, and therefore, by the universal law of adaptation to circumstances, no arrangement whatever existed by which any money could be spared, or our labour exchanged, for the growth of other countries: but bread is an article of overruling necessity, to the possession of which every other consideration, whether mercantile or political, must give way.

In the three last months of 1838, in addition to the enormous advance of the price of provisions; in addition to the abstraction of upwards of 300,000*l.* weekly from the accustomed channels of convenient occupation; our currency had to suffer an abstraction of more than five millions sterling, for the payment of 1,812,294 quarters of foreign wheat, introduced into consumption from the 10th of October till the 5th of January inclusive. Nor did it stop here: even this enormous sum made no visible impression in filling up the deficiency, we shall not say of one bad harvest, but of a number of successive insufficient harvests, as shown by the almost exhausted stock before the harvest of 1838. At the commencement of last year, prices still went on increasing until they reached an average of 80*s.* per quarter; the weekly absorption of capital became greater and greater; the importation of foreign supplies continued, until the whole quantity of foreign wheat introduced into consumption, from the 10th of October, 1838, to the 10th of October, 1839, inclusive, amounted to 4,355,778 quarters, at a cost of more than twelve millions sterling.

Now admitting, as we always do in these views, that about 52*s*. per quarter is the fair average price at which all interests in this country have been sustained, and that the average of this period was about 20*s*. higher, it follows that not only have sixteen millions sterling of the national income, during this year, been paid and consumed in bread, more than the average, and thus abstracted from other employment, but that *three-fourths* of this excess of price has actually been paid for wheat, the produce of other countries, and abstracted, for reasons we have already considered, from the available currency of the country. We only compare this with what should be an average; but, in order to show again the great extent of fluctuations in our available current means, to which these charges subject us, let us put the three last years in comparison with the three preceding years :—

Years.	Total cost of Wheat.	Total cost of Foreign Wheat.	Years.	Total cost of Wheat.	Total cost of Foreign Wheat.
	£.	£.		£.	£.
1834	36,933,333	101,750	1837	44,666,666	499,430
1835	31,400,000	34,654	1838	51,666,666	4,594,014
1836	38,800,000	51,177	1839	56,533,333	7,515,864
	107,133,333	187,581		152,866,665	12,609,308
			More paid in this period	45,733,332	12,421,721
				107,133,333	187,681

This table shows that, during the last three years, we have nationally spent in wheat 45,733,332*l*. more than in the three preceding years, and paid the sum of

12,421,727*l*. more in the latter than the former period for foreign wheat.

In order to place the operation of these principles, during the last two years, more clearly before the reader, we submit to his attention the following Table, showing the quantity of wheat which entered into consumption in each month in 1838 and 1839; the general average price at which the same was cleared; the cost in sterling money of each such monthly clearance, calculated at 15*s*. per quarter less than the general average of the time; and the amount of bullion and deposits, as shown by the Bank returns in each month during that period. (*See next page.*)

	Wheat and Wheat-flour cleared for consumption.	General average price.	Cost of Foreign Wheat taken into consumption.—At 15*s*. less than the average.			Bullion held by the Bank of England.	Deposits in the Bank of England.
1838.	*Quarters.*		£.		1838.	£.	£.
Jan. 5	1,619	53/0	3,076		Jan. 11	8,895,000	10,992,000
Feb. 5	1,569	53/3	3,000		Feb. 8	9,543,000	11,266,000
Mar. 5	759	54/11	1,514		Mar. 8	10,015,000	11,535,000
April 5	1.081	56/4	2,234		April 5	10,126,000	11,262,000
May 5	1,914	58/3	4,139		May 4	10,002,000	11,006,000
June 5	2,939	61/3	6,796		June 1	9,806,000	10,786,000
July 5	851	61/7	2,109		„ 29	9,722,000	10,426,000
Aug. 5	9,584	67/8	25,237		July 26	9,749,000	10,424,000
Sept. 5	14,891	68/0	39,461		Aug. 24	9,746,000	10,298,000
Oct. 5	*1,514,046	72/11	4,384,424		Sept. 21	9,615,000	10,042,000
Nov. 5	12,537	65/10	31,864		Oct. 19	9,437,000	9,327,000
Dec. 5	7,295	71/6	20,603		Dec. 13	9,362,000	9,033,000
1839							
Jan. 5	278,416	76/1	850,328		Jan. 10	9,336,000	10,315,000
Feb. 5	168,130	79/7	542,924		Feb. 7	8,919,000	10,269,000
Mar. 5	234,183	74/5	695,718		Mar. 7	8,106,000	9,950,000
April 5	517,848	72/1	1,478,024		April 5	7,073,000	8,998,000
May 5	188,191	70/1	518,309		May 2	6,023,000	8,107,000
June 5	153,777	71/1	431,216	Total 8,685,779*l*.	„ 30	5,119,000	7,814,000
July 5	504,536	71/4	1,421,109		July 1	4,344,000	7,567,000
Aug. 5	23,821	70/0	65,507		„ 25	3,758,000	7,955,000
Sept. 5	4,242	71/6	12,483		Aug. 22	3,265,000	8,029,000
Oct. 5	811,679	71/9	2,303,139		Sept. 19	2.816,000	7,781,000
Nov. 5	123,160	67/2	321,242		Oct. 18	2,522,000	6,734,000
Dec. 5	17,468	67/5	45.780		Dec. 12	2,887,000	5,952,000

This table deserves close examination, and affords a most instructive illustration of the action of the theory and principles of which we are treating.

* Of this 630,000 quarters had been imported, and paid for in former years, before 1838, leaving 884,046 quarters of this quantity of the import of that year.

It will be seen that during the first half of 1838 the prices of wheat were moderate and tolerably steady (although gradually advancing), and that a most trivial quantity was cleared for consumption. From this time until September prices advanced so rapidly that, early in that month, the averages had risen so that wheat was admitted at the lowest duty, at which time more than one million and a half of quarters were cleared for consumption. During the whole of this year (1838), the bullion and deposits, and especially the former, display a very uniform condition; and the large clearance of foreign wheat, which took place during September, appears to have had little influence on them.

This fact may be satisfactorily explained in the following manner:—Of the quantity cleared up to this period, 630,000 quarters had been imported, and the payment therefore provided for in former years; a further quantity of 869,245 quarters had been imported during the six weeks preceding this large clearance; of this a considerable portion was held in continental ports on English account of former purchases, and therefore not to be then provided for; and a further large portion of this quantity was imported from near ports during the month of September, when the low duty became a matter of certainty (the quantity imported in this month amounted to 533,771 quarters); and as the practice is for the shipper to draw upon the importer at three months, the payment for such new purchases would not become due until the close of the year, or the beginning of the year

1839; accordingly towards the close of the year we remark a gradual though not extensive diminution of bullion.

During the two months succeeding the 10th of October, the clearances and imports were alike trifling, and it is not until the month ending January 5th, 1839, that we find an important quantity imported or cleared, and from this time forward, until the 5th of November, the quantities imported and cleared for consumption continued unprecedentedly large. The greatest part of old purchases, held on British account, as well in this country as abroad, having been now exhausted, the transactions of the following periods show their full natural action on the currency and the floating capital of the country.

We accordingly find, that month after month displays a rapid diminution both in the bullion and deposits of the Bank during the whole of this period; the former falling from 9,336,000*l*., on the 10th of January, to 2,522,000*l*. on the 18th of October; and the latter falling from 10,315,000, on 10th of January, to 5,952,000*l*. on the 12th of December.

Adding together our estimated amounts of the cost of the wheat cleared from the 5th of December, 1838, during the following year, it amounts to 8,685,779*l*. In this period we find a most uniform corresponding reduction taking place in the amount of bullion, until we find, from January till October 5th, 6,814,000*l*. abstracted from the country. To this sum should be added the credit of 2,500,000*l.*, which the Bank obtained on Paris. the drafts for which may be said to represent so much bullion exported. In this way we see clearly how our imports of wheat have been provided for, and how our bullion has been disposed of.

We would crave attention to the reduction in the amount of the deposits on two grounds:—

First.—For the same reason that so large an importation of wheat finds no corresponding commodity of exchange except bullion, as having a common value everywhere, viz., its being *uncertain* and *accidental*; we believe that its amount must always be abstracted, in great measure, from that portion of the capital of the country constituting the currency, or convenient medium of exchange; or from that portion which constitutes the stock of what is termed the money-market. This is chiefly represented by the *deposits* with bankers throughout the kingdom; the whole amount of which, it has been shown, is in some measure indicated by the deposits in the Bank of England. These transactions being *accidental*, a small portion of the usual fixed commercial capital is directed into this channel. or kept available for its uses; and, therefore, when the demand does arise, it can only be abstracted from the sources referred to; were the demand equal and certain, the same amount of transactions thrown over a large space of time with any degree of uniformity, not only would a regular medium of exchange in other commodities be the necessary consequence. but also would a suitable share of the capital of the country find its way into that trade, like any other, for its convenient conducting; and thus not only would the derangement in the currency be prevented, as caused by an abstraction of bullion, but also the derangement of the money-market, inseparably associated with the currency, would be prevented, as at present caused by such large amounts being accidentally abstracted from its stock, which usually finds employment in contributing to the general convenient conducting of the commerce of the country, by discounting bills of exchange and otherwise.

Secondly,—As we have throughout these views shown how an unusually high price of provisions must tend to a contraction of the currency, and the floating capital of the country, by directing an unusual portion into particular channels for investment, and stagnating the capital employed in other interests, from which this abstraction of their usual portion takes place, it must be plain that this deficiency must become evident, by a diminishing amount of the deposits with bankers.

Before taking leave of the period embraced in this inquiry, we will draw the reader's attention to the following Table, exhibiting the same principles of connexion between the prices and operations in wheat and the amount of bullion and deposits held by the Bank, during the whole period of inquiry:—

	Period.		Deposits.	Bullion.	Average Prices of Wheat.	Amount paid for Foreign Wheat.	
			£	£			£
	Feb. 2,	1828	9,198.140	10,347,290	56/9	1827	1,195,580
	„	1829	9,553,960	6,835,020	60/5	1828	1,912,159
	„	1830	10,763,150	9,171,000	66/3	1829	3,495,813
	„	1831	11,213,530	8,217,050	64/3	1830	4,190,891
	„	1832	8,937,170	5,293,150	66/4	1831	3,828,519
3 months ending	April 3,	„	8,969,000	5,354,000			
	July 3,	„	9,020,000	5,780,000	58/8	1832	710,533
	Oct. 2,	„	10,861,000	7,401,000			
	Jan. 1,	1833	11,737,000	8,983,000			
	April 2	„	12,777,000	10,068,000			
	July 2,	„	12,045,000	10,673,000	52/11	1833	156,114
	Oct. 1,	„	13,057,000	10,905,000			
	Jan. 1,	1834	13,101,000	9,948,000			
	April 1,	„	14,011,000	9,431,000			
	June 3,	„	14,539,000	8,645,000	46/2	1834	101,750
	Aug. 26,	„	15,384,000	8,272,000			
	Nov. 18,	„	12,669,000	6,781,000			
	Feb. 10,	1835	12,535,000	6,693,000			
	May 5,	„	10,726,000	6,197,000			
	July 28,	„	11,561,000	6,203,000	39/4	1835	31,654
	Oct. 20,	„	14,227,000	6,186,000			
	Jan. 12,	1836	19,169,000	7,060,000			
	April 5,	„	14,751,000	7,801,000			
	June 28,	„	13,810,000	7,362,000	48/6	1836	51,177
	Sept. 20,	„	14,118,000	5,719,000			
	Dec. 13,	„	13,330,000	4,545,000			
	March 7,	1837	13,260,000	4,048,000			
	May 30,	„	10,422,000	4,423,000	55/10	1837	449,430
	Aug. 22,	„	11,005,000	5,754,000			
	Nov. 14,	„	10,242,000	7,432,000			
	Jan. 11,	1838	10,992,000	8,895,000			
	April 5,	„	11,262,000	10,126,000	64/7	1838	4,594,014
	June 29,	„	10,426,000	9,722,000			
	Sept. 21,	„	10,040,000	9,615,000			
	Jan. 10,	1839	10,315,000	9,336,000			
	April 5,	„	8,998,000	7,073,000			
	July 1,	„	7,567,000	4,344,000	70/8	1839	7,515,864
	Sept. 19,	„	7,781,000	2,816,000			
	Dec. 12,	„	5,952,000	2,887,000			

It will be observed that, from 1828 to 1832, the bullion diminished, under a large import of wheat, from 10.347,000*l.* to 5,293,000*l.* Here prices became lower, imports decreased, and became quite trivial; the stock of bullion gradually rose again to 10,905,000*l.* in the end of 1833. With some fluctuations of lesser importance, it continued at a convenient amount until the results of the extensive speculations of 1836 reduced it, in March, 1837, to 4,048,000*l.*, from which it rapidly recovered, in April, 1838, to 10,126,000*l.* It remained very stationary during that year; but in 1839, under the heavy import of wheat, was reduced in December, to 2,887,000*l.*, and, but for the credit on Paris, before alluded to, would have been reduced even much lower.

Similar corresponding fluctuations are observable in the deposits; the two lowest points being, in 1832, 8,937,170*l.*, after a continuance of high prices and large imports, from 1828 to 1831 inclusive; and in December, 1839, only 5,952,000*l.*, after the high prices and huge inports of that year; and the largest amount being, in a remarkable extent, in the four cheap years without imports, 1833, 1834, 1835, and 1836.

From the whole tendency of these facts and arguments, it will be plain to the reader that it is, as we said before, not to high or low prices, but to the continued fluctuation that we ascribe chiefly these most dangerous and extensive influences on the currency; nor can it be a matter of any surprise, when we view the enormous amounts to which these fluctuations have extended. that the occurrence of monetarial difficulties should have been as frequent and severe as they have been; the only surprise is, that they have not been felt to a much more serious extent; which only gives some evidence of the extensive resources, wealth, and enterprise enjoyed by this country.

Having now, we are afraid rather tediously, glanced at the history of the fluctuations which have taken place during the last eleven years, let us direct our attention to the general result, not only of this period, but of the whole time exhibited in the table, from 1817.

We find, from beginning to end periods of scarcity, high prices, and large importations, succeeded by periods of plenty, low prices, with little or no importation; and thus, period after period succeeding each other in the most uniform cycles which we could well imagine. Confining our attention exclusively in the present places to the influences these rapid changes have exercised on the currency, as shown by the tables and facts already given. we naturally come to the following conclusions, as the irresistible consequence of such fluctuations; consequences which ever have, and ever must continue to be, experienced as long as we are all subject to such changes.

In the periods of *scarcity*, high prices, and large importations, an extensive contraction of the currency must take place, not only by the exportation of the precious metal to purchase an accidental supply of wheat, but also by abstracting much of the capital of the country otherwise usefully employed in agricultural pursuits, where it is absorbed in improved and extended cultivation; and so far as these improvements or extensions are carried consistently with the wants of the community, no absorption of capital could be more useful; but stimulated by a pretended legislative protection of prices which have never been realised, experience teaches us that these operations have always been carried to such an extent as to produce a period of prices as much below a remunerating rate as they had before been above it. The effect of which is, that the capital which is thus absorbed, during dear years, becomes wasted and worthless in a short time, by calling into existence so much more productive power than can be profitably consumed, pressing prices far below the cost of production; and, instead of being beneficial to the agricultural interest, only leaves them in ultimate losses and disappointments. It was thus that from 1817 to 1820 the severe contraction of capital was experienced; it was thus that from 1827 to 1831 a similar difficulty occurred, and it is thus that at this moment the national income and capital is so much absorbed in an extravagant price of provisions and the payment of foreign supplies, that the currency has become so much exhausted and curtailed as to be quite insufficient for the usual wants of other branches of trade and industry.

Then following such periods we find uniformly periods of extreme low prices, which have, in some respects, even a more violent influence on the currency than the periods of high prices. So small a portion of the national means being consumed in these years in the purchase of food. causes, year after year, so great an accumulation of wealth, such an expansion of the currency, such a depreciation in the value of money, and so much difficulty of finding profitable employment for it, that a spirit of daring enterprise and speculation is engendered, which has at different periods not only disburthened the country of all superfluous means, but threatened it with dangers and evils of the greatest magnitude. Thus we find that the extreme low prices, with an absence of foreign purchases in 1821, 1822, 1823 and 1824, produced the effects above described, and brought on the speculative fever in the spring of 1825, which ended in the panic of the winter of that year; and thus again we find that the accumulated means from the low prices of 1832, 1833, 1834, and 1835, brought about another period of great excitement and speculation, and which produced the panic of 1836.

It has often been a subject of remark by practical men, without referring to the real causes, that there appeared periodically to exist a plethora in the currency or available capital of the country, which brought about these periods of excitement and wild speculation, opening up channels through which the redundancy flowed, not only to the cure of the disorder, but much to the danger of the patient. Such were the years 1825 and 1836.

In the former year, to say nothing of the millions that were absorbed and buried for ever, with as much utility as if they had been committed to the deep, in the innumerable mining speculations abroad and at home, and many other objects, which seldom knew a longer existence than was requisite for the mere expenditure of the capital; to say nothing of these, we will give a list of only *nine* of the foreign loans made out of the redundant capital of this period, in the end of 1824 and beginning of 1825, which, at their present value, show an actual loss to the country of upwards of *ten millions* sterling.

Nine Loans made in 1824 and 1825.	Nominal Amount of Loan.	Contracting Price.	Actual Amount at the Contracting Price.	Present Value.
	£		£	£
Colombian, 6 per cent. loan	4,750,000	88½	4,203,750	1,050,937
Buenos Ayres	1,000,000	85	850,000	255,000
Peru	750,000	77	577,500	101,062
Ditto	616,000	78	489,480	85,659
Mexican, 5 per cent.	3,200,000	58	1,856,000	417,600
Ditto, 6 per cent.	3,200,000	85	2,872,000	861,600
Guatamala, 5 per cent. . . .	2,000,000	73	1,042,988	—
Greece, 5 per cent.	800,000	59	472,000	—
Ditto, ditto	2,000,000	56½	1,130,000	—
Total paid up, and total present value. . . .			13,493,718	2,771,858
Total loss to the country.				10,721,860
			13,493,718	13,493,718

The extensive and injurious speculations in American securities, and other objects equally destructive, which occurred previous to the panic of 1836, are too recent and well known to require any further notice than merely to mark them as the result of the unnatural redundancy of capital at that period, as the means by which the apparent plethora of capital was reduced.

But independent of the wild speculations which these years induce, and the absolute destruction of capital which results therefrom, there is another mode by which the available currency is, perhaps, even more extensively influenced.

The greatly increased means of the whole community during these years to consume articles of luxury, the produce of arts and manufactures, giving an increased stimulus to these branches of industry, causes a great absorption of capital to take place in the extension of their productive powers, equal to the excited demand of the moment, but which only can be said to be profitably invested capital as long as the demand is equal to the produce, which only is the case until the existing excitement wears off by the arrival of a period of high prices of provisions, when we find that a large amount of capital has been sunk to supply a mere momentary demand, and is no longer of any value to the community.

Again, at these periods of a redundant capital, internal improvements and speculations in railways and other objects have been undertaken, under this un natural excitement, to a much greater extent than the real actual wealth of the country would warrant; and, before they have been completed, have drained more of the floating capital into their channels than a due regard to existing industries and the proper condition of the currency render desirable. For, however beneficial such improvements ultimately proved, it must be clear that they should never be attempted to such an extent as to endanger the abstraction of capital from the permanent and existing channels of the industry of the country.

Finally, then, it would appear, from the whole of these considerations, that the necessary tendency of the fluctuations which we have shown to exist in the annual portion of the national income absorbed in the supply of the first necessaries of life, is to produce continued and violent fluctuations in the condition of the currency, or floating capital of the country; and we think, when we have compared the theory with the facts, and seen the correspondence in point of time when the great and marked convulsions have taken place, the conviction of the close connexion which we have endeavoured to prove must be irresistible.

Both reasoning and evidence clearly demonstrate that with these large fluctuations there is, and must be, a continued action on the currency, rendering it, at one time, inconveniently full, and productive of the wildest and most destructive speculations, and, at another, so contracted that the whole community, from the Chancellor of the Exchequer down to the poorest artisan, are subjected to the most grievous pressure and distress It is plain that the Bank of England, and the bankers generally throughout the country, as being the dealers in money or currency, must be the first to feel the changes which we have described; but it is equally plain that they can have little to do with creating them, and almost as little in controlling them. They can do much by wise and prudent conduct, by a timely contraction of their own liabilities, to render their own position more secure against the effects of a coming storm, and ultimately to steer safely through it; but beyond this they have little or no power.

They are pressed by necessities, arising out of the causes we have described, into a course of policy which the world are too apt to think the influencing cause of the evils which afterwards become developed; and hence the public very generally attribute, as we before stated, all these derangements and convulsions in the currency to the imperfect construction of our banking system, and especially of the Bank of England. As in the beginning of these remarks we disclaimed any intention of entering into consideration of the principles of banking or management of the currency generally, we shall not here inquire whether this institution is the best that could be devised for the professed objects; whether its powers are too limited or too full—whether its functions are incongruous or not; for we are convinced that, however imperfect it may be, or however perfect it may be made, the country will ever remain subject to violent changes and fluctuations in its currency, as long as the real causes which produce the rapid changes and fluctuations in the price of the first great necessaries of life shall continue to exist.*

We have already, in a former work, traced these fluctuations as the imperative offspring of the existence of laws attempting to control and regulate the supply and price of these first necessaries; of laws which have separated, by most unnatural violence, the great leading interests of the country; which have called into existence feelings of animosity and jealousy among parties who had, in reality, only one common and indissoluble stake; and which have created a continued and never-ending strife, in which each party in his turn is the great loser, and by which neither party is ever permanently advantaged. Until these laws are erased from the statute book—not altered, not amended, for alterations and amendments will only produce new difficulties, new incongruities, new false positions, in which we shall have everything to learn over again—but swept for ever away; until we find all the great leading interests of the community going on in one uniform and fair compact, whereby energy, industry, and capital shall have a free, full, and unfettered exercise of their functions; when men will no longer deceive themselves into a reliance on legislative enactments for partial ends;

* While we thus avoid the subject of banking or the management of the currency as irrelevant to the considerations immediately under review, we are not insensible of the immense benefits which will accrue to the community by the adoption of correct and wise principles in relation thereto.

and when we shall no longer "refuse to ourselves the benefit of that provision which Providence itself has made for equalising to man the variations of climate and of seasons—until then, we shall in vain look for any uniformity in the condition and prosperity of the country, for any theory or plan of conducting the monetarial arrangements of this great and enterprising community with any degree of certainty and success.

PART II.

FLUCTUATIONS OF COMMERCE, MANUFACTURES, &c.

THE rapid and violent fluctuations in the manufacturing and commercial prosperity of this country, which have occurred in late years, have equally excited the astonishment of the thinking economist, and puzzled his ingenuity satisfactorily to account for them.

During a time of extensive and protracted warfare, when strong and unnatural barriers are raised to interrupt the usual course of production and consumption; when the productive ability of entire countries is paralysed and destroyed by being the seat of lengthened campaigns; when more of labour's creation is often destroyed by rapine, plunder, and devastation in one day, to appease the wrath or gratify the passions of the triumphant conqueror, than would suffice to minister to the wants and reproductive energies of a whole kingdom for a long period; it is an easy matter to understand that great and sudden changes should be experienced by the trading interests of the whole mercantile world. But that such fluctuations should still continue to be experienced after nearly the whole civilised world may be said to have reposed in peace for a quarter of a century, during which period intelligence has made more progress, productive energy acquired more strength, and consumptive ability, extending hand in hand with civilisation, has obtained a wider and richer field than ever could have been hoped for by the most sanguine lover and well wisher of his race, is indeed a matter, at first sight, of great difficulty to reconcile.

And this difficulty is certainly much increased when we consider what constitute the true fundamental grounds of industrial and mercantile prosperity, and its uniformity:—*a productive ability, on the one hand, to administer to the necessities, tastes, and pleasures of the community; a consumptive ability, on the other hand, to absorb the creation of production.*

Now, it requires no argument to show that the extent to which productive ability will be stimulated and called into existence, will depend much on the extent and power of the consumptive ability. But let us shortly inquire what constitutes this consumptive ability:—in a few words, it is production alone, it is labour alone—whether it be that of the present moment, or the accumulated recompense of past toil:—in other words, it is the price paid for labour, and the profits or interest of capital which, whether taken in the light of merely accumulated labour, or, as an active instrument of present labour, is, perhaps, the most important element in production:—for we see by its application to mechanics, the power of one labourer is multiplied one hundred-fold and more; by its application to commerce, the labour of exchanging the productions of the most remote corners of the globe is reduced from an utter impracticability without it, to an almost insensible amount by its aid.

Well then, consumptive ability,—whether arising from the rents of land or houses, the value of which have alone been created by past labour; whether found in public functionaries, civil, military, or naval; whether in the interest derived by the capitalist for his loan—the profits of commerce, the produce of the soil, the wages of labour, are all resolved into two simple things—the price of labour, and the interest of capital; or, in other words, the two only elements of production.

It would therefore follow, that, in order to increase or diminish materially the consumptive ability, one or both of these elements should be correspondingly increased or diminished; and it would therefore be no great matter of surprise if we saw a community evincing great energy and industry one year, and utter imbecility and indolence another year: that such periods should be marked by a very different amount of consumptive ability: but consumption certainly could not be materially abridged, until productive energy had failed:—on the other hand, if we see a nation steadily becoming richer and more industrious, with a productive ability uniformly increasing, we have necessarily to expect that its consumptive ability must, in like manner, advance as uniformly; and until a reaction takes place in the former, no change should be experienced in the latter.

This natural and necessary inference cannot, however, be said to be at all applicable to the experience of this country; and it is no wonder that many attempts should have been made to account for so obvious a departure from the natural order of things —for the violent and constant changes which have occurred in the relation of production and consumption. —and thereby, for the continual derangement and excitement which have followed each other at rapid intervals, and which have time after time shaken the whole commercial fabric to its base.

It is a common and favourite mode to arrive at an object by the shortest possible mode: and therefore, in the inquiries which take place as to the cause of certain effects, it is not unusual to mistake some of the other symptoms as the cause, instead of merely as the co-existing effects of a common cause.

In the eager inquiries which have occupied the public mind from time to time as to the cause of the disorders of which we now speak, we think we discover a striking illustration of this tendency. In all these investigations the chief, if not only causes which have been relied upon have been: first—An imperfect banking system, by which the capital of the country has been capriciously managed; by which, in the popular term, a power has been given to certain establishments, especially the Bank of England, to "*tamper with the currency*;" by which at one period money has been rendered plentiful and of easy acquirement, and has given a most unnatural stimulus to speculation and production:—and at another period very scarce and difficult to obtain, and thereby cramped the facilities of commerce and production: and, secondly, That, at particular periods, overtrading, as it is termed, prevails to a great extent, stimulated by excessive and easy credit producing wild speculation, which ultimately ends in a serious reaction, producing all the panic and dismay which have attended our commercial crises. It must be admitted that many reasons have existed to direct the public mind to these two points; but it is not difficult to show that there can be no truth in alleging that they are the first cause of the serious occurrences to which we refer, the continued fluctuations in the condition of the industrial and commercial prosperity of this kingdom.

With regard to the former reason, after having so fully gone into a consideration of it, in the last chapter, it would be superfluous to repeat the arguments which we there use to show that no banking establishment, much less the Bank of England, powerless and dependent as it is for its existence on credit only, could exercise such an influence on this great and powerful community. Whether we speak of the action of the Bank of England, or of the action of the whole banking establishments in the kingdom, it must be clear that they can only act, as they are acted upon, by the source from which their power of action is derived. Now inquire what is the source of power:—the wealth of the community from time to time, which finds its way into the hands of bankers for employment, and who are therefore the agents through whom the surplus or spare capital of one portion of the public finds a safe, prudent, and profitable employment by another portion of the community.—A, B, & C, have money to lend or invest for an uncertain period; they have no sufficient knowledge or reliance on their own judgment to undertake the task of lending themselves, especially as they may require the money again at a day's notice; they lend to their banker, from whom they can always rely on obtaining it when required. The banker, then, having a connection of borrowers, as well as lenders, distributes these sums intrusted to his care in such loans and other ways as enable him to make a profit; but always having at the same time his means sufficiently available to repay his creditors whenever they require it. The business of a banker may therefore be said to be, that of borrowing at one rate of interest from one portion of the public, and lending at a higher rate of interest to another portion; the difference being the remuneration for the undoubted guarantee which his known wealth and respectability infuse into the transaction, and for the facility of always being able to receive it back when required. It is true, there are some bankers who have a large available capital of their own always employed, and so far these bankers are more independent of external influences; to this class the Bank of England certainly does not belong. It is also true, that there is a certain power amongst bankers of creating money by paper issues, but this is a most weak and inefficient source of means. In a country where only a large denomination of notes prevails, and those always convertible, such paper issues can only be sustained to a certain proportion of the whole circulation. There may be moments when by violent attempts more than a usual proportion is sustained, but those periods must be of very short duration; as a rule, if the whole circulation increases or diminishes, the portion of it which is paper convertible on demand must also in like manner increase or diminish.

In comparison, therefore, of these two last modes of bank action on the public, viz., their own private and independent capital, and the power of creating money by paper issues — the first mentioned, viz., that of deposits, bears a most indisputable and overtowering importance. The amount of deposits of banks is their great strength and power. The wise and active employment of deposits, is the greatest and truest source of bank profits. Even in Scotland, where a paper circulation prevails to a much lower denomination than in England, deposits are still the greatest and most available power of business and source of profit.

Seeing, then, that any increase or diminution of the power of bank action must proceed from the public, that power can only become greater when money is becoming more abundant with the public, and cannot fail to become much weaker when the public means are diminishing, or suffering any unusual or extraordinary absorption; and it would, therefore, be more correct to say, that in any correspondence which is seen between the action of banks, and the oscillations in the trade and commerce of the country, the former is rather the effect of the latter, than the cause; and perhaps truer still to say, that they are equally the effects of some common cause.

With respect to the other alleged cause of these derangements and fluctuations, that they proceed from and are caused by overtrading, and an excess of credit called into existence simply by the will or caprice of the moment, it will be no difficult matter to show that such a state of things were utterly impossible. It is utterly impossible that any production whatever could take place upon credit; except where an inconvertible paper currency existed of a very low denomination, which could not last long without the most alarming depreciation;—but, circumstanced as we are in this country, with a convertible paper currency only, and that only of a large denomination, no production whatever can take place that is not represented by real capital.

True it is, as far as the immediate agent of production is concerned, all may be done upon credit; he may buy his raw material upon credit; he may pay the wages of labour by an advance from his banker; he may sell his goods to a merchant at a lengthened credit, and receive an acceptance for the amount, which he may convert into money; and, to put an extreme case, he may thus actually become possessed of capital instead of investing it by this process. True it is, to put a case advanced in a recent pamphlet, written to prove that the objects of our present consideration are the cause of these evils,—that these goods so produced (amounting to £2000) may be sold and resold nine times within a few days, and that for each sale a bill of exchange may be drawn and discounted: and that amongst these individuals, from the producer to the last seller, an amount of capital to the extent of £20,000 may thus be created. True it is (to follow another illustration of the same writer), the same goods may be then consigned to a distant market, and an advance made by the acceptance of the party to whose care they are intrusted payable at a distant date, which may also, by similar means, be converted into cash. True it is, that by this extreme, though quite possible proposition, capital to the extent of £22,000 may, by the multiplied credits of those parties, find its way to their possession; but just as true it is, that every shilling of this sum must be advanced from the real substantial capital or money of some one or other of the community. The immediate parties who give the credit may only be enabled to do so by themselves receiving credit; the parties who discount the bills may only be enabled to do so by re-discounting them again and again, but at every stage, and ultimately every shilling must represent the real capital of some one or other. The only possible mode in which production could take place on credit, in the broad sense affecting the community, would be to suppose, that the labour that produced from beginning to end could be supported by credit; that the muscle and sinew, the physical energy, which to-day is exhausted, by calling into existence a new object could wait two, three, or four months to be replenished; for it would not be enough, even that the labourer should be able to give a credit upon his labour; for then it is obvious that he is either a capitalist himself, or indebted to some capitalist;—day by day, nay, hour by hour, the exhausted energies must be replenished; they can give no credit,—they cannot wait *the result* of markets.

All the means, therefore, by which these various credits are supported from beginning to end (excepting when an inconvertible paper currency of low denomination exists), must be supplied from the real absolute capitals and money of some one or other of the community, whether the exchange of the commodity be confined to two parties only, or extended to any number. Now this capital, or accumulated labour, existing as it does in the community, is as urgent for employment in order to give it any value to its possessor, as is the use of the sinew and the muscle of the present labourer to him. To either, inactivity is unprofitable and waste. Each, therefore, are simple merchantable commodities, the value of which, and the facility of acquiring their assistance, depends only on the relative proportion of supply and demand. If, therefore, credits become abundant and excessive, and *trade* or production is thereby extravagantly stimulated, it can only be because the supply of capital seeking employment is very great; and, if credit becomes very contracted, and the facilities of trade much impaired, it can only be by the amount of capital seeking employment being much lessened—the simple effects, it is true, being exaggerated by the competition which in the first case exists to invest, and the greater risks that are then taken; and the second place, by the increased caution by the market of demand being more in the hand of the suppliers; but, in both instances, it is simply a question of amount of supply in relation to demand. It would therefore appear, that both of these popular modes of accounting for the sudden and frequent fluctuations of trade are only part of the co-existing effects arising out of the great fluctuations in the amount of capital available for trading purposes at different periods.

It has already been shown how difficult it is to conceive that the wealth or capital of a country, of uniform industry and perseverance, can fluctuate much; but this is not necessary, as the same effect will be produced if we can show that that capital suffers any very material and imperative change in its direction from time to time.

In the preceding chapter we have entered into so much evidence to show the great extent of such changes in the direction of the national income and floating capital of this country, by the fluctuations which have continually been going forward in the amount absorbed at different periods, in payment for the first necessaries of life, whereby great and violent changes are shown to have occurred in the state of the currency and money market; and we believe, by a careful investigation, that we shall find that the same cause has exercised over commerce and trade all the fluctuations of which we have spoken.

If our reasoning, and the facts displayed to illustrate our position, have proved at all satisfactory to the reader, with respect to the influence which the fluctuations in the price of wheat have exercised over the currency and money market, we believe that the applicability of the same facts and the same reasoning will not fail to be more satisfactory and conclusive on the present subject of consideration.

In considering the influence which the large fluctuations of the amount of the national income and means absorbed from time to time have exerted over our industry and commerce, there must necessarily be a considerable similarity to the arguments and illustrations already used, in reference to their effects on the currency and money-market ; and to prevent any tedious repetitions of these arguments, we must take it for granted, that the reasoning in the previous chapter is always clearly before the reader

By the policy pursued by our laws, the interests of this great country have been divided into two great sections, the agricultural and commercial : but it must be very plain to every thinking mind, that these interests, ultimately interwoven with each other, and entirely dependent upon each other, and having no ultimate and final interest distinct from each other, never could have suffered this unnatural severance but by the exertion and interposition of unnatural laws, which have ever proved impracticable and futile, because they were unnatural ;—because they affected to give a support to one interest, which, if it should have any effect at all, was to be a direct charge on the only other interest which was expected to support the protected one ; and, therefore, in the exact proportion that the law should prove successful in its object, must have had the direct tendency to weaken and impoverish the objects on which they relied.

The laws of Providence and the laws of nature are mutual dependence ;—a principle calculated to bind in the strongest harmony the best interests of all classes and portions of the community; and any legislative attempt to sever these mutual interests and reliance, while it may have given to the whole tone and arrangements of the social system, and prosperity of the community, a most unfavourable and unhappy direction, never succeeded in the object it had in view; nothing has tended more to lower the estimation and influence of legislative wisdom than their abortive attempts to control the natural and imperative current of national and mutual interests.

But treating things as they are, such a severance, however unprofitable to all parties, has been effected.

We must admit, that the first and most imperative call upon the national income of the country, upon its consumptive ability, must be the first necessaries of food; that to this provision all other considerations must give way; that every thing else must be considered relatively as luxuries, which are indulged in only in proportion to the ability remaining after the first necessaries are secured.

If, therefore, the cost of these first necessaries is very changeable and fluctuating, the ability to consume all other products must be equally fluctuating; and the fluctuation of the former must necessarily prove the cause of the fluctuation of the latter.

Confining our consideration of these principles, as we have hitherto done, to *wheat*, the first universal necessary of life, we have shewn in page 10, that at the average price of a number of years the actual cost of this article to the country has been 41,600,000*l.*; and taking this average as the correct amount of the annual expenditure which should be so absorbed it necessarily follows, that in proportion as it rises above or sinks below that average, the national means for sustaining other branches of industry must necessarily increase or diminish.

The fluctuations which have occurred in the amount of national means, so absorbed, have been carefully given in a table, page 13. This table shews that the means thus absorbed gradually fell from *seventy five millions* in 1817, to *thirty-three millions* in 1822: then gradually advanced to *fifty-three millions* in 1829; then again fell to *thirty-one millions* in 1835, and finally, again, advanced to *fifty-six millions* in 1839.

In this manner has the most imperative portion of the national expenditure varied and fluctuated, and leaving therefore so much less in some years, and so much more in other years to expend in all other objects of lesser necessity, of taste and luxury; the obvious and necessary tendency of which must be to give in some years a most unnatural excitement and encouragement to manufacturing and commercial pursuits, and in other years to withdraw from such pursuits not only the portion of the public income which they had enjoyed more than their proper share, but to reduce it as much below the fair proportion as it had been before above it, has been sufficiently alluded to in the preceding chapter, in the obvious and close relationship such considerations have with the currency.

We will now endeavour, as shortly as possible, to trace the effects of these fluctuations on manufactures and commerce, as exhibited by the occurrences since 1832. The four preceding years had been marked by a continuance of high prices of wheat, and by a low stagnant state of the manufacturing and commercial interests.

In 1832, the sum absorbed in the price of wheat was *six millions* less than the preceding year, and we find that in that year trade began to evince symptoms of a more active character.

In 1833, a further reduction took place in the sum absorbed in the price of wheat to the extent of *four millions*:—a further improvement and steady extension of commercial prosperity was visible during this year.

In 1834, a further reduction took place in the sum absorbed in the prices of wheat of *five millions*—which was again accompanied by a further increased demand for the products of commerce and manufactures.

In 1835, a further reduction took place in the sum absorbed in the prices of wheat of *five millions*, making a total difference of *twenty-one millions* in this year as compared with 1831, in the portion of the national income and means thus absorbed. During this year, and the beginning of the following, the demand for the products of manufacturing skill, for the luxuries wafted to our shores by our commercial enterprise, rose to an amount unprecedented (in relation to our means of supplying them) in the annals of commerce; while the agricultural interests sunk year after year into a state of poverty and ruin.

It may appear somewhat unaccountable, that the former interest should have flourished so much, while the latter should be so depressed; but it must be borne in mind, that the portions of the agricultural interest who experienced this suffering were only the landlords and farmers, while the great bulk, the large mass of consumers represented by the labouring classes, received really higher wages in these years than formerly, in consequence of the great demand for labour called into existence in the manufacturing districts, and in carrying into effect all the schemes of internal improvement, by railways, &c., to which the unnatural abundance of capital, set free in those years, gave rise

We would now inquire what was the imperative consequence of this state of things?—a demand for manufactured goods and commercial products, which could hardly be met by existing means; a price for the products of agriculture, which brought certain ruin and difficulty on all whose capitals were engaged therein.

The natural and imperative consequences ensued. Every effort was used to extend the means and facilities of extending production on the one hand. Factories were reared on all hands — the productive ability of machinery was increased by new improvements and accelerated movement—ships were built—mercantile establishments sprung into existence—and banks were created day by day ; in short, all the necessary and contributary means suited not alone to the present enormously increased action of commerce, but to a belief that the increase would continue at the same rate, rapidly arose on all sides, while the capital engaged in agriculture was year after year suffering greater and greater depreciation, and consequently tending to discourage production.

In this most unnatural position, therefore, at this moment were we placed : we were calling at an enormous rate productive ability in manufactures to supply the supposed demand of the future, while the means of future subsistence were daily suffering diminution.

The unnatural excitement and speculation which arose out of the plethora of free capital in 1835 and 1836, lead, as we have shewn in the last chapter, to the panic of 1836-37.

The character and symptoms of this crisis demand a most minute investigation in reference to its general connexion with trade. It was most strikingly a money crisis, and a money crisis only * a disturbance of the

* When we use the term "*money crisis,*" we do not mean to assent to a most prevalent opinion, that it was brought about by a redundant and extravagant paper issue, which we believe to be an error, but into which we shall by-and-by inquire more particularly.

channels of connexion between producer and consumer, and not a disturbance in any general relative ability of consumption and production.

The approach of this crisis was not marked by any diminution in the demand for the products of industry, but on the contrary, this demand continued for many months with unabated vigour, after the commencement of the monetarial crisis. and suffered no check until the channels of interchange were entirely choked by the want of confidence which ensued.

Great as were the monetorial powers and means of the time, a spirit of extensive enterprise was encouraged and called into existence, and future commercial and financial liabilities contracted, which, as they became due, proved to be greater than the ability which **existed** for their provision. But, in the first instance, these difficulties were confined to a few of the leading parties, who had entered most extensively into these liabilities; and altogether may be said to have been confined to foreign commerce: and that chiefly by the sudden reduction which took place in the price of every commodity, in consequence of the urgent demand for money to meet the extravagant engagements which had been promoted by the unnatural excitement and speculation of the previous two or three years. Towards the middle of 1837, when this panic arrived at its greatest height, there were certainly considerable symptoms of a depression in manufacturing industry; but we believe these arose altogether out of the derangement of the channels of supply, and not out of any abatement in the actual consumption; which, whether it be considered in relation to a foreign or home demand, we will hereafter shew suffered no diminution, but, on the contrary, exceeded that of any preceding year. The elasticity which every interest displayed in recovering its natural position, immediately the unnatural pressure of overloaded liabilities was removed, sufficiently shewed that this crisis was a mere reaction of the unnatural abundance of money and excitement of commercial enterprise arising therefrom, which we we have shewn had been called into existence at this period, and not of any substantial derangement of the ability of consumption and production, which must ever be regarded as the only great source of general prosperity.

We are ready to admit, that during this crisis, from September 1836 until September 1837 (but felt chiefly from February until July of the latter year) larger losses were incurred by individuals, and a greater difficulty was experienced in sustaining engagements than perhaps ever before existed in the commercial world.

The enormous amount of foreign credits, especially American, which had been granted, and the huge liabilities which arose out of them (promoted by the great abundance and facility of obtaining money for some time previously), found our money-market in a condition of comparative exhaustion: and hence the competition which arose to obtain money and support credit, led to great sacrifices, and a sudden and intense depression of prices. This chiefly took place in the months of *March, April,* and *May.* On the first of June, the crisis reached its summit, but the public mind was relieved from the suspense in which it had been held for some time, by the protection which the Bank of England had extended to some leading houses being withdrawn, and their consequent suspension of payment. Immediately after this event confidence became greater and greater every day ; prices gradually improved, and before the close of the year things had assumed their usual appearance ; and although many individuals lost large sums of money by the sudden depression of prices during this period, yet, as a whole community, the amount of wealth did not suffer much contraction : production and consumption went on without much interruption, the price of food was still moderate : a large portion of the national income was still available for the consumption of manufactures : this will appear by the following analysis of the cotton trade of 1836 and 1837 :

	Cotton wool taken into consumption.	Exported in Goods and Yarns.
1836	363,684,232 lbs.	198,868,910 lbs.
1837	368,445,035 ,,	207,576,839. ,,

We therefore consider this crisis in the character of a mere temporary reaction, the effects of which soon disappeared.

In the commencement of 1838, every branch of industry assumed a most active but substantial appearance, every description of produce obtained a fair and moderate value; and the great engines of increased productive power, which had been called into existance by the excited demand which had prevailed for two or three years, sprung into great and energetic action. In the absence of any speculation or excitement, all the new manufacturing establishments, all the increased mechanical power, and labourers of every class, found in this year a full employment: and never was there, to all external appearances, more reason to look forward to a continuance of existing prosperity: an enormous advance had been made in the economy of production, reducing the price and increasing the consumption of all articles of manufacture, and the well-poised relative condition of all the leading interests of the country gave great assurance of durability.

In the midst of this security, however, towards the close of the year, a cause of embarrassment, which had been secretly and unwittingly in silent operation for some time, began to shew itself. The depressed condition of the agricultural interest for some years had not failed to discourage production, as much as the increased impulse of the manufacturing interest had tended to encourage it. The lavish consumption of wheat, for some years, and the diminished efforts of production evinced themselves towards the autumn of this year, by rapidly rising prices consequent on an exhausted stock. In addition to this alarming symptom the harvest was not only late, but to every appearance threatened to be very deficient. As we have now arrived at the end of a period of low and moderate prices, at the point when, by the necessary operation of cause and effect, we are about to suffer a great and violent change in existing interests, we crave attention to the following statistical evidence of the rapid and uniform advance of our manufactures during the period under review.

The cotton trade offers the safest evidence on this point; being an article altogether imported, and no part produced at home, the Custom-house returns furnish an unerring guide to the progress of its consumption. It is also the article of our most important manufacture.

Years.	Cotton taken into Consumption.
1832	259,412,463 lbs.
1833	293,682,976 ,,
1834	302,935,657 ,,
1835	326,407,692 ,,
1836	363,684,232 ,,
1837	368,445,035 ,,
1838	460,756,013 ,,

The following is the weekly consumption of Cotton Wools in each of these years in bags:

1832	1833	1834	1835	1836	1837	1838
16,650	17,217	17,165	18,157	19,978	20,794	24,312

shewing in seven years an increase of 7,662 bags weekly, or 398,464 yearly: or of 201.343,550lbs. in the consumption of this great staple of our manufactures: while in the preceding seven years (during which period wheat ranged at very high prices), the increase in the consumption of cotton wool was only 70,702,784lbs. The two periods stand thus:

Years.	Average price of Wheat.	Progress of the consumption of Cotton Wool during seven years of high prices, and seven years of low prices of wheat.			
1825	66/6	202,546,869 lbs.	1832	58/8	259,412,463 lbs.
1826	56/11	162,889,012 „	1833	52/11	293,682,976
1827	56/9	249,804,396 „	1834	46/2	302,935,457
1828	60/5	208,987,741 „	1835	39/4	326,407,692
1829	66/3	204,097,037 „	1836	48/6	363,684,232
1830	64/3	269,616,640 „	1837	55/10	368,445,035
1831	66/4	273,249,653 „	1838	64/7*	460,756,013
	Increase	70,702,784 lbs; or 35 per cent.		Increase	201,343,550 lbs; or 80 per cent.

We have seen in the former chapter that in the autumn of 1838 we commenced an expenditure of more than £300,000 weekly, as the price of bread, above the fair average cost of that article, which continued during the whole of the following year, 1839; during which period foreign wheat, at a cost of thirteen millions sterling, and other grain at a cost of two millions more, were taken into consumption. It became obvious that so large an additional amount of our expenditure being directed into this channel, could not fail to act with great effect in the consumption of all other articles of less importance; and that so large a sum being required to pay for foreign supplies could not

* The price of wheat was moderate in 1838 until towards the close, when it rose to a very high range, which shows a high average, but the effects of which were experienced in the beginning of the following year.

fail to derange the financial arrangements by which our commerce and industry were supported. The cause, however, continued in operation for a long time before its effects became very apparent. Merchants, manufacturers, dealers, wholesale and retail, must always act by anticipation. Provision must be made before the hour of demand. The manufacturer continues his industry and his purchases of raw material from the merchant, in anticipation of his usual demand; the dealers order their usual supply for an approaching season, anticipating the same consumption as before; and it is not until some time has passed, until the dealer is disappointed in the demand from the actual consumers, that, failing to replenish his stock to the ordinary extent, the deficiency falls back upon the manufacturer, and ultimately upon the merchant, for the raw material, and the suffering artizan for his labour. It was not, therefore, until the spring of 1839 that any material falling off was experienced in the demand for the products of our chief manufactures. From this period the effects of the high prices of wheat, in lessening the consumption of manufactured goods, became daily more and more apparent. The usual extensive preparation for the spring demand (when nature, gladsomely arrayed in new attire, invites us to be so also) proved much too great; disappointment was experienced, and derangement rapidly ensued. It became evident, that if the enormously increased productive power was continued in full operation, manufactured goods would soon have scarcely a price at all, from the competition which must ensue. Mills were, therefore, by common consent, put on short work, and production checked in every possible way: but here arose two new evils; it soon became apparent, first, that in proportion as production is checked, its cost is enhanced in all mechanical operations by a given amount of capital invested with its whole management, producing so much less than before; and, second, that a great number of working men must be thrown either altogether or partially out of employment, and the whole ability of consumption being thus lessened, was soon felt to re-act again on the demand for production.

Such is the mutual dependence on each other in the social system, that no sooner does one branch of industry fail than all others immediately feel the shock; and every day, by the action and re-action of cause and effect, fresh numbers are added to the list of the unemployed and distressed.

If one class of producers cease to be fully employed, while at the same time the necessaries of life are considerably dearer, it is clear they can no longer purchase the labour of other classes of producers to the same extent as before. The means of the latter classes being thus abridged re-acts again on the former, and thus all classes of labourers are, sooner or later, drawn into the position of having a much smaller demand for their products; and, therefore, independently of the high price of provisions, their ability to consume becomes day by day lessened; the necessary action of which is to create a supply of labour very disproportionate to the demand, and thereby, with half work and dear food, to cause a reduction in the price of the little labour required.

In this manner, week after week and month after month, the depression became greater, and extended itself to every class of industry throughout the kingdom; and fully justified the worst anticipations which existed as the necessary consequences of the diminution of national means to consume the products of manufacturing industry.

In illustration of the effects of the present Corn Laws, the consideration of this year is very important and interesting; as it is the first since 1831 in which prices have risen so high as to allow of a free importation, or of an importation to any extent, with the exception of the last three months of 1838, the effects of which we have already shown, were experienced in the year under notice. We will therefore endeavour to show how the influences, of which we have spoken have acted upon the interests of trade, by examining the comparative result of 1839 with the preceding year, in which inquiry we shall be guided only by official, or other undoubted authority.

Much disputation has taken place as to the relative importance of the home and the foreign trade of this country; we are however assured, by every calm reflection, that ultimately the one must ever depend in a great measure on the other. A foreign trade can only be supported by an ability of consumption of the articles taken in exchange, which necessarily implies a proportionate consumption of our home production; and it is evident there is no attempt to send articles to a distance for sale as long as there is consumption at home.

Whatever may be the difference of opinion as to the relative importance of the two classes of trade (into which we have not here leisure to inquire), it must be obvious that the home trade furnishes a much more accurate criterion of the real condition of the nation and business generally than the foreign trade, for the two following reasons: first, a large portion of our foreign trade consists in consignments on speculation of the demand in foreign countries, which often increase in the proportion that parties are disappointed of an actual demand for consumption at home, but which, in reality, may be considered a mere transfer of goods from the warehouse of the owner in this country to that of his agent in some other, without being any nearer to actual consumption; and, secondly, because it is possible, but not probable, that for some time at least reasons should exist for an increasing consumption of goods in foreign countries, while our home consumption was much depressed.

One thing, however, must be obvious, that in proportion as the supply prepared for home consumption proves to be too great for it, there must be a tendency and an effort to diffuse the surplus over foreign markets: there are two motives for this operation; first, the quantity cannot be consumed at home—an extended field must be sought, and the surplus is necessarily pressed on other markets; and, second, by the practice in business it is usual for the parties receiving consignments of goods for sale in foreign markets, to make advances in anticipation of the ultimate result of such sales; and, therefore, if parties are disappointed of a home demand, a facility of obtaining means to meet their engagements is thus afforded, of which they have otherwise been deprived.

It is therefore clear, that a large export trade may equally prove two things:—first, a demand from foreign countries, temporarily independent of our condition; or, second, a very depressed home consumption, by which the surplus production is pressed into other channels to find consumption, and in the mean time to afford the facility of obtaining advances in the current, and apparently regular mode of business.

It was therefore to be expected, that when any sudden cause arose to disappoint the usual arrangements which had been made for the home supply, the surplus on such occasions should be forced into an export trade, for the two reasons we have given.

With these preliminary remarks, we will proceed to the proposed comparison of the trade of 1838 and 1839; in which we shall find, as all our arguments lead us to anticipate, a great reduction of our home consumption with an increase in our exports of manufactured goods in the latter year as compared with the former.

In this inquiry, we will direct our attention chiefly to the cotton trade, not only because it is by far the most extensive branch of our manufactures, but being exclusively of foreign produce, the custom-house accounts furnish a perfect and unerring guide to its progress.

With respect to the home consumption of our manufactures, there is no official data to guide us, nor has there been any attempt hitherto to arrive at any correct estimate of its amount. We trust, however, that the mode we have adopted will appear sufficiently clear and accurate, to obtain a correct estimate of the home consumption.

COTTON TRADE OF GREAT BRITAIN.—1838.

		BAGS.
January 1st, 1838, stock on hand		409,057
Imported into Liverpool	1,329,142	
„ „ London . . .	46,764	
„ „ Glasgow . . .	53,156	
		1,429,062
Total supply		1,838,119
Deduct exported	102,370	
Stock left, December 31st . . .	498,929	
		601,299
Total number of bags consumed,		1,236,820

At an average weight of 346lbs., making 426,090, 116lbs.

of cotton wool spun in this year, of which was exported from England in manufactured goods as follow :—*

WEIGHT OF YARN IN MANUFACTURED COTTON GOODS EXPORTED FROM ENGLAND IN THE YEAR 1838.

Description.	Number of yards, &c. of each description.	Length of each piece.	Number of pieces of each description.	Weight of yarn in each piece.		Total weight of yarn exported in goods.
	Yards.	Yards.		lbs.	oz.	lbs.
Calicoes, Printed & dyed	264,724,867	28	9,454,459	4	4	40,181,451
Calicoes, Plain . . .	282,817,754	24	11,785,323	6	0	70,711,938
Cambrics and Muslins.	5,845,521	20	292,276	3	0	876,828
Velveteens, Velvets. Cords, &c. . . .	4,698,077	60	78,135	22	12	1,777,570
Quiltings and Ribs . .	472,202	60	7,870	18	0	141,660
Cotton & Linen, mixed	1,870,473	40	46,762	8	0	374,086
Ginghams and Checks	2,516,576	20	125,829	3	8	440,401
Ticks, checked and striped	212,553	50	4,251	20	0	85,020
Dimities	89,802	60	1,497	12	0	17,964
Damasks and Diapers .	18,332	36	509	10	0	5,090
Nankeens	383,786	50	7,676	8	8	65,246
Lawns and Lenos. . .	18,250	20	912	2	8	2,280
Imitation Shawls . . .	106,572	12	8,881	2	8	22,202
Lace, &c.	81,987,421	40	2,049,685	0	8	1,024,842
Counterpanes & Quilts	96,307	No.	96,307	7	0	674,149
Shawls & Handkerchiefs	808,924	Doz.	808,924	2	8	2,022,310
Tapes, Bobbins, &c.. .	1,205	..	51,205	1	0	51,205
Hosiery	447,391	..	447,391	2	8	1,118,477
Unenumerated	119,190	£.	Sterling.	10	0	1,191,900

Total Weight of Yarn Exported in Manufactured Goods, in 1838, 120,784,629.

* For the data of these calculations, &c., in this table, we are indebted o Mr. Burnes, of Manchester (so deservedly known as a great authority in cotton statistics), obtained through Richard Cobden, Esq.

	lbs.
Total of yarn in manufactured goods . .	120,784,629
,, ,, as such	113,753,197
,, ,, Thread	3,362,983
Total weight of yarn exported	236,900,809
To which add ⅐th, to show the quantity of Wool	33,842,972
Total weight of cotton wool exported in goods and yarn	270,743,781
Shows cotton wool consumed at home, in manufactured goods, and the Scotch trade	155,346,335
	426,090,116

COTTON TRADE OF GREAT BRITAIN.— 1839.

		BAGS.
Jan. 1st, 1829, Stock on hand		498,929
Imported into Liverpool . . .	1,015,357	
,, ,, London	51,231	
,, ,, Glasgow . . .	41,962	
		1,109,550
Total supply		1,608,479
Deduct exported	121,659	
Stock left, Dec. 31	370,276	
		491,935
Total number of Bags consumed		1,116,544

Or, at the average weight of 346 lbs.: — making 384,928,079 lbs. of cotton wool, spun in 1839,—of which was exported from England, in manufactured goods, as follows :—

WEIGHT OF YARN IN MANUFACTURED COTTON GOODS, EXPORTED FROM ENGLAND IN THE YEAR 1839.

Description.	Number of Yards of each description.	Length of each piece.	Number of pieces of each description.	Weight of yarn in each piece.		Total weight of yarn exported in goods.
	Yards.			lbs.	oz.	lbs.
Calicoes, Printed and Dyed	278,064,831	28	9,930,887	4	4	42,207,019
Calicoes, Plain . .	316,001.128	24	13,166,713	5	12	75,708,599
Cambrics and Muslins	5.168,731	20	258,437	3	0	775,311
Velveteens, &c. . . .	4,396.771	60	73,279	22	12	1,667,036
Quiltings and Ribs .	215,373	60	3,589	18	4	65,599
Cotton and Linen . .	1,910,745	40	47,769	8	0	382,152
Ginghams and Checks	2,681,391	20	131,070	3	8	469.245
Ticks, checked, &c. .	326,981	50	6,540	20	0	130,800
Dimities	92,254	60	1,538	12	0	18,455
Damasks and Diapers	24.108	36	679	10	0	6,790
Nankeens	121,258	50	2,425	8	8	20,612
Lawns and Lenos . .	47,840	20	2,392	2	8	5,9 0
Imitation Shawls . .	27,652	12	2,304	2	8	5,760
Lace, &c.	91,531,094	40	2,288,277	0	8	1,144,138
Counterpanes, &c. . .	142,708	No.	142.708	7	0	998,956
Shawls and Handkerchiefs	686,616	Doz.	686,616	2	8	1,716,560
Tapes, Bobbins, &c. .	81,432	..	81,432	1	0	81,432
Hosiery	516,156	..	516,156	2	8	1,300,390
Unenumerated . .	159,341	£	Sterling.	10	0	1,593,341

Total Weight of Yarn Exported in Manufactured Goods in 1839,—128,298,236

	lbs.
Total weight of yarn in manufactured goods	128,298,236
.. „ Exported as such .	99,043,539
.. .. Thread	2,711.798
	230,053,673

	lbs.
Total weight of Yarn exported . . .	230,053,673
To which add $\frac{1}{7}$ to show the quantity of Wool	32,864,810
Total weight of Cotton wool exported in goods and yarn	262,918,483
Shows Cotton wool consumed at home in manufactured goods, and the Scotch trade	122,009,596
	384,928,079

Which leads us to the following comparison of the Cotton trade of 1838 and 1839 :—

	lbs.
Quantity of cotton wool exported in a manufactured state, in 1838 . .	270,743,781
do. do. 1839 . .	262,918,483
Deficient in the latter year, all in yarns	7,825,298
Quantity of cotton wool consumed at home in manufactured goods, and the Scotch trade, in 1838 . . .	155,346,335
do. . 1839 . . .	122,009,596
Deficiency in the latter year, in home consumption	33,336,739
do. do. Export	7,825,298
Total deficiency of cotton wool manufactured in 1839	41,162,037

Of this deficiency the whole of the portion in the export is in yarns, which, in that state, may be estimated at *one shilling* per lb. for the weight of wool. The deficiency shown in the home trade must be considered altogether as manufactured goods of every kind; the value of which, as a fair general average, is calcucated at 2*s*. 4*d*. per lb. of cotton.*

The deficiency as thus shown, on the whole trade, will stand thus:—

7,825,298 lbs. in yarn	.	1*s*. 0*d*.	391,264
33,336,739 ,, goods	.	2*s*. 4*d*.	3,889,286
			£4,280,550

The deficiency of the consumption of cotton manufactures in 1839, as compared with 1838, was therefore upwards of *four millions of pounds sterling*; of which sum *one-fourth* may be called the price of the raw material, and *three-fourths* the representative of *labour, interest of capital, and profit,* in all the different branches of *spinning, weaving, dyeing, bleaching, printing, &c.* and it becomes therefore evident

* This we believe to be a correct calculation; as we have tried it with the whole accounts of the last three years, as shown by the customs entries for export, which were as follow:—in

1837. Exported in manufactured goods 114,709,861 lbs. of cotton wool as manufactured goods:—at the declared value of £13,640,181,—or 2*s*. 4.¾*d* per lb.

1838. Exported in manufactured goods 138,039,576 lbs. of cotton wool as manufactured goods:—at the declared value of £16,715,857.—or 2*s*. 5*d*. per lb

1839. Exported in manufactured goods 146,626,555 lbs. of cotton as manufactured goods:—at the declared value of £17,694,303, or 2*s*. 5*d*. per lb.

that the cotton interest alone has suffered an abstraction from its income, in the last year, as compared with the preceding, in *labour*, *interest*, and *profit*, of the large sum of *three millions two hundred and ten thousand pounds.*

After calmly examining these facts, can any one be surprised at the *ruin* which has crowded the Gazettes with bankrupts, and the famine which has wrought such wreck in the cotton manufacturing districts, during the last year?

All the other leading branches of manufactures have shared a similar fate during this period. In every instance, as far as can be discovered, the quantity of raw material consumed has been greatly diminished; and in every case a greater proportion of the amount of what production has been created has been forced into an export trade, for the want of a home consumption, which is therefore shown to have diminished, not only by a great diminution of the whole quantity manufactured, but by a large increase of the portion forced abroad.

The following statements will show the result of the leading articles of manufacture:—

Quantities taken into consumption and exported in 1838 *and* 1839 *of the following articles:—*

WOOL.

			lbs.
Taken into consumption,	1838	. . .	56,415,460
Ditto	1839	. . .	53,221,231
Less, cleared for consumption		. .	3,194,229

		£
Woollen goods exported, 1838		6,179,604
Ditto	1839	6,679,287
More, exported		499,683

FLAX, &c.

		cwt.
Taken into consumption, 1838		1,625,830
Ditto	1839	1,228,894
Less, cleared for consumption . . .		396,936

		£
Linen manufactures exported, 1838 . .		3,566,435
Ditto	ditto 1839 . .	4,237,095
More, exported		670,660

SILK.—RAW, WASTE, THROWN, &c.

		lbs.
Taken into consumption, 1838		4,887,456
Ditto	1839	4,757,639
Less, cleared for consumption . . .		129,817

		£
Silk Goods exported, 1838		777,280
Ditto	1839	865,768
More, exported		88,488

EXPORTED, HARDWARE AND CUTLERY.

	£
In 1838	1,498,327
„ 1839	1.819,000
More, exported in 1839 . . .	320,673

As may be expected, we find all the articles, contributary to the manufacture of the above great staple articles, falling off greatly in consumption also. The following table will show the comparison of the consumption of the two years under review of the following articles :—

CLEARED FOR HOME CONSUMPTION.

		1838.	1839.
Barilla and Alkali .	cwt.	77,759	59,607
Indigo	lbs.	3,020.562	2,719,503
Lace-dye	„	633,869	539,599
Logwood	tons	14,107	17,937
Madder	cwt.	109,385	97,645
Madder-root . . .	„	83,725	81,219
Shumac	„	208,251	171,222
Olive Oil	galls.	2,037,987	1,815,692
Train. &c., do. . .	tuns	28,014	22,348
Palm do.	cwt.	276,809	266,427

Cochineal and logwood are the only articles which are an exception to a great decrease.

From all these official statements it becomes sufficiently plain that the home consumption of the whole of our leading articles of manufacture has been greatly reduced during the past year, not only to the extent of the diminished quantity actually manufactured, as shown by the falling off of consumption of the raw material, but also by the additional quantities exported to relieve this market of a pressing excess. But although this pressing excess has apparently been disposed of, it is not in reality so. It has only been removed from this market, and diffused over other markets, where it has also created an excess; the consequence of which is, at this time, that great sacrifices are being made in these distant markets, which all fall upon the British merchant and manufacturer, on whose account such goods were exported.*

It is therefore obvious that, although the effect of the diminished ability to consume the produce of manufacturers, in consequence of the increased portion of the national means absorbed in a high price of provisions, is first apparent on the home consumption, it must ultimately tend also to destroy and to derange our foreign markets in a twofold manner; first, by the large excess thrown upon them from this country, by which they become glutted, and the more healthy demand of direct purchases superseded; and, secondly, in consequence of the great falling off of the consumption in this country of such articles of their growth as form their ability of exchange, their power of consumption necessarily becomes contracted.

There is still one other mode by which the mercantile

---

* Illustrative of this operation, we may quote the following from an American correspondent to one of our leading journals: "I would wish to give a hint to those of British manufacturers who *continue to send over goods to this country to be sold at forced sales, at almost any price. If the practice is continued, the loss will be enormous.*" The forced *sales* are, however, only the effect of forced *exports*.

interest becomes greatly injured at such periods. When, by the sudden demand for grain, the import can only be secured in exchange for *bullion*, then, according to every authority on the currency question, it becomes a duty with the managers of the currency, whoever they are, to contract it in the same proportion that there appears a tendency for the bullion to lessen, in order to raise the value of money, and prevent a further abstraction of bullion. Well, be it so, and admit that they succeed: what is the result? The same quantity of wheat must still be obtained, and it must be paid for: the principle is that by raising the value of money so high, the price of goods is depressed so low, that at last, instead of taking gold at a very high price, they take goods at a very low price; instead of taking a small quantity of bullion, they are induced to take a large quantity of goods, as compared with the ordinary and real comparative value of the two commodities.

If, therefore, this attempt of raising the value of money means anything, it is simply depressing the value of goods so low, comparatively, that the foreigner is induced to take the latter, instead of the former, in exchange.

Suppose this to be true—it is obvious that this is another motive from the same common cause of forced exports, at ruinous prices; and it is not necessary to accomplish the object that the exports should take place to the countries from whence we derive the grain: these countries may require none of our products at that particular time; or we may find intermediate countries with whom a forced exchange may be made of our goods for bullion, at a smaller sacrifice than could be with the producer of grain; but it is nevertheless the forced exports of our goods at a low price that enables us to satisfy such purchases of grain with bullion so obtained.*

We will not here inquire whether any part of the depression of prices and the forced exports have arisen from a voluntary contraction of the currency, or whether they are altogether referable to a diminished demand for home consumption, as in either case the first cause is the same; and the ultimate effect is to charge the mercantile and manufacturing interest with the whole cost of correcting the derangement.

Having now, we are afraid rather tediously, traced the course of trade since 1832, we would now crave

* In speaking of the monetarial derangement in the United States last year, Mr. Biddle says: " There remains to be added the *vast quantity of foreign merchandise which has been poured in upon us for a market* to swell the amount of our imports, during the present year, far beyond the proceeds of our exports. Immense amounts of the precious metals have already been exported within that period; it is believed that the port of New York alone has witnessed the departure of probably not less than twelve millions of dollars, the fruits chiefly of her collections, for the sales of foreign goods, here and elsewhere; the packets of England, departing every five days, all take their quota; and the great steamers, each with her millions, vie with each other in accelerating their speed to replenish with our means, ere it be too late, the exhausted vaults of the Bank of England."

attention while we shortly apply our general principle to the facts.

We say that the chief cause of the fluctuating character of our trade and manufactures arises from the great fluctuation in the amount of the national income which is absorbed in a number of consecutive years, as compared with others, for payment of the first and imperative necessaries of life ; thus leaving in some years a much larger portion of the national means to be expended in manufactured goods, than can be regularly and eventually maintained.

Considering wheat as the most universal first necessary of life, we regard it as an article which fluctuates less in the amount of consumption than any other ; with all classes of society, not absolutely in want, the consumption is nearly the same at all times ; and with the very poorest classes everything else is curtailed or given up before bread. As therefore the consumption does not materially increase with lower prices, or diminish with higher prices, and as we have seen that these prices fluctuate very much, it follows, that the whole amount of means absorbed in the purchase of this article must fluctuate at the same rate as the price.

It also follows that as the means of the community to purchase manufactures, and other articles of a secondary consideration, must depend entirely upon the amount of income left, after securing the first necessaries, the demand for the former must fluctuate exactly in proportion to the price of the latter. Admitting these obvious principles, it follows that if we could maintain a uniform price of wheat, by which the amount of income necessarily absorbed would be always the same, then only could we expect a uniform condition of the trade.

But, if by the operation of our Corn Laws, we have alternately periods of very high prices, and of very low prices, the general condition of trade must oscillate correspondingly. Thus, if the price of wheat continues unusually high for three or four consecutive years, trade must remain restrained and stationary; and thus, if prices fall much below the average rate, the demand for manufactures must receive a great impulse; and, as in both cases, the effect is accumulative, if low prices continue for a number of years, the influence is correspondingly great.

Referring to the table page 13, we find that, during the extremely high prices which ruled from 1817 to 1820, trade was extremely depressed; great distress existed in our manufacturing districts, and the peace of the country was materially interrupted; but no sooner did prices fall in 1820, than an improvement was visible; –a further decline took place in 1821; all complaints vanished, and trade became active: in 1822, a further decline took place,—the influence was more and more evident on manufacturing industry which, in this year, received a great impulse, the effect of which, with moderate prices, continued until the speculative mania of 1825, with a high price of wheat and a considerable importation, caused a most serious re-action, and which produced the panic of 1825-26.

The great excitement which had prevailed, and the increased demand which had been experienced for the products of our manufactories, during the two or three preceding years of very low prices of wheat, had naturally called into existence an amount of productive power, equal to the demand. In the beginning of 1826, when the effects of the crisis and the high price of grain greatly reduced the demand, the increased productive ability which had thus been called into existence from a temporary cause, added to the other existing circumstances, created a great depression in all branches of business. In 1827, there was a general sign of improvement, but in 1828, the price of wheat advanced materially, and continued very high, with extensive importations, until 1831, during which period, especially in 1829 and 1830, trade was reduced to an extremely low ebb; and the peace of the country was once more threatened by an ill employed population.*

* The following table shows the sum expended in each year in support of the Poor in England and Wales, and bears a remarkable coincidence with the principles under consideration, and the description we have just given of this period:—

YEAR.	£.				s.	d.
1818	7,822,735	Following	1817	Price of Wheat	94	
1819	7,468,383	,,	1818	,	83	8
1820	7,330,256	,,	1819	,,	72	3
1821	6,959,249	,,	1820	,,	65	10

The rapid extension of business which took place under the influence of low prices from 1832 to 1836, and forward until the autum of 1838, with the sudden and disastrous check it received in 1839, in consequence of the rapid advance in the price of wheat, have already been sufficiently considered.

Having now fully considered the fluctations to which commerce and manufacturing industry are subjected, by the fluctuating price of wheat, we will shortly examine the relative results of these fluctuations to this and the agricultural interests.

We have found that each interest, at opposite periods, have experienced similar effects—each interest has had periods of alternate excitement and depression—which have been attended by equally ruinous consequences to each.

The landed interest has had periods of very high prices (as from 1828 to 1831)—much above the average prices,

1822	6,358,702	,,	1821	,,	54	5
1823	5,772,958	,,	1822	,,	43	3
1824	5,736,898	,,	1823	,,	51	9
1825	5,786,989	,,	1824	,,	62	0
1826	5,928,501	,,	1825	,,	66	6
1827	6,441,088	,,	1826	,,	56	11
1828	6,298,000	,,	1827	,,	56	9
1829	6,332,410	,,	1828	,,	60	5
1830	6,829,042	,,	1829	,,	66	3
1831	6,798,888	,,	1830	,,	64	3

which drew into it a much larger portion of the national income than could be sustained. The natural consequence, however, was (and the natural corrective), profits being thus forced much above the ordinary rate, the greatest part of the excess of capital which thus flowed into the agricultural interest was invested in improved and extended cultivation; and just in proportion as the price, and consequently the profit, was above the average, did the inducement exist to improve and extend cultivaton to secure these advantages. This naturally led to an over productionin the exact proportion to which prices had been forced above the average and remunerating rate; and which, as a necessary consequence, led to a reduction of prices as much below the average and remunerating rate, as they had before been above it: and thus we find that after this period from 1831 prices regularly fell every year until 1835, from 66/3 per quarter in the former to 39/4 in the latter year. Of what advantage, therefore, did the high profits made from 1828 to 1831 prove, when, by the necessary tendency of such profits, losses to a corresponding amount arose from 1832 to 1836?

On the other hand, manufacturers have had periods of very extensive demand increasing year after year, as the prices of wheat became lower and more ruinous to the farmer (as from 1832 to 1836). He was then enjoying a demand for his products as much above the proper average rate as provisions were below it. We have given abundant evidence of the rapidly increasing demand for such products, while wheat fell from 66/3 per quarter in 1831 to 39/4 in 1835. In the history of the world there is not an instance of so rapid an increase of manufacturing production as arose out of the unnatural stimulus afforded by these extreme low prices. The great and profitable demand which existed under the excitement had the natural effect of forcing into existence a sufficiently increased productive power not only to accomplish all the demand of the time, but to provide for a further increase at the rate experienced by each individual party. We consequently find that productive ability to a most unexampled extent was called into existence at this period, but which did not come into full operation until 1838. In 1835, when most of the cotton-mills not only worked very long hours, but in very many instances with two distinct sets of work-people, continued in full operation night and day, with the greatest possible effort under a most excited demand, the whole productive ability of our cotton manufactures was equal to a weekly consumption of cotton wool of 18,157 bags; but in 1838 it had advanced to a weekly consumption of 24,312 bags, showing an increased power of working up 6,155 bags every week by the great extension of manufactories and expensive improvements in machinery.*

* While the foregoing was at press, we have received a most interesting communication from John Sturrock, Esq., banker, in Dundee, to whom we had addressed inquiries relating to the progress that town had made since 1828, the period which we have so closely examined; and the statistical facts which he furnishes, with his observations thereon, are so truly illustrative of our principles, that we must crave the reader's particular attention to the following extract from them:—

In 1828 the productive ability of Dundee in flax-spinning was

But, as the fundamental cause of this excitement was too great to be permanent—as this extensive demand

equal to 500 horse-power; it advanced very slowly until the end of 1832, when it was equal to 615 horse-power: from this time until 1836 the progress was very rapid, having in these three years increased to 1309 horse-power. The continued impulse of the great demand in 1835 and 1836 induced a still further extension, until it amounted in 1839 to 1695 horse-power.

The progress stands thus:—

Flax-spinning power in	1828—500	horse-power.		
Advanced in four dear years to	1832—615	,,	,,	
,, ,, cheap years to	1836—1309	,,	,,	
,, ,, ,,	1839—1695	,,	,,	

Up to the end of 1836 the whole productive ability of the town was kept in full operation. The reaction which took place in 1837 threw about 200 horse-power out of working: part of which were again set to work in 1838: but by the end of 1839, and up to this time, out of the whole existing 1695 horse-power, only 951 are employed, and 744 are standing idle. The comparison is thus:

1828,	existing,	500	horse-power;	employed,	500	horse-power.
1832	,, ,,	615	,,	,,	615	,,
1836	,, ,,	1309	,,	,,	1309	,,
1837	,, ,,	1456	,,	,,	1256	,,
1839	,, ,,	1695	,,	,,	951	,,

We thus see, by the excited prosperity of the cheap years, a productive ability was called into existence which could not ultimately be used, and there is no doubt that a large portion, if not the whole, of the advantages obtained in the good years, have been since lost and sunk in unproductive power. The cost of flax-mills is about 400*l.* per horse-power. The portion now standing in an unproductive state shows a sunk loss of 297,000*l.*; but, large as this sum may appear, to it must be added the depreciation which the existence of this surplus necessarily inflicts on all those that are employed; as well as the losses which must arise from a branch of industry of which there must always be, was based on a price of provisions much below the cost at which they could be produced,—a reaction sooner or later was an imperative consequence; and we find that prices gradually rose, but continued moderate, until the end

---

with such an excess of productive ability, a large surplus in the market.

The depreciation in the value of the existing mill property, since 1836, is thus stated :—

These mills have cost . . .		£678,000
Of which are employed	£380,400	
,, unemployed	297,600	
		678,000
Their present value is not above .		339,000
To which add depreciation on manufactories and machine-shops of all descriptions . .		121,000
Makes a loss in sunk capital, since October, 1836, of . .		460,000

This loss to individuals is a loss to the nation ; therefore what benefit can years of prosperity be either to individuals or the community, when they are, necessarily, succeeded by a loss of the whole advantages, and producing innumerable evils in the derangement and ruin which ensue ? Mr. Sturrock observes, with great truth, in reference to this loss—

"The value can never be restored, unless our rulers adopt measures for having a *free trade with all the world*—admitting at the *same duty* the *same articles* from *every quarter*—and, above all, a *free trade in corn*, that our population may be freed from the situation in which they are at present placed, when they *eat* as much as they *can get*, but do not *get* as much as they *can eat*.

"Thus, by the starvation of the people, are the two ends of the year made to meet.

of 1838 (the very year in which the increased productive ability first showed its great power), when it was discovered that low prices and a lessened production had exhausted the ordinary stock of wheat; prices rose suddenly, and large imports were required from abroad; and so much did the enhanced prices of wheat reduce the consumption of manufactures in 1839, that the productive ability, which we have seen was capable of working up 24,312 bags of cotton weekly in 1838, was only called to exercise its powers to the extent of 20,348 bags weekly in 1839, and that at ruinous prices to the

---

"The long-continued depression of mercantile affairs is breaking down the spirits of the people and *demoralising them*. They are become callous—think nothing of becoming bankrupts—and many of them have failed twice since 1836.

"The disastrous consequences which have resulted can only be first alleviated, and then eventually removed, by allowing all nations freely to exchange with us, that markets may be found for the necessaries and luxuries of life, which, from our not-to-be-estimated productive powers, can be furnished to an unlimited extent—for what bounds are there to human wants?—and what reason is there why the population of our country should not be quadrupled?

"By a free intercourse the *status* of the world would be generally raised, and our own country, from its wealth, from the confidence which exists between man and man, its ingenuity, perseverance, and skill, would assuredly progress in a much greater ratio than any other."

The state of things we have described as existing in Dundee, leads us naturally to the consideration that, if so much mechanical power be stagnant, how much physical power and skill must be stagnant with it. We learn from this report that *wages are now twenty-five per cent. lower than they were in 1836, when wheat was half the present price.*

producers. It is therefore plain that a productive ability equal to working about 4000 bags of cotton, weekly, or 200,000 bags in this year, remained stagnant, unprofitable, and just as useful as if it had never existed.

The extraordinary excitement which cheap years of wheat produce in the demand for manufactures, and the great profits which are then secured by this interest, lead only to a time and consequences correspondingly ruinous, by calling into existence a productive ability which cannot be regularly maintained, and which is not only so much positive loss of capital, but, by the general law of competition, when the supply is greater than the demand, reduces the whole product to ruinous prices.

The result, therefore, is, that each of these leading interests is alternately introduced into periods of great prosperity, but which necessarily lead to periods of equal depression, when all the advantages obtained in the former period are lost and destroyed. There is no permanence in the success of either; and these fluctuations are always proceeding in their course of operation, although it is only at the extreme points that public attention is much attracted by the consequences.

The only way in which these crying evils could be remedied would be by maintaining a uniformity of the price of the first necessary of life, which we have shown is the great acting impulse. If this happy object could be obtained, then the two interests, commercial and agricultural, could only go on hand in hand—progress together or recede together. As there would exist no undue exciting causes for over-production on either side, each would produce regularly and uniformly nearly the precise quantity required for consumption; no re-action would, therefore, take place, which, while it depressed the one interest, unduly excited the other; but they would advance steadily together, regularly affording to each other additional means of extension, and tending continually to the benefit of each other, instead of as it is at present—that the two interests are alternately rising on the ruin of each other.

We have sufficiently shown in a former work that this most desirable uniformity never can be experienced under the operation of the present law, or any other law which tends to restrict the supply of a regular and uniform quantity—which forbids the excess of one country to flow into another to equalise a deficiency created by accident or a change of circumstances; but which, on the contrary, by holding out delusive promises of a maintenance of extremely high prices, tends to give a most unnatural and excited impulse to production, and thus imperatively induces a course of violent fluctuations which are ruinous to all and beneficial to none.

When these laws were first enacted in 1815, Lord Grenville, and the other peers who subscribed his celebrated protest against them, with great sagacity foresaw all these effects. The following extract from that enlightened document is so true in principle, has proved so true in practice, and is so universally applicable to all mercantile legislation, that it well deserves to be suspended in every senate-house in the civilised world :—

"We cannot persuade ourselves that this law will ever contribute to produce plenty, cheapness, or steadiness of price. So long as it operates at all, its effects must be the opposite of these. *Monopoly is the parent of scarcity, of dearness, and of uncertainty.* To cut off any of the sources of supply can only tend to lessen its abundance; to close against ourselves the cheapest market for any commodity must enhance the price at which we purchase it; and to confine the consumer of corn to the produce of his own country is to refuse to ourselves the benefit of that provision which Providence itself has made for equalising to man the variations of climate and of seasons."

PART III.

FLUCTUATIONS OF COMMERCE, MANUFACTURES, &c., OF THE CONTINENT.

The effects which our Corn Laws produce on continental industry and commerce, and the tendency that these effects necessarily have to re-act again on this country, are well deserving of our consideration.

By the imperative operation of our Corn Laws we have clearly seen that the demand for foreign grain can only be at uncertain periods, considerably apart from each other. For years successively these countries are altogether excluded from our markets, and, when at last they are admitted, it is at the very highest prices. This circumstance necessarily produces in these countries fluctuations even to a greater extent than are experienced in this country.

The extensive demand which was experienced from 1828 to 1831 for continental wheat, at very high prices, gave a similar impulse to its production that the high prices of that period exerted in this country; and the consequence was that, as soon as our prices fell to the point at which foreign wheat could no longer be admitted, the continental producers had two difficulties to contend with—first, a greatly increased production stimulated by high prices; and, secondly, the entire loss of the market which they had enjoyed to some extent for three years. Under this two-fold cause the price of wheat fell to an extremely low point; the average price in Dantzig, in 1835, being only 23*s*. per quarter.

During these years of low prices on the continent the same effect on manufacturing industry was experienced as in this country. Throughout Germany, Russia, France, and Belgium a very rapid progress was made in the industrial arts; a great quantity of capital, which would otherwise have been invested in agriculture, being diverted to these objects. The very low prices of the first necessaries of life leaving a large surplus to consume other products, an excited demand arose in exact proportion to this lowness of price.

With the continuance of low prices, and exclusion from the market, a re-action in agricultural production necessarily ensued, which became reduced to a limit of their own consumption.

When, therefore, a large demand arises for this country, such as was experienced last year, the prices on the continent are raised, even in a much greater proportion to their average prices than those of this country, by the inevitable process which we have examined in the Appendix to the second edition of the "Influences of the Còrn Laws," &c.

By this means the income of the continental countries,

especially of France, Belgium, and others, which consume chiefly wheaten bread, is absorbed in a proportionably greater degree in payment for the first necessaries of life; and leaving, therefore, so much less to expend in the products of other industries. The same reasons, therefore, that are acting in this country to contract the demand for manufactures, are acting in a stronger degree in the very countries from which we abstract, by the compulsary force of high prices, the quantity of food needed to make up our deficiency.

In proportion, therefore, to the amount of our accidental necessity of importing their produce, we raise the prices so much on them, that we reduce their means, for the time being, to consume their own manufactures, and therefore the difficulty is still greater to induce them to take any portion of our manufactures in return. At first sight this may appear a strange contradiction; that, by paying a country high prices for its produce, its power of consumption is thereby diminished; but we do the same in this country; we pay one class of producers a very high price for their produce, and are unable to consume the usual quantity of the produce of another class; and, although in this country the evil is rendered greater by our having to pay for the deficiency, while the continental countries receive the price of their surplus, yet, as concerns the ability of the masses of consumers, it is very much the same; in both cases the advantage of these high prices, being altogether accidental and not regular, goes to enrich the few, while the great masses, who are the chief consumers everywhere. suffer merely so much abstraction from their ordinary means to enjoy other things. Hence we find that during the past year the falling off of manufacturing industry on the continent has been as great as in this country, and in many instances greater; for not only have they had a diminished ability of consumption, but they have also had to contend against the forced exports from this country; as an intelligent correspondent in Belgium writes, in relation to the decrease of the cotton trade of that country during the past year, that it was "partly owing to the high prices of bread-corn, but more especially to the competition of British manufactures, which, notwithstanding a high protective duty, have been imported and sold at such low prices as to compel our manufacturers materially to curtail their operations."

The following comparative statements of the trade of some of the most important continental countries, in 1838 and 1839, will show that the same corresponding effects have attended extremely high prices of provisions as in this country.

TRADE OF BELGIUM, 1838 & 1839.

COTTON WOOL.

	BAGS.		BAGS.
Stock, January 1, 1838 .	2,566	January, 1839	3,881
Total imports in 1838 .	39,552	" "	22,766
Total supply " " .	42,118	" "	26,647
Stock left, December 31 .	3,881	" "	5,207
Consumption, 1838 . . .	38,237	" "	21,440

Showing a falling off of 16,797 bags in 1839.

SHEEP'S WOOL.

	BAGS.		BALES.
Stock, January 1, 1838 .	4,600	January, 1839	2,460
Imports in . . . 1838 .	9,756	„ „	7,982
	14,356		10 442
Stock, December 31 „	2,460	„ „	2,150
Consumption of 1838	11,896	„ „	8,292

Showing a falling off of 3,504 bales in 1839.

This table refers only to the wool imported by sea; of that brought by land from Germany and the north of France we have no account.

These are the chief articles of manufacture in Belgium, except linen, the raw material of which being produced in the country, we cannot ascertain the quantities; but in all the leading articles, contributing to manufactures, dye stuffs, oils, &c., the falling off has been on the same scale.

COTTON TRADE OF FRANCE 1838 & 1839.

COTTON WOOL.

	BAGS.		BAGS.
Stock on hand, Jan. 1, 1838 . .	63,500	January, 1839	62,000
Imported in „ .	390,978	„ „	342,100
Total supply „ .	454,478	Total „	400,100
Stock, December 31, 1838	62,000	Stock, December 31, 1839	75,000
Consumption „	392.478	Consumption „	329,100

Showing a falling off of 63,378 bags in France and the neighbouring parts of Switzerland, in 1839.

The woollen and silk trades of France are so much of an inland character that we cannot arrive at any comparative statement; but the consumption of dye stuffs, &c., has also fallen off greatly in 1839.

COTTON TRADE OF HAMBURG FOR THE SUPPLY OF GERMANY in 1838 & 1839.

COTTON WOOL.

	BALES.		BALES.
Stock, January 1, 1838	16,600	January, 1839	7,960
Imports in „ „	42,224	„ „	40,956
Total supply „ „	58,824	Total „	48,916
Stock, December 31, „	7,960	Stock, December 31, 1839	8,880
Total „ „	50,864	Total „ „	40,006

Showing a falling off of 10,828 bales in 1839.

And, in addition to all these deficiencies of the consumption of cotton wool, the continental countries have purchased from this country less cotton yarn to manufacture into cloth, by 14,700,000 lbs., in 1839, than in 1838.

But not only does it appear that a great falling off has taken place in the consumption of manufactured goods in the continental countries during the last year, but also that the same effect has been experienced with reference to other articles of colonial produce, of which we may quote *coffee*, as one of the chief articles of consumption.

The consumption of Belgium, as shown by the deliveries

in Antwerp; of France, as shown by the deliveries in Havre, and of the parts of Germany, drawing their supply from Hamburgh, as shown by the deliveries of port, were :—

1838.			1839.		
Antwerp .	17,642	Tons	Antwerp .	15,411	Tons.
Havre .	20,014,000	Demi Kils.	Havre .	15,550,000	Demi Kils.
Hamburgh	56,256,000	lbs.	Hamburgh	48,000,000	lbs.

The falling off of the consumption of manufactures and colonial produce on the continent has a two-fold effect on our manufactures and commerce: first, the excess which is everywhere experienced in the manufacturing districts on the continent compels them to force their goods into foreign markets, at the time that we are doing the same, and thus tends still further to deluge these markets; and secondly, as in ordinary times, a considerable portion of the supply of raw material, as well as colonial produce, consumed on the continent is furnished, either directly or indirectly, by means of British commerce, and in exchange for British manufactures, it follows that, in proportion as the consumption falls off on the continent, our trade must be lessened with those countries which originally produce these articles. For example, a large portion of the cotton wool consumed in Belgium and Germany is imported from the East Indies and America by us, in exchange for our manufactures, and re-exported by us to those countries. The same is the case, to a very large extent, with respect to indigo and many other articles. The returns for nearly the whole of our exports to the

Brazils, and other parts of South America, as well as St. Domingo and many other places, are made in produce ultimately consumed on the continent; the discriminating duties in favour of our own possessions excluding the produce of these countries from consumption here. It is thus seen that the extremely high prices to which food is accidentally raised throughout Europe by the necessary actions of our Corn Laws, inflicts the most serious and extensive evils to our commerce in many ways not visible at first.

If we had not the continental countries as customers for the coffee and sugars which we receive in exchange for our manufactures from St. Domingo (where coffee is the only exchangeable commodity they can offer), and the Brazils where it is the chief one, and the same exclusive principles continued which at present exist in favour of our own colonies, we should necessarily be deprived of these markets for our manufactures altogether.

The extent of our trade with neutral countries is, we believe, very generally under-rated: we find that about *three-fourths* of the whole of our exports of British produce and manufactures go to foreign countries, with which we have no other relationship than the strong bond of mutual interest; while only *one-fourth* of such exports go to our own colonies. This very extensive foreign trade, being carried on to a great degree, in exchange for commodities which we are practically prohibited from using in this country, we are only enabled to continue it by finding consumers in other countries for such produce.

Independent, therefore, of the vast quantity of foreign produce which is shipped, direct, on British account, to the continent, the re-exports of such articles from this country forms one of the largest branches of our trade. In 1838, we re-exported, in the latter mode, chiefly to the continent:—

Coffee	11,293,290	lbs.
Sugar	374,697	cwt.
Tea	2,577,877	lbs.
Cotton	30,644,469	„
Sheep's Wool . .	1,897,860	„
Raw Silk . . .	166,767	„
Indigo	5,143,891	„
Pepper	3,077,109	„
Tobacco	13,294,212	„

Besides gums, dye stuffs, wines, spices, furs, and other articles to a vast amount, all of which may be considered as the payment for our manufactures sent to the various places from which they were imported; thus the consumption of cotton wool on the continent is one of the modes by which the growers in America are able to purchase our manufactures.

It must, therefore, be obvious, that if any circumstance occurs materially to diminish the rate of general consumption, on the continent, of those articles which we receive from other countries, in exchange for our manufactures, it must tend to reduce the consuming ability of our customers, by lessening the demand for their produce, and, ultimately, the demand for our manufactures.

It is therefore clear that we are interested in the uniform prosperity of the continental countries equally as merchants and as manufacturers; and we cannot but think that the popular jealousy which exists against the advancement of those countries not only displays a spirit of culpable selfishness, but at the same time ill accords with a true and enlightened view of our own interests. In proportion as any country improves and advances, the general field of consumption is expanded, and must be beneficial, directly or indirectly, to producers everywhere: indeed two nations might exist, who had not one transaction directly with each other, and yet their prosperity might most materially depend on each other; and while either was using means to injure the other, the greatest force of such injury might fall upon itself: such are the indirect and insensible modes by which different countries act upon each other. Neither national nor individual interests require to be guarded by a policy resulting from jealousy or envy; but are best promoted by the exercise of a free, liberal, and benevolent principle, by which all are rendered prosperous and happy, and are only thus capable of again reflecting prosperous influences.

PART IV.

FLUCTUATIONS OF LABOUR.

It is impossible that these violent fluctuations in the demand for labour and the price of food can exist, without exercising effects equally violent on that portion of society whose only exchangeable commodity for their daily bread is their labour.

Very little reflection will shew us that the changes which take place in the condition of the working-classes, must be exactly corresponding in character and time with the fluctuations in the industrial world which we have examined: a little investigation on this subject may prove very useful.

It is a plain and easily-understood principle that the value of labour, like money, or any other merchantable article, must be regulated entirely by the proportion which the supply and demand bear to each other. These two elements, however, of regulating value, are acted upon by numerous secondary causes; and, like all other articles, there will always be a tendency for an adjustment between the two. If the supply be larger at any one time than the demand requires, the price of the whole must necessarily fall in proportion to the excess, until, in course of time, low prices increase the demand, or, failing this, until the supply itself was reduced; if, on the other hand, the demand materially exceed the supply, the price of labour would rise until the enhanced cost reduces the consumption, or until the supply was increased, so as to be equal to the demand, to which there would be a strong tendency.

So far as to the price of labour generally, and with respect to any particular kind of labour, the principle is exactly the same. There are many considerations which influence the supply;—the time and expense necessary to acquire the knowledge;—the degree of certainty of demand and remuneration when acquired; —the healthiness and agreeableness, the respectability and station which society accords to the occupation. The demand for all or any must depend on the power of consumption; but as we have before seen that this power must ultimately be regulated by productive ability only, the proportion between the demand and supply ought always to remain nearly the same; and there can be no doubt that they would, were it not for the violation of their regulating laws by the interference of partial legislation attempting to promote particular interests; by which, although the object intended never was and never can be accomplished, a derangement ensues which leads to ruinous changes and fluctuations, afflictive of serious injury in their operations to all parties.

The two great distinctions into which we have seen society severed by such violence, are the agricultural and manufacturing.

It will be useful for the purpose of illustration to know

the relative proportion which these two classes of labour bear to each other. In 1831, the proportion of labour in England, in the two great subdivisions of industry, was 761,348 families agricultural, and 1,182,912 manufacturing, or about 50 per cent. more of the latter than the former; and there is every reason to think that at this moment the difference is even much greater in favour of the latter industry. In 1811 the difference was only 33 per cent., but gradually rose to 50 per cent. in 1831, and there is no doubt has still continued to advance since the last census.

This is important to know in a consideration of how and when labour is likely to be influenced by these fluctuations: for it is clear that labour generally must be influenced by the condition of that interest which retains and consumes the largest portion; and that, therefore, the position of manufacturing industry as employing the largest portion, must always be the index to the general state of labour.

If the manufacturing interest be prosperous, as in 1835, the great improvements and extensions which in such periods take place in our sea-ports and manufacturing towns, and by public undertakings of various characters, such as *railways, canals, &c.*, give a great impulse not only to the demand for manufacturing labour, but also for what may be called common labour; and therefore, at such moments when *provisions* are at the *lowest price*, and the *landed interest* in the most *depressed state*, wages of *all* kinds of labour have been highest. In 1835 and 1836, when the agricultural interest was at the lowest point of depression, one of the great causes of complaint was, that labour was higher than it had been some years before, when the price of wheat was double. At this period, therefore, the whole of the labouring classes have three great advantages,—*full employment, high wages,* and *a low price of provisions;* they experience to its full extent the excitement which then prevails in the commercial world; labour of every description becomes greatly in demand, and commands high prices; the condition of the labourer everywhere becomes greatly improved; he inhabits a better class and a better furnished house; he contracts habits of comparative luxury. In every way his expenditure and engagements rise in proportion to his means;—marriages are numerously contracted; a great impulse is given to the increase of population by the extraordinary demand for labour. So great was this demand, that at this period there were instances of large manufacturing establishments standing still only for a want of work-people. In this state of prosperity, the working classes made great progress in intelligence and taste; and, generally speaking, their condition was materially advanced.

This would certainly be a most pleasing picture, arousing most gratifying reflections, if it were not alloyed by a conviction that this state arose out of a false and artificial excitement which could not be maintained, but which, on the contrary, must, ere long, lead to a *depression* as great as was the *excitement.*

But it can be no matter of surprise that this class should fail to discover, that the enjoyments and prosperity of the present could not last—that they should act as if it were to continue so for ever—that they should do all things in relation to the existing causes of the moment, without looking forward to the future. It cannot be matter of surprise that this class should do so, when we have seen all classes in their turns have committed the same error;—that the agriculturist cultivated during dear and excited years, in reference only to the existing state of things, and found, by doing so, that he brought loss and ruin upon himself by calling into existence a power of production at an expensive rate, greater than could be consumed at prices consistent with the cost; that the manufacturer, in his turn, used every effort to create a productive power equal to the demand he experienced, at the time of the greatest excitement, but which, by the time it was ready for full operation, was not required, and therefore may be called so much sacrifice of the profits of past years—that, in fact, all mankind are governed by the influences of the present, without much reference to the future.

We have already shown how delusive and ruinous to all parties such policy had proved, with what certainty a re-action succeeded such excitement; and it is now our melancholy duty to trace this re-action on the condition of the labourer.

We have already seen that from obvious reasons the fluctuations in the condition of the labourer (even agricultural) must correspond with those of the manufacturing classes; and, in addition to those reasons already given, it must also be obvious that when the latter interest is greatly depressed, there must be a large quantity of labour usually employed in it, which, at such times, will come in competition with common labour, which, being of a less skilled character, is easily taken up by many not usually employed therein. It therefore necessarily happens, from all we have seen, that when provisions are at the highest point, manufacturing industry at the greatest depression, labour is least in demand and lowest in price. Our manufacturing and seaport towns, instead of absorbing and drawing towards them a portion of the country labour as before, (and so preventing any redundancy which might otherwise have been felt in the agricultural districts during depressed times,) now throw back upon the country a considerable amount of labour—there is no longer any great demand for internal improvements; and thus, when the agricultural interest is in a high state of prosperity and extension, the increased supply of labour prevents any increase of price.* Then comes the reverse of the labourer's former position; he is injured—he is compromised in *three* most distressing ways—*deficient employment, low wages, and a high price of provisions.*

The experience of the past year and the present

* We are quite aware that in some solitary instances during high prices, a slight advance has taken place in the price paid for agricultural labour: but this has not been general by any means, and may be termed rather the exception than the rule; and in no case has wages been raised at all in proportion to food; and in many cases among agriculturists have the money wages been lowered.

moment furnishes a most melancholy evidence of this deplorable experience of the whole labouring classes—of the existence of these ill-assorted elements of their condition: they are now called upon to relinquish all the habits of comparative comfort and luxury into which prosperous years introduced them; thousands of comfortable cottages built for them in the manufacturing districts and suitable for their means a few years ago are now empty, while several families are crowded into single garrets and cellars: the intellect that was partially expanded, the taste that was a little cultivated, are now of no use but to render less endurable the degradation which has come over them: the impulse that was given to an increase of population and physical productive ability only tends now by its consequences to swell the amount of evil and difficulty. Instead of the comparative plenty which was in all ways enjoyed only a few years ago, the most deplorable starvation and want now exists. Their marriages are denounced as "*improvident*," because the altered state of affairs renders the obligations arising from them a burthen to themselves and the public. Improvident! Let the landowner excuse the improvidence of making laws which give deceptive promise of high rents which last for a year or two, and then fall lower than before, but on the strength of which an extraordinary scale of expenditure is incurred, which ends in embarrassment and mortgage—let the farmer excuse the improvidence of being led to an expensive culture of waste and barren lands, by the excitement of high prices and an expectation of their continuance, but which produce only ruin and disappointment—let the manufacturer excuse the improvidence of creating factory after factory, and swelling the amount of his productive power equal to the wants of the moment, but which prove superfluous when done; and then will there be no difficulty in finding much more excuse for the misfortunes of these poor innocent victims of such laws—laws which teem with mischiefs of the gravest character to every possible class of the community, but which weigh with the heaviest and most oppressive anguish and suffering on the unemployed and starving labourer—doomed to see the only relicts of better times, the fruits of an "*improvident*" marriage, endeared to him the more from their innocent suffering, daily pining away before his eyes by want and disease. There is surely an awful responsibility for all this human suffering resting somewhere; and wherever it rests, a wilful ignorance of these facts can be no excuse; *if investigation be petitioned for, be implored for, information offered, evidence tendered, and all disdainfully rejected*, the responsibility for the consequences, for every pang of suffering, and for every crime arising therefrom, must rest upon the inflictors of this wrong.

There are two ways in which these times of depression act with increased hardship upon this class of sufferers: first, they are more than any other class innocent either of the original or immediate cause; and second, with this class only it becomes a consideration of daily support. The landowner, the farmer, and the manufacturer, are not immediately dependent upon the present moment for their daily food, but the poor labourer relies only from day to day on the result of his toil for the existence of himself and those dependent upon him; when his labour, therefore, fails him, he is at once reduced to want. That a serious amount of crime and disease should arise out of such a state of destitution is only to be expected.

We find that there never have been times of serious and alarming crime, of public commotion and disturbance, of disregard to the laws of the country, excepting at such periods of high prices and want of employment. The disturbances which threatened the peace of the country in 1818 and 1819, the frame-breakers, the Ludites, and the serious occurrences in Manchester, were all promoted by this cause; but how soon all trouble and anxiety ceased on a return to low prices and full work. Again in 1829 and 1830 the same reason can be justly assigned for the violence of that period. The great distress and consequent discontent which prevailed in France in the manufacturing districts during 1829-30 led to the disturbances, and at length to the revolution in the latter year. By referring to the table, page 15, of the prices of wheat in France, it will be found that it was dearer for the two years preceding 1830 than had been the case for many years. Although on such occasions many engaged most prominently in agitation are not of a suffering class, yet all the attempts of such men would ever be in vain, if idleness, want, and starvation did not predispose the mind to crime, partly from desperation—partly from a delusive hope to alleviate their grievances and improve their future condition.

Nor is it to the labouring classes of this country alone that these fluctuations in the price of food exercise so severe a wrong. We have already shown that the manufacturing industry of the continent must necessarily suffer a depression as great as that of this country from the same cause; and therefore we find that during the last year, and up to the present moment, the working classes in France and Belgium particularly are suffering proportionably with those in this country; and we believe that sooner or later a similar action and re-action will be experienced in the productive labour of the whole world, deranging the whole social economy of this class, creating a great mass of misery, disease, and crime, and interfering most materially with the onward progress of moral and intellectual improvement.

Who, then, we ask, have been benefited by the Corn Laws? Who are interested in their maintenance?

Every class of society under their operation has been artificially excited in an extraordinary manner at particular times by false prosperity, which has been followed by an imperative re-action, bringing with it ruin and disappointment to all in their turn.

The deceit began with the law itself;—it professed, it promised what it never could fulfil; and just in proportion as people believed it could fulful its pretensions, did it fail; just in proportion as the landowner and his dependants believed it would secure to them the high prices it professed to uphold, was the effort made by each to secure to himself as large a portion of the benefit as possible. High rents were promised; extensive and enriched cultivation ensued, an immense increase of production was the consequence, in the great eagerness to reap the advantages of this law. This law was passed in 1828: before 1833 the struggle to reap its benefits and the competition for its promises had been so great, that overproduction, disappointment, and distress already were visible as the result. A parliamentary committee inquired into the agricultural distress of this period without any satisfactory result as to its cause; the tendency of the law still went on for two years more; the competition which had been created in productive power for high prices still so much further depressed the condition of the landed interest, farmer and landlord equally, that in 1836 another parliamentary committee was obtained to inquire into their distress. The evidence before this committee teems with the most instructive lessons of the necessary operation of such laws. The whole tendency of this evidence was to prove that the Corn Laws had, by inducing an expectation of high prices, raised rents very high; had called into cultivation a vast quantity of new land; had increased, by expensive modes, the productiveness of that which was in cultivation; had produced thereby a greatly increased supply, which being much more than could be consumed, reduced prices to a destructive rate; to the ruin of the farmer, to an impossibility of collecting the rents in full, to an ultimate reduction of rents, to a depreciation in the quality of cultivation; and, in many instances, to a complete abandonment. (See Appendix.)

With such evidence before us, how can we doubt the baneful effects that these laws have produced on the landed interest?

We have already sufficiently considered how the necessary re-action of these laws influenced the whole of the other classes of society; the capitalist, the merchant, the manufacturer, and the labourer;—to all they have been productive of constant and most injurious fluctuations and derangements. It may however be said that these fluctuations may be accounted for by the natural tendency which the human mind has to excitement and depression; each state necessarily producing the other by simple re-action.

We are free to admit that such impulses are evident and visible in the daily transactions of the world; but we cannot conceive that any one large class of men of one given pursuit should always be uniformly, and at the same time, and for periods of considerable duration, under the same impulses. We cannot suppose that the whole agricultural classes continue excited simultaneously for a few years, while the whole manufacturing classes are depressed—that the latter should thence become all excited, while the former become all depressed, except by supposing that some strong influencing cause existed which acted upon each as a class.

We must admit that there are some of the apparently more immediate causes of the depressions and excitements both of the money market and manufacturing pursuits, which we may be charged with having passed over without sufficient consideration, more particularly the derangements which have been so constantly occurring in our connexions with the United States, which, from the great extent of our business with them, cannot fail to exercise a most important effect upon us : but if we have passed them slightly over, it has not been because they have not seriously engaged our attention, but because the more we have examined and considered them, we can only treat them as part of the effects ; in the first place, as owing their origin altogether to the first great influencing causes of the fluctuations in this country. But, for the great excitement and unnatural abundance of money which prevailed in this country in 1834, 1835, and 1836, could the American crisis of 1837 have occurred?—and there would be little difficulty to show, if our limit admitted, that most of the speculative spirit which has existed in America, has been promoted in a great degree by the unnatural and extensive facilities afforded in this country at particular times, and consequently re-action and depression have never been experienced here without producing even to a more intense degree similar effects there, as they rely in every way so much upon their credit with this country.

To trace all the evils of the necessary tendency which we have shown these laws have in rendering the whole existence of present circumstances uncertain and fluctuating, would be a task of too serious a magnitude to undertake. From what we have seen, we must feel assured that they are opposed in their operation to every effort of civilisation, to every effort of advanced and improved society, to every effort of science and discovery. The first and great object of all being to render uniform and certain the present and future supply of the great necessaries of life, by distributing and equalising with certainty and speed the gifts which Providence plentifully bestows upon some parts of the earth to other places where they are required, and thus producing a feeling of reciprocal benefits and mutual reliance which cannot fail to advance the best and most enlightened interests of the whole human race.

APPENDIX.

The following extracts from the Evidence given before the Parliamentary Committee in 1836, will show how far the opinions of the parties selected to be examined on the condition of agriculture, and the facts which they speak, agree with our theory. It will be borne in mind that this is the period in the fluctuation of great depression in wheat. As may be expected, from a number of men selected from all parts of the country, the different notions and opinions relative to the value and effect of the Corn Laws which are entertained will be found in all their different shades and forms; but what we want chiefly to show is the facts to which they speak:—that the Corn Laws gave delusive hopes to the landlord and farmer of high prices, which never could be maintained—that both were thereby entrapped to press their productive powers to an extent inconsistent with the consumption of the country by an expensive and ruinous outlay; that a reaction took place, in consequence of the excess of supply, by which prices were reduced as much below the fair average price, as the temptation had been held out of obtaining a price above it; that by this state of things the farmers had expended much capital on these improvements, and become ruined: the landlord was disappointed in the rent he expected: another reaction took place, land fell into bad cultivation and became unproductive—the excess of previous years became gradually consumed, after which the lessened production is inadequate to the consumption of the country—prices rise, and at the highest point the foreign grower pours in his accumulated excess of several years. The English farmer had forced, by great additional expense, large crops of wheat, which he sold below the cost of production. He then lessens his production until it is very small, and when prices consequently rise very high, the foreign grower is chiefly benefited by selling his large excess at a price double that at which the English grower sold his excess a few years before.

It is curious to observe in this evidence, that wheat, the chief object to which protection has been directed, and which was so much encouraged in 1829-30 and 1831, was at this period, 1836, the only article that was pointed to as the certain ruin of the farmer; and that now, at a distance of four years, fluctuation has placed it in the same position again in which it stood in the first-named period:—

From the Evidence of Mr. John Ellis.

Mr. Loch. With regard to the question of low prices, have you ever considered how those low prices might be affected by the present system of Corn Laws?—Latterly they have not been affected at all by the Corn Laws, because we are living entirely on our own growth. I have thought a good deal upon the Corn Laws, and if I had been asked that question two years ago, I should have said, without hesitation, that it would be desirable to abolish the present system so as to have a fixed duty; but since I have seen that we can grow so much more than we want ourselves, I doubt whether that would be a safe plan to resort to. But I think the present duty is too high—for this reason, that I think it gives a fictitious value to land, that it gives the farmers an expectation that something is to come to their relief that can never arrive, and on that account it holds up the value of land fictitiously.

Then you think it induced the tenants to make larger offers

than in the result they have been able to pay?—I think so; farmers are naturally prone to expect high prices, and they have been expecting something that was not likely to happen.

Then what alteration would you recommend?—Mine is a vague opinion, but I should propose to retain the fluctuating duty, and to reduce it one-half. I think that that would be all the protection that we ought to have.

Mr. Clay. When you say " reduce it one-half," do you mean that you would make it begin at 60*s.* instead of 70*s.*?—Yes.

Mr. Clive. Would you take off the extreme ends of the duty altogether?—I think it might be left where it is, only changing from 70*s.* to 60*s.*

Chairman. Would you stop at the two last stages of the scale, and have a fixed duty of 5*s.* and never a lower duty than 5*s.*?—That is a point upon which I have not thought; but I should not think that would be a bad plan, because I think the 5*s.* would be no injury to anybody.

Mr. B. Baring. You object to the present scale of Corn Laws, because it encourages delusive hopes in the farmer's mind; is not the farmer undeceived at present?—I think the farmer is anxious for some change in the Corn Laws, he does not know what; but he finds that he has not got the advantage that he expected to get. The fact is, that it is the seasons and himself that have brought these low prices upon him.

The present Corn Laws no longer continue to raise their delusive hopes?—I cannot say; the men that occupy the poor soils are not very intelligent men.

Would not any change encourage other delusive hopes?—Not if you were to lower the duty.

It is for the advantage of the farmer to raise prices, is it not?—I do not think so, I am not of that opinion, I do not think it is the advantage of the farmer to have very high prices.

What do you consider most advantageous to the farmer?—A steady price; that the farmer when he goes to take land should look to some steady price, and not look to adventitious circumstances to help him out of a difficulty.

What is the effect upon the market of the present Corn Laws?—It has no effect at all now; the supply of corn is a mere supply and demand amongst ourselves.

In the long run what has been the effect of the present Corn Laws?—It has tended to keep up the price when we have had bad seasons.

Do you think the present scale has had the effect of creating greater fluctuations of price than there would have been under a more reduced scale?—That is a question that I cannot answer, not having been in the corn trade, but I am certain that the Corn Laws have raised delusive hopes in the farmers.

Mr. Clay. You are decidedly of opinion that steadiness of price is the circumstance most important to the farmer?—My opinion is not in accordance with that of most people with respect to the interests of landlord and tenant; up to a certain point I hold that they go together, that it is the interest of the tenant to keep the land in good condition, as it is of the landlord that he should do so; but his landlord's interest is to have a high price to enable him to pay a high rent; I do not think it is the tenant's interest to be clamorous about a high price; it makes very little difference to me whether I pay a high price or a low price, and I think the country thrives better all round me if the price is a moderate one; it is better for me not to have a high price, provided my expenses are in proportion.

The farmer is a capitalist, and it is of importance to him to be able to calculate the returns upon his capital?—Just so.

He would do that better and feel more certainty if he were sure of a steady price of wheat?—Yes, he would.

Supposing that the present system or any system of Corn Laws tends to produce fluctuation in the price of wheat, that must be ruinous in its consequences to the farmer?—There is no doubt of it.

Mr. Miles. Do you think you could do without protection altogether?—Not in the present state of things; I think we must come to that ultimately, but we must go by easy steps.

But you think that the poorer class of farmers at present look at 60*s.* as the price at which wheat can be maintained?—Yes.

Is it your opinion that upon the average of years prices can attain to that height?—It is my opinion that they cannot, and that they will not attain 50*s.* with fine seasons.

And the consequence is that the poorer farmers have fallacious hopes raised?—Yes.

From the Evidence of Mr. John Hancock.

Mr. Sanford.—Have you any observations to make with regard to the state of agriculture in the neighbourhood with which you are acquainted, which you would wish to add to the evidence which you gave in 1833?—Yes, certainly it is worse than it was. Wheat has gone down from 1*s.* 6*d.* to 2*s.* a bushel.

In consequence of the low price of wheat has there been much less land sown to wheat the last year?—I should think much less; one-fourth, and from that to one-fifth.

From the Evidence of Mr. Robert Hatch Stares.

Chairman. Are you acquainted with the condition of the farmers of a considerable district of Hampshire?—Yes, I value the land occasionally, therefore I have an opportunity of knowing the situation of many of them in our own county.

Comparing their condition at the present time with their condition in 1833, is it better or worse?—Decidedly worse.

To what do you attribute that?—Low prices.

From the Evidence of Christopher Comyns Parker, Esq.

Chairman. What is the condition of the farmers in that part of the county of Essex with which you are so well acquainted?—The condition of the farmers in part of my neighbourhood has been very bad.

Where farms have been re-let to new tenants, have those tenants gone on in improvements in draining, and so on?—I have never seen more improvements in draining, liming, and chalking, than within the last three years.

Do you consider that the distressed state of those farmers can be at all attributed to the rents not having been lowered sufficiently in time?—I should say very materially, the landlords not prudently lowering their rents earlier than they have done.

Do you think the total reduction of rent would have been less if the rents had been lowered sooner?—I know farms that men of capital were occupying that were 25*s.* and 30*s.* an acre, and they offered a pound, and they have since been let for 12*s.* to 14*s.* and 15*s.* an acre, and I believe that had they been reduced to 1*l.* at that time, those tenants would now have been in possession of them, and they would never have been impoverished in their cultivation.

From the Evidence of Mr. William Cox.

Chairman. For the last three years have you been farming that land to a profit?—Decidedly not to a profit.

Are the farmers doing well or ill that occupy land of that description?—A great part have failed: and more than half the rest, if they were to reckon, would be insolvent.

Chairman. What is the condition of the labourers in your neighbourhood?—The labourers are not well off in Buckinghamshire.

Are there many out of employment?—We have not so many

out of employment as we had; there are very few out of employment now, in consequence of the railroads and other public works.

Chairman. Have new tenants been found for unoccupied farms?—For some of them there have, and some of them are in the landlord's hands; a nobleman has two on hand near Aylesbury.

Were those farms exhausted by the tenants before they left them?—One of those alluded to had as good a tenant upon it as any in the country.

Have those farms been offered to be let at a reduced rent? —I cannot say; but I know the landlord would not occupy that description of land, if he could get good tenants.

Mr. Loch. Are those farms in a good state of cultivation? —One was in the hands of a very excellent farmer.

In what condition did he leave it?—I think it was left in good condition.

Has there been any draining or other improvement made in the farm?—The proprietor has drained it since he had it on hand.

Was the other farm in good condition?—I think it was..

Mr. Clive. Were the buildings in good repair?—Yes, they were new.

Adapted for the convenience of the farm in all respects?— Yes.

Mr. Loch. Then why did the tenants go?—They went because they had lost a good deal of money.

Chairman. If the rent of those farms had been reduced after the war to a proper level, do you think those farmers would have left those farms?—There is one of them that I would not have without rent at all.

Sir Robert Price. What was the rent?—I suppose 15*s.* an acre.

Chairman. Why would you not have it without rent?—Because I should lose money.

From the Evidence of Mr. John Brickwell.

Marquis of Chandos. What is the state of the part of the county in which you reside?—I hear complaints from the farmers whom I meet, that they cannot pay their way; that produce is selling so low, they are very much distressed: that is the general complaint when I meet them.

Was there not a farm in the neighbourhood of Buckingham which was thrown entirely out of cultivation?—There are two; this was in the parish adjoining that in which I live; one adjoining my own farm let three years ago at 5*s*. an acre, and wheat was then 7*s*. per bushel, and now wheat is 4*s*. 6*d*., that farm can be of course worth nothing; the persons who see it all refuse it at any rent.

On what ground do they refuse it?—Because the price of produce will not answer.

At what did that farm let several years ago?—At about 20*s*. an acre; it was a poor farm, rather wet clay land.

How many years ago?—I should think about 1826 or 1827; I do not know what the exact rent was; I believe it might have been about 20*s*. an acre, and now it is worth nothing.

Should you say that the cultivation of Buckinghamshire has fallen off within these last eight or ten years?—I should say so in the neighbourhood in which I live.

In what respect?—The land is getting very foul and over-cropped; in some places driven further than it should be.

From the Evidence of Mr. John Houghton.

Marquis of Chandos. Have you not arable farms in the county of Buckingham, over which you are steward?—Yes, I have.

What is their state now, compared with the state of the

grazing farms to which you allude?—On the heavy clay lands the distress is very great, more than it is on the turnip and barley lands, or grass land.

How do you account for that distress upon the clay lands? From the low price of wheat.

Do you find that the capital of the farmers has been diminishing?—Certainly; I think the great distress has been on the heavy land farms.

Have the farmers been paying their rents out of their produce, or out of their capital?—If you take the heavy clay land, certainly out of their capital.

The chief complaint is on account of the depression in the price of wheat?—Yes, that is where the farmer is suffering most; that is where he looks for his rent in the spring of the year, when he should have the price of his wheat to raise the money for his rent; when he is looking for a large sum of money to meet his payments; when he comes to thresh out and carry to market, his expenses almost take the whole price.

Mr. Cayley. Can you assign in your mind any particular reason for the estate alluded to becoming so much diminished in value as to fall within the grasp of the mortgagee?—My opinion is this, that it is that description of soil that will grow nothing in its present state but wheat, and wheat has been so very low in price that persons have not been found to purchase it.

From the Evidence of Mr. John Rolfe.

Marquis of Chandos. What is the rent you pay for land? —Twenty shillings per acre.

Do you use wheat for any other purpose but that of human food now?—I have not done it; some have ground wheat for the pigs: some have given it to their horses, but that was principally the grown wheat of the last harvest but one.

What is the cost of the cultivation of your farm per acre now, as compared with what it was some years ago?—The cost of cultivation is very much the same; there is a little difference in the price of labour.

Mr. Cayley. Can you state how rents are paid in your district?—Rents have heretofore, till the last two years, been very well paid.

How have they been paid since 1833?—They have been paid very badly.

Even on the light soils you speak of?—Yes.

What will become of the landlord?—We shall be all beggars together.

Do you think then that the tenants of this country to a great extent hold their farms upon sufferance only, and at the mercy of the landlords?—Yes, I do.

To what extent should you say that was the case?—I should say that one-half at least in your neighbourhood are subject to that. In the parish where I reside, to my own certain knowledge, if the landlord was to say, I will have the whole of the rent that is now in arrear, the tenant must give up.

Then you mean to say that one-half of the tenantry in your district are insolvent?—Yes, I do.

Has the reduction in rent been equal to the fall in price of corn?—Certainly not: nor if the whole of the rent was reduced it would not be equal.

Mr. Miles. When any farms are untenanted in your district, is there any difficulty in getting tenants?—Yes.

From the Evidence of Mr. John Kemp.

Marquis of Chandos. With regard to wheat, you state that the market is down as regards that; can you assign to the Committee any cause for that depression in the wheat market?—No, I cannot; unless it is from the productions of the seasons; in the last three years there has been a great improvement in the average quantity per acre on our growth, and consequently the supply has been greater.

Do you consider, then, the quantity of wheat in the market has been the cause of the depression of the price?—I should say so.

Has the capital of the farmers in your neighbourhood, and under your knowledge, diminished or not?—Very much diminished.

Has any land gone out of cultivation in your neighbourhood?—No, I believe not; there has been a great quantity of land left on hand with the landlords, and they have taken it and farmed it themselves; that has been very much out of condition.

What is the state of the small farmer about you; the man who rents an hundred acres?—As bad off as the poor man.

Are farmers paying rents from their profits or their capital? —From their capital.

Have the rents been sufficiently reduced in your neighbourhood, do you think, compared with the reduction in the price of corn?—Certainly not, compared with the price of corn; I think in many instances, if the tenants were farming without paying any rent, they would not be able to do more than to keep themselves up.

Suppose the landlords sued their tenants for all arrears, what do you think would be the consequence to the landlords?—They would have all the farms on their hands.

You consider then that the tenants now are merely holding their farms on the sufferance and at the mercy of the landlords?—In many cases that is the case; where they are not, they have borrowed capital to carry on their farms with.

From the Evidence of Mr. William Thurnall.

Mr. Cayley. Do you think that as yet they have reduced rents equivalent to the reduced price of corn?—If my landlord would offer me my farm rent-free, as we have had the prices lately, I would not accept it.

Do you know many farms similarly circumstanced that you would not take rent-free ?—I scarcely know one.

What, in your opinion, is the condition of the tenantry generally in your neighbourhood ?—I think verging on insolvency, generally in the most desperate state that men can possibly be.

You say that you are an oil-crusher, do you sell as much oil-cake as you used to do ?—Not a fourth ; I have sold more oil-cake than all the crushers in my neighbourhood do now ; there are five in that trade, and in rape-dust, which is very considerably used in our neighbourhood ; the trade is reduced to a mere nothing, in consequence of the farmers not being able to purchase it.

In consequence of the farmers not using this rape-dust, can they grow as good crops as they used to do ?—*Certainly not, and the land will feel it in the course of a year or two very materially indeed.*

You say that you sell less oil-cake and less rape-dust ; do you get as well paid for that as you used to do ?—No, that has caused me many unhappy moments ; I believe at this moment my book debts with the farmers are not worth ten shillings in the pound ; there are two farmers in the Cambridge gaol at this moment, and I dare scarcely open a letter, knowing the state of the farmers, fearing that it may contain notice of some bad debt or other.

Are those men who are verging on insolvency, men of prudent character and industrious habits ?—I am speaking only of that class of men.

And yet those men are on the verge of ruin ?—Yes, not only in Cambridge, but, generally speaking, great part of Norfolk, Suffolk, and Essex.

From the Evidence of Mr. Robert Babbs.

Marquis of Chandos. Do you believe whether the farmers are paying their rent out of their capital or out of the profits of their farms?—I believe the farmers have been paying their rents out of the capital they employ.

Is that your case?—It has been my case.

Has the land been cropped harder in your neighbourhood than it used to be?—I think it has.

What is the state of the small farmer as compared with the man that occupies largely?—I think he is very little better than a pauper, a 40 acre farmer.

From the Evidence of Mr. Charles Howard.

Mr. Cayley. Taking the period since the last Committee sat in 1833, what do you consider to be the comparative state of the farming interests now and at that time?—Decidedly and progressively worse.

Do you take into your consideration every species of land, or one species of land more than another?—I think upon the sheep farms, the upland farms, from the increased demand which there has been for sheep, the distress has rather decreased; sheep have been very high.

Then with respect to the low land farms?—Their situation has been progressively much worse.

Have the Holderness farmers in your opinion been paying much rent, or has the cultivation paid the expenses in the last three years?—The rents have been considerably reduced; but those reduced rents have been paid from the capital of occupiers.

From the Evidence of Mr. James Grinding Cooper.

Chairman. Where do you reside?—At Blythburgh, in Suffolk.

What is the state of the farmer?—The condition of the

farmer I consider to be bordering on ruin; he is not so well off as he was in 1833.

Do you know any farms untenanted in that part of Suffolk?—I know a farm that has been untenanted till within the last month or so; the landlord could not let it; but I think he has let it within the last month or six weeks.

Was it let at a reduced rent?—I believe at a very reduced rent.

To a man of capital?—I believe to a man of capital at the present time.

Do you know any other farms that have been without tenants?—I have known a small farm last year without a tenant; it was a considerable time in letting.

What sort of land was that? The principal part of it very heavy land.

From the Evidence of Mr. Samuel Byron.

Chairman. Do you rely entirely or mainly upon your wheat crop?—The small farmers do rely almost entirely on the wheat crop.

To what do you attribute the low price of wheat?—I attribute it in the first place to an abundantly great harvest, in the next to the great quantity of grazing land that has been converted into tillage.

From the Evidence of Mr. Robert Hope.

Mr. Loch. Have you ever thought anything about the present Corn Laws, whether they are beneficial to the farmer, or not?—Yes, they have been often discussed; but it is a very general feeling among those that pay Corn-rents, that they have not been hitherto beneficial, but the very reverse of being beneficial.

What is your reason for that opinion?—It induced men to offer more than has been well realised by the price of corn, because it was generally expected from the Corn Laws, that prices would be kept up to something like what they promised; that the import of foreign corn would be restricted, and by that means keep up the price of the home growth to 70*s*. or so.

Is it the operation of the law, or some other cause, that has made the price of wheat so low, in your opinion?—I think the law has had nothing to do in bringing down the price of wheat; I think it is the favourable seasons and the abundant crops.

The favourable seasons and the abundant crops have affected the price of wheat, not the Corn Laws?—Yes.

Then how has the Corn Law disappointed your expectation?—Because it led those that took farms at money-rents to give a much higher rent than they would have done.

Then they did not calculate upon such favourable seasons?—They did not expect that a series of favourable seasons would ever reduce prices at the rate we have seen the last six months.

Then is it the opinion of you and those other gentlemen that have considered the subject in the way you mention, that the present Corn Law ought to continue, or do you think that that any change would be beneficial to the farmer?—From what we experienced in the year 1831, I am disposed to think that a change would be more beneficial to the farmer, by reducing the scale at which foreign corn is imported.

By reducing the limit?—Yes.

How would that be more favourable to you?—Because prices were run to the top of the scale in 1829; before any foreign corn could be imported, they were run up so high as 70*s*. a quarter; when we could not grow so much wheat as we paid in rent, and had the price only run up to 60*s*. a quarter, we should just have had so much less money to make up the deficient quantity of wheat.

Then it is as affects corn-rents that your observation applies?—It applies entirely to that.

Mr. Sanford. You have stated that the existing Corn Law you consider is prejudicial to the farmer; is your opinion founded upon the circumstance of there having been a miscalculation as to the effects to be produced by the Corn Laws, or upon the working of the Corn Laws themselves?—I think by the present working of the Corn Laws that it may run prices too high for the interest of the farmers in years of scarcity; before any foreign corn can be admitted into the country, prices may be run up so high as to be prejudicial to the interest of the farmer; because in such a year as we had in 1831, we could not grow so much wheat as we had to pay in rent.

Mr. Clay. If the result of this Corn Law should be to produce great fluctuations in price, you would think that effect would apply to all farmers?—I think it has been prejudicial to those that even pay a money-rent, because I am sure that if it had not been for the Corn Laws, they would not have given so high a money-rent.

Mr. Sanford. That proceeded from a miscalculation, upon their part, as to the effect to be produced by the Corn Law?—It was merely a miscalculation.

From the Evidence of Mr. Andrew Howden.

Mr. Cayley. If you had been sold off in 1820, do you think you would have been better off than you are now?—I do not know that mine is a fair case to be taken as a general case, because I started very poor in life, and I have had a hard struggle, and other circumstances that contributed to assist me: I am the only remaining farmer in the parish where I was brought up; except myself, there is not a farmer nor the son of a farmer remaining within the parish but myself.

What is the reason of their having all gone away?—The money-rents that were exacted of them; they all conceived that they were to have 80*s*. a quarter, and their calculations were made upon that; it soon appeared that that could not be realised, and they were not converted, and ruin has been the consequence.

Then there has been a great change of tenantry in your neighbourhood?—There has been.

And that has been caused by the fall of prices?—Yes, and the want of accommodation on the part of the proprietors.

The proprietors have not reduced their rents in proportion? —They now have generally done so; but they were later in doing it than the circumstances required, and therefore the tenantry fell.

In your opinion, did the Corn Law that was made in 1815 deceive both the landlord and the tenant?—It did; I believe that the calculation upon which they took at that time was almost universally 4*l.* a quarter.

The general impression was, that the Corn Laws then made would have the effect of keeping wheat at the price of 80*s.*, and both landlord and tenant were deceived in that?—Yes.

There was some other cause at work, which brought the price down?—I do not know.

If the Corn Law had not the effect of keeping up the price, something must have reduced the price?—It did reduce; but as to the cause, I shall not pretend to say.

The Corn Law having promised a price of 80*s.* failed to perform it?—Yes.

From the Evidence of Lawrence Oliphant, Esq., M.P.

Mr. Cayley. Have you ever made a comparative estimate of the increase of the growth of wheat, and the increase of the population since the fall of prices?—I believe it was a very general opinion, at the time of the first Corn Law in 1815, that this country could not produce anything like what it consumed. The consequence was, both the farmer and the proprietor conceived that, by getting the ports shut up at a particular price, the monopoly would be complete with regard to our own produce. It certainly was so, but the increase of cultivation has far outstripped the consumption, and our low prices are now attributable simply to two or three good years, and the increased cultivation by bone manure and furrow draining.

From the Evidence of Mr. William Bell.

Mr. Loch. In your opinion, can Parliament do anything to relieve the farmers?—I am not satisfied that they have the power of doing anything; if they did anything, I think it would only shift the burthen to the consumer.

Have you ever thought whether the Corn Laws affect the farmer beneficially or otherwise?—The present Corn Laws have operated of late as a complete prohibition against the sale of foreign corn, and I cannot conceive that any other protection can be given beyond a monopoly of the market.

Do you conceive that a system of average, such as the present, or a fixed duty, would be beneficial to the farmer?—I am not sure that a fixed duty would not be ultimately the most satisfactory; but it is a difficult question, because a fixed duty in scarce seasons would not be submitted to.

Upon the whole, are you satisfied with the present Corn Law?—I should consider it a complete protection against foreign corn.

And you would make no alteration?—Unless an alteration was made to a fixed duty.

Mr. Handley. What is your reason for supposing a fixed duty would be preferable?—By the present Corn Law, whenever the price approaches near the rate at which the foreign corn can be brought into the market with a profit, the prices may possibly be run up to that rate by artificial means; thus a great quantity of corn would be improperly liberated and thrown upon the market, and this might probably depress the market for the whole season; now at a fixed duty that could not take place.

Do you consider that a fixed duty would have the effect of preventing fluctuation?—I think so; I think it would make the price more uniform.

You are aware that there are two articles of agricultural produce that for years were subject to a fixed duty, namely, wool and tallow; are you aware whether or no they have not fluctuated very considerably in price?—They have fluctuated very much; but I understand that wool was only at a penny a pound, a mere nominal duty.

Has the foreign corn imported into this country been the surplus corn of Europe, or has it been grown expressly for this market?—I believe that it is the surplus corn of Europe; this is the best market they can bring it to.

If by a fixed duty you made this market a certain market, is it your opinion that considerable tracts of country might not be brought into cultivation on the Continent expressly to supply this market?—Perhaps they might to a certain extent.

Would not that be prejudicial to the farmers of this country? —They would probably take something else from us in lieu of that.

Under the present system of Corn Laws, when a prohibition lasts so many years as it has done, is not that the best protection against the growth of foreign corn for the supply of this market?—I have stated distinctly that I think the farmer has no reason to complain of the present law; that it is a sufficient protection to him.

Have you ever considered what would be the proper amount of fixed duty?—My notion would be, if a fixed duty was to take place I would lay it on as high as the country could bear it, and I would reduce it gradually 1*s.* or 2*s.* every year, till it came to a nominal duty; and during the operation of that, the landlord and tenant would come to an adjustment, and the land would find its natural value.

If such then be the effects on those interests, which were intended to be benefited and supported by the present Corn Laws, on what principle can their continuance be defended or sought for?

The Economist

Around 1843 Wilson began writing for the *Morning Chronicle* and for *The Examiner*. Unhappy with the space allowed for his articles Wilson decided to start a new weekly with his own money and some help from Lord Radnor (1779–1869). *The Economist* was first published on 2 September, 1843 and at first Wilson wrote most of the paper. Wilson's paper was helped by the Anti Corn Law League and despite his reservations about the confrontational manner of some of its provincial leaders he joined in the League's campaign. The difference in style was alluded to by Prentice in his description of a League meeting in Drury Lane Theatre on 15 March 1843: 'I knew that he was closely argumentative, relying more upon statistical figures than on figures of speech, and trusting more to facts and reasonings than to rhetorical flourishes.'[1]

The first issue of *The Economist* appeared on 2 September 1843. One hundred years later in a centenary volume of essays its then editor wrote that in view of the journal's initial commitment to the policy of free trade, it avoided becoming doctrinaire by adopting a quantitative approach.

> *The Economist* was barely two months old when its first statistical supplement appeared; its index of wholesale prices was the first in any country to be regularly calculated and published. From the start it was the deliberate purpose of the paper to put every argument to the test of the facts so far as they could be ascertained, and if they were not readily available to go in search of them. Something of this intention is possibly to be read into the choice of the title for the paper. 'Economist' – especially without the adjective 'political' . . . indicated a cast of mind in approach to all problems, rather than a specialist profession in some. An economist was a particular variety of philosophic radical, one who believed in testing his sophistry against his calculations.[2]

After Wilson's death in 1860 *The Economist* remained a family paper. It was held in trust for his six daughters and their descendants, and only in 1928 was it sold.

[1] Prentice, *History of the Anti Corn Law League*, vol. 2, p. 58.
[2] *The Economist 1843–1943 A Centenary Volume*, Oxford University Press, 1943, p. 5.

The Economist:

OR

THE POLITICAL, COMMERCIAL, AGRICULTURAL, AND FREE-TRADE JOURNAL.

PRELIMINARY NUMBER: AUGUST, 1843. (AND PROSPECTUS.

CONTENTS.

"If a writer be conscious that to gain a reception for his favourite doctrine he must combat with certain elements of opposition, in the taste, or the pride, or the indolence of those whom he is addressing, this will only serve to make him the more importunate. *There is a difference between such truths as are merely of a speculative nature and such as are allied with practice and moral feeling. With the former all repetition may be often superfluous; with the latter it may just be by earnest repetition, that their influence comes to be thoroughly established over the mind of an inquirer.*"—CHALMERS.

IT is one of the most melancholy reflections of the present day, that while wealth and capital have been rapidly increasing, while science and art have been working the most surprising miracles in aid of the human family, and while morality, intelligence, and civilization have been rapidly extending on all hands;—that at this time, the great material interests of the higher and middle classes, and the physical condition of the labouring and industrial classes, are more and more marked by characters of uncertainty and insecurity. In vain has the hand of ART (led on and guided by a complete glare of SCIENCE, aided by INDUSTRY of unsurpassed intelligence and perseverance, nurtured and fertilized by CAPITAL almost without limit) developed the resources of the human mind and the material creation in a manner which has at once astonished and exalted the world;—in vain have all parts of the earth been brought nearer and nearer to us;—our Indian territory within forty days' journey, the great American continent within ten days' sail, our continental neighbours and very part of our own country separated only by a brief space of a few hours;—in vain the producers and consumers of the whole world, the administrators of mutual wants, the encouragers of mutual industries, have been brought in easy and close collision and contact, and thus facilitated the supply of every want, and the demand for every exertion of human skill and industry;—in vain do we acknowledge all these unequalled and undoubted elements of national prosperity: for at this moment the whole country—every interest without exception,—the owner and occupier of the soil, the explorer of our great mineral world, the manufacturer who gives form, shape, and utility to the produce of nature, the artisan, the labourer of every description, the merchant and shipowner (the great links of exchange), and the capitalist who facilitates the operations of all,—every one of these interests stand at this moment CONFESSEDLY in a condition of the most unprecedented depression, anxiety, and uneasiness. And what rather adds to this anomaly than in any way accounts for it, is, that our population has been rapidly increasing, not only in numbers, but also in great skill and productive ability.

But while Art, Science, Intelligence, and Enterprise have been thus engaged for the last half century in behalf of our country and the human race, in what manner has legislation been occupied? Let cool and calm deliberation determine this question. In the early part of that period the little time which could be spared by the legislature from the excitement of political strife, the struggle for political power and place, was occupied with the stirring events attendant on the long and continued wars in which we were engaged, and the principles of commercial and industrial legislation attracted little of its attention. Under such circumstances it was not difficult for those interests who possessed great political influence to obtain enactments which they supposed would be beneficial to themselves. Unfortunately, however, both governments, and classes, and individuals have been too apt to conclude that their benefit could be secured by a policy injurious to others: and too often the benefit proposed has even been measured by the injury to be inflicted: hence all the laws which were framed under this influence had a tendency to raise up *barriers to intercourse*, *jealousies*, *animosities*, and *heartburnings* between *individuals* and *classes in this country*, and again between *this country* and *all others*; and thus, under the plea of *protecting* individuals or classes against each other, and the whole against other countries, was the system of COMMERCIAL RESTRICTION completed by the enactment of the corn and provision laws, passed in 1815; *amid the utter forgetfulness on the part of the legislature, that it had no power or privilege which could enable it to confer a favour or wealth on any one part of the community, without abstracting as much from others; in fact, that it possessed no inherent source of productiveness which could enable it to be generous.*

The policy of England, always, but especially at this particular time, looked up to by all the world as the highway to greatness, was eagerly followed in her commercial regulations by other countries; navigation laws, hostile tariffs, prohibition of English manufactures, were resorted to by other governments, each in a way according to the notions they had of their own interests, in imitation of, or opposition to the policy of England.

each country inflicting on itself as much mischief and injury as England had done by similar policy.

It was thus while *Art, Science, Capital, Commercial Enterprise*, and *Labour* were eagerly demanding a greater arena to multiply and extend their benefits to ALL, that legislation, ignorance, and prejudice associated with short-sighted selfishness, were actively engaged in frustrating all these nobler efforts and designs. And so far had they succeeded in creating a war among the material interests of the world, that in 1819 the collision occasioned thereby threatened the most serious consequences to our Social and Commercial existence. This crisis caused reflecting men to turn their attention to the hitherto neglected science of Political and Commercial Economy. The philosophy of Adam Smith found a clear and able enunciator in Ricardo. The political and legislative application of these great principles, so eloquently put forth to a wondering but ignorant audience by Burke, found an ardent, warm, and able echo in Huskisson. The philosopher wrote, and was not refuted. The legislator debated, and by his earnestness, industry, and eloquence, aided no doubt by the pressing exigencies of the time, gained a partial triumph over the ignorance and prejudice which ruled; and shadowed out for the first time the principles of Political Economy into the embodyment of FREE TRADE as their practical result. He saw that our interests and commerce had far out-grown the narrow limits which ignorant legislation had assigned them; that all the up-heavings and convulsions in the country were but the external symptoms of the fierce struggle which was going forward between our rapidly-advancing productive power, earnestly demanding a larger field of exchange, and the principles of restriction and monopoly, blindly and vainly attempting to confine them to their ancient and narrow limit: that it was a severe contest between intelligence, which pressed forward, and an unworthy, timid ignorance obstructing our progress.

He commenced his commercial reform by revising our truly Anti-Commercial Navigation laws; he followed that effort by revising the import duties on the raw materials of manufactures, of silk, wool, flax, &c.; he reduced the differential duty on coffee and wine, and by these and various other changes, but far more by the broad, intelligent, and enlightened arguments by which he supported his policy, gave great and cheering hopes that the emancipation of industry and commerce was at hand. Under the salutary influence of these reforms the country recovered, and with returning prosperity, discontent was dispelled,—peace was restored. Every measure was attended with eminent success. With reduction of duties he increased the revenue; with protection, removed or lowered, he increased the competition and import, without injury to the producer at home. Increased supply only tended to stimulate demand. The Minister and his principles became equally popular. The silk weavers in Macclesfield, who declared themselves ruined by his policy in 1825, drew his carriage triumphantly into the town in 1830, on his last and fatal journey to Liverpool. The Free-Trade Minister died, and left no successor. The progress of his policy was thus arrested at its outset, and was soon forgot in the stormy political events of 1830.

In 1831 commenced the great Reform struggle: fascinated with the excitement, intoxicated with the success, the country totally forgot the *ends* of good government in the struggle for its *means*:—its *means* were obtained, its *ends* were neglected. The Corn Laws and Commercial restrictions were denounced on the hustings, but unheard of in Parliament; and it is a serious reflection on the intelligence and wisdom of the times, that the greatest popular political influence which ever existed in this country, scarcely achieved one important act of liberation to commerce and industry; that it left the Corn Laws and all the great glaring monopolies and restrictions as it found them: it spent its whole strength in things good, but good only as a means to an end. A succession of a few good harvests, and the development of Huskisson's then neglected principles, sustained our onward progress for some years,—until we reached the end of 1838,—when the occurrence of a single bad harvest, proved to all thinking men the critical point at which we had arrived. Wealth abounded, useful productions were multiplied beyond all precedent, but the field of exchange had become so narrowed, that the most serious national sacrifices were required to supply the deficiency of the first necessary of life during the three following years.

Twenty years had passed away: six millions had been added to our population: art, science, ingenuity, and industry had been working their miracles—but legislation still sought to confine the country in the same swaddling clothes in which it had been wrapt a quarter of a century before; and, with the exception of the few acts of Huskisson, no means had been taken to afford a wider field for our increasing numbers and powers.

The fierce struggle for more room, for wider markets, for freer exchange, visible in 1819, was now again, as before, exhibited by new upheavings and convulsions—productive energy and intelligence were again in keen antagonism with monopoly and restriction. The great manufacturing population was the first to suffer, but that sympathy between all the different parts of the state, the existence of which has always been overlooked in framing restrictive and protecting laws, gradually extended the mischief, until it reached every interest in the country: the lessened means of consumption on the part of the artisans of one class reacted generally on the demand for the produce of their fellow artisans of other classes; which again reacted more strongly on the shopkeepers and small dealers; again affecting the wholesale dealer and importer;—the consumption of articles of foreign growth being thus curtailed in quantity and price, the power of our foreign customers to consume our manufactures was again, in their turn, lessened; and thus reacted once more on the producing classes at home; trade had a constant tendency to contraction; the shipping interest became deeply depressed; capital became profitless; the revenue suffered: new taxes became needful: consumption was thus once more lessened; and at last, though not with less certainty, the agricultural interest, that interest which is most strongly protected by law, *but far more strongly by the stern necessity which exists for their produce in priority to all other articles*, was involved in the common lot of *increased charges, diminished demand*, and *lower prices*: and thus the narrow policy of restriction and protection worked mischief to all, benefit to none; for where is the interest which does not at this moment confess itself in a state of depression without parallel?—It is no longer complaints of a class, or of classes, it is a universal national embarrassment;—an embarrassment which has disturbed and complicated our commercial relations over the whole world.

WHERE IS THE REMEDY?—who is the man that would remain as he is?—who is the man that would go back into greater restrictions, into a narrower field; into less demand? All now begin to feel and acknowledge that want of consumption is the true cause of depression and low prices,—that the real cause of all our evils is found in the want of employment for the labour, energy, and capital of the country *as it now is*: but how is that to be remedied?— Only by extending our markets abroad, by increasing our exports: but we can only increase our exports by being willing to INCREASE OUR IMPORTS, and this can only be done from those large productive countries, the produce of which, at this time, is practically prohibited. No revision of the tariff will be of any practical benefit which will not admit in the greatest abundance all the first necessaries of life, and which does not open the markets of those great countries which produce them. It is of no avail to open freely our ports for articles of small and trifling consumption, to open our trade to small and comparatively unimportant spots on the ocean;—if we will really extend our trade, we must be willing to take freely and *regularly* articles of extensive consumption from countries of wide and rich territory, having great wants. We must be willing to take the corn of Prussia, Poland, and America; the sugar and coffee of Brazil, Cuba, and Java; *and by the acts indicated in these two lines* give to our great population, round whose well-being we have discovered all other interests revolve,—the two-fold blessings of ABUNDANCE and EMPLOYMENT.

We must retrace the whole of that narrow and ignorant legislation which seeks falsely and in vain to prop up and protect individual interests—which has only deceived and misled; we must rely alone on the great principles of public good for public prosperity. We must relieve industry and capital from all restrictions; we must know that there is no safety for our great active population but in the freest intercourse with the producers and consumers of all the world; in short, as the only true guarantee for prosperity and peace, we must honestly and fearlessly carry into *practice* those principles which all parties are ready to advocate in *theory* involved in

FREE TRADE.

To no country in the world that ever did or does exist are these principles of the same first importance that they are to us, for in no country does so large a portion of the *population* and *property* depend on commerce and industry alone, in order that they shall have *any* value. We believe that this important and critical fact has been entirely overlooked, or has never been considered in one tithe of its importance. Let us consider what a huge portion of our *property* and *reliance for employment* consists of, and depends upon, the vast variety of factories, mills, and other manufacturing establishments, and their numberless aiders, assistants, contributors, and ministers, found in every variety in manufacturing districts; our extensive and rich kingdom of minerals; our canals, railroads, and various facilities of internal transport; our endless variety of public companies; our huge and splendid commercial marine; our docks, basins, and public warehouses; and our great cities attached to and dependent on the same interests.

Now the important fact to which we wish to draw attention is, that the labour and property thus involved, not only depend on *trade*, but on a SUFFICIENT EXTENT OF TRADE, to retain *any* value whatever. As long as they are profitably employed they represent their full amount of cost in the sum of national wealth; and are of their full amount of utility in affording employment to the population: but with an increasing population and ingenuity always at work, supply must have a constant tendency to increase. If the demand for the produce of our factories be not correspondingly increased, but on the contrary, diminished, competition must become greater and greater, until all profit ceases; the capital is *sunk*, and until there is a loss competitors will persevere. When that period arrives, when the price of the goods will not repay the labour and cost of the raw material, *then the whole of this property vanishes*, and its means of giving employment to labour, and its various contributors, ceases: *for of* what value or utility is a factory, and all its magnificent and complicated machinery and arrangement, with its steam-engine still and motionless? As long as our mines of iron and of coal yield a profit, they represent at least the whole value of the labour employed in exploring them, and generally much more in the form of rent or royalty; but increase the quantity of iron or coal *without an increase of demand*, and competition will lower the prices, so that first all rent will vanish, and as soon as the price does not pay the expense and labour of raising the mineral, we are no richer with coal or iron fields than if they were beds of quicksand: their power of employing labour is at an end, and all the money invested ceases to be national wealth. As long as railways and canals are profitable, they truly represent in real wealth the capital invested: but diminish the amount of traffic only so much as pays the profit—until the receipts do not cover the necessary wear and tear and expenses—and they are no longer wealth. Increase our number of ships, without proportionably increasing the consumption of articles of foreign growth—first the competition will destroy the merchant's profit and yield only freight, but next competition will reduce freight, until the wages and expenses are not covered; and then all wealth in ships ceases: and the capital invested in them is so long an absolute abstraction of national wealth. With a given amount of trade all this wealth is secure, with a little less it vanishes. And let us well consider that it is not the mere surplus of these various interests that thus suffers, *for no man will consent voluntarily to be the surplus*:—no man will close his factory, blow out his furnace, lay by his pit, or lay up his ship, until they become a source of loss. It is true the weakest must go first: the worst factory must be closed, the poorest mines must be laid by, and the worst ship must be laid up first; and then follow the next in degree; but the moment a little diminution of supply lessens the loss, a portion of the idle start afresh into competition. It may be coolly said, this state of things must cure itself in time, if it were only by a course of ruin; but, be it remembered, the population still goes on increasing, ingenuity and invention are still at the highest pressure of necessity, and as one class of competitors are destroyed, another class are immediately in their place. We can safely refer to each and all of these interests, if this is not a literal description of their present condition. The want of more trade prevents that trade we have being profitable: the excess of produce beyond the demand lessens the value of the whole producing ability; and this must continue as long as demand keeps not pace with production, as long as no effort is made to extend our markets, as our population and productive ability increase. But inasmuch as consumption is only created by production, the two should always in a natural state of things keep pace with each other; the demand for productions should always increase as they become abundant and cheap, for abundance implies great production, and great production an extensive means of consumption. Then why do we find this country so great an exception to this natural law? Because by our

RESTRICTIVE SYSTEM

we *limit the supply* of one great class of productions, and thus practically *limit the demand* for all others, however much we affect to encourage our commerce. During the last thirty years one great class of producers at home has been limited by the nature of the country and Acts of Parliament. The land has given employment to *no portion* of the increase of the population: the whole additional six millions of our people, since 1821, have been thrown upon other employments. In 1821, 4,790,000 of the population were engaged in producing food for, and consuming the products of, the remaining 9,600,000: in 1842 the number of 4,790,000 of producers of food and consumers of manufactures is somewhat reduced, while the consumers of food, irrespective of the producers, are increased to 14,400,000; but th law practically enacts that the 14,400,000 in 1842 shall be fed by the same means that fed the 9,600,000 in 1821; and moreover, for such is the effect, that in 1842, 14,400,000 manufacturers, dealers, various producers, professions, &c., shall only have the same number of customers with whom to exchange for the first great necessaries of life as the 9,600,000 had twenty years ago; and thus there has been a constant tendency for the produce of the rapidly increasing number to exchange for a smaller quantity of the produce of the stationary number, or, in other words, while agricultural produce has all along maintained a high price, all other kinds of goods have fallen rapidly during the period; and the demand being thus far stationary, while the supplies were increasing so much, there was a constant tendency during the whole period to an excess of production on one hand, only because the same constant tendency existed to a limited and deficient production on the other hand. Had the producers of food kept in the same proportionate increase of numbers and quantity as the other class, there had remained the same relative value and demand for the produce of each, and excess or over-production would not have arisen in the one case nor deficiency in the other. *This excess, or what is termed over-production, is precisely that surplus which we have before shown has been so long, and still is, undermining the commercial and industrial existence of the country*;—for however great the struggle may be among farmers to occupy, or of labourers to cultivate, this fixed quantity of land, their numbers do not increase: they only require the same number of ploughshares, the same quantity of saddlery, the same number is still only to be shod and booted, still only the fixed number of backs to be clothed, still only the same number of consumers of colonial produce; while the class who depend for food on this fixed number, and who seek to minister to their wants of ploughshares, of saddlery, of shoes, of clothing, who import and supply foreign produce, and have other occupations, are six millions more since 1821, and still *increase at the rate of one thousand per day*. In another eight years, if the increase goes on in the same proportion, in 1851, while the food producers remain at 4,790,000, the other classes will have increased to 17,000,000; and if it be possible that suicidal restriction and monopoly still prevail, it must require a still larger portion of the conflict of the large class to *obtain the produce* and *minister to the wants* of the smaller class; and it is an important fact, that the great competition to occupy, and to labour upon, this fixed quantity of land, has a constant tendency to keep the largest portion of even this smallest class in the utmost poverty and depression.

Thus far as regards the power of exchange in the home trade for the first great article of food:—next as to the greatest foreign article of consumption, and therefore of exchangeable ability, SUGAR. Here again the same principle has been acted upon, the same result has followed. Restriction and monopoly have again here attempted to confine the supply of the 27,000,000, which we now are, to the same means which supplied 21,000,000, twenty years ago. In 1821, the quantity of sugar available for the consumption of 21,000,000 of people was 4,170,178 cwts.—in 1842 the quantity similarly available for the consumption of 27,000,000 was only 4,082,312 cwts., being actually 93,366 cwts. less. The competition, therefore, of 27,000,000 to obtain only the same or a less quantity in exchange for their articles of produce, has had the constant tendency to cause a smaller quantity of sugar to exchange for a larger quantity of goods. The same quantity of sugar which exchanged, twenty years ago, for a given quantity of manufactures, iron or hardware, will now command at least three times the quantity of those articles. Thus, while the supply of these great necessaries is limited to a given quantity, the chief effect of increased production at home is to lower its exchangeable value for the article of which the quantity is fixed. If the producers of our sugar increased in the same proportion as the consumers have, the same relative value would be always maintained between the goods of this country and that article, because the demand would always increase in proportion to the supply; but the restriction affects us in two ways; first, by making sugar dear, and secondly, by making our goods cheap; inasmuch as we limit our market in other sugar growing countries in consequence of the practical prohibition to consume their produce. And thus it is, with these restrictions, that we have a constant tendency to that surplus or excess of one class of productions, which weighs down and depresses the great industrial interests of the country: that we have every day a greater tendency to that little trade, which makes trade profitless, and which brings about the exact state of things which at present exist.

There is no cure, there is no remedy, for all these evils but increased demand; there can be no increased demand without increased markets; and we cannot secure larger markets without an unrestricted power of exchange, and by this means add to our territory of land, as far as productive utility is concerned, the corn fields of Poland, Prussia, and above all, the rich and endless acres of the United States; to avail ourselves of the vast and rich productiveness of Brazil, Cuba, Java, &c.; and thus, at the same time that a plentiful and proportionate supply of all the great necessaries of life would be maintained, we should always, in exchange, have a corresponding demand for our increasing productions at home; the equilibrium of the various classes of producers would be restored and maintained. With free trade we might go on increasing our productions without limit, for in this only natural state of things increased production could only create the power and means of increased consumption. There is no other remedy. It is in vain that deputations of distressed interests pass resolutions merely affirming their distress; seek interviews with Ministers of the Crown only to repeat their resolutions, without an opinion to offer as to the cause or cure; all will be in vain until they have this important truth palpably and at all times before them, that they are increasing by millions, while the law practically prescribes only a fixed, stationary quantity of the great necessaries of life for their consumption, only the same number of customers with whom to exchange their productions, whatever may be the quantity: until this conviction compels them to demand an unrestricted exchange, until they demand FREE TRADE as a simple act of justice and policy.

But we may be told these are all only opinions, well enough reasoned and difficult to answer, and perhaps very like the truth; but the experiment is great—we want something more than opinions. Well, then, we will endeavour to prove and illustrate every opinion we have offered to the full; and that by our own experience in four of the most important articles of the consumption of this country—Coffee and Sugar, as representing the Colonial interests; Wool and Corn, as representing the Home or Agricultural interests.

COFFEE AND SUGAR.

Previous to 1824 these two articles had been equally the objects of the greatest protection and care. The duty on Coffee was

West India . . .	1s. 0d. per lb.
East India . . .	1s. 6d. ,,
Foreign	2s. 6d. ,,

Since that period Coffee may be termed the pet article on which free trade has tried its experiments, and Sugar, on the other hand, the peculiar pet of protection.

In 1825 Mr Huskisson experimented on Coffee. He reduced the duties on

West India to . . .	6d.
East India . . .	9d.
Foreign	1s. 3d.

In 1835 the duty on East India was reduced to 6d., and a law was afterwards enacted that any coffee, of whatever growth, if imported from a British possession eastward of the Cape of Good Hope, or from that place, should be admitted at 9d. duty. So that practically the alteration made the duties thus:—

West India . . .	6d.
East India . . .	6d.
Foreign . . .	9d.

And 1d. for extra freight.

Therefore, instead of 50 per cent. protection, which West India coffee enjoyed against East India growth, and 150 per cent. against that of foreign growth; since 1835, the protection against East India has been entirely removed, and the protection against foreign reduced to 50 per cent. Here, then, is a great experiment of free trade, which, when it was begun in 1824, was denounced by the West India interest as the greatest chimera that had entered the head of a minister. Now let us see the result:—

In 1824 our total imports of coffee were .	lbs. 50,674,249
,, 1840	70,250,766

In 1824, of the total quantity imported, we consumed:—

		lbs.
Of West India, at the duty of	1s. 0d per lb. .	7,947,390
East India . .	1s. 6d. ,, .	313,513
Foreign . . .	2s. 6d. ,, .	1,540
		lbs. 8,262,943

In 1840, of the total quantity imported, we consumed—

		lbs.
Of West and East India, at the duty of . . .	6d. per lb.	14,443,399
Foreign . .	9d. ,,	
and with the additional charge of 1d. for freight say	10d. ,,	14,143,433
Foreign direct . .	1s. 3d. ,,	77,504
		lbs. 28,664,336

In 1824 the amount of revenue at the high rates of duty was	. . .	£420,988
In 1840 " " " low rates		921,551

In 1824 the price of good Jamaica coffee in bond, with the high prohibitory duty, was—

In January	. .	113s. to 118s. per cwt.
July	. .	99s. — 101s. "
November	. .	97s. — 100s. "

In 1840, with the low duty and reduced protection, the price was—

In January	. .	125s. to 132s. per cwt.
July	. .	124s. — 128s. "
November	. .	120s. — 125s. "

The result may, therefore, be said to be an increased import of 20,423,000 lbs.; and increased consumption of 20,402,000 lbs.; with the former lowest duty reduced to one half, and the differential duties comparatively abandoned, the *revenue more than doubled;* and notwithstanding the enormous increased supply of East India and foreign coffee, which, at the old rate of duty of 2s. 6d. per lb., would have been practically prohibited, the price of Jamaica coffee in bond to the merchant and planter higher than in 1824.

On this extraordinary result we must for a moment dwell, and reflect. The consumption of 1824 was 8,262,943 lbs., or 73,776 cwts. at an average price of 100s. per cwt. in bond, which represented 368,880*l*. of value. In 1840 the quantity consumed was 28,664,336 lbs., or 255,931 cwts.; and considering the large portion of East Indian and foreign coffee,—if calculated at only 80s. per cwt.—represented 1,023,724*l*. of value.

The first reflection in thinking of all the interests involved in this is, the additional number of ships which are required to carry 255,931cwts. instead of 73,776 cwts.,—the employment of landing and warehousing it,—the increase of business to the importing merchant and the Mincing-lane brokers, in passing 1,023,724*l*. through their hands instead of 368,880*l*. The increase of business, again, which the distribution throughout the country by the wholesale dealer, and the retailing by the shopkeeper, of 28,664,336 lbs., instead of 8,262,943 lbs.; the blessing of this increased supply to the community, the revenue receiving 921,551*l*. instead of 420,988*l*.—and in the midst of these advantages,—the producer receiving actually a higher price than he did for the little quantity in 1824—all are benefited: no one is injured.

But stay: this is only half the benefit. We want goods—manufactures or minerals, to export in payment of this coffee, to the amount of 1,023,724*l*., in place of 368,880*l*. New labour is set to work throughout the country to produce them; this labour communicates ABILITY TO CONSUME MORE FARM PRODUCE, more of other kinds of manufactures, of other colonial or foreign produce. Then again, we have larger business for the export merchant, for inland carriers, for labourers in the docks; and once more,—all this additional demand for ships to carry the increased outward cargoes; and throughout, great additional legitimate demand for capital to conduct the transactions.

All this is very consistent with the condition of a population increasing at the rate of one thousand a day; and were this article the rule instead of the exception in our commercial policy, we should have no complaint of the lack of trade, of deficient revenue, or of surplus population.

Reflecting on these operations shows us how truly foolish is the distinction which men are constantly attempting to draw *between the value of a* HOME *or a* FOREIGN TRADE. All these increased transactions, arising out of the import and payment for coffee (or be it corn or any other article), is exactly what makes a good home trade; the ability to consume circulates from one class to another; artisans of one class give employment to those of another by spending their wages: these, again, circulate in an accumulative manner; every additional man that we employ assists immediately by his consumption to find employment for others; and all unite in increased consumption of the fruits of the earth; the benefit circulates throughout all classes, and creates what is termed a good home trade: but the truth is, foreign trade and home trade are in effect synonymous terms; and equally synonymous are the terms "*native industry*" and "*foreign industry*"—the former being used to convey the idea of labour in cultivating our land, and the latter being used to convey the idea of that labour which is imported in exchange for our manufactures. Very little reflection will show that the value and demand for "*native labour*" in cultivating the soil, depends much on the demand which is caused by the consumption of those employed in manufacturing for the foreign markets, and that the whole demand for the labour of the latter class depends exclusively on our being able and willing to take from other countries such things as they value less than the goods which we have to offer: and this article will always be found to be that which such countries can cultivate most profitably: exchanges thus can only be a source of mutual advantage. The *coffee*, the *wool*, or the *wheat* which we import in exchange for the produce of the looms of Manchester and Leeds, the anvils and furnaces of Birmingham and Sheffield, just as much represent native industry, as does the wool shorn on the Brighton Downs, or the wheat grown on the fields of Kent or Essex. The truth is, that as every article which we import can only represent directly or indirectly some article which we export, it must always follow that the more we extend our imports, the more we encourage that labour, "*native industry*" by increasing a demand for those articles which are required in exchange for our increased imports.

In order to show most indisputably that the increased consumption of coffee was caused by the changes in the duties referred to, we subjoin the annexed tabular history of the article since 1820, distinguishing the three periods of the different rates of duties; and also distinguishing the proportions furnished under the different rates of duties during the whole period:—

COFFEE.

YEARS.	Cleared for Consumption. British Plantation.	East India.	Foreign Plantation.	Total.	Rates of Duty. British Plantation.	East India.	Foreign Plantation.	Nett Revenue.
			First Period—Old Rates of Duty.					
								£.
1820	6,316,932	295,943	1,131	7,103,400	1s.	1s. 6d.	2s. 6d.	342,828
1821	7,336,040	206,177	784	7,383,001	"	"	"	384,233
1822	7,494,213	171,717	2,116	7,668,121	"	"	"	367,242
1823	8,218,342	233,397	561	8,454,920	"	"	"	429,613
1824	7,947,390	313,313	1,540	8,262,243	"	"	"	420,988
			Second Period—Huskisson's Rates of Duty.					
1825	10,622,376	487,743	2,849	11,082,970	6d.	9d.	1s. 3d.	315,809
1826	12,409,000	791,370	2,733	13,203,323	"	"	"	336,170
1827	14,476,088	898,190	1,210	15,366,376	"	"	"	399,680
1828	16,151,229	973,410	2,994	17,127,633	"	"	"	440,245
1829	18,495,407	974,376	6,197	19,476,180	"	"	"	484,975
1830	21,007,966	989,185	3,971	22,691,122	"	"	"	579,283
1831	21,301,966	1,234,721	3,940	22,740,627	"	"	"	583,731
1832	20,906,301	1,970,635	17,301	22,952,177	"	"	"	580,338
1833	20,941,194	1,790,319	1,471	22,741,984	"	"	"	581,241
1834	22,274,673	1,456,604	2,418	23,765,696	"	"	"	614,636
	British Possessions.		*Third Period—Duties as Fixed by the late Ministry.*					
1835	23,292,920	duty equalised.	2,196	23,295,046	6d.	6d.	1s. 3d.	652,124
1836	24,945,434		2,224	24,947,690	"	"	9d. if imported from the Cape, &c.	691,616
1837	26,343,792		3,169	26,346,961	"	"		686,445
1838	22,530,361		3,217,742	25,748,073	"	"		685,004
1839	18,041,542		8,647,121	26,832,108	"	"		779,853
1840	14,495,331		14,130,924	28,664,338	"	"		921,551
1841	17,171,409		10,640,357	28,421,466	"	"		896,283
1842	17,338,296		11,243,633	28,583,931	"	"		770,163*

* Half of the year came under the reduced Duties of the last Tariff, of 4d. per lb. on all Coffee produced in British Possessions, and 8d. on that of foreign growth, however imported.

During the first period in the above table, the total consumption remains nearly the same, showing only a very slight increase. With the lowering of the duty the increase is so rapid, that in the fourth year of the second period it is more than doubled, and more revenue is secured at half the former rates of duty. It will be observed that still the former proportions of differential duties on East India and foreign coffee were retained during this period, and that, in consequence, the consumption of those kinds (especially of foreign, still subject to a very high duty) did not materially increase. From 1830 for several years the consumption remained nearly stationary, until we arrived at the third period, when the differential duty was repealed on East India, and *practically* greatly reduced on foreign growth; and from this period another great and rapid increase of consumption took place. The law by which foreign coffee was admitted at the duty of 9d. if shipped from the Cape, or British possessions eastward thereof, did not operate materially till 1838; and then it will be seen how rapidly the supply of that description and the general consumption increased. Under this change the revenue increased about *thirty-five per cent.* in two years.

In further illustration of this principle. The duty on coffee was again reduced by the tariff of last year; and the quantity consumed increased on that of the previous year, while the consumption of sugar and all other leading articles was materially reduced. Indeed, the loss of revenue last year was less on coffee, with a reduction of thirty-three per cent. of duty on colonial (from 6d. to 4d.), and practically twenty-five per cent. (from 10d.—including 1d. for extra freight—to 8d.) on that of foreign growth, than occurred on sugar, the duty of which was not reduced at all.

SUGAR.

We are not aware of one reason which could induce under the same circumstances in every respect an extended consumption of coffee, that would not in all and every way apply to sugar; but we can enumerate many most important ways in which the consumption of sugar should be increased, not applicable to coffee. It is much used for the food of infants; and if cheap, for this purpose alone medical men consider it would be an incalculable blessing to the poor; it is used largely in cooking, in preserving, in confectionery, &c.; and another reason for a great increase of sugar during the period alluded to, would be, that independent of the enormous increase of the consumption of coffee, the consumption of tea has also increased from 23,784,838 lbs. in 1824, to 32,252,628 lbs. in 1840. For our present purpose of comparison, two lines will dispose of the slavery argument: if it applies at all, it does as much to coffee as sugar; and indeed more, for if our purpose be to coerce the Brazilians into our views, then to them coffee is an infinitely more important article of growth than sugar: and gold, silver, and copper apply as much as sugar can to the argument, both in Brazil and Cuba. With all these advantages, let us examine how this PET OF PROTECTION has proceeded during this period. In 1824 the duty on sugar was—

West India . . .	27s. per cwt.
East India . . .	37s. "
Foreign . . .	63s. "

In 1824 Huskisson was given to understand that he must not touch sugar; in 1830 the West India duty was reduced to 24s., the East India to 32s.; which was just so much more put into the pockets of the producers as long as the 63s. on foreign sugar was continued. In

1836 the duty on East India was equalized, but that on foreign not touched; and the duties now stand:

British Possessions .	. 24s. per cwt.
Foreign . .	. 63s. "

—a protection to the British colonial grower against the foreign grower and British consumer of upwards of one hundred and fifty per cent. In 1824 we imported—

	cwts.
West India Sugar .	. 3,935,549
East India and Mauritius	. 271,848
Foreign . .	. 205,750
	cwts. 4,413,147

The duties being as before stated.

In 1840 we imported—

	cwts.
West India Sugar .	. 2,217,681
East India and Mauritius	. 1,043,737
Foreign	. 774,427
	cwts. 4,035,845

The duties being equalized on East and West India, but still 63s. on foreign.

In 1824 the revenue from sugar was .	£4,641,945
1840	4,449,035

The result is, therefore, *a diminished supply of* 377,302 cwts., and with the rates of duty very little changed, *a loss of revenue* of 192,910*l.*; and it is well worthy of remark that this account would have been a much more deplorable one, but for a little free-trade principle applied in it, viz.: that simple act of justice to our East India possessions so long opposed by the West India interest;—equalizing the duties of East and West India sugar. By looking at the two statements, it will be seen that West India sugar was actually reduced in quantity 1,717,868 cwts.; while East India and Mauritius had increased 771,889 cwts.*

We must again pause and reflect. The supply of sugar was 377,302 cwts. less in 1840 than 1824. The population had increased between 1824 and 1840 upwards of five millions, but not one ounce of sugar more for their consumption. The amount of British shipping in 1824 was 2,559,587 tons, and in 1840, 3,311,538 tons; an increase of 751,951 tons, but not one hogshead and not one bag of sugar more to bring home; or if more bags, fewer hogsheads. Docks have increased, warehouses enlarged, but no more sugar to land or stow away. The merchants in Broad street have so multiplied that the drawing-rooms, dining-rooms, bed-rooms, and attics of our ancient merchants have been turned into counting houses for the increased modern numbers, and even that not sufficient, they are pressed into Austin friars and Tokenhouse yard; but among them all, not one cwt. of sugar more to sell. The brokers in Mincing lane, after filling "the lane" from the cellar to the attic, have betaken themselves to the neighbouring streets, but not one additional contract for sugar in a whole year for the swelling numbers. Money has accumulated in Lombard street, but no more bills drawn against sugar to discount, or warrants to advance upon than in 1824. Wholesale and retail grocers throughout the country have multiplied in full proportion to the population, but the same amount of sugar trade is only to be divided among them that existed twenty years ago, and every one connected with the article cries out, *there is no profit by sugar;* the fact being, that while the quantity has continued fixed, the competition to carry it, to sell it, and deal in it, has greatly increased, and this is exactly the way in which the littleness of the trade makes what trade there is without profit. But the shipowners, the merchants, the brokers, and the wholesale dealers, are so disinterested in the midst of all their crushing and elbowing for the sugar business, that they send men to parliament whose chief and great service is to maintain this *fixity* of quantity, and prevent a larger business for them.

But this is only half the mischief;—no more sugar coming home requires no more goods and manufactures to be sent out; there is no more work for the artisans, with all their increased numbers; no more ability communicated for the consumption of farm produce, or other articles; no more trade for the export merchant; no more freight for the shipowner, to pay for our sugar than twenty years ago.

Now it is quite impossible to form a precise estimate of what would have been the increase of the consumption of sugar had it been subjected to the same treatment as coffee. We have already shown that there is nothing in its character or uses that should prevent a corresponding increase of consumption, but, on the contrary, which would rather induce a greater increase: then, the only other consideration is, would the facilities of obtaining supplies have been as great? The history of the island of Java during that period is perhaps the best reply to the question. In 1826 the quantity of sugar shipped from that island was 23,565 cwts., and in 1841 it had increased to 1,252,041 cwts.;* and there we should find upwards of *seven millions* of *free* industrious people as consumers of our manufactures, living under the Dutch Government, which would only be too glad of an opportunity of entering into closer trading relations with us. Then we have the whole of the foreign West India islands, and the whole of the sugar-producing South

* It is proper to remark that the year 1840 was one of a smaller supply of sugar than usual, but we have taken that year as being the last of which the complete accounts have been published; but, as all our arguments proceed on the fact that the supply of sugar has not increased, it would have been equally applicable had we taken 1842, in which, as before remarked, the supply of sugar available for the consumption of this country was 90,000 cwts. less than in 1824.

* This increase has been so rapid and uniform, that to many the following table will be of great interest:—

SUGAR EXPORTED FROM JAVA AND MADURA.

	cwts.
1826	23,565
1827	38,357
1828	31,301
1829	91,227
1830	129,339
1831	144,077
1832	292,705
1833	251,129
1834	443,911
1835	523,162
1836	607,398
1837	831,063
1838	873,030
1839	990,393
1840	1,231,125
1841	1,252,041

American continent; so that there is no reason to suppose that the supply would not have proportionably increased with a freer state of trade.

Had such been the case, we should at this moment be in possession of revenue to the amount of five millions annually more than we are; and be in the enjoyment of an abundant supply of sugar, the immense increase of trade which would arise out of its import, and the export of goods of various kinds to the amount of some millions annually to pay for it. But it will be said by some, this act, just and fair and advantageous as it might have been to the English consumer and trader, would have been ruinous to our colonial possessions; but, from the evidence we have produced respecting coffee, that does not at all follow. Such people always forget that we cannot increase our supplies without in every way creating more trade, and thereby communicating to the whole country such an increased ability to consume the commodity; and that our experience proves that prices are less affected by increased supplies, than by that narrow and contracted consumption consequent on a narrow and contracted trade. This, indeed, we believe to be the real reason why restriction *never* succeeds, and why free trade *always* succeeds.

We cannot quit the subject without remarking, that during the period of which we have been treating, Java, Cuba, the Brazils, under all the discouragement of little demand, have produced so much sugar, and at such low prices, that our own merchants trading to those countries have, at three separate times during that period, made application to our government for permission to introduce the sugar prohibited by a duty of 63s. per cwt. for the purposes of agriculture: first spoiling it in the presence of an officer in such a way that it could not be converted into purposes of food.* Sugar so abundant that it could be used for manure and feeding cattle, but prohibited to minister to the wants of a British public, or exchange for British labour; and is it to be believed that in the face of this fact Government and merchants can see no plan for the relief of commerce, or employing an idle population?

WOOL, &c.

In 1819, a duty of *sixpence* per lb. was put on foreign wool, for the purpose of protecting the home growth, against a reduction of price: but in 1824, Huskisson, after a hard struggle with the landed interest, succeeded in reducing the duty to its present rate, viz. —*one penny* per lb. on all wools of value above one shilling per lb., and one *halfpenny* on wools under that value. In both Houses of Parliament, this reduction was strongly opposed, and Lord Sheffield wrote a pamphlet against it, in which he contended, as the West Indian interest did with respect to coffee, that if more wools* were required, we could produce them.

In 1820, with the sixpenny duty, the import of foreign wool was 9,775,605 lbs., yielding a revenue of 131,035*l*. In 1823, the year before the change was made, the consumption of foreign wool was 18,787,329 lbs., and the price of South Down fleeces, in that year, was fifteen pence per lb. With the reduction of the duty, the imports rapidly increased, until they arrived at the maximum in 1836, when the quantity imported amounted to 64,239,977 lbs., in which year the duty yielded a net revenue of 189,324*l*.; and in the face of this huge increased foreign importation, the price for South Down fleeces rose to eighteen pence per lb., being a higher price than they ever were during the protection of sixpence per lb., with a foreign competition of only 9,775,605 lbs. It would appear also, that the home growth materially increased, as by some evidence collected before the House of Lords, the produce of England in 1800 was 323,269 packs; and in 1828, 384,392 packs of 240 lbs. each.

If Lord Sheffield could have proved to the House of Lords in 1823 that the imports of foreign wool would, under the proposed act, increase to 64,000,000 lbs. in 1836—the eloquence and earnestness of Huskisson, and the influence of Lord Liverpool, had been all in vain, and we might to this day have had a duty of 6d. per lb. on foreign wool; for Lord Sheffield's successors, in restrictive advocacy, seem to be more powerful now than he was then; and in that case, it is a serious subject of consideration, how much real advantage to the country would have been lost which has been gained.

In 1820 almost the whole import was from Germany and Spain. In 1836 our imports were, from—

	lbs.
Germany	31,766,194
Spain	2,818,137
Australia	4,996,645
Other countries . . .	24,659,001
	64,239,977

Independent of the supply from Australia, we have received from new countries—chiefly Russia, Denmark, Italy, Turkey, the coast of Barbary, the States of Rio de la Plata, Peru, and Chili, 24,659,001 lbs.; now by far the largest portions of these wools are of such low qualities, that the duty of 6d. per lb. would have been a complete prohibition; in some few instances more than the whole value.

Let us again consider what this approach to free trade has done. The import of 1820 represents 48,878 bags of 200 lbs. each, and reckoned at an average price of 2s. 6d. per lb., was of value 1,221,950*l*. In 1836 the import equalled 321,190 bags, and reckoning the average price only at 1s. 8d. per lb., on account of much

* It is a very curious fact in scientific discovery that the most profitable invention which was ever patented in this or any other country accidentally arose out of a similar application to Government. The application was to admit sugar for agricultural purposes; the Government applied to Mr Howard, the accomplished chemist, brother to the late Duke of Norfolk, to try some experiments for the purpose of ascertaining if sugar could be so effectually adulterated that it could not be again converted for culinary uses. For this purpose he mixed all kinds of noxious materials with it, but the question remained whether they could be again separated, and in the experiments to ascertain this he discovered that not only could they be separated but that the sugar was better and purer. Out of this arose Howard's patent for sugar refining and the use of the vacuum pan; the annual net income of which from licences granted for its use at the rate of *one shilling per cwt.* yielded in some years between twenty or thirty thousand pounds. One house in London alone paid four thousand pounds per annum.

* Canning getting hold of this pamphlet, in a moment of wicked sarcasm altered the W of this word into F.

of a lower quality coming, was of value 3,353,313*l*. The shipowner has had freight for 321,199 bags, instead of 48,378 bags. The merchants had consignments, and the brokers in Coleman street and Basinghall street had to sell to the amount of 3,353,313*l*., instead of 1,221,930*l*. Bills to the amount of 4,000,000*l*. additional had to be negotiated; the wheels of industry were set in active operation throughout the manufacturing districts to work up that quantity; the population was employed, *a great consumptive ability communicated for farm produce*, and the produce of other trades. Then, again, we had to export goods to all that additional amount in payment for these imports; new trade was opened up at home to produce them; additional foreign trade and employment of ships, in exporting them, and a large portion of this wool found its way back to the very people who grew it, manufactured cheaper and better than they could have done it, and having communicated all the blessings and advantages which we have above described to this country, *all* or much of which we should have lost had monopoly prevailed in 1823.

During the whole period from 1824 to 1842, it is uniformly the case that the years of largest imports were those of highest prices, both being caused by the existence of greater demand. This fact, and all our experience proves, that prices do not depend on limiting quantity, but on increasing consumption. Limit quantity, the immediate and temporary effect may be to raise prices; but the next and permanent effect is to reduce demand, owing to the reduced means arising from a narrowed trade and less employment, and thus permanently to reduce price. Increase quantity, the first and temporary effect may be to lower price, but the next and permanent effect is to increase demand by the increased means arising from a larger trade and more employment, in producing or procuring the greater quantity, and the price is permanently increased. While the import of wool has fallen 20,000,000 lbs. since 1836, the price of home-grown wool has fallen from 18d. to 10½d. per lb., owing to the bad trade.

WHEAT.

Wheat, the first great necessary of life, has been professedly by the Legislature put entirely out of the category of our regular foreign trade, and a scheme devised to be entirely prohibitory in ordinary years: there is only a device by which it may at a time of extraordinary pressure be let in. This has always been supported on the allegation that, in ordinary years, we grow enough for our consumption. Now this is exactly the opinion which Lord Sheffield held of wool, and the West India planters and merchants of coffee, in 1824. The former took upon himself to measure the manufacturing energies of the population which has since risen in Yorkshire; the latter to measure the palates for coffee of twenty-one millions of people; and the Legislature now professes, by Act of Parliament, to gauge the appetites of twenty-seven millions of people and their increasing numbers for bread. If any man had predicted in 1824 that in 1840 we should consume 20,000,000 lbs. of coffee and 40,000,000 lbs. of foreign wool more than we did then, it would have been treated as the wild dream of a visionary; but if he had added, that all this would be done, without lowering the price of colonial coffee or home-grown wool, his prediction had been received with a smile, but not thought worthy of a reply. But with the experience before us we hesitate not to express our most conscientious conviction, that with a free trade in corn we may go on from year to year increasing our import; *that ten years hence we may annually import* 10,000,000 *quarters of wheat without permanently lowering the average price of home-grown wheat one shilling, and certainly keep the price much more uniform than at present.*

At this moment we have more than one million and a half of paupers in our workhouses; we are said to have a population of ten millions who live on potatoes and oatmeal; and some millions who eat much less wheat bread than they would do if they could obtain it. At the same time we have thousands of tons of shipping lying idle, labourers of all classes without work, mills and workshops standing still, capital wanting employment; and there are in the great corn-producing countries millions of backs to be clothed, or better clothed, if they could. Now the eaters of potatoes and oatmeal are not customers to the wheat grower; the paupers are a great charge instead of being profitable consumers; the idle and the half idle are but poor customers.

Make our trade in wheat free, entirely free:—your idle ships would find employment, your sailors work; your labourers at the docks would receive wages for landing, delivering, turning, &c.; your flour mills would be put more in work; more capital would be profitably employed. Well, then, if other countries send wheat they want something for it; that is, something that we have that is less valuable to us than the wheat, for otherwise the transaction would not take place. They want our manufactures or our minerals, or they want the coffee, sugar, or cotton lying in our docks, or our gold and silver, all of which we have received directly or indirectly for our manufactures, and which we still continue to receive. Something they *will* have to the full value of their wheat. If by all the labour which we thus call into operation by importing, distributing, manufacturing, collecting, and again exporting, we can empty our workhouses of one-half of their inmates, make them profitable consumers, and thus save three to four millions a year of poor rates;—if we thus improve the condition of the ten millions subsisting on potatoes and oatmeal, so that they can eat bread; of the other millions so that they can get bread enough; of those who at present have just enough bread so that they can purchase butchers meat, butter, cheese, vegetables, and fruit; of others, that they can consume more foreign produce, more wine and other luxuries; of others, again, a little higher, that they "*require more servants, more gardeners, keep more horses and more grooms;*" and thus improve the condition of all classes by creating more labour, by making a large and good home trade, and by giving more employment for ships and capital;—to whatever extent we would import wheat and other produce of land, that of this country would only bear a proportionably safer and higher price; but a price, however high, that could not be injurious to the consumer, because it would be his good condition that drew the price higher, after him, whereas at present his necessities and lowering condition drag the price down, after him, without affording him substantial relief. By an increase of trade, whether it be the import of corn or any other article, the producers here can only be advantaged. By the reduction of trade, though it were all in wheat and wool that we reduced it, they could only be injured. Burke truly said, in a debate in 1770, "There is no such thing as the landed interest separate from the trading interest." If more security than this reasoning is required for the result, we refer to the successful issue of the same principles with coffee and wool.

But some will say, wool is a raw material of our manufacturers, and should not be taxed, for in proportion as wool is free and abundant, trade will increase. We reply, wheat also is a raw material like wool, with this exception, that wool enters into only one kind of fabric, while wheat enters as the chief component part of all goods that are made: no kind of trade can be prosperous without increasing the consumption of wheat.

But the most striking thing which ought to excite the suspicion of the most superficial observer about protected interests, is *that they are constantly in distress.* In all inquiries into agricultural distress it has always been the grower of wheat who preferred complaints—that pet article of protection; we have never heard a word of complaint about wool, low as the price sometimes is. Again, with the West India interest, nothing is said about the *free tree of* coffee, but sugar is never unremunerating. While we are writing we receive accounts from the Mauritius, by which, on the 13th April, it appears Sir William Gomm, the Governor, had given great displeasure by refusing to convene a public meeting at the request of the planters to "devise extraordinary measures for their relief;" and in their disappointment they had determined to apply to the Queen.

Now, if we had been asked yesterday to say what spot on the globe had a right to be peculiarly prosperous, we should have said the Mauritius. Since 1827 their exports of sugar have increased from 204,344 cwts. to 696,652 cwts. last year, all of which we take from them at the high protective price, amounting to about 1,803,304*l*., while they take from us goods only to the amount of 320,000*l*. The *extra price* which this country pays them for their sugar more than the same article could be purchased for, of the growth of Java, Cuba, or Brazil, is on the above quantity 520,000*l*., so that, in effect, they get their goods from us for nothing, 200,000*l*. into the bargain, and the natural price of the world for sugar (24s. per cwt.) without the duty, and yet they are appealing for "*extraordinary measures of relief.*" There appears a singular blight to rest wherever monopoly and restriction breathe; while all seems freshness, vivacity, and strength amidst the *freedom of competition.*

Now, then, we ask the reader to stop and reflect,—what, if narrow-minded restriction had succeeded against Huskisson in 1824, had coffee, wool, silk, and flax shared the same fate as sugar, wheat, and the hundreds of other articles in our tariff, and been confined to their ancient limit—what now had been the condition of the shipowner, the merchant, the capitalist?—what now that of the manufacturer, the home trade, the pressing population? The workhouses:—what now would have been the condition of the farmer and the landlord, with a population whose employment would thus have been so much more restricted than it is even now?—what now would have been the state of the revenue, the public peace, the safety of the institutions of the country, and of the CROWN itself?—perplexed as all interests may be now, what had they been had monopoly prevented any extension of our industrial resources? and what, we may be permitted to demand triumphantly in the name of Huskisson, had been the high and thriving condition of all these interests at this moment, had the principles which he was permitted partially to apply to coffee, wool, silk, flax, &c., been applied more perfectly, and to all the great and important articles of consumption—to corn, sugar, and the numerous articles which fill up the list of our trade?

If we would convert our increasing population into a source of increased moral and political greatness, instead of constant alarm and uneasiness; if we would profit by, and truly enjoy all the great and miraculous blessings which art, science, ingenuity, and unwearying industry, throw profusely at our feet; if we would convert into a real national benefit that great and unrivalled manufacturing superiority which we possess, and give full development to the skill and industry of the most patient, intelligent, and active artisans in the world, and raise them from a state of pauperism to a state of manly sober independence; if we would diffuse these blessings in the widest sense to the whole human family, and in return communicate that rich provision which Providence has made in other climes to our now needy and starving population at home; if we would call into active and profitable occupation the great accumulated capital which is now stagnant in our coffers; if we would see the most splendid commercial navy ever owned by a country once more floating freely on the ocean; if we would truly avail ourselves of all the advantages which the wonderful facilities of intercourse with all countries of the globe now offer; if we would no longer be satisfied to see the great continent of America brought close to our little island, the rich plains, the large cities of the European continent almost intermingling with our own, for the mere purposes of curiosity or recreation; if we would convert them into means of administering to the happiness, prosperity, and mutual wants, to the physical and moral improvement of the human family; IF WE WOULD GIVE TO THE OWNER AND CULTIVATOR OF THE SOIL AT HOME THE BEST AND ONLY TRUE SECURITY FOR PROSPERING AMID, AND BY REASON OF, THE PROSPERITY OF THE GREAT COMMUNITY BY WHICH HE IS SURROUNDED; we must emancipate commerce and industry from those trammels and restrictions, with which short-sighted jealousies and unwise legislation have fettered them; feeling, at the same time, assured, that mutual dependence is the only true and safest guarantee for independence.

But to whom are we to look? On what are we to rely for this great act of emancipation? Not to political parties or their leaders; they are dependent on the public will: it may be used by them as a means to an end, but that can only be as public opinion willeth. IT IS WITH PUBLIC OPINION THAT WE HAVE TO DO. With party strife, with political struggle, we have no connexion, further than we can bring public opinion to make the hitherto neglected interests of industry and commerce the great battle ground, and free trade the great object of the contest. And, therefore, to public opinion we will now shortly address ourselves.

If public opinion, if popular influences, have their political privileges, they have also their corresponding moral and civil responsibilities, and a neglect of the duties which they involve, may be of greater injury to a country than the most unprincipled traitor ever inflicted. It is worse than idle to blame governments and legislatures, while public opinion alone can "make or mar them."

If, however, we find in public opinion strange and inconceivable inconsistencies, strong prejudices and ignorances, and find it guilty of a singular neglect of the first great and material interests of the state, we must admit that there has been a marvellous neglect of the means of informing the public mind on these all-important subjects. Men of rank and birth, likely to become legislators, have been sedulously taught the dead languages, ancient philosophy and history, and have been versed in classical acquirements and curiosities; men in the middle ranks, destined for merchants, traders, or manufacturers, have been taught the modern popular sciences, mathematics, geography, chemistry, &c.: but strange to say, the principles of feeding the country, of conducting commerce, of securing national prosperity, have been as yet no part of the education of any class. These important duties have been left to mere accident; it had indeed been well had ignorance been as unobtrusive, as intelligence has been neglectful.

When we consider how much pure commercial economical science has been converted to political expediency, how much, unfortunately, all the higher principles are sacrificed for party purposes; how much pains have been taken to entangle free trade with notions of reciprocity; and more than all the insidious way in which monopoly and restriction have coiled themselves round our interests under the pretence of raising a revenue to the State, in the most dangerous of all shapes—by differential duties; —we can hardly wonder that public opinion has shown itself confused and undecided on this subject. The country, however, is now suffering so much from the operation of bad principles, that men must rouse themselves from the apathy in which they have so long remained, and every man who has a stake in the country must feel it his duty to investigate and learn for himself, for the real and true interest of every man, whoever he may be, is to arrive at a correct opinion on these all-important principles; on the aggregate result of which the country must either rise or sink.

For ourselves we have very strong opinions, formed after long observation, experience, and reflection, and which the further observation of every day tends only to make stronger,—of the pressing necessity of adopting, without delay, a distinct line of free-trade policy as the only means of securing the peace, safety, honour, and prosperity of our common country: and it is under this strong conviction that, among other efforts which we consider it our duty to use to press these principles, we have organised a weekly paper, solely for the purpose of advocating these principles, and ministering in other useful ways to the material interests of the country; to the advancement of commerce and industry in every form; and while we advocate and disseminate correct principles, it is also a specific part of our plan to render it a medium of practical usefulness to commerce, manufactures, and agriculture, on a scale not hitherto attempted; and also to combine with these the political and general news of the week.

And now we beg to submit the following detail of the plans which we have thoroughly organised to carry into effect these objects of our ardent desires, in the following

PROSPECTUS

of a weekly paper, to be published every Saturday, and to be called

THE ECONOMIST,

which will contain—

First.—ORIGINAL LEADING ARTICLES, in which free-trade principles will be most rigidly applied to all the important questions of the day—political events—and parliamentary discussions; and particularly to all such as relate immediately to revenue, commerce, and agriculture; or otherwise affect the material interests of the country.

Second.—Articles relating more especially to some practical, commercial, agricultural, or foreign topic of passing interest; of the state of the revenue, foreign treaties, &c.

Third.—An article on the elementary principles of political economy, applied in a familiar and popular manner to practical experience; especially in relation to the laws of price—wages—rent—exchange—revenue—taxes—and the relation between producers and consumers abroad and at home; proved and illustrated by the experience of this and other countries.

Fourth. — PARLIAMENTARY REPORTS: Giving at greater length all discussions peculiarly interesting to commerce and agriculture, and especially involving the principles of Free Trade.

Fifth.—POPULAR MOVEMENTS: A report and account of all popular movements throughout the country in favour of Free Trade.

Sixth.—GENERAL NEWS: A summary of all the news of the week,—the Court—the Metropolis—the Provinces: Scotland and Ireland.

Seventh.—COMMERCIAL: Under this head a careful and elaborate account will be given of the trade of the week; with special notices of changes in fiscal regulations; state and prospects of the markets, especially indicating the progress of stocks and consumption; of imports and exports; latest Foreign News, likely to influence future supply; the state of the manufacturing districts; notices of important new mechanical improvements; shipping news; an account of the money market, and of the progress of railways and public companies.

Eighth.—AGRICULTURAL: Under this head we will give frequent articles on improvements in agriculture; on the application of geology and chemistry; on new and improved implements; and in every way, to the utmost of our power, assist that true and independent spirit which is everywhere rising among the *best* landlords and farmers, to rely on the only safe support agriculture can have—*intelligence, ingenuity, and perseverance,* instead of *deceptive protection.* We will give a general detail of incidents, state of crops, markets, prices, foreign markets and prices converted into English money; and we have made an arrangement to communicate, from time to time, in some detail, the plans pursued in Belgium, Switzerland, and other well-cultivated countries.

Ninth.—COLONIAL AND FOREIGN: In which we will furnish the earliest information respecting the trade, produce, political and fiscal changes, and other matter interesting; and, particularly, we will endeavour to expose the evils of restriction and protection, and the advantages of free intercourse and trade.

Tenth.—LAW REPORTS: These we will confine chiefly to such as are particularly important to commerce, manufactures, and agriculture.

Eleventh.—NOTICES OF BOOKS: Confined chiefly, but not so exclusively, to such as treat of the foregoing subjects; including all treatises on political economy, finance, or taxation.

Twelfth.—COMMERCIAL GAZETTE: Price currents and statistics of the week.

Thirteenth.—CORRESPONDENCE, INQUIRIES, &c.: Under this head we especially invite every one to apply for information on all the topics herein enumerated, which we do not furnish, or which is not given in such detail as may be required. We have made an arrangement by which inquiries shall be replied to in the next number, if received by Thursday morning, on all subjects enumerated in this prospectus:—POLITICAL ECONOMY AND COMMERCE; FOREIGN COMMERCIAL REGULATIONS; TARIFFS, RATES OF DUTIES, AND PORT REGULATIONS; EXISTING COMMERCIAL TREATIES; POINTS OF COMMERCIAL LAW; GENERAL STATISTICS, connected with our trade for the last twenty years, or earlier, when they exist; AGRICULTURAL STATISTICS AND IMPROVEMENTS; and on other practical and mechanical subjects required.

EXTRA MONTHLY STATISTICAL AND PARLIAMENTARY PAPER NUMBER:—In each month we will publish an extra number, devoted exclusively to statistics, and the preservation of the statistical parts of documents laid before parliament; many of which, of great value, never at present reach the public eye, or at least in a very limited way. There can be no question that, whether we speak of the economist, the legislator, the merchant, or the trader, statistics must form the most important ground-work of the whole of his reasonings, opinions, and actions; they are, in short, the fundamental facts on which all his opinions and actions must be based to be true; it is difficult to estimate their importance. At the same time we must remark, that however powerful and useful they may be as an instrument, they cannot be used with safety without considerable knowledge of the peculiar subjects, and without the exercise of great discretion in drawing results. This we will endeavour to aid by explanatory notes and observations in the collection and arrangement. Our plan is,—to divide this monthly number into two parts, one for permanent statistics, in which we will commence and collect together in alphabetical order the statistics of our revenue and trade, including exports and imports, navigation, agriculture, and currency for the last twenty years:—the trade with our colonies, and of our colonies with each other, and with this country:—and various interesting statistical statements which we can get relating to the same subjects in foreign countries: the other part we will apply to the statistics of the day: the comparison of our trade, imports, exports, consumption, stocks, &c., of all the leading articles of commerce, between the current year and the corresponding period of the preceding year: and other matters useful and interesting to the material interests of the country.

And at the end of each year, we will furnish a title-page and general index to the whole paper, including the statistical numbers, so that the whole may form a useful volume of reference to the economist, the politician, the merchant, and manufacturer, the agriculturist, and the general reader.

We have made such arrangements, and under such superintendence, as will secure the accomplishment of all that we propose, in a way which we trust will render our objects and exertions useful to the country:—we have no party or class interests or motives; we are of no class, or rather of every class:—we are of the landowning class; we are of the commercial class interested in our colonies, in our foreign trade, and in our manufactures: but our opinions are that no one part of these can have any lasting and true success that is not associated and co-existing with the prosperity of all.

And lastly—if we required higher motives than bare utility, to induce that zeal, labour, and perseverance against all the difficulties which we shall have to encounter in this work—we have them. If we look abroad, we see within the range of our commercial intercourse whole islands and continents, on which the light of civilization has scarce yet dawned; and we seriously believe that FREE TRADE, free intercourse, will do more than any other visible agent to extend civilization and morality throughout the world—yes, to extinguish slavery itself. Then, if we look around us at home, we see ignorance, depravity, immorality, irreligion, abounding to an extent disgraceful to a civilized country; and we feel assured that there is little chance of successfully treating this great national disease while want and pauperism so much abound: we can little hope to improve the mental and moral condition of a people while their physical state is so deplorable:—personal experience has shown us in the manufacturing districts that the people want no acts of parliament to coerce education or induce moral improvement when they are in physical comfort—and that, when men are depressed with want and hunger, and agonized by the sufferings of helpless and starving children, no acts of parliament are of the slightest avail. We look far beyond the power of acts of parliament, or even of the efforts of the philanthropist or the charitable, however praiseworthy, to effect a cure for this great national leprosy: we look mainly to an improvement in the condition of the people. And we hope to see the day when it will be as difficult to understand how an act of parliament could have been made to restrict the food and employment of the people, as it is now to conceive how the mild, inoffensive spirit of Christianity could ever have been converted into the plea of persecution and martyrdom, or how poor old wrinkled women, with a little eccentricity, were burned by our forefathers for witchcraft.